Following His Own Path

SUNY series, Translating China
———
Roger T. Ames and Paul J. D'Ambrosio, editors

Following His Own Path

Li Zehou and Contemporary Chinese Philosophy

JANA S. ROŠKER

Cover photo: Li Zehou, Autumn 1979, Beijing China. Photograph by Yu Jian. © Li Zehou.

Published by State University of New York Press, Albany

© 2019 State University of New York

All rights reserved

No part of this book may be used or reproduced in any manner whatsoever without written permission. No part of this book may be stored in a retrieval system or transmitted in any form or by any means including electronic, electrostatic, magnetic tape, mechanical, photocopying, recording, or otherwise without the prior permission in writing of the publisher.

For information, contact State University of New York Press, Albany, NY
www.sunypress.edu

Library of Congress Cataloging-in-Publication Data

Names: Rošker, Jana, 1960– author.
Title: Following his own path : Li Zehou and contemporary Chinese philosophy / Jana S. Rošker.
Description: Albany : State University of New York, [2019] | Series: SUNY series. Translating China | Includes bibliographical references and indexes.
Identifiers: LCCN 2018000362 | ISBN 9781438472478 (hardcover) | ISBN 9781438472461 (pbk) | ISBN 9781438472485 (ebook) Subjects: LCSH: Li, Zehou. | Philosophy, Chinese—20th century. | Philosophy, Chinese—21st century.
Classification: LCC B5234.L4874 R67 2018 | DDC 181/.11—dc23
LC record available at https://lccn.loc.gov/2018000362

10 9 8 7 6 5 4 3 2 1

自反而縮，雖千萬人，吾往矣

*If I reflect on myself and ascertain that I am upright,
I will continue to follow my way
against thousands and tens of thousands
(Mengzi, Gongsun Chou I: 2.6)*

Contents

Acknowledgments ix

Notes on References, Bibliography, and Translation xi

Introduction xiii

1. Li Zehou and His Time 1

2. Central Concepts 47

3. Upgrading and Modernizing Traditional Chinese Philosophy 103

4. Exploring the Beauty of Humanity 183

5. General Evaluation and Impact 251

Appendix: General Scheme of Ethics (Lunlixue zong lanbiao 倫理學總覽表) 277

Notes 279

Bibliography 315

Glossary of Specific Terms, Phrases, and Titles (Chinese-English) 335

Index of Proper Names 349

Acknowledgments

The assistance of numerous individuals and institutions contributed to the accomplishment of this work. First of all, I would like to express my gratitude to Professor Li Zehou, simply because without him, this book would never be possible. His broad wisdom, his insightful inventiveness and exhilarating theories were always a precious source of incentive, making the writing of this book on his philosophical system for me a wonderful and exciting journey through the labyrinths of his fascinating thought.

I am very grateful to the faculty of arts at Ljubljana University and to all the colleagues from the Department for Asian Studies for their support of my efforts in writing this book and for providing all the necessary facilities that we all too often take for granted. My research in Taiwan and China, where I could obtain most of the important sources and secondary material, were supported by the Slovenian Research Agency (ARRS, research program P6—0243), the Center for Chinese Studies at the National Central Library in Taipei, and the Deng Delong grant. I am also grateful to the Department of Philosophy at the National Taiwan University in Taipei for allowing me the opportunity to do research in their library as a visiting scholar. All these activities enabled me to exchange ideas with many other scholars working in the field of Chinese philosophy, which benefited my study enormously.

I appreciate the help and support of many friends and colleagues, from whom I have drawn a lot of warmth, stimulation, and professional, as well as personal assistances. I am immensely grateful for their constant support and stimulating conversations, which have been the most exquisite springs of my inspiration. I would like to thank (in alphabetical order of their surnames) Andrej Bekeš, Bart Dessein, Raoul David Findeisen, Guo Qiyong, Fabian Heubel, Huang Chun-chieh, Lee Hsien-chung,

Lee Ming-huei, Lin Ming-chao, Lin Yue-huei, Karl-Heinz Pohl, Geir Sigurðsson, Wang Hui, Nataša Vampelj Suhadolnik, Maja Veselič, Wu Xiaoming, Igor Ž. Žagar, and many others. Karyn Lai, Andrej Ule, and Kai Marchal have read different sections of the manuscript before the final submission, and provided valuable comments. I would also like to thank the two anonymous reviewers for their timely, diligent, thorough, as well as extremely attentive work. I am very grateful for their insightful remarks, which have helped me to substantially improve the manuscript.

My very special appreciation goes to Roger T. Ames for his interest in my book, and especially his trust, care and wisdom. I would also like to thank him and Peter Hershock for their readiness to include this book into the new series they are editing, and for all the supporting efforts they have put into its production. This book owes much to Christopher Ahn for his wonderful editorial guidance, his constant availability, and his professional help.

I am also very grateful to Klara Hrvatin for helping me with the editing and formatting of the manuscript and preparing the glossary and bibliography before the final submission. My earnest appreciation also goes to Mai Shaikhanuar-Cota, who took the time to proofread it and who helped me to iron out many mistakes, both stylistically and grammatically.

Most of all, I wish to tell my partner Téa Sernelj how grateful I am for her unceasing love, involvement, and support. My sons Janko and Nils are also a great comfort to me with their warm chats and unfailing encouragement, which has always sparkled my mind's eye.

Notes on References, Bibliography, and Translation

Because of the small number of Chinese family names, the reference style of this book does not follow the common Western styles. In addition to their surnames, the given names of Chinese authors are included in the references (for instance, Hu Weixi 2002, 14 instead of Hu 2002, 14). To distinguish between sources that have been published by Chinese authors in English and the ones that have been published in Chinese by the same authors, the first and last names of the authors of Chinese material will not be separated by a comma. In contrast, in references to their works written and published in English or other Indo-European languages their surnames will be followed by a comma. For example: a reference to Li Zehou's article written in English: Li, Zehou 1999, "Subjectivity and 'Subjectality': A Response," *Philosophy East and West* 49(2): 174–83, the source is cited within text as (Li, Zehou 1999). His work in Chinese: Li Zehou 李澤厚 1999, *Zhongguo sixiang shilun* 中國思想史論 *(On Chinese Intellectual History)*, *Hefei: Anhui wenyi chuban she* is cited within text as (Li Zehou 1999). Such specific conventions do not apply to sources written by non-Chinese authors.

Unless otherwise indicated, all translations from classical and modern Chinese contained in this book are my own.

Introduction

Li Zehou is undoubtedly one of the most distinguished, significant, and influential Chinese philosophers of our time and one of the rare Chinese intellectuals whose work acquired broad readership outside of China. Since the late 1970s, Li has propelled a number of views that have had a deep and lasting impact on Chinese intellectuals. Even his critics acknowledge his scholarly influence and academic accomplishments (Ding 2002, 246). Because Li belongs to a group of exiled intellectuals, his contribution towards contemporary Chinese thought and culture is rather complex. The same holds true for his brand of philosophy, which has been variously characterized as "neo-traditional," "neo-Kantian," "post-Marxist," "Marxist-Confucian," "pragmatist," "instrumentalist," "romantic," and more. Despite this complexity, which cannot be reduced to any dominant philosophical categories or currents, he doubtless belongs to the most significant modern scholars of Chinese history and culture, especially considering the fact that his work was central to the Chinese Enlightenment (*qimeng* 啟蒙) of the 1980s.[1]

Even though Li deals with complex philosophical ideas, he is able to express them in multifaceted texts, successfully combining logical analyses with narrative and emotive elements. His philosophy has helped modify and transform antiquated patterns of Chinese intellectual discourses. His innovative, imaginative, and unique approach to a wide range of basic theoretical problems, grounded in solid arguments and analyses, has created new styles of intellectual investigation into the post-Mao period and presented a new challenge to the tedious and monotonous theories delivered by the official Party ideologists. Li's ambition to fill "old bottles with new wine" often took the form of a reversal or inversion of words or phrases that were central to his philosophical endeavors. Three key phrases warrant mention.

1. The most famous example is his reversal of the nineteenth-century slogan "(preserving) Chinese substance and (applying) Western functions," which became "(assuming) Western substance and (applying) Chinese functions" (from *Zhongti Xiyong* 中體西用 to *Xiti Zhongyong* 西體中用).

2. Li likewise inverted Lin Yusheng's "creative transformation" to "transformative creation" (from *chuangzaoxingde zhuanhua* 創造性的轉化 to *zhuanhuaxingde chuangzao* 轉化性的創造).

3. Finally, he gave new meaning to Marx's vision of a non-alienated relation between men and nature,—the "humanization of nature," by complementing it with the reversed phrase "naturalization of humans" (from *zirande renhua* 自然的人化 to *rende ziranhua* 人的自然化).

During the creative urgency of this period, when it seemed that aesthetics offered the most effective redemption from the difficult experiences of the Cultural Revolution, Li offered young Chinese people new, exceptionally creative interpretations of art, philosophy, and literature. He launched many views that have had great impact not only on the Chinese, but also on global theories of ethics, humanism, aesthetics, and philosophical anthropology. Mainly by remaining loyal to the conceptual framework of Marxist historical materialism, he simultaneously drew selective inspiration from the works of Kant, Hegel, Heidegger, the Frankfurt School, Lukács, Piaget, Lacan, and Habermas. One of his main contributions to contemporary Chinese—and, to a certain extent, to contemporary Western philosophy—lies in his deepening of the problem of the active and autonomous human potential in post-revolutionary modernism through his neologism "subjectality" (*zhutixing* 主體性). Li uses this concept to ground human agency in the historically conditioned and environmentally subsumed—but nonetheless conscious—subject. In doing so, Li upgrades the Marxist view of consciousness as a solely mechanical reflection of the material world and, even more importantly, refutes the passivity of the subject. With this concept he created a revolution in the name of beauty. This radical re-interpretation of the notion of subject achieved scholarly distinction with the publication of his book *Pipan zhexue de pipan: Kangde shuping* 批判哲學的批判: 康德述評 (*Critique of Critical Philosophy: A New Approach to Kant*). In this book, Li places the central framework of Kant's philosophy upon a social and materialist foundation by simultaneously recovering the original Marxist definition of human beings as *homo faber*—as living beings developed through practice and able to make use of tools in a systemic, continuous way. Humans, in Li's view, recreate both their environment and their inwardness into something he calls "humanized nature."

A second important neologism in which Li's philosophy, especially his philosophical anthropology, is rooted is the concept of *sedimentation*. With this geological metaphor, Li expresses the historical process of continuous, gradual, and successive shaping of epistemological, ethical, and aesthetical forms of human inwardness. The greatest challenge to the modern and postmodern subject was the problem of a meaningful context. Proceeding from his conception of an active subject, he points out the pragmatic reasoning that also defines the concept of *subjectality*. This led to his construction of the evolutional path of the subject, which began in the Neolithic era and led to the contemporary human subject. To Li, the main driving force of evolutionary development is subjectality. The crucial formations that enable and mark the creation of different stages of this development can be seen in various forms of dynamic cultural sedimentation. In his best-known book *The Path of Beauty* (*Meide licheng* 美的歷程), Li argues that art is the central unfolding imprint of the psychological condition of human ontology—of the subject's existence in the world. The concept of sedimentation brought Chinese thought into dialogue with world philosophy, while giving the specifically-Chinese experience of human evolution a historicized and activist role. In *The Path of Beauty* and the subsequent *Four Essays on Aesthetics* (*Meixue sijiang* 美學四講), Li creates an innovative synthesis of Marxism, classical Chinese moral philosophy, medieval aesthetics, and continental rationalism. He insists that science and technology produce beautiful things that can be appreciated as aesthetic objects, especially considering their origin. These beautiful things can be seen as products of human endeavors on our human path towards the unification or reconciliation of nature (or heaven) and human beings (*tian ren heyi* 天人合一).

Li Zehou's thought seeks to respond to an era that is defined not only by attempts to revive various traditions, but by efforts to harmonize or reconcile cultural heritage with the demands of the dominant economic, political, and axiological structures of a globalized world. His thought can be described as the search for a synthesis between Western and traditional Chinese thought, driven in order to elaborate a system of ideas and values capable of resolving the social and political problems of the modern way of life. He attempts to reconcile Western (especially Kantian and Marxist) theories with traditional Chinese (especially Confucian, and also to a certain extent, Daoist) ideas, concepts and values, to create a theoretical model of modernization that would not be confused or equated with "Westernization."[2,3]

By renewing and rethinking traditional Chinese values and knowledge, Li makes an important contribution to contemporary philosophical discourse. His work can be seen as an ongoing effort to rediscover and renew traditional Chinese (especially Confucian) *ideational* tradition, by not only aiding China on its path to future material and spiritual development, but also making a unique and valuable contribution to world philosophy. In spite of the basic cosmopolitan nature of his work, he still remains loyal to specifically Chinese theoretical and methodological approaches. Li's complex philosophical and essayistic opus cannot be understood without an understanding of the historical, political, and ideational context to which he belonged.

1

Li Zehou and His Time

Historical and Ideational Background

Li Zehou was born on the threshold of the third decade of the first Chinese republic, the Republic of China, which was established after the decay of the empire in 1911. In the era of Li Zehou's birth, the Chinese intellectual arena developed mainly in the spirit of confronting the challenges of Western thought while simultaneously trying to develop and to modernize China's own philosophical and ideational tradition. Let us take a short glimpse into the complex developments that marked this significant and crucial era.

Chinese Culture in the Twentieth Century: Crises and Syntheses, Dilemmas, and New Hopes

At the threshold of the twentieth century, a stern debate among Chinese intellectuals arose from conflicting opinions on how best to assume Western thought without dropping the core of the Chinese ideational tradition and the cultural identity linked to it. Confronted with this quandary, numerous scholars adopted the position of the conservative political theorist Zhang Zhidong 張之洞 (1837–1909), who became famous with the slogan "(Preserving) Chinese essence and (applying) Western functions" (*Zhongti Xiyong* 中體西用).[1] In addition to this group, two more radical streams began to take shape among the Chinese intellectuals of this time (Rošker 2008: 130). The first of these supported the total abolition of Chinese tradition and a comprehensive Westernization of Chinese thought and culture (*Quan pan xihua* 全盤西化). The second promoted the revitalization and reawakening (*Fuguzhuyi* 復古主義) of the classical tradition in the form of a new leading culture.

Regarding the political situation, the epoch of the First Republic (1911–1949) was still determined by a profound crisis and general instability. Under the facade of legislatorial democracy, governmental policies were defined by authoritarian drives and power fights among competing generals. With the start of World War I, the Chinese came to be witness to the complete failure of European political theories as the chief Western powers entered into a seemingly endless spiral of bloodletting and devastation (ibid.). These events unsurprisingly diminished the previous Chinese passion for progressive European thought, and those who had seen in Western science, culture, and philosophy the most forward-thinking phase of human civilization were quite upset by this experience.

The demands for a comprehensive transformation of Chinese culture and thought that had arisen from the different rejections of the outdated Confucian tradition finally exploded in the May 4th Movement (*Wusi yundong* 五四運動), which began on 4 May 1919 with student demonstrations in the Square of Heavenly Peace (Tiananmen Square) in Peking. This movement would soon come to play a critical role in the ideational, political, and cultural modernization of Chinese society. *New Youth* (*Xin qingnian* 新青年), a key publication founded in 1915 by Chen Duxiu 陳獨秀, rapidly became the leading journal of its kind for a new generation of Chinese intellectuals. The essence of the new China manifested itself in cries for dismissing outmoded and dogmatic Confucian doctrines and eliminating traditionalist social and political configurations, which were seen as hampering the free advance of individuals and society. The journal and the movement it represented also promoted equality between the sexes and "free love," as well as the termination of economic and political control by the elite classes.[2] For the modern "new intellectuals," who belonged to the main agents of the May 4th "Cultural Revolution," this was seen by numerous scholars as the "Chinese Enlightenment" movement, as these demands formed the elementary and necessary precondition for a more just dissemination of the ideational and material resources of Chinese society. Of course, all these requirements were naturally linked to the need for basic changes in the overall mindset of Chinese people. *New Youth*, for instance, published its articles in a colloquial language (*bai hua* 白話), thereby giving crucial momentum to the successive elimination of ancient or classical Chinese (*wenyan* 文言) that had up to that point represented the official literary language and the only acceptable form of public writing. It was an archaic language, which differed drastically from modern Chinese, and could only be learned through the costly and lengthy procedure of a classical education. The exclusive application of classical Chinese, which was accessible only to a small minority of the elite classes, meant that the overwhelming majority of Chinese citizens were entirely cut off from any form of written culture, even if one was not completely unschooled. Thus, the so-called Colloquial Movement (*Bai hua yundong* 白話運動) became a keystone of the new Chinese culture. This ideational progeny of the May 4th Movement first revealed itself in the blossoming of the "new literature" (*xin wenxue* 新文學), which was written by the so-called New Intellectuals and that was profoundly influenced by Western literary canons, streams, and forms. The new literature differed significantly from traditionally Chinese literary creations, not only in terms of language, but also in its subject matter and content.

Because this was a gradual process of incremental changes, it is not surprising that the notion of the "May 4th Movement" in a broader sense generally also refers to the entire epoch between 1915 and 1921 (ibid.). Often it is also denoted as the "New Culture Movement" or the "May 4th Cultural Revolution." However, only a few years after its commencement, the May 4th Movement would slowly lose its influence and become absorbed in the fight between Communist and Nationalist parties, which added more pressure to an already unstable internal political situation. The military and political conflicts that were supplemented by the lingering corruption and incompetence of the leading Nationalist Party sounded much like the prelude to the Japanese occupation of Manchuria in 1931, followed by the overall Japanese offensive six years later (ibid.). With the end of World War II—known as the Anti-Japanese War in China—the struggles between the Communists and the Nationalists exploded into a civil war. This concluded in 1949 with the triumph of the Communists and the establishment of the People's Republic of China under the leadership of Mao Zedong 毛澤東 (1893–1976). The political governance of the defeated Nationalist Party immigrated to Taiwan (台灣) (the island of Formosa), where it founded an exile government that continued the political tradition of the Republic of China.

In the People's Republic of China (PRC), censorship of the previous Nationalist government, which had been applied unofficially in all spaces of public life, was substituted by a methodical intellectual control that permitted almost exclusively the "correct" interpretations and reproductions of Marxist thought in firm agreement with the varying interests of the reigning elite. The Communist Party government renewed the system of high education, which had been founded in China at the start of the twentieth century grounded on the American and British models. This "Communist" transformation of universities was rooted in the ideological directions voiced by Mao Zedong in his renowned Yan'an speeches (1942) on intellectual, literary, and cultural policy.[3] All these material and ideational reforms were followed by an epoch of immense, centralized campaigns directed against both the modern and the traditional ideological opponents of the new government. Various endeavors to release China from this oppressive bondage resulted in the short-lived "Hundred Flowers Movement" (1957), which was fast smothered by a new "Anti-Rightist Movement" (1957–1959). The disaster of the utopian economic-political campaign of the "Great Leap Forward" (1958) was followed by the epoch of the "Great Proletarian Cultural Revolution" (1966–1976). The Cultural Revolution, which was rooted in the power struggles and conspiracies within the highest cadres of the governing elite, was quite successful in totally destroying all the newly founded educational structures and in pitilessly eradicating several millions of intellectuals. Even those who were spared this fate were mostly exiled to rural areas to experience the hard life of the "peasant masses" (ibid., 144) and thereby come to understand crucial matters of life and politics. After a decade of this movement, which was marked by political and economic chaos, ideological repression, and an impermeable barrier on accomplishing any valid intellectual work, China experienced two decades of relative internal stability and a gradual "liberation of thought" under Deng Xiaoping's 鄧小平 policy of external openness and economic liberation. This era, however, was violently interrupted on June 4, 1989, with the bloodbath of several thousand Chinese students who were demonstrating for a swifter and more genuine democratization of Chinese society on Beijing's Tiananmen Square. Chinese intelligentsia responded to this tragedy either with apathetical nihilism or with a fatalistic withdrawal from intellectual activities (Rošker 2008, 139–50). After that, the free advance of contemporary Chinese thought was somehow jammed for several more years, with open debates on these issues only slowly reemerging in the final years of the millennium.

While evaluating Li's philosophy, we must not forget that he was born into the era when the development of modern Chinese thought, which had begun to emerge at the end of the nineteenth century, had been interrupted for almost four decades. Furthermore, while during the past few decades contemporary Chinese culture and thought have at last slowly begun to awaken from a long slumber, we must consider the vast scale of time and space that determined the unfolding of the Chinese tradition. In any case, this new awakening, which began in the 1980s and that resembles in many respects the so-called Golden Period of Chinese thought during the era of the Warring States (戰國, 475–221 BC), seems well-prepared to face the challenges of the global age (ibid., 150). Being one of the central figures of this era in Chinese philosophy, Li Zehou has contributed significantly to the resolution of problems brought about by these challenges. However, before focusing upon his life and work, we must provide a basis for a deeper understanding of his theoretical thought. Hence, we will first take a short look upon the general position and the main content that were elaborated by Chinese philosophers of this period.

The Main Philosophical Currents and the Role of Aesthetic Thought

Despite the great, though at times almost unbearable, political and ideological pressures[4] in the latter half of the twentieth century, a number of theorists were sufficiently subtle and creative (and certainly also sufficiently courageous) so as to plant the seeds of new theories that combined Western (especially Kantian and Marxist), Confucian, Daoist, and even Buddhist approaches. While maintaining a Marxist perspective, they tried to reconstruct Chinese philosophy and methodology. Through this combination of commitments, they were perhaps more culturally representative than many other Chinese philosophical figures from the 1940s through the 1990s (Cheng, Chung-ying 2002, 381). Li Zehou doubtless belongs to this group of such innovative and spirited scholars.

Parallel to the cultural development, the historical era of the modernization of Chinese philosophy can also be roughly divided into three periods, with the first being that of active modernization, lasting approximately from 1910 to 1937. This was the period of the systematic, extensive, and qualitatively profound introduction of Western discourses. We must not forget that the start of World War II, which began in

China with the Japanese occupation of Manchuria in 1937, represents the beginning of the period of theoretical stagnation, which lasted for more than four decades (Rošker 2008, 139–50). During the 1940s, theoretical work on philosophy was silenced by the cataclysm of war, while with the founding of the PRC, a Sinicized ideologization of Marxist theories necessarily prevailed in this so-called "socialist society": the result was that, until the 1970s, philosophy was mainly viewed as a tool for the theoretical underpinnings of Maoist policies, and as a means for the mass ideologization of society. The popularization and simplification of those aspects of Marxist–Leninist and Maoist thought, which were regarded functional for current political trends was one of the main tasks of the Chinese intelligentsia of that time. This period was marked by a specific shift in discourse, caused by the increasingly broader politicization of everyday life, and philosophy was increasingly substituted by forms of symbolic speech (ibid.). In this context, abstract notions no longer served as methodological tools for formulating or constituting new systems of thought but, as with the doctrines of orthodox Confucianism, appeared on a formal level as expressions of various ideological directions together with their proponents (ibid.).

The further development of innovative theories, in the sense of a systematic formulation of philosophical contents, began in the early 1980s. In the post-Maoist China of the last two decades of the century, there were interesting attempts to Sinicize dialectical materialism, as well as increasingly frequent efforts to fuse Chinese and Western traditions of thought. While the latter can be found primarily in the new methodological foundations of contemporary Chinese thought, irrespective of the specific theoretical area, the Sinicization of Marxist discourses mostly appears in two other theoretical currents: the first of these was primarily determined by dialectics, logic, and modern linguistic theories, and the second by the ethical and aesthetic aspects of the synthesis of Marxist and traditional Chinese thought. Li's philosophy has immensely contributed to the developments of the latter current.

The third period, which began with the simultaneous external opening and internal liberalization of China, can be designated as the period for the dissemination and critical evaluation of the most influential currents of Western thought. At the threshold of the third millennia, philosophy as an academic discipline exists in China within the framework of what we can call three different "scopes of content" (Li, You-Zheng 1997, 97–98):

- the scope of (Sinicized) Marxist and post-Marxist philosophy (including the so-called neo leftist philosophy);
- the scope of traditional, primarily classical Chinese philosophy;
- and the scope of introduction and exploration of the history of Western philosophy.

With respect to comparative studies, contemporary Chinese thinkers who confront Western discourses have mainly set themselves two major tasks in terms of application. The first task is to understand and interpret the old in the new and interpret the traditional in the modern. Because the West represents the new and the modern, the second task is to understand and interpret Chinese tradition in light of the West and to understand and interpret Western tradition in light of China (Cheng, Chung-ying 2002, 372). Thus, the reinterpretation, renewed awareness, and reflection upon traditional values, adapted for the present time, is of crucial importance for the preservation of cultural identity. This task is more problematic than it seems at first glance, since a paradigmatic evaluation requires objective or generally valid valuation criteria. Li belongs to those contemporary Chinese thinkers who have intensively worked on such approaches, which has led to the germs of a more consistent, flexible, and autonomous axiology of philosophical theory, suited to the demands of the present time. These theoretical innovations have clearly shown that such approaches can be found and modernized within the ever-present system of dynamic, situationally-determined interrelativeness of the Chinese ideational traditions.

The renaissance of contemporary Chinese thought has primarily manifested itself in the elaborations on and developments of Marxist thought; the quests for syntheses between Western theories and the classical Chinese, particularly Confucian tradition; as well as in a new, specifically Chinese liberalism.

A new, powerful stream of thought, which emerged amidst all this discourse, was Chinese aesthetics. For the first time a wide-ranging discussion on questions related to the connection of art and philosophy, form and content, emerged in the 1950s. This discussion, "The Great Debate on Aesthetics" (*Meixue da taolun* 美學大討論), dealt mainly with the meaning, function, and the possibilities of aesthetics. It was a broad and significant debate on questions regarding aesthetic thought and was later followed by a new wave of controversies in the 1980. This new, even more important and influential aesthetic discourse was rooted in mutually quite opposing views. These views will be introduced in detail in later chapters of this book. This discourse became well known under the name "Aesthetic Fever" (*Meixue re* 美學熱). Karl Heinz Pohl rightly points out that modern Chinese aesthetics formed an important part of the historical struggle with Western thought.

> Because of a similarity to art-philosophical aspects of Western aesthetics, the Chinese, in general, understood and still understand their own rich tradition of poetic rather than systematic reflections on the essence of literature and art as "aesthetics." The "Aesthetic Fever" (*Meixue re* 美學熱), that broke out in China during the eighties of the 20th century can be understood from this eminent role that aesthetics played and still plays in the history of Chinese ideas. (Pohl 2001, 2)

In the 1980s, the Chinese people were already quite exhausted because of the omnipresent and never-ending political debates, pressures, and campaigns. One of the most attractive characteristics of aesthetics—and hence, one of the reasons for the outburst of the "Aesthetic Fever" in that time—was its apolitical nature. It constituted a realm that was relatively free of politics (ibid., 9). Besides, the philosophy of art as an important part of aesthetics offered the people several ways of connecting with their own ideational and cultural tradition. As we shall see later, Li was doubtless the most important figure in these movements and debates.

General Overview: Li Zehou, His Life, and Work

Main Biographical Data and Crucial Publications

Li Zehou was born in 1930 in the Chinese city of Hankou, a part of the Wuhan urban area north of the Yangtze River. When he was four years old, his family moved to Changsha, the capital of Hunan province, where he spent his childhood and early youth. In the early 1950s he graduated from the Department of Philosophy at Peking University. In the early 1980s, he was a researcher and professor at the Research Institute of Philosophy at the prestigious Chinese Academy of Social Sciences (CASS, *Zhongguo shehui kexue yuan* 中國社會科學院). In 1955, he was one of the founders of the prestigious Chinese journal of philosophy, *Philosophy Research* (*Zhexue yanjiu* 哲學研究). The journal published his first influential theoretical essay when he was only 26. This essay, which will be introduced and analyzed in detail in later chapters of this book, was based on his critique of the aesthetic theories that had been prevailing in China at the time. Almost immediately, it brought him great fame not only as a promising theoretician, but also the less splendid reputation of being a "rightwing scholar."

Soon after the beginning of the first wave of the so-called Aesthetic Fever (*meixue re* 美学热), Li became one of the most visible proponents of this influential discourse, taking part in all of the most important controversies that decisively formed its development.[5] It is not coincidental that he belongs among the pioneers of modern and contemporary Chinese aesthetics. During the latter half of the 1960s, like many other nonconformist intellectuals, he was consigned to re-education in a working camp in the province of Hebei. During this exile, he wrote numerous essays and also began to work on his longer, more complex, and more mature works.

In the following years, his influence grew continuously and gradually he obtained the reputation of being one of the most important Chinese theoreticians of the twentieth century. His impact upon younger intellectuals, especially students, grew so strong during the 1980s that, after the massacre at the Tiananmen Square in 1989, he was severely criticized for "poisoning a whole young generation" and his works were forbidden for several years. In addition, he was prohibited from leaving the country until 1992. Thanks to constant pressure from abroad (especially by American and German academic and political organizations), he was then allowed to visit the United States and Germany. He was appointed visiting chair professor at Colorado College and taught there for several years. He still resides in Boulder, occasionally assuming shorter research and teaching positions at other universities and abroad, including Hong Kong and China.

The above-mentioned sparse biographical data should only serve as the crucial signposts marking the most important transfers and stations on the winding path of his life, consisting of two always creatively interconnected trails of personal experiences and professional work. However, before introducing this path in a more detailed and contextualized way, I would like to set out a rough list of his most important publications. Li is an extremely productive writer, having published a wide range of articles, essays, and more than thirty books. This makes it rather difficult to decide which ones deserve a special mention. Here, I will try to point out some of the most influential ones in the fields of aesthetics, epistemology, classical Chinese and comparative philosophy, historical ontology, and political studies.

Li began working on aesthetic issues in the 1950s when he was still in his twenties. Soon after he entered Peking University, he published several articles on aesthetics. He gained a lot of attention in intellectual circles as early as 1956 with the publication of his first mature theoretical essay entitled "On the Aesthetic Feeling, Beauty, and Art" (*Lun meigan, mei he yishu* 論美感, 美和藝術). However, his most famous work on aesthetics is *The Path of Beauty* (*Meide licheng* 美的歷程). This book, which is generally considered to be a classic of modern Chinese aesthetics, was published in 1981, with the English translation appearing in 1994 in Oxford.[6] His other important works include *The Chinese Aesthetic Tradition* (*Huaxia meixue* 華夏美學, 1988) and *Four Essays on Aesthetics* (*Meixue si jiang* 美學四講, 1989). These three books, all translated into English, comprise the core of his opus on aesthetics. In later years, they were reprinted and published together in his famous collection *Three Books on Aesthetics* (*Meixue sanshu* 美學三書).

Li is also significant in terms of his research on classical and traditional Chinese philosophy. As a student, he investigated the philosophies of the important premodern scholars and reformers of the Qing Dynasty, Tan Sitong 譚嗣同 (1865–1898), and Kang Youwei 康有爲 (1858–1927).[7] The results of these investigations were later compiled into *Studies on the Thoughts of Kang Youwei and Tan Sitong* (*Kang Youwei Tan Sitong sixiang yanjiu* 康有為譚嗣同思想研究) published in 1958. A good decade later, immediately after the Cultural Revolution in 1979, he published the first book of his trilogy on traditional Chinese thought, *On Pre-Modern Chinese Intellectual History* (*Zhongguo jindai sixiang shilun* 中國近代思想史論). The other two were *On Ancient Chinese Intellectual History* (*Zhongguo gudai sixiang shilun* 中國古代思想史論, 1985) and *On Modern Chinese Intellectual History* (*Zhongguo xiandai sixiang shilun* 中國現代思想史論, 1987). In 1980, his essay "A Reevaluation of Confucius" (*Kongzi zai pingjia* 孔子再評價); was especially important because it proved that Li was the first contemporary Chinese philosopher who strove for a rehabilitation of Confucianism, which after 1949 was gradually thrown to the dustbin of history and marked as "feudalistic ideology." At the threshold of the new millennium, he wrote several additional books in this field: a reinterpretation of Chinese classics, *Reading the Analects Today* (*Lunyu jindu* 論語今讀); and an important collection containing his specific theories on the development of Confucianism and its influence upon Chinese culture, *Five Essays from 1999* (*Jimao wu shuo* 己卯五說). In *Pragmatic Reason and the Culture of Pleasure* (*Shiyong lixing yu legan wenhua* 實用理性與樂感文化), Li elaborated on the philosophical, spiritual, emotional, and ideational grounds of traditional Chinese culture. In this context, we should also mention his treatise, *Contemporary Currents of Thought and Chinese Wisdom* (*Dangdai sichao yu Zhongguo zhihui* 當代思潮與中國智慧). In recent years, Li upgraded his theories in these fields and published the results in 2015 in a relatively tiny compilation *From Shamanism to Rituality: Explaining Rituality as a Return to the Humanness* (*You wu dao li, shi li gui ren* 由巫到禮, 釋禮歸仁). These works partly include a comparative perspective grounded on Li's broad knowledge of traditional and modern Western philosophy.

Among the works that provide an overview of his own philosophical system and explain the crucial concepts of his theory are *Wode zhexue tigang* 我的哲學提綱 (*The Outline of My Philosophy*) and *An Outline of Philosophy* (*Zhexue gangyao* 哲學綱要). His ethical thought is summarized in *An Outline of Ethics* (*Lunlixue gangyao* 倫理學綱要), published in 2010.[8] *What Is Morality* (*Shenme shi daode* 什麼是道德) (2015) is based on his important differentiation between ethics and morals (*lunli daode erfen* 倫理道德二分) and on ethical and philosophical debates that he carried out in 2014 at Huadong Normal University in Shanghai.

Li's epistemological works are also very important and rather influential, especially those based upon his critique and elaboration of Kant's philosophy. In this context we must certainly point out his extensive and probably most difficult work, namely, the *Critique of Critical Philosophy: A New Approach to Kant* (*Pipan zhexuede pipan—Kangde shuping* 批判哲學的批判: 康德述評). Published in 1979 it was written during his detention in a re-education camp during the Cultural Revolution. Li's reinterpretation of Kant's subjectivity and its integration into his newly coined concept of *subjectality* (*zhutixing* 主體性). Subjectality can also be found in his "four outlines." The first, "An Outline of Kant's Philosophy and the Construction of Subjectality" (*Kangde zhexue yu jianli zhutixing lungang* 康德哲學與建立主體性論綱, was first published in 1981 as a speech given at a conference organized to celebrate the two hundredth jubilee of Kant's *Critique of Pure Reason*. The second outline followed four years later, *A Supplementary Explanation of Subjectivity* (*Guanyu zhutixingde buchong shuoming* 關於主體性的補充說明). Subsequently, Li wrote two more supplements on these explanations, *The Third Outline on Subjectivity* (*Guanyu zhutixingde di san tigang* 關於主體性的第三提綱) (1987), and *The Fourth Outline on Subjectivity* (*Zhutixingde di si tigang* 關於主體性的第四提綱) (1989). All four outlines were later republished in the Taiwanese edition of his *The Outline of My Philosophy* (*Wode zhexue tigang* 我的哲學提綱, 1996). He explains the most important feature of this concept in English in "Subjectivity and 'Subjectality': A Response," which was published in *Philosophy East and West* in 1999.

Li also wrote several works on philosophical anthropology. "An Outline of the Origin of Mankind" (*Renlei qiyuan tigang* 人類起源提綱) was written in 1964 but was first published in 1985 under the slightly different title, "On the Origin of Mankind (An Outline)" (*Shilun renlei qiyuan* 試論人類起源 /提綱/). Also, his *Historical Ontology* (*Lishi bentilun* 歷史本體論) was later republished in a more complete and expanded form with the title *Anthropo-Historical Ontology* (*Renleixue lishi bentilun* 人類學歷史本體論). Much of the content from these two books and from "An Outline of the Origin of Mankind," were originally also part of the aforementioned, concise collection entitled *The Outline of My Philosophy*.

One very important work from the broad range of his writings in political philosophy is *Marxism in China* (*Makesizhuyi zai Zhongguo* 馬克思主義在中國), published in Hong Kong in 2006. Li's reinterpretations of Marxist theories can also be found in *Farewell to Revolution* (*Gaobie geming* 告別革命) coauthored with Liu Zaifu 劉再復.[9] In *A Response to Michael Sandel and Other Matters* (*Huiying Sangdeer ji qita* 回應桑德爾及其他), first published in 2014, he discusses his own system of political philosophy and places it in relation to Western liberalism.[10]

An extraordinarily prolific writer, Li also published an endless series of articles and essays on a wide variety of topics. Some of the most important ones appeared two influential collections: *Following My Own Way* (*Zou wo zijide lu* 走我自己的路) and *A Collection of Various Essays* (*Za zhu ji* 雜著集).

The Beauty of Being Alive: Exciting Theories and Creative Practices

Li Zehou was born into a refined but poor family. In spite of their poverty, his parents both cherished and valued education and the intellectual development of their two sons. His father was an official with the post office and had a good command of the English language, a rare asset at the time. His mother was an elementary schoolteacher. As soon as he could read, his parents provided him with opportunities to immerse himself in the rich waters of traditional literature. At the same time, he and his younger brother were raised in accordance with Confucian values and norms. According to his own recollection, no one was supposed to even touch their chopsticks at lunch before the grandmother, the oldest member of the family, started eating. In such ways, he learned "to control himself from the earliest times" (Yang Bin 2015, 3).

Li Zehou was twelve years old when his father passed away. In that year as he hiked in the highlands, Li came upon a startling view of a meadow covered with gorgeously blooming mountain flowers. Overwhelmed by the beauty of the moment, he suddenly became aware of his own mortality. He found himself wondering what, then, was the sense of this beauty, for it seemed meaningless, ephemeral, and empty. The young Li experienced a kind of existential crisis, leading him to skip school for three days (Li Zehou 2016b, 605). It was after this crucial moment that his interests, already very broad, gradually became more centered upon philosophical questions, and were later increasingly connected with aesthetics.[11] By pursuing aesthetics, he hoped to find the answers to the eternal questions of how we perceive and value beauty, and what it means for humanity. Ultimately, it was philosophy and especially aesthetics that helped him understand that, as an individual, he would always be deeply influenced by the laws of social development; even though individual life is tragic, one could more easily understand that it is the laws of shared development of human communities that raise human purpose to the level of the sublime. It was probably also because of this brief but critical experience that his later philosophy never left the sphere of human life, leading his theory to proceed from the basic fact that "the human being is alive."

This is how Li found his own path, to which he remained loyal all his life. It was not the easiest one, because the driving force that led him over this untrodden route was not a reward in the form of power or fame. This was the path he had to follow because there was no other way. He often recalled his mother, who, after losing her husband at a young age, had to raise and educate her two children all by herself, which at the time was anything but easy, especially given the fact that the entire family had to rely only on her low teacher's salary. In order to offer both her sons possibilities for a better future despite their present poverty, she had to work additional jobs, working from early morning until late evening. When neighbors tried to comfort her by saying that her sons would repay her efforts in the future, she would always reply:

> I only know that the fields have to be cultivated. I am not waiting for the harvest.
>
> 只問耕耘, 不求收穫。 (Li Zehou 2003a, 19)

In Li's case it was not necessarily a struggle for survival, but rather a struggle to fulfill his intellectual needs, to feed his rampant curiosity, and sate his passionate craving for answers. He always felt an aversion to simply stepping into the footsteps of others, or simply reading what was required of him to read. It is therefore unsurprising that he often obtained valuable insights from blacklisted literature. At the age of fifteen in high school, he discovered Karl Marx. Four years before the establishment of socialist China, the work of this influential, but daring European theoretician still belonged to the forbidden literature—at least at his conservative high school. Studying socialist theory during that period was thus an exciting adventure. By secretly reading Marx, young Li felt just as thrilled as he would thirty years later when he secretly read Kant in a Maoist reeducation camp.

Although he successfully passed the entrance exam to the best high school in his native province, he had to enroll in the teacher's secondary school, because the latter provided students with free food. In exchange, in order to obtain his diploma after he graduated, he was obligated to teach for two years in an elementary school. But he had to find the teaching position himself, which was not an easy task, because at that time he already had gained the reputation of a radical leftist intellectual. Hence, he could not attend the entrance examination for universities before 1950, although he had graduated from secondary school in 1948 (Li Zehou and Liu Xuyuan 2011b, 73).

Being away from home, he was unable to see his mother before she died in 1949 at the age of 41. But in the next year, Li fulfilled her (and his own) dream when he passed the entrance exam for admission to Peking University, where he planned to study philosophy. He also passed the entrance exam to local Wuhan University. With an option to select between the two, he chose the more prestigious Peking University. The only problem was that he did not have enough money to buy a train ticket to Beijing. To overcome this barrier, he tried to sell blood, but because of bad health, he was rejected. As a result of problems such as these, Li finally arrived in Peking more than a month after classes had started. He was an extremely poor student, but optimistic and happy at the same time. Every month, he would send most of his scholarship money to his young orphaned cousin who attended high school in his home province. As a result, he used to brush his teeth with salt instead of toothpaste, which he couldn't afford. But Li did not lament his poverty: after each solemn celebration of the official feasts, he used to linger at one of the open fires at Tiananmen Square to have fun with his fellow students and friends through the night right until dawn.

Almost immediately after enrolling and attending lectures, Li became driven by a strong desire to carry out independent research so he started working on Tan Sitong's philosophy. However, without an advisor's guidance, this was a task was too difficult as he learned that Tan's thought was philosophically immature and full of self-contradictions. In 1952, he began to investigate Kang Youwei's work. Kang Youwei had been Tan Sitong's teacher. The essay that resulted from these studies was published in 1955 and, according to Li, this was his first published academic article (Li Zehou 2011b, 74). Years later he still held Kang in the highest esteem, seeing him as a representative of the "middle way." Kang was one of the very few people who knew exactly how to choose the "proper measure," a concept that will be elaborated in detail in the later chapters of this book. While Zhang Zhidong could be seen as a conservative and Tan Sitong as a representative of radical ideas, Kang was, in Li's view, a good example of someone who would agree with his proposal of "Western substance, Chinese application."[12] Similar to Li, Kang also always emphasized the importance of individual freedom and a gradual change of the existing social order (Li Zehou 2016, 84–85).

Several years before the beginning of the infamous "Great Debate on Aesthetics" (*Meixue da taolun* 美學大討論), which was originally intended to establish Marxist aesthetics in China (Li Zehou 2001, 22), Li was already interested in the philosophical investigations of beauty. By the time he attended first grade at the Department of Philosophy, he was used to reading English essays on aesthetics on his own, although they were not part of the official curricula. His graduation thesis, however, was linked to his research in Kang Youwei's and Tan Sitong's thought.

After graduation in 1954, several of his professors—including Feng Youlan 馮友蘭, the famous pioneer of the Modern Confucian thought—wanted him to remain at the university, but student representatives and the personnel department sent him to Shanghai. However, because of his severe tuberculosis, which constantly caused him to cough up blood, he was sent back to Beijing after only a few days. In February 1955, he was assigned to the Department of Philosophy at the Chinese Academy for Sciences (*Zhongguo kexue yuan* 中國科學院), later renamed the Chinese Academy of Social Sciences (CASS), where he worked during the 1950s and 1960s as a junior researcher. The library there was excellent, much better (and richer) than the one at Peking University. Here, he was able to access even the latest material on Western theories.

Fragile Dreams of Freedom and Different Horizons

From the very beginning, Li had planned to focus on Chinese intellectual history, but as soon as he discerned that there was a public intellectual debate that revolved around the question whether beauty was subjective or objective, he immediately became absorbed by it.[13] At that time, it had already become quite clear that Li was following his own path, and a rather unique one at that. He opposed both main interpretations prevailing in the Chinese academic world of that period. Beauty for him was not objective as a part and parcel of some internal texture of objects, nor was it purely subjective—created by the mind of the beholder. He saw beauty as social, originating from the material practice of humankind. In this sense, it was objective, but simultaneously subjective, although this subjectivity was not of an individual nature but of a more general social nature. For Li, beauty was something that resulted from the inner aspect of the Marxist notion "humanization of nature."

In 1956, right at the beginning of the "Great Debate," he published "On the Aesthetic Feeling, Beauty, and Art." In this essay, Li established the foundations of his theory on aestheticism, that beauty or aesthetic feeling is determined by objective sociality. In this essay, he introduces ideas that were very close to his central cultural-psychological concept of *sedimentation* (*jidian* 積澱), which he would establish later. This concept, based on Li's critique of the prevailing aesthetic theories of Zhu Guangqian 朱光潛 and Cai Yi 蔡儀, together with his elaborations on the importance of "image thinking" (*xingxiang siwei* 形象思維) almost immediately brought him the ambiguous prominence of a "rightist."

In 1959, he was accused of being related to the so-called Hu Feng 胡风 contra-revolutionary clique and was branded as a person with "problematic thought" (*sixiang wenti* 思想問題). While he survived the continuous interrogations and investigations that followed during this campaign, that marked the arrival of politically more rigid times, his close friend Wang Chengshao 王承紹 committed suicide because of the permanent attacks. Wang was not the only one to commit suicide. After the Hu Feng process, many intellectuals lived in fear, and many committed suicide. The atmosphere was oppressive and the last relics of the previously euphoric mood had vanished. Many writers and researchers ceased to write. The number of literary and theoretical works fell dramatically, their subjects and forms impoverished. The faith of the intellectuals in the Communist Party and in a "New China" suffered a severe setback. Li remained calm and buried himself in books, especially works on topical Western theories. In these works, he found a new freedom. And since freedom seldom comes alone, he also found love. In 1963, he married Ma Wenjun, a bright, independent-thinking young actress and dancer.

Two years after that, a far less romantic event swept over China: the "Great Proletarian Cultural Revolution." Li did not actively participate in any of the campaigns and did not join any ideological fraction. He preferred to remain at home and rarely went to his office. He frequently asked for sick leave and stayed home, reading books and writing articles that he did not publish, because at that time, they were simply unpublishable. The kinds of articles that could have been published were not the ones he wanted to write (Yang Bin 2015, 40). From 1964 until 1966, he was sent to a re-education working camp at the May 7th Cadre School in Henan province for two years before he was reunited with his wife. During this time, the concept of image-thinking, which belonged to the most important aspects of Li's theoretical work, was severely criticized.[14] In 1973, his only child was born. In this period, he wrote numerous essays and also began to work on his longer, more complex works, among others his first major theoretical monograph *Critique of Critical Philosophy: A New Approach to Kant*. Li Zehou remembers that he started to work on the book in the early 1970s, during his stay at the cadre school (Li Zehou 2002a, 4).

He managed to smuggle into the re-education camp an English volume of Immanuel Kant's *Critique of Pure Reason*. There he used to read it secretly, under the cover of *Chairman Mao's Quotes*, pretending to be deeply immersed into the study of this universally enforced reading. In some way, his cynical comments on this situation are quite logical: "In a difficult situation it is good to read a difficult book" (Li Zehou 2008e, 318). However, the fact that he took precisely this book along to the re-education camp was mainly the result of a highly pragmatic decision. It was relatively light, which was ideal since the weight of the luggage he was allowed to take with him was very limited. Also, the book was complex and difficult to understand, which meant that, although a small book, he could read it slowly and it would keep his mind busy and give him intellectual satisfaction for the longest possible time (ibid.).

Li had long been interested in Kant's philosophy, but he always put a thorough and systematic study and reinterpretation of his work on the back burner because his primary interests were in the study of aesthetics and the history of Chinese thought (Li Zehou 1990a, 3). During this period in particular, in which the Gang of Four dominated Chinese culture, it had become completely impossible for him to follow his original academic interests seriously. At that time Yao Wenyuan 姚文元 issued a directive that the history of Chinese thought could only be studied and analyzed in terms of the "battle between Confucians and Legalists."[15] Li refused to deal with Chinese intellectual heritage in such a way (Li Zehou 1996b, 461). In a certain sense, Kant's philosophy was even safer to deal with, for one could always claim that Kant, like Hegel, belonged to the predecessors of Marx, which meant studying Kant could be justified in the sense that Kant served as a background for a better understanding of Marx's philosophy (ibid., 464).

After returning from the re-education camp, Chong remarked that Li "withdrew from public view and began writing his commentary on Kant" (Chong 1999a, 103). That four-year period was a time of immense suffering: "Culture was in turmoil, (Li) had no access to many indispensable sources, and on top of this he had to cope with health problems" (ibid.). The first draft was completed around the time of the infamous Tangshan earthquake while he was in an earthquake tent.

Li started his writing under the pretext that it was in response to the campaign "Criticize Apriorism" (*Pipan xianyanlun* 批判先驗論), which was an important part of the general campaign "Criticize Lin Biao, Criticize Confucius" (*Pi Lin pi Kong* 批林批孔) (ibid.).[16] According to his later explanations, an important reason for writing this text, which turned out to become one of his most difficult and complex books, was to indirectly express his own thought and establish his own theory (Li Zehou 1996b, 6; 2008e, 318). Although the book was draft form and relatively incomplete (but nevertheless systematic), it represents a version of his pragmatic (or practical) philosophy of subjectality, based on the paradigm of anthropo-historical ontology. Wrapped in such a complex system, he tried to critically but subtly express his opposition to the then dominant ideologies (ibid.). His main goal was to clarify the relation between Kant and Marx (neither of whom, in his view, was understood very well in China and to provide a creative development of the synthesis of their philosophical contributions. In this book, Li tries to supplement Kant through Marx, and vice versa. For him, the "intersection" of these two theories was of utmost importance (Li Zehou 2016,154). However, he went even further. Li took elements from both philosophies that he valued most. At some point, he disagreed with both philosophies and from then on, he developed his own theory and followed his own way. He created the great majority of his new, self-coined concepts during this period while reading Kant's epistemology and writing this "Kant book," in which he systematically connected Kant and Marx, positing their philosophies in a mutually complementary relation.[17] With this work Li's own way was paved with a solid theoretical frame. He often admits that, while interpreting Kant, he actually wrote his own philosophy (Li Zehou 2016, 153).

Finally, the ice of autocratic policies began to melt. Li was an extremely productive author, and he was even more so in the 1980s, in the decade that followed the Cultural Revolution. This period was marked by a successive, but longingly awaited liberalization of critical thought, representing one of the most intellectually vivid and creative periods in China's history.

During this time, Li actively and most instrumentally participated in the "Aesthetic Fever." He also resumed and intensified his research in Chinese ideational tradition. In the early 1980s, he coined the term "emotion-based substance" (qing benti 情本體), in order to describe the ontological and moral foundation of traditional Chinese social reality. This paradigm also formed the basis of the Chinese traditional religious morality that could serve as a regulative principle for the exaggerated individualism inherent in modern social morals. However, in this decade, which was not only the most intellectually vivid and creative period in post-Mao China, but also the most critical one, Li Zehou highlighted the importance of modern social morality, which guaranteed important values such as respect for individual integrity and freedom, public reason, human rights, and the legal system. In spite of the regulative role of religious morality, social morality is important as a basis of reasonable, fair, and democratic political systems. For Li it formed the basis for individuals to freely decide on the beliefs of their "private virtue" (religious morals) and find values and meaning in the teachings and ideas of various spiritual or ethical discourses. Only on such a basis can religious morality in turn truly serve as the "regulative and properly constitutive" standard of social morality. Chinese authorities regarded such statements as heresy. In their view, these were expressions of "bourgeois individualism" which could undermine the legitimacy of official ideologies and the collective foundation of the socialist system. In spite of his "heresy," Li soon joined China's most influential intellectuals. His contribution to what is widely regarded as the new Enlightenment movement in the post-Mao China cannot be overestimated (Lin, Min 1992, 974). Considering the fact that the theoretical renaissance in the intellectual world was a compulsory condition of the economic and political reforms, it soon became obvious that Li was at the forefront of those who initiated changes through his works on Kant and modern Marxism, the history of both classical and modern Chinese thought, and aesthetics.

In this period, Li's concern with philosophical questions at a deeper level has had an increasingly greater impact on numerous Chinese intellectuals. His notion of human subjectality has directly influenced the shaping of a theory of *zhutixing* in contemporary Chinese literature. His theory of anthropo-historical ontology has led to a critical reconsideration of the conformist version of the Marxist epistemology and theory of perception by several Chinese theoreticians. In addition, he was one of the first Chinese scholars who openly pledged for a "rehabilitation" of Confucius (Kongzi 孔子) as the representative symbol of Chinese intellectual heritage, and for a critical revival of Confucian thought. Countless debates on aesthetics, epistemology, ethics, or traditional Chinese thought were inspired by Li Zehou's theories. In various intellectual, artistic, and cultural circles, his ideas have been extensively quoted as authoritative, and he has virtually become the "intellectual icon or guru of many university students" (Lin, Min 1992, 975).

Besides his attempts to re-bridge various social dichotomies—individual freedom and social or historical necessities, alienation and progress, subjective emotions and objective laws—Li was mostly regarded as a bridge between the older and younger generations. His huge impact and massive attraction were felt by an entire generation of Chinese youth who regarded him as an inspirational intellectual leader, comparable to the roles of Jean-Paul Sartre or Herbert Marcuse in Western culture. Li's popularity reached a genuinely huge dimension. His books almost always sold out within days of publication, and there were hardly any student dorms without at least a volume of his *Critique of Critical Philosophy*, even though the book is extremely complex and difficult to read. We could probably track this impact to two main reasons: Li's openly declared love for beauty and his appreciation of freedom. Both factors were tightly connected to emotions and to the longing for unpredictable and inexpressible wings of our life. This was a yearning that was (with good reasons) hidden in the subconscious desires of young Chinese people living in the 1980s. Until then, notions of beauty as well as freedom had been considered taboo and were handled with care by the official and governing institutions under the claim that—like their underlying feelings—they were not easy to control and thus politically highly dangerous. These notions were also both connected to the creativity and spontaneity that were widely misused not so long ago through the massive emotional manipulations that were committed by Cultural Revolution and its leaders.

Li's popularity among Chinese youth was doubtless due to his emphasis on individual autonomy and democracy, and his questioning of formal authority (Li Zehou 2002, 1–19), a "disobedience" that also found expression in his theoretical essays. It is not coincidental that the notion of *subjectality* (*zhutixing*) is at the center of his theory. *Subjectality* is based upon the notion of an active subject forming an independent entity as a potential bearer for the realization of ideals (Li Zehou 2002b, 174). It is not difficult to understand the seeds of this attraction. Li sincerely and genuinely believed in the Chinese youth, in their intellectual, emotional, and creative potential. As one of the central representatives of the post-Mao Enlightenment movement, he criticized the remains of traditional gerontocracy that suppressed any form of creativity and independent thought.

Li openly condemned the academic authorities who demanded from young people only blind obedience, memorization of prescribed texts, and uncritical accumulation of factual knowledge, and encourage them to believe in themselves, "Young people should be confident; they should not allow themselves to be swallowed and overwhelmed by the huge piles of old Chinese papers . . ." (Li Zehou 1985c, 4). Just like

China itself, young people exploring its culture should also leave the old, outdated things behind them and go towards the future (ibid., 5). Li saw the innovative potential possessed by the young people as something Chinese society still did not value enough. For him, the automatic authority of the old was a relict of the remote past.

> I always feel this is the heritage of primitive societies. In primitive societies, it was clear that people who lived the longest and who had gone through the most things also possessed the best "education." But pre-modern and modern societies are not like that; there are many young people among the genuine inventors. Although they are not so experienced and they don't possess so much knowledge, they can discover a lot and generate numerous important inventions.
>
> 我總感覺這好像是原始社會的遺風。在原始社會誰的鬍子長，誰的權威就最大。因為他活得長，經歷的事情多，「學問」當然也最大。但近現代社會並不是這樣。真正的創新家經常有青年人。他們並沒有那麼多的學問、知識、經驗，卻偏偏能做出非常重要的發現或發明。(ibid.)

Li was convinced that China could not rely exclusively on experts with tons of accumulated data-driven information, but that it also needed thinkers, and since youth is the best time to develop one's ability to reason and to think independently, young people should make the most of it and should not waste their youth living in fear of the authorities.[18]

It was not surprising that immediately after the 1989 Tiananmen Square tragedy Li, found himself on the black list of Chinese intellectuals who were marked as "black hands" (*hei shou* 黑手) and reproached for attempting to manipulate students for their own goals. Li Zehou was mentioned by name in the official report of the "turmoil" as one of the elite scholars causing chaos. "Open letters signed by Li along with other intellectuals . . . were cited as evidence of his complicity in initiating and supporting the turmoil" (Lin, Min 1992, 990). As a socially committed intellectual, Li signed a critical protest letter initiated by Bei Dao 北島 and Chen Jun 陳軍 back in 1988, demanding the release of political prisoners and connecting the respect of human rights with the creation of a more positive atmosphere for the implementation and realization of the reform program (ibid., 992). In February 1989, he also signed a petition requesting the release of Wei Jingsheng 魏京生, a human rights activist known for his involvement in the prodemocracy movement (Yang Bin 2015, 133).

Only a few days before the massacre, as the situation at Tiananmen Square was obviously turning into a direct conflict between the students and the government, Li, together with eleven other intellectuals, signed an urgent statement confirming the important role students play in promoting freedom and democracy as necessary parts of the reforms. They urgently demanded that the government avoid using violence against the students (Lin, Min 1992, 993). At the same time, they also hoped to convince the most radical wings of the students to withdraw from the square because democracy could only be reached through gradual reforms. Li spoke to the students and tried to convince them to withdraw from the square, saying: "Please be reasonable, enough is enough! Let's stop for now—you can come back another time! I am against the continuation of this confrontation!" (Yang Bin 2015, 141). He was also against the two radical manifests that were issued by the students in the next days and strongly opposed their hunger strike. At that point, he remained "sympathetic, towards the movement, but without supporting it" (ibid.). He repeatedly emphasized that enlightenment must be integrated by the system, and that it cannot remain trapped in a movement. Democracy has to be implemented gradually, it cannot be rushed.

As a result of his criticism of the Chinese government's response to the protests and massacre he was branded a "thought criminal" and was forbidden to leave Peking. In 1991, following massive international pressures, he was granted permission to leave the country and visit the United States and Germany. In the United States, he was given a permanent residency shortly afterward.

Li Zehou has lived mostly in the United States since 1992, lecturing at various American universities and returning to his homeland only for short sabbaticals. However, despite the hospitality of the American government, he still maintained his critical, somewhat provocative, and freethinking spirit.

> Politicians like to use the name of culture as a flag to cover their real interests and intentions. Therefore, we cannot take governments as representatives of cultures. . . . Further, as Edward Said says in his *Culture and Imperialism*, "There are far too many politicized people on earth today for any nation to

accept passively the finality of America's historical mission to lead the world." Thus, a harmonious coexistence of multiple cultures with the same modern material civilization will be the future of mankind, a future for which we have to struggle. (Li, Zehou 1999a, 1)

Even though he was mainly living abroad, Li remained faithful to the Chinese culture throughout. He increasingly took after traditional Chinese scholarly ideals, always attempting to combine "the critical detachment of a serious scholar with a deep commitment to society that was the traditional mark of a member of the Chinese intelligentsia" (Lin, Min 1992, 971). He also returned to Chinese intellectual history, which—besides epistemology, ethics, and aesthetics—has always belonged to his central interests. His recent investigations into classical and traditional Chinese thought have also led to the creation of several new and important ideas and concepts, such as the unity of shaman and (Confucian) gentleman (*wujun heyi* 巫君合一) or the notion of emotional cosmology. In his later years, he also created numerous reinterpretations, redefinitions, and new explanations of previously existing theories.

Practically none of his contemporaries saw the modern Western challenges to Chinese culture in such a comprehensive way as Li did. He emphasized the holistic unity of technology, institutions, ideas, and values in the multifaceted development of intercultural interaction. As Lin Min rightly points out, the deep structure of Chinese tradition, with its integrated social, political, and cultural dimensions is actually the main topic of his academic undertakings (ibid., 975).

Rocky Relationships with Confucius, Kant, and Marx

In creating his theory, Li relied on three central sources of inspiration: early Marx, Kant, and Confucius. From a young age he was very much influenced by the earliest representative essay of the former, namely, the *Economic and Philosophical Manuscripts from 1844*, in which young Karl Marx promoted his theory of human value and estrangement—in contrast to his later works, which dealt mostly with economic theories revealing the operational mode, the historical conditions, and the structural foundations of capitalist societies.[19] Early Marx was influenced by Hegel's dialectical view of history, whereby he replaced Hegel's idealistic foundation with Feuerbach's materialistic and humanistic groundwork. Li assumed the early Marxist supposition, according to which the essential nature of human beings is that of a *homo faber*—or a living being capable of (and defined by) the free production (and reproduction) of their own existential conditions. In addition, Li has also assumed the Marxist view of historical development that is based upon material foundations.

Later on, when Li was first acquainted with Kant's transcendental philosophy, the young Chinese philosopher was very much impressed by his emphasis upon the idea of human subjectivity and the human subject as an independent, free, active, and morally autonomous agent. Kant's conception of subjectivity, however, was rooted in the existence of the transcendental forms that decidedly influenced and reshaped the (human perception of) objective realty. While for Kant, these forms were *a priori* (independent of any kind of [individual or social and historical] experience), Li, who also presupposed the existence of similar forms of subjectivity, placed them into a framework of a dynamic historical development.[20] The roots of such a view are doubtless to be found in Hegelian understanding of reality. Nevertheless, since Li aimed to place his dynamic and changeable forms onto materialist foundations, his theory can be seen as a form of, or a discourse belonging to, historical materialism. He tried to relocate Kant's transcendental forms into a dynamic and historical context, defined by the principles of a materialist development of humankind. At the same time, Li modified the teleological and deterministic Hegelian–Marxist view of social development through the exciting element of the (morally aware, yet unpredictable) human subject, her free will and his autonomy. In this sense, the meeting point of Marx and Kant was for him particularly relevant (Li Zehou 2016, 154). In this framework, the mental forms of human consciousness were no longer completely fixed, static, and therefore constant or even predetermined. Like sedimented layers of clay and sand from ancient times, they seem to be fixed from an individual's viewpoint. However, from the viewpoint of humankind as a historically (through millions and millions of years) evolving entity, they are not *a priori*.

In creating his anthropo-historical ontology, Li Zehou was mainly following early Marxist theories. He was highly skeptical towards Marxist economic theories and criticized the crucial concepts elaborated by Marx in his *Capital* through the lens of Kantian "transcendental illusions." In this context, he exposed that Marx summed up the "two-fold character of commodities" in the "two-fold character of labor." The crucial point was that Marx saw "exchange value" as a product of "abstract labor," since for him, the exchange of commodities was an act characterized by a total abstraction from use value.[21] According to Li, ideas such as socially necessary labor time, which were derived from the concept of abstract human labor, do make sense in rational analysis, but since they are completely separated from actual circumstances of concrete human lives, they are not empirically operational. Marx has completely separated the concept of labor from its concrete empirical environment; he abstracted the "labor-power" from the actual labor and from the concrete historical practice of making and using tools. This has caused him to slip into an abstract Hegelian idealistic speculation, in which he aimed to prove his concept of surplus value through a unified and homogenized, abstract idea of the "expenditure of human labor-power." In this abstract construct, the class struggle and the proletarian revolution became necessary, since Marx did not consider any of the complex, historically determined elements (as for instance the developmental stage of technologies in different societies and cultures). In Li's view, such elements are decidedly influencing the development of societies, which was in Marx's view determined by the relations between the class of the owners of the means of production and commodity-possessors on the one hand, and the working class, on the other. According to Li, this idea of class struggle between capital and labor has led Marx to the necessity of eliminating the market-guided production of commodities, which he replaced with planned economies, in which social distribution should be organized according to the maxim: "From each according to his abilities to each according to his needs." In Li's view, such a logic is problematic (Li Zehou 2006a, 141).

> At the same time, I believe that this logic has no necessary relation with the core part of the historical materialism, which I am emphasizing, namely with the using and making of tools (and the formation of human language, which stems from it).
>
> 同時我也認為這一邏輯與我強調的唯物史觀的核心部分，即使用一製造工具的實踐（以及由之而產生人類語言）並無必然的關係。(ibid.)

Li considers these abstracted concepts as a form of Kantian "transcendental illusions."[22] In Li's view, they represent conceptions of objects that can only be thought of, but not known, because they are shaped through abstract reasoning without any empirical foundation (ibid., 148). They are ideal illusions produced by the transcendental reason. Such transcendental illusions are still actively effective in guiding and organizing human thought, for they help us to achieve the greatest possible unity of reason (Kant 1998, 389/B359). Li emphasizes that they positively influence human ability to act and to change the world and have a profound philosophical significance.

Because of their transcendental nature, because they are completely separated from the empirical world, they cannot be directly applied in concrete strategies and policies of actual societies.

> The system of equal distribution that has been implemented in the past in our people's communes was such a case: it seemingly aimed to achieve justice and equality. However, because it has not considered or taken into account the multifarious other aspects and complex empirical factors, it resulted in stagnation and regression of productive forces. The economic wages were overall equal, but the living standard and the quality of life of the people were stagnating or even deteriorating.
>
> 列入以前我們人民公社所採取的工分制, 就因為沒有考慮, 計算其他方面的複雜經驗因素, 貌似公正, 平等, 造成的卻是生產力的停滯和倒退; 經濟收入大體平等了, 人民生活水準和質量卻停滯或下降了。(Li Zehou 2006a, 146)

In Li's view, this was also the reason why Marx's economic studies could not be developed in the framework of a general economic theory and why his theory of labor value was replaced by various concrete price theories. Although Marx's theory of labor value has a great historical, philosophical, and ethical significance, it completely lacks empirical operability.

In Li's philosophy, Kant's and Marx's theories were reshaped, modified, and upgraded in a theoretical framework that differed from the original. He agreed with Marx's presumption that tools represent the basic means of production. Nevertheless, he saw Marx's further evolvement of this theory as problematic because he saw it as being one-sided: progress from means of production to the relations of production and then on to the superstructure only concerned the external developments of the relation between the manufacture and use of tools. At this point,

Li was more interested in their internal influences; i.e., the ways in which the making and use of tools has reshaped the human mind. Li was interested in establishing and investigating the phenomenon of the cultural-psychological formations that were shaped in human inwardness in this process. For Li, this was a phenomenon tightly linked to the central questions of humanness (*ren xing*), for it could reveal the actual difference between human beings and animals (Li Zehou and Liu Xuyuan 2011b, 77). In order to proceed a step further on this path of reasoning, Li also offered his own, unique hypothetical definition of this difference outside of the constructs of behavioral norms, ethics, upright posture, language, or the construction and employment of tools. All these features are not uniquely and specifically human for they are also displayed by some kinds of animals. Li identifies the crucial difference in the fact that, for human beings, tools are a universal necessity (ibid.). If humans had only their bodily biological conditions to rely on, they could never survive (as human beings). In Li's view, this is also why humans are "supra-biological" beings.

Kant, on the other hand, saw the universal necessity in a completely different way, positing that *a priori* forms of reason were parts of a specifically human cognitive structure that is separated from and prior to experience. He never explained the origins of these forms. He merely emphasized their transcendental nature. Li took it upon himself to solve the riddle of the geneses of these forms. In contrast to Kant's view, he proposed a theory that held that "experience can be transformed into the transcendental (「*jingyan bian xianyan* 經驗變先驗)" (ibid.). The individual transcendental forms of cognition are shaped in this theory from collective human experience through historically long periods of sedimentation and can thus also be equated with the cultural-psychological formations (ibid.). Li explains:

> Ancient Greeks said, "Human beings are rational animals,"
> and Franklin said, "Human beings are tool producing animals"
> I want to connect these two opinions and investigate how
> "the tool producing animals" became "rational animals."
>
> 古希臘說「人是有理性的動物」，富蘭克林說「人是製造工具的動物」——而我是要把這兩個定義結合起來，即研究人怎樣由「製造工具的動物」變為「有理性的動物」。(ibid.)

Li held that this process of changing experience into the transcendental was especially clearly visible in China. Here, reason was not only shaped as a part of epistemology, but also of ethics and specifically Chinese aesthetics. These two discourses elevated biological animal capabilities into rational forms (ibid.). As we will see, this process started and finished in Chinese culture with emotions—reason and emotionality were intermingled in a specific mental formation, which Li termed "emotio-rational formation" (*qingli jiegou* 情理結構).²³ This epistemic structure is a part of the cultural-psychological formation, which is an antipode of the more basic; i.e., the techno-social formation.

These forms that encompass different layers, among which there is also a layer of the so-called cultural sedimentation. Li explained his understanding of the origins of the specifically Chinese culture: it is a (unique) culture of "rationalized shamanism." For Li, the process of rationalizing the shamanistic ceremonies was a crucial factor in the shaping of this culture that he named "the culture of pleasure" (*legan wenhua* 樂感文化), embedded in the bosom of the above-mentioned "emotion-based substance" (*qing benti*), which was defined by the "one world view" (*yige shijie guan* 一個世界觀) and regulated by the "pragmatic reason" (*shiyong lixing* 實用理性). Li was the first theoretician who dared in 1980 to emphasize that Confucius was not a "reactionary" supporter of the "slave-owning class" and their exploitative ideologies (Moody 1974, 311), but rather a great ancient scholar who managed to preserve the rationalized external forms of ceremonies or rites (*li* 禮) that were established by the Duke of Zhou (Zhou Gong 周公²⁴), in order to further rationalize their internal forms and to lay foundations for a popularization of the elementary virtue of humaneness (*ren* 仁), which comprised reason with emotions. The structure of humanness (*ren jiegou* 仁結構) is a central part of the cultural-psychological formation (*wenhua—xinli jiegou* 文化—心理結構) accumulated in the mental forms transferred from generation to generation in the Chinese culture. Li emphasizes that without the contribution of Confucius, the developmental procedures of the specifically Chinese culture could be following completely different trajectories.

Proceeding from his own understanding of these three great thinkers, Li worked to establish his own theoretical system. He saw this work as a "transformative creation" (*zhuanhuaxingde chuangzao* 轉化性的創造), for it was embedded in, but by no means limited to, Confucian, Kantian, and Marxist discourses. His system cannot be seen as a mere blend of these philosophies—it exceeds a plain "synthesis of Kant and Marx" by combining their thought with Hegel's and, above all, with that of Confucius (Bruya 2003, 134). This book aims to show, inter alia, that Li Zehou's thought comprises several inventive essential features that cannot be found in the work of previous philosophers.

Theoretical Innovations

This section will offer a rough and schematic overview of the main ideas that shape and define the essential grounds of Li Zehou's theoretical system. The most significant concepts that were formed in the process of its establishment and the specific mode of their interrelatedness will be introduced in greater detail in the following chapters.

Li is one of the most significant contemporary Chinese philosophers working in the fields of aesthetics, traditional Chinese and Comparative philosophy, ethics and epistemology. Partly due to his status as a political dissident, he is also one of the best-known living Chinese intellectuals in the West. When in the late 1970s he emerged in China as an eminent intellectual leader "whose status and influence in China is probably comparable to that of Sartre in France" (Liu, Kang 1992, 121), Li's appeal to the younger generation has been enormous. Many consider him a "mentor of spiritual Enlightenment" (ibid.).

Li established a new foundation in the study of Marxism, which represented the primary subject of learning in China of that period. He went all the way back to Marx's intellectual origins, the pioneers of enlightenment, and the German idealist philosophy, to search for a solid theoretical foundation for Marxist theories. As we have seen, he seemed to have found this foundation in Kant, rather than in Hegel. In Li's view, Kant laid the ultimate grounds for a modern concept of an enlightened human subject, thereby providing possibilities for a new kind of reflection on humankind, nature, and society.

Li's reflection of the important, basic question regarding the essence, the specific features, and the evolvement of humanity, was rooted in a synthesis of Kantian transcendental subjectivity and Marxist historical understanding of material practice, in which the systematic producing and using of tools was seen as the basis and the ultimate reason for the evolution of the human species. The internalization and continuous gradual accumulation of this material practice changes experiences into transcendental forms, which shape and develop human subjectality. In contrast to the mechanistic and deterministic Hegelian-Marxist view, and (again) in accordance with Kant's understanding, the human subjectality also represents an important factor of social and individual development.

Li also made great contributions regarding the rehabilitation and philosophical revival of traditional Chinese, especially Confucian philosophy. He was the first one who pointed out the relation between shamanistic cultures and rituality and who explained why and how the tribal system and rationalized shamanism were the most important origins of Chinese culture. In addition, he also presented a pioneering contribution regarding the origins of the traditional Chinese tripartite unity between religion, ethics, and politics. And last, but certainly not least, Li proposed a completely new interpretation of the essence of Chinese intellectual history, replacing the Kong-Meng tradition in the role of a leading thought current with the Zhou Gong-Kong tradition.[25]

His research into the Chinese tradition also always remained inherently linked to the quest of Chinese modernity. He often emphasized that it was "a first step in the transformation of the traditional into the modern" (ibid., 986). Li is convinced that a deep and comprehensive understanding of Chinese intellectual history is a necessary and indispensable precondition for finding a workable reconciliation of the contradictions between the old and the new, the Chinese and the Western. Only on such a basis could one begin to develop a "transformative creation" (*zhuanhuaxingde chuangzao*), stepping on a new middle path that leads to a balanced, but sensible future.

We have already noted that Li's popularity among Chinese youth was primarily due to his emphasis on beauty and individual autonomy. Here, we could also expose his quest for democracy, and his questioning of formal authorities, a disobedience that also found expression in his theoretical essays (Li Zehou 2002, 1–19). Therefore, it is not coincidental that the notion of subjectality (*zhutixing*) is at the center of his theory. As he points out, it should not be understood in the epistemological sense of subjectivity (*zhuguanxing* 主觀性), but as a collective or individual human subject as an active agent striving for the realization of ideals (Li Zehou 2002b, 174). Li wanted to define the role of human agency in a way that was neither determinism nor voluntarism. In the 1980s, he suggested a new philosophical anthropology (also known as his "theory of practical subjectality") that moved between two poles. On the one hand, man is different from animals because of their capacity to mold their own environment in a goal-directed way. For Li, subjectality is real, if mankind can indeed to a great extent control its own destiny. On the other hand, human control over nature is subject to limitations that are partly determined by the level of technology and social organization in any given society (Chong 1999, 437). He attributes the widespread appeal of Maoist voluntarism in China to the belief in the transformative power of human will, unaided by science and technology.

Li's general philosophy is based upon the so-called anthropological ontology (*renleixue benti lun* 人類學本體論), a post-Marxist methodological tool that he created in order to supersede and elaborate upon traditional Marxist theory (Li Zehou 2002b). Li accepted and advocated Marxist materialism while simultaneously opposing the mechanistically abstracted view of dialectical social development. Like Marx, Li also emphasized the ideal of "humanization of nature" (*zirande renhua* 自然的人化), which he completed by the oppositional notion that was inspired by Daoist discourses. Li called this complementary antipode of the humanization of nature "naturalization of humans" (*rende ziranhua* 人的自然化). Both processes and their mutual interaction will be described in greater detail in later parts of this book. For now, we shall leave the former aside, for it is tightly linked to several other crucial concepts of Li Zehou's theory. The humanization of nature is the process in which human beings through their self-initiated action transform physical nature into an integral part of humanness.[26] Li slightly alters the original Marxist notion. In contrast to Marx, who mainly emphasized the relation between human beings and the external nature, Li understood it as a process directed not only towards the external, but also towards their internal worlds, for both of them are constitutive parts of humanness in the sense of the traditional Chinese notion *ren xing* 人性.[27] In this framework, Li's concept of subjectality (*zhutixing*) is of prime importance as it encompasses all constitutive elements of humanness that include naturalness, sociality, biology, historicity, individuality, rationality, sensitivity (Li Zehou 1994, 465). In this context, humanness marks the human pole of the static difference between human beings and all other beings and entities. However, from the viewpoint of a dynamic difference between human beings and the objective (or sacral) world, humanness is the internal part of subjectality, which is a product of sedimentation (*jidian*). Li aims to denote with this metaphor, borrowed from geology, the endless process of human evolution in which sense data, experiences, and laws arising from the external world are being internalized and accumulated in specific forms of human mental structures. Similar to natural sedimentation, this sedimentation of humanized nature also consists of several layers. Li mainly distinguishes between three basic levels of such accumulations. He calls the fundamental layer (by far the largest one) "sedimentation of species" (*wuzhong jidian* 物種積澱). This layer comprises universal forms that are common to all human beings. Li calls the second layer "cultural sedimentation" (*wenhua jidian* 文化積澱). It consists of forms, linked to specific thought and behavioral patterns, linguistic structures and other factors shared by people belonging to particular cultures. The third layer (the topmost) is "individual sedimentation" (*geti jidian* 個體積澱), which co-creates our intimate value systems, worldviews, emotions, habits, as well as modes of thinking and feeling[28] (Cauvel 1999, 156). All three layers form a dynamic entity. The changes in the highest (topmost) layer are the fastest and occur the most often as they follow human life experiences. The changes are the slowest in the most fundamental, deepest universal layer of sedimented forms of human species. From the viewpoint of an individual life, or even from the viewpoint of many generations, this level is fixed and static—for our limited sense organs cannot perceive or comprehend changes that took place gradually over a long historical evolvement that lasts several millions of years. Hence, these forms falsely appear to us as static and unchangeable.

On the other hand, the subjectality, which is formed by the process of sedimentation, is additionally defined by four dimensions (or two pairs of contents), which overlap and mutually influence each other. The first two dimensions of human mental forms are the external techno-social formation (*gongyi—shehui jiegou* 工藝一社會結構), which pertains to social and material production, and the internal cultural-psychological formation (*wenhua—xinli jiegou* 文化一心理結構).[29] In addition, human subjectality also comprises the human community or "the great self" (*da wo* 大我) and the human individual or "the small self" (*xiao wo* 小我) (Li Zehou 2016, 173).[30] The mutual interaction between these four dimensions shapes human subjectality. Although these dimensions are complementary, interdependent, and even though they mutually influence each other, the external techno-social formation, which is connected to the material practice of making tools, grounds all later dimensions. Li argues that this production predates all symbolic and artistic activities by hundreds of thousands of years (Li, Zehou 1994, 2). "The great self," or the communal or collective aspect of subjectality, is also a dominant entity in comparison to "the small self"; i.e., the individual aspect. In this sense, subjectality has been incorporated as an entity that embraces and simultaneously transcends any social group (Feng Qi 2001–02, 813).

Human action as a driving force for the humanization of nature consists of two inherent ontological structures: the first, which is of a biological-technical nature, Li calls techno-social substance (*gonju benti* 工具本體) while the second, which is culturally determined, he calls it psychological substance (*xinli benti* 心理本體). In parallel with these definitions, Li also distinguishes between two different kinds of subjectality. The first refers to the personal identity of an individual and the second to communities and to humanity as a whole.

Hence, the concept of subjectality (*zhutixing*), in the sense of an objective human existential entity, is by no means limited solely to the level of the individual (including their ability to establish interactive relations with their environment); it also implies various kinds of human community (societies, nations, classes, organizations).

> The so-called subjectality has precisely this meaning. The subject of humanity appears through the social realization of material reality, (based upon material production). This is the objective level of subjectality. This level is elementary and manifests itself in the structural connection between technology and society, as well as in social existence. Simultaneously, it also embraces the subjective level of social consciousness, which manifests itself in culturally conditioned mental structures. Therefore, the mental structure of subjectality is not primarily the subjective awareness of an individual in the sense of his sensations, desires etc. This notion refers primarily to the results of human history that manifest themselves in structures of spiritual and intellectual culture, as well as in structures of ethical and aesthetic consciousness.
>
> 所謂'主體性'也是這個意思. 人類主體即展現為物質現實的社會實現活動 (物質生產活動是核心), 這是主體性的客觀方面即工藝—社會結構亦即社會存在方面, 基礎的方面. 同時主體性也包括社會意識亦即文化心理結構的主觀方面. 從而這裡講的主體性心理結構也主要不是個主觀的意識, 情感, 慾望, 等等. 而恰恰首先是指作為人類歷史成果的精神文化, 智力結構, 理論意識, 審美享受。(Li Zehou, 2001, 43)

While Marx was interested in sociality, the post-Marxist theories were, according to Li, exaggeratedly focused upon the latter, individually conditioned type of subjectality. In his philosophy, Li tries to go "from Marx to Kant and also from Kant to Marx," but he does not simply copy these two great thinkers. Rather, he uses Marx as his starting point to reexamine issues initiated by Kant and then deals with unsolved problems arising from these considerations (Ding 2002, 247). He places these discourses into a framework that is closer to traditional Chinese philosophy, especially to the Confucian treaties, which were in his view strongly marked by the notion of pragmatic reason (*shiyong lixing* 實用理性). It is a form of reason, rooted in the conditions and requirements of human life in communities and societies. It furthermore functions through the interaction of rational and emotional factors, which are seen as equal parts of the emotio-rational structure (*qingli jiegou*) and grounded in the ontology of the emotion-based substance (*qinggan benti* 情感本體).

Li's concept of subjectality manifests itself in the *homo faber* nature of humankind, which was shaped and developed through material practice. Subjectality springs out from the ontology of two substances, which are (at least *prima facie* and only to a certain extent) similar to the Marxist material base and ideational superstructure. These two substances cannot be understood as *noumena*, but rather only as an ultimate reality, origin, or root of the concrete phenomena grounded in them. The two substances are the techno-social or instrumental substance (*gongju benti* 工具本體) and the psychological substance (*xinli benti* 心理本體). They are reflected in the two types of sedimented dynamic structures, which he termed the techno-social formation (*gongyi—shehui jiegou*) and the cultural-psychological formation (*wenhua—xinli jiegou*) respectively. Neither belongs to static and fixed structures, for they are both highly modifiable and changeable. In particular, the cultural-psychological formation is profoundly influenced by the languages, modes of life, and the specific cultural traditions in which human beings live. In China, which Li sees as a "culture of pleasure" (*legan wenhua*), it manifests itself as emotion-based substance.

In this process of human genesis the making and using of tools was of crucial importance. For Li Zehou, this feature was by no means arbitrary but must rather be seen as a universal necessity, instrumental for the genesis, evolution, and survival of human beings. But this is not the only factor that conditions and defines humankind. In the process of its development, humankind could not have survived if it had not learned to apply the "proper measure," a concept that Li names *du* (度). *Du* is a typical classical Chinese category, which is tightly linked to the contents and basic approaches of the Confucian classics *Zhong yong* 中庸 (*The State of Equilibrium* or *The Mean*). It belongs to the crucial and pivotal concepts of Li Zehou's philosophy and will therefore also be introduced and analyzed in great detail in later chapters.

As noted, Li also tries to introduce into this framework the traditional Chinese concept of humanness (*ren xing*), which he sees as the unification of sensitivity and rationality, nature and culture, as well as the instrumental and psychological substances of subjectality. This unification is not achieved by the mechanical addition of these elements, but through the dynamic process of the humanization of nature, and thus through interaction between human subjects and natural objects. In this process, sensitivity and naturalness are transformed by rationality and social factors. The essence of this transformation manifests itself in the sense of beauty or aesthetic feeling (*meigan* 美感), which means that Li understands the philosophy of beauty (aesthetics) not only as the highest form of human philosophy, but also as a potential instrument for further developing the Marxist understanding of history. For him, beauty in philosophical terms basically concerns the problem of human subjectivity, although it is objectified through collective sociality, and even though it is, in scientific terms, reduced to the problem of the dynamic and changeable cultural-psychological mental structure (Ding 2002, 248). Thus, an investigation of the subjective dimension of beauty can provide the basis of the future development of historical materialism.

Li explains the essence of beauty in terms of the Marxist concept of humanized nature:

> Nature as such is not beautiful. Beautiful nature is a result of socialized nature, i.e., a result of the objectification of human essence. The socialization of nature is therefore the basis of its beauty.
>
> 自然本身並不是美; 美的自然是社會化的結果, 也就是人的本質對象化的結果. 自然的社會性是自然美的根源。 (Li Zehou 2002a, 23–24)

For Li, the sense of beauty or aesthetic feeling (*meigan* 美感) as the essence of the transformative humanization of nature is the ultimate stage in the realization of aesthetic awareness (*shenmei yishi* 審美意識). Because aesthetic feeling differs from aesthetic relations, attentiveness, and experiences, as well as from aesthetic capacities, intuitions, and sensitivity, questions concerning the aesthetic feeling are essentially epistemological ones (Li Zehou 2001, 142, 157). Although aesthetics as such cannot be reduced to epistemology: "The philosophical foundation of aesthetics as science is epistemology. The aesthetic feeling is the crucial problem in this specific area of inquiry" (Li Zehou 2002a, 2).

Li rejects the view of beauty as an independent quality, inherent *a priori* in the objects of our perception. Similarly, the sense of beauty cannot exist as an independent element of our individual consciousness, defined solely by our sensitivity.

> Our direct (intuitive) perception of concrete images already implies a number of extraordinarily complex contents from social life, including our comprehension and understanding of life itself. This means that perception embraces our recognition of relations between things.
>
> 在 . . . 各別事物的具體形象的直覺本身中，即已包涵了極為豐富複雜的社會生活的內容，包涵了我們對這種生活的了解和認識，而這，就正是包涵了我們對事物關係的認識。 (ibid., 7)

The sense of beauty is therefore of a sensitive, as well as of a supersensitive nature. It unifies contradictions between logic and intuition, usefulness and uselessness (Feng Qi 2001–02, 813). Specific elements of this unity automatically express themselves in certain forms. However, the sense of beauty also transcends specific limitations of these concrete forms, for it represents the sedimentation (*jidian*) of social rationality, inherent to human sensations. Li saw history as a process that reached its ideal goal in the domain of aesthetics, which he understood as the union of nature and freedom.

In his principal aesthetic work *The Path of Beauty*, Li states that while aesthetics in Chinese tradition never formed an independent academic (or theoretical) discipline, it can still be found in the majority of the most influential philosophical teachings (Li Zehou 2003, 45–49). Like most other dominant discourses, aesthetic treatises were also based upon rationalism, free of any religious or mystical ideas (ibid.).[31] Li sees this kind of rationalism in Confucianism, as well as in Daoism. In his view, even though both currents were established in opposition to each other, they were still linked as two complementary philosophical streams. The complementary and mutual roles played by Confucianism and Daoism are an important thread that has run through all traditional Chinese aesthetic thinking. Chinese Philosophy, including aesthetics, has been guided by the practical rationality of daily life, human relations, and political concepts, rather than by any abstract and abstruse rationalist theory (Ding 2002, 253).

> But how can such a "complementarity of oppositions" be realized on a concrete level? I believe that the very concept of the "naturalization of humans," as theorized by Zhuangzi and other Daoists, as well as the concept of the "humanization of nature," as found within the tradition of "rituality and music" in Confucian discourses, represent concepts that are based upon such a relation of simultaneous opposition and complementarity.
>
> 那麼, 這個'對立的補充'是如何具體進行呢? 我以為, 道家和莊子提出了'人的自然化'的命題, 它與'禮樂'傳統和儒門仁學強調的'自然的人化'恰好即對立, 又補充。(Li Zehou 2003, 265)

As we shall see later, Li's interpretation of his notion of the "naturalization of humans" appears as a counterpart to the Marxist "humanization of nature."[32] This interpretation is based upon the classical Chinese concept of the "unity of heaven (nature) and humans (*Tian ren heyi*)," which, according to Li, not only expresses the unification of nature and individual human consciousness, but refers primarily to the unification of nature and the material actuality (including productive relations) of the entire human community.

In the chapter "Humanization of Nature and Naturalization of Humans," we will see how and why the specificity of classical Chinese aesthetics becomes evident in the concept of the "Unity of heaven (or nature) and man" (*tianren heyi* 天人合一), which implies both complementary aspects. Such a unification of oppositions could, according to Li, provide a methodological foundation for the further development of theoretical interpretations of beauty and thus for the elaboration of a new global aesthetics.

As to the central issue that defines modern Chinese philosophical discourses—which position to assume vis-à-vis Western thought, Li inverts the famous slogan "(preserving) Chinese substance and (applying) Western functions (Zhongti Xiyong 中體西用)," instead proposing to "(apply) Western substance and (preserve) Chinese functions (Xiti Zhongyong 西體中用)." Actually, his view of China's confrontation with the West does not differ fundamentally from those who advocated the appropriation of Western technology and the preservation of Chinese ideologies. The reason for Li's inversion of their slogan is, at first glance, purely terminological.

> I understand the word "substance" (*ti*) differently from others. In my opinion, it primarily expresses social substance.... I have always stressed the fact that social existence represents the substance of society, and that "substance" (*ti*) for me means social existence, which for the most part was not defined by ideology.... Therefore, so-called technology is not a "function" (*yong*); just the opposite—technology belongs to the category of substance (*ti*).
>
> 我用的'體'一詞與別人不同，它首先指得是社會本體 . . . 我曾經強調社會存在是社會本體，把'體'說成是社會存在，這就主要不是意識形態 . . . 所謂科技不是'用'，恰好相反，它們屬於'體'的範疇。(Li Zehou 2002b: 155)

The concept of *ti* 體, or "substance," which the proponents of the original motto intended as the "substance of tradition," is understood by Li in Marxist terms as the material basis and social existence of society. In this regard, Li explains that he understood "Western substance" (*Xiti* 西體) primarily as modernization, which cannot be equated with Westernization, even though modernization undoubtedly began in the West (ibid., 156).

However, the concept of *yong* 用, understood as "function" or "application" in the sense of the particular way of life, has crucial significance for Li, for it defines the concrete circumstances of individuals in a society. To illustrate this concept, he replaces the traditional terms of essence and function with the very contemporary "hardware" and "software":

> Even though the hardware of material life (refrigerators, air-conditioners, televisions, etc.) are in unlimited use throughout the world, the software of human life (economic organization, political systems, customs, behavioral patterns, world views,

value systems, particularities of thought, etc.) differ with respect to various political and cultural traditions.

因為儘管物質生活上的硬件 (冰箱, 空調, 電視機等等) 世界通用, 並無國界; 但人們的生活軟件 (經濟組織, 政治體制, 生活習慣, 行為模式, 人生態度, 價值觀念, 思維特徵等等), 卻因不同政治, 文化傳統而不相同。

Because Li believes that identification with one's own historical tradition is a necessary prerequisite for the development of any society or individual, the "Chinese function,"—or the methods of modernization that correspond to specific Chinese social conditions, is of fundamental importance for the future of the Chinese state, society, and culture (ibid., 158).

> The "function" (yong) is of crucial importance, for it defines the question about which mode of transition towards a modern society really is easier and healthier. . . . We must not necessarily imitate and appropriate the already accomplished form of the Western model as the object of our aspirations for "transformation." Instead, we can create new forms and models in accordance with the specific conditions of Chinese history and contemporary Chinese reality. . . . The basic emphasis lies in the "creation" of new, and not in the "transformation" of already existing Western forms. "Creation," of course, is much more difficult than "transformation," since it implies many more attempts and possible mistakes, with many more necessary changes and urgent corrections. However, I still believe that it is worth paying this price, for it is the only way to discover the model and form that corresponds in factual terms to specific Chinese circumstances.

關鍵在 '用', 如何中國能真正比較順利地健康地進入現代化社會 . . . 不一定要以西方現成的模式作為模仿, 追求, '轉化' 的對象. 可以根據中國自己的歷史情況和現實情況創造出一些新的形式, 模態來 . . . 但強調 '創造' 新形式, 而不是 '轉化' 到西方的既定形式這一基本思路. 當然, '創造' 比 '轉化' 會需要更多的嘗試錯誤, 需要更多的修補改正, 但我以為, 付出這些代價是置得的, 因為它實在能夠尋找一些最適合中國情況的模態和形式。 (ibid., 385)

Li's view of the relation between past and present, tradition and modernity, Chinese and Western societies, as well as economy and culture, is paradigmatic for his entire philosophy. This is why we shall touch upon the above-mentioned issues many times and elaborate on them further in the later chapters of this book.

Impact and Critiques

Precisely because he frames an innovative and independent system, Li is not only one of the most famous, but also one of the most controversial contemporary Chinese theorists. Leftist critics often reproach him with "pseudo-Marxism." Rightists denounce him for "degenerating into the dogmatism of outworn Marxism" (Ding 2002, 257). But in his own view, even politically motivated criticism merely confirms his independence of thought, though he acknowledges that he was very lucky not to have become a severe victim of such criticism during the period of the Cultural Revolution.

> Interestingly enough, in my homeland I was attacked as an "Anti-Marxist" and "liberalist," while people from abroad (naturally including numerous compatriots) reproached me for being a "dogmatic Marxist" and a "conservative." Such criticism stopped bothering me long ago. But still, I am infinitely grateful that they did not occur at a time when such criticisms were written in large letters on the "Big-Character Posters."
>
> 有趣的是，海內批我是'反馬克思主義'，'自由化'，海外（當然也包括許多'海內'）批我是'死守馬克思主義''保守派'... 因之對所有批判,我幾乎已心如木石，無話想說. 唯一感激的是，好些批判不是當年大字報體。 (ibid., 352)

Some scholars consider his theoretical frameworks to be "a mixed stew" of Marx, Kant, and other philosophers, or, at most, a "creative imitation" of those figures (ibid.). Many theoreticians categorize him as a current follower of the eclectic school. However, Li seems to accept and even welcome such criticism.

> Someone has called me an "eclectic," since I deal with the Chinese history of thought as well as with Western philosophy,

and with aesthetics . . . I gladly accept such criticism, since I never wanted to become a specialist who spends his whole life studying a single classic.

據說有人曾說我「雜」，又是中國思想史，又是外國哲學，又是美學 . . . 我欣然接受。因為我從來不想作一生治一經的專家。
(Li Zehou 1996, 5)

Several scholars criticize Li for his ignorant attitude towards the supposedly decisive role of language in the process of human evolution and for his favoring pragmatic rationality.

Liu Kang, for instance, reproaches Li Zehou's theory of sedimentation with a "relentless privileging of rationality" (1992, 130). In his view, Li's account of rationality negates the problematic field of the unconscious as an antagonistic Other to the rationality of the Subject. According to Kant and Freud, subjectivity is based on the conflict between desires and sense experiences on the one hand, and laws of reason on the other. Liu believes that a rationality unifying the two essentially incompatible domains cannot be simply achieved by a pre-linguistic material practice of tool-making, which causes the former to coalesce into the latter. However, it must be pointed out that here, Li Zehou is proceeding from a different paradigm, because for him sensuality and reason are not embedded in an antagonistic, mutually exclusive relationship in the first place. Rather, they represent a correlative and complementary pair of the same entity, namely of a humanness or inborn human quality (*ren xing*) that is not seen as a fixed predisposition, but rather as dynamic and changeable unity of many different factors (Li Zehou 1994, 461).

Liu Kang further emphasizes that Li's "dismissal of important recent discoveries concerning language" was a "very serious flaw" in his thought (Liu Kang 1992, 130). He elaborates on this by adding that what Li has painstakingly belabored in order to explain the constitution of "subjectivity," namely the process of internalization and sedimentation, "errs at the critical moment where the antagonistic nature is embodied in symbolic and linguistic practices" (ibid.).[33] In this context, Liu also indicates that some critics emphasize language, or symbolic formation, as a meeting ground for Piagetian biological developmental models and Freudian psychoanalysis (Liu Kang 1992, 139).[34] However, as Michael Balter shows, new research reveals that the creation and the development of language was tightly linked to the needs for the production of tools and for the mediation and transmission of the skills which are necessary for it (Balter 2015). According to Balter, new studies conclude that "the art of conversation may have arisen early in human evolution, because it made it easier for our ancestors to teach each other how to make stone tools—a skill that was crucial for the spectacular success of our lineage" (ibid.). Therefore, with respect to the classical question about what distinguishes humans from other animals, it remains difficult to find an unambiguous answer. Although most theories from the twentieth century prefer the supposition that our *differentia specifica* is language and not the making of tools, it is, in fact, still impossible to prove which evolution, the linguistic or the tool-producing one, was prior and of a greater impact to the specific development of the humankind. This is not surprising, especially concerning the fact that words (in contrast to the relics of tools) leave no traces in the archaeological record. Notwithstanding the view that human language can also be seen as a kind of tool, both language and tools have certainly evolved in mutually complementary relation, as a part of the broader, general human ability of problem solving (McGrew 1993, 167).

Li often acknowledges that language and material practice are correlative and that they complement each other. For him, practice is primary and decisive, because it is necessary for human survival. It hence contains an ontological dimension. Li points to Heidegger and emphasizes that in Heidegger's *Being and Time*, he also denotes tools as a basic fact of life and that he exposed the existential importance of everyday life (Li Zehou 1994a, 18; Heidegger 1967, 69–71). Li also grounds his hypothesis with Wittgenstein's *On Certainty*, noting that Wittgenstein also claims that it is our acting, (not certain propositions), which lies at the bottom of the language-game (Wittgenstein 1975, 17).

Liu Kang also points out that Li is "acutely aware of this lack of engagement on the part of Chinese thinkers with the Western contemporary philosophy of language, power, and history" (ibid.). In this context, Li writes:

> This might be one of the future developmental streams of the materialistic view of the history. It will no longer deal merely with external structures of productivity, but will also concentrate upon questions linked to the inherent formations of humankind, which might gradually become a crucial point of future periods. Linguistics already comprised the center of

the philosophy of the twentieth century. Alongside educational sciences that explore the comprehensive growth, development, and formation, it might become the most important and central science of our future.

這可能是唯物史觀的未來發展方向之一。不僅是外部的生產結構，而且是人類內在的心理結構問題，可能日漸成為未來時代的焦點。語言學是二十世紀哲學的中心，教育學一研究人的全面生長和發展、形成和塑造的科學，可能成為未來社會的最主要的中心學科。(Li Zehou 1994, 474)

However, in his *Critique of Critical Philosophy*, Li also predicts that education and psychology should (and probably will) ultimately replace the language-centered humanistic and philosophical pursuits of the twentieth century (Li Zehou 2007, 281; 2016, 33). In his view, the limitation of language and the borderlines between the linguistic and conceptual sphere on the one, and the world of social reality on the other side, must be surpassed in order to fully restore humanness to humankind (Li Zehou 2015, 6).

Woei Lien Chong criticizes the general theoretic value of Li's theory by questioning his fundamental methodology: "The problem with this method, of course, is that it tries to show that *histomat* is true by using arguments which themselves rest on the assumption that *histomat* is true" (ibid.)[35] However, such critiques miss the point precisely because historical materialism is not a theory, but rather a method or a basic approach, which Li applied in order to provide a system based on a certain perspective of reality. It is a basic perspective that can be applied in the same way in which classical German philosophers, for instance, have applied the perspective of objective idealism. In the theory of science, it is not approaches or methods that have to be proven, but rather the consistency and reliability of the theories of which they are a constitutive part and which can be either verified or falsified.[36] (We will nonetheless be dealing with the functions and application modes of this method within Li's system in the last part of this book, for these utilizations certainly had a powerful impact upon his theory as a whole.)

Moreover, such critiques are grounded in the false assumption that Li's specific application of the *histomat*—its paradigms, laws, and outcomes, could be placed into and then proven or at least evaluated within a theoretical system belonging to models that have prevailed in the history of Euro-American thought. However, there are good reasons to assume that his system cannot be fully understood if we limit our observation and evaluation of his theories merely to perspectives inherent to such frameworks. In order to prove this point, we will take a broader look at Li's philosophy and his theoretical system as such in the last chapter of this book.

A similar critique, which is also mainly focused on Li's application of historical materialism, can be found in Lee Ming-huei's evaluation of Li's interpretation of Kant's philosophy. First of all, Lee reminds us that in his *Critique of Judgment*, Kant explains the essence of beauty with transcendental principles of unity of nature and teleology, as a bridge connecting the natural world with the world of freedom (Lee Ming-huei 2016, 34). He also points out that Li Zehou sees beauty as a form of freedom, a form which unifies natural and cultural elements in the sphere of humaneness, comparable to the unity of human beings and nature (*tian ren heyi*), which represents a core paradigm of traditional Chinese philosophy. Hence, Lee Ming-huei (rightfully) wonders whether such a holistic unity can really be established on the basis of a materialistic worldview.[37]

He also questions the legitimacy of Li Zehou's "evolvement" of Kant's philosophy, pointing out that his view of practice (which, as we have seen, represents the core of Li's modification of experiences into the transcendental) can be compared to Kant's, for it is too obviously rooted in the Hegelian (Aristotelian) and not in Kantian (Platonic) understanding. According to Lee Ming-huei, Li's basic approach is grounded on a completely different paradigm than Kant's. Lee believes they cannot be directly compared, since their similarity is only a formal one (ibid., 35–36). On the other hand, it is commonly known that Li aimed to upgrade a synthesis of Marxist and Kantian philosophy. In the logic of his double approach, it is therefore completely understandable that his historicist understanding of practice could be traced back to Hegelian approaches, for, as already mentioned, Marx places Hegel's objective idealism on a materialist foundation. Although Lee Ming-huei's critique is directly directed towards Li's system, it is actually questioning the very foundations of Marxist philosophy, for it is based upon the presumption that a material view of practice cannot be directly combined with elements of idealist (or transcendental) philosophy. Li, on the other hand, was explicitly referring to "intersections" of Marxist and Kantian philosophy, and not to any form of amalgamation based on mutual compatibility of the two systems.

In post-Mao China, an anti-Marxist climate prevailed in wide circles of the academic world. It is therefore quite easy to understand that at the threshold of the new millennium, Li was often seen as a conservative or at least a neo-conservative theoretician. However, as Wang Jing points out (1996, 95), anyone brave enough to keep repeating about how tool making, and, by effect, how the mode of production rather than abstract human nature governs the course of history unavoidably asks for the stigmatic label of conservatism. The fault finders, who classify him in this way, mostly do not understand that because romantic, harmless humanism prevailed in Deng Xiaoping's China as the new religion, it is precisely those who dare to swim against the sentimental current of humanism that truly deserve to be called radical (ibid.).

2

Central Concepts

The previous chapter provided us with insight into the general characteristics and specific features of Li Zehou's theoretical system. In this chapter, we take a closer look into the deeper structure of his philosophy by providing an analysis and interpretation of the central concepts that make up the paradigmatic foundation of his thought.

Sedimentation

Sedimentation is an innovative, fresh, and invigorating concept. Gu Xin emphasized that due to the lack of suitable existing words, the term was created by Li himself (Gu Xin 1996, 215). In reality this term, which is borrowed from geology and describes in a metaphorical way different layers of mental forms in human psychology, had been used by several modern European phenomenologists before Li.[1] But as we shall see later, they understood and applied the term in a different way than Li did. It is not very likely that Li borrowed the term from Western phenomenology because even in his twenties as a young university graduate with a very limited access to the central works of Western theories, Li obviously spontaneously associated the shaping of these geological forms with fluvial deposits. Li described sedimentation for the first time in his essay, "On Aesthetic Feeling, Beauty, and Art," which was published in 1956 in *Philosophy Research* (*Zhexue yanjiu*).[2] This pivotal notion regards a fundamental philosophical idea—linked to several other central concepts that constitute the basic theoretical platform of Li's system (as for instance to subjectality, the humanization of nature, the naturalization of humans)—as the shaping of inborn human qualities (or the so-called humanness *ren xing*), and thus to the very substance and existence of human beings (Li Zehou 1987, 238).

Li describes this notion as "the accumulations and deposits of the social, rational, and historical in the individual through the process of humanizing nature" (Li and Cauvel 2006, 94). Li's conception of sedimentation is based upon the metaphor of the geological stratification of layers of clay, soil, dust, and rocks that are formed and deposited over many millions of years. The mental forms of humanness are shaped by the accumulations of experiences, which is comparable to movements of glaciers, their rising and disappearing, the erosion and the modifications of earth's crust by continental drift, and so on. All these result in the formation of layers that change at different rates. The surface is more variable than the bedrock, which is relatively static and fixed (Chandler 2016, 170). The entire structure and each layer is modifiable, changeable, and moveable, subject to the never-ending process of the evolution of our planet.

The complex process of human sedimentation can be categorized into three levels where such layering takes place: sedimentation of species, cultural sedimentation, and individual sedimentation.[3] The process of sedimentation itself involves four dimensions, which form Li's notion of subjectality. These dimensions are the external techno-social formation (*gongyi—shehui jiegou*), which pertains to social and material production; the internal cultural-psychological formation;[4] the human community or "the great self" (*da wo* 大我); and the human individual or "the small self" (*xiao wo* 小我)[5] (Li Zehou 2016, 173). Li makes a distinction between these three different stages of sedimentation, namely:

1. elementary (primitive or original) sedimentation (*yuanshi jidian* 原始積澱),

2. artistic sedimentation or sedimentation of art (*yishu jidian* 藝術積澱),

3. vital sedimentation or sedimentation of life (*shenghuo jidian* 生活積澱).

Li describes elementary sedimentation as "the most fundamental sedimentation, formed from the process of material labor" (Li and Cauvel

2006, 134). This type of sedimentation began as part of the techno-social dimension at that crucial moment in history when humans began to produce and employ tools (*gongju* 工具) in a systematic and continuous way. This practice enabled them to modify the world around them, and at the same time themselves (Sernelj 2016, 99). Thus, this primary process of sedimentation was formed from material work. In this context, it is important to note that the most important part of elementary sedimentation was social. Because this process of sedimentation is "dynamic and continues to occur, the cultural-psychological formations created by primitive sedimentation are more flexible and subject to variation than the *a priori* structures described by Kant" (Chandler 2016, 169). Elementary sedimentation provides a foundation for artistic sedimentation. Li remarks that this level of sedimentation was formed when early humans started to appreciate that the tools they produced were useful in making their communities more comfortable and secure. At the same time, the pleasure they felt in making and using the tools led to the beginning of their sense of beauty (Li and Cauvel 2006, 134). The saturation of this form of sedimentation leads to vital sedimentation, which represents the basis of artistic creation. In this sense, sedimentation can be viewed as a process that constitutes aesthetic sensibility in human mental construction. These specific forms of sedimentation are the reason for the difference between human beings and other animals, because the inherent cultural-psychological formations, created and transferred in sedimentation processes, have enabled humans to create material and psychological practices that became a part of society (ibid.). According to Li, sedimentation can be interpreted in a broad or in a narrow sense. In the broad sense it refers to the development and constitution of human minds. In the narrow sense it refers to the constitution of aesthetic sensibility in human mental construction (Li and Cauvel 2006, 167).

Sedimentation, in the broad sense, can be compared to Jean Piaget's notion of *internalization* (*neihua* 内化) (Gu, Xin 1996, 215). Some scholars (e.g., Liu, Kang 1992, 124) even believe that Li's entire theory of sedimentation is largely a variation of this concept, based on Piagetian theory of cognitive and affective development. However, in Li's view, Piaget's theory was *biologistic*, since it neglected the social factors and the active role of humans in making and applying tools.[6] Hence, Li tried to combine Piaget's theories that unfold the *a priori* categories according to universal patterns in growing children with his technology-oriented interpretation of Marx (Chong 1999, 129). For Li, the *a priori* as such is already a product of social activities: patterns of mind are influenced by the specific mode of production in each stage of social development, forming particular cultural-psychological formations and leading individuals to view the world in a certain way and to act accordingly. In this context, Li writes:

> My theory is closer to Jean Piaget's, which emphasizes that logic and mathematics come from the abstraction of activity itself. Piaget came to this conclusion through the study of child psychology. But he did not connect psychology with anthropology to raise "subjectality" and "sedimentation" as a philosophical problem. (Li, Zehou 1999e, 175)

Li created the concept of sedimentation to study how rational elements shape human sense experience, how social factors manifest themselves in individual minds, and how historical developments become part of human mind. In other words, sedimentation is the process in which rational, social, and historical elements are accumulated in the individual mind. This process takes place through the so-called humanization of nature.[7]

One of the crucial points in the process of sedimentation is to establish a set of mental forms, comprised of three parts: the cognitive, the moral, and the aesthetic substructures. Li employs "three utterances—internalization, condensation, and sedimentation of reason, respectively—to depict the formation of these three different substructures" (Gu, Xin 1996, 215). As already mentioned, sedimentation in the narrow sense particularly refers to the social and historical formation of universalized aesthetic forms among human species. Sedimentation is a significant element of Li Zehou's aesthetics of practice (*shijian meixue* 實踐美學) and also of his theory of subjectality, which will be introduced in detail in the next section.

Dynamic Layering of Mental Formations

In Li's theoretical system, sedimentation is a notion that belongs to the field of historical or anthropological ontology.[8] It describes a dialectical process of human evolution, in which activities and practices that have been carried on through long periods of several million years gradually formed the dynamic categories of the mind. Li denotes these categories, formations, or dynamic structures as sedimentations or mental layers of psychophysical formations. These are commonly seen as generating human consciousness. One of the main reasons for his elaboration of this evolution of cultural sedimentation, which formed the contemporary subject and which he saw as a dynamic conception of a sensuous moral reasoning in action, lies in his interpretation of the crucial problems that are facing modern societies. As Li sees it, modern subjects living in modern societies lack a meaningful context (Jensen 2005, 463) and, as such, Li formed the neologism of sedimentation in order to expose the experience of the individual as a historicized, activist subject.

Sedimentation represents a specific stage of human experience in which form and content, the natural and sociocultural, and the senses and reason are unified to form a complex and coherent entity. Many scholars believe that, in certain aspects, it could be compared to Carl Gustav Jung's archetypes, which are embedded in the collective unconscious. However, Li's sedimentation is a dynamic entity and therefore less ahistorical than Jung's notion (Chong 1999, 129). The existence of Jung's collective unconscious implies that individual consciousness is by no means a *tabula rasa*, it is rather subject to predetermining influences. Jung points out that

> it is in the highest degree influenced by inherited presuppositions, quite apart from the unavoidable influences exerted upon it by the environment. The collective unconscious comprises in itself the psychic life of our ancestors right back to the earliest beginnings. It is the matrix of all conscious psychic occurrences, and hence it exerts an influence that compromises the freedom of consciousness in the highest degree, since it is continually striving to lead all conscious processes back into the old paths. (Jung 1990, 112)

Li's sedimentation is also a kind of collective unconscious. While Jung's archetypes are fixed and static structures, belonging to the conceptual framework of transcendental forms, Li absolutely denies the existence of such mental phenomena: "Human psyche is not a dead thing like a table or a chair. It is a continuously evolving, developing, and progressing process. Thus, sedimentation and cultural-psychological formation equally belong to such vital, lively processes" (Li Zehou 2014, 3).

Li's sedimentation is not biologically inherited, rather, it is the product of a dynamic, ever-changing process of psychocultural development. In such processes, it is the dominant mode of production of a certain type of society that produces a particular cultural-psychological formation that then leads the individuals that belong to this society to view reality in a certain way and to act in certain ways (Sernelj 2016, 98). Jung presupposes that the archetypes gained from a remote past are *a priori* or primordial patterns existing in human collective unconsciousness. Li's theory of sedimentation, on the other hand, is fundamentally different because it emphasizes the dynamic process of continuous change, which is a result of the impact of the material development of society upon the psychological-cultural formations in human mind (ibid.).

This psychological-cultural formation is collective only in the sense that all members of a certain culture or society obtain and possess the same cultural code, which manifests itself in particular modes of behavior, customs, and value systems. An additional difference between the two concepts lies in the fact that Jung—in contrast to Li—bestowed on his archetypes a mystical and religious dimension. He regarded them as symbols, reflecting the ever-unique experience of divinity and possessing the ability to offer human beings a premonition of the divine, while at the same time guarding individuals from its immediate experience (Jung 1990, 8). For him, these symbols are embedded in a complex cognitive system and manifest themselves through religion or other mystical practice. In Jung's view, they can be discovered through artistic creation, which arouses them from the realm of collective unconscious, surfacing to the conscious level. According to Téa Sernelj, such an interpretation of religion and such attempts to draw parallels between mythology and an individual mind prove a tendency toward bold generalization that ignores important cultural distinctions (Sernelj 2016, 99). Besides, they are latently dangerous for as soon as they are linked to any kind of axiological evaluations, they can lead to implicit forms of racism.

Jung's view is also completely different from Li's interpretation of the forms and symbols that have been sedimented in the cultural-psychological formation of the human mind. According to Li, rituals, songs, dancing, and myths gradually formed poetry, literature, music, painting, and other forms of artistic expression, along with social and political institutions. All these culturally determined phenomena were formed in the process of material (or technological) production and development of society, which modified the spiritual production of humans. Although in a certain sense and to a certain degree, they certainly represent some sort of "frozen images of the remote past" (ibid.). They still cannot exist in people's minds as something static and immutable, because they were transformed through a complex and ever-changeable historical process. In Li's theoretical framework, the structure of sedimentation layers is dynamic and can thus be regarded as a form of collective unconscious only in the sense of a cultural identity gained through the process of socialization as well as hereditary cultural code of the society we were born in. In this context, it is important to understand that this congenital cultural code or cultural identity as a form of collective unconscious is by no means composed of primordial forms—as Jung suggests in his theory of archetypes—but is constantly changing in accordance with the material and spiritual development of society. By laying stress upon the crucial function of the material and technological impact on the sedimented cultural-psychological formations contained in the human mind, Li has bestowed the idealistic and speculative nature of Jung's view with important components derived from the Marxist historical materialism. Simultaneously, he also upgraded the Marxist theory of social developments by pointing to the important role assumed in these processes by factors belonging to human psychology.[9] Thus, the superficial resemblance between Jung's collective unconscious and Li's concept of sedimentation is quite irrelevant if we take into consideration the above-mentioned differences (ibid.).

According to Li, the sedimentations or forms of the mind are likewise different from Kant's *a priori* forms and categories, which are equally governed by fixed and unchangeable, abstract and static laws. Due to the fact that they are subject to human agency and tightly linked to historical and social processes, they are necessarily dynamic and modifiable. Although Li believes that human sedimentations are categories or forms of mind that are independent of any individual, community, or society at any particular moment in time, he still thoroughly emphasizes that they are not independent of humankind as a whole over long periods. Thus, they cannot be viewed as categories that are absolutely independent of all experience. In other words, according to Li Zehou, the forms and categories of understanding are only *a priori* from an individual's viewpoint, whereas they are derived from experience and are thus *a posteriori* from the viewpoint of society and communities. For Li, the main weakness of Kant's doctrine of the *a priori* was that it ignored history. Hence, being a highly dynamic concept, sedimentations naturally also change as human beings evolve, as the cultures they live within become more complex and as they individually develop new modes of perceiving the world through thinking and feeling.

Sedimentation and Habitus

Li's concept of sedimentation might be compared with the notion of *habitus* as developed, by Pierre Bourdieu, who also often stressed the corporeal nature of social life and emphasized the role of practice and embodiment in social dynamics. In Bourdieu's theory, the habitus is a system of structuring dispositions rooted in social practice and is always oriented towards practical functions. It represents a mental formation that includes thoughts and feelings and is characterized by a set of acquired categories, sensibilities, dispositions, and taste. Its contents are a complex product of embodying social structures. Habitus is created through a social rather than individual process. It leads to patterns that are enduring and is transferrable from one context to another. But it also shifts in relation to different contexts in time and space. According to Bourdieu, habitus refers to the mental structures through which people apprehend the social world. These structures are essentially the product of the internalization of the structures of that world (Bourdieu 1989, 18). Habitus is not only a system of schemes for generating practices, but also a system of perception and appreciation of practices. In both dimensions, its operation expresses the concrete social position in which it was formed. Thus, it produces practices and representations that can be classified or differentiated (ibid., 19). Similar to Li's sedimentation, habitus is not static, fixed, or permanent, but can be modified in various situations or over long periods of time. It is mainly developed through the processes of socialization and determines a wide range of dispositions that shape individuals in a given society. Further it is a durable set of dispositions that are formed, stored, and recorded and that exert influence to mold forms of human behavior. Habitus can vary in accordance to particular social environments because unstable social domains may produce unstable systems of dispositions that generate irregular patterns of action. It can reinforce cohesion as well as stimulate change and innovation (Navarro 2006, 16).

Habitus can be viewed as a product of sedimentation of experience, and as a result of long-lasting, continuous socialization. Bourdieu draws upon Maurice Merleau-Ponty's philosophical concept of *embodiment* as a part of his model that incorporates social experiences into the concrete corporeal. Merleau-Ponty also employs the notion of sedimentation. For him, experiences and abilities, accumulated through long historical periods settle into "habitual dispositions" (Flynn 2011, 9), which are seen as products of sedimentation of intersubjective practice. It is within this context that he emphasizes the need to distinguish between the body as it is at a given moment and the body that he calls a "habitual body" (Merleau-Ponty 1962, 101). He also emphasizes that the very core of consciousness involves a so-called world-structure, which comprised an interaction of sedimentation and spontaneity (Rosenthal and Bourgeois 1991, 87). In this aspect, Merleau-Ponty is quite comparable to Li Zehou, who also emphasizes the complementary relation between the laws of history and the coincidental nature of human decisions and actions (Li Zehou 1994a, 40).

Nonetheless, Merleau-Ponty's understanding of sedimentation is different from Li's, especially regarding the question of which particular elements and which aspects are being emphasized or treated. This tiny formal difference brings along substantial divergences in the general connotations of the two theories. First, Merleau-Ponty is not so much interested in the origins of sedimentation (or the causal laws by which it is determined), rather he discusses its functions and implications. According to him, sedimentation is accumulated on the universal "prepersonal" level that is connected both to the world and to the concrete living body. Second, Merleau-Ponty does not deal with Li Zehou's first or the second level of sedimentation—with the sedimentation of species and the cultural sedimentation—but rather distinguishes several levels of sedimentation within the structure of the given (or living) subject. Hence, his theory of perception is taking place on Li's third (the smallest) level of sedimentation, namely, on the level of individual sedimentation. It is exclusively on this level and in this context that Merleau-Ponty distinguishes between the prepersonal and personal levels. The former is prior to the latter and therefore occurs prior to explicit reflection. Besides, it is also constitutive of the concrete experience of the lived bodily subject. In this structure of prepersonal and personal levels of the subject, the further layer of sedimentation is that of the personal activities of the subject that spontaneously reforms different components into the preexisting sedimented world, and productively rebuilds itself in its reactions, which then becomes accumulated in the next layer of sedimentation. This next layer, on which Merleau-Ponty focuses, is also deposited in the concrete existence of the individual rebuilding of him- or herself. The sedimented experiences are hence actions and experiences that, once mastered, must never be learned again, as for instance, riding a bicycle or swimming.

In Li's view, however, the most relevant dimension of sedimentation is its historical and social nature. Although the changes taking place on the level of individual sedimentation are most clearly observable and even though they have the greatest influence on the concrete lives of the living empirical subjects, the impact of these changes upon the entire structure of human sedimentation, which lies in the center of his interest, is certainly trifling. It is not a coincidence that Li often emphasizes that precisely because of Western post-Marxist theoreticians' exaggerated emphasis on the individual human subject, his theory and his central concepts cannot be compared to the views of existentialists or others.

Li's theory of perception is also tightly connected to the human material practice. In Li's theory, the origin of what Merleau-Ponty calls "habituated body" also lies in the production and use of tools. As we shall see in the section on epistemology, Li's theory of perception emphasizes that the origin of human comprehension is not to be found (merely) in the external stimuli and in the sense-data, nor is it derived from them, but rather it is found in the internalized laws, experiences, and operational skills accumulated in the process of sedimentation that represents the internal aspect of the humanization of nature.

Epistemological Foundations and the Shaping of Human Beings

Like the views laid out above, Li's concept of sedimentation is a historical one and, as such, it thoroughly manifests itself in human practice, largely influencing its concrete forms and co-creating its development. Li called this specific approach to sedimentation "historical" or "anthropological" ontology. With sedimentation, he metaphorically refers to the hidden structure of human enculturation. Layers of human experience, human aesthetic sensibility, and our practical rationality are being sedimented, through millions of years, in the unconscious realms of our mental forms that Li calls cultural-psychological formations.[10] The theoretical foundation for Li's theory of sedimentation can be traced back to his critique of Kant's epistemology, that knowledge is not merely the result of the mind passively receiving sensory data, but also of its actively synthesizing sensory data into objects. Li aimed to formulate an alternative epistemology to replace "not only the Kantian *a priori* but also the doctrinaire Marxist 'mirror' theory of knowledge" (Chong 1999, 128).[11] In this way, he turned Kant's transcendental philosophy into an empirically grounded theory of human "cultural psychology" that is seen as an independent factor of human historical development at the level of culture.[12] However, his effort to counter such determinisms by reaffirming human agency could lead to a theory of voluntarism, which Li explicitly wanted to avoid. Woei Lien Chong believes that when Li brought Kant in to overthrow the naive reflection theory of knowledge, he also had to build in a safety valve to prevent the turn toward Fichtean idealism (Woei Lien Chong 1999, 128). Once the form in which the external reality occurs in the human mind is viewed as a product of the synthesizing function of consciousness and the sense data (as it was viewed by Kant), then it is quite easy to slip into the idealistic conclusion that it is consciousness that constitutes experience.

Li points out that the solution to this dilemma could already be found in Marx's early work, because it was Marx who discovered that both the "transcendental ego" and the idea of the "thing in itself" were fundamentally historical and social (ibid.). They are both equally the results of sedimentation of accumulated experience in individual minds, not in terms of content but rather in terms of forms (*xingshi* 形式) or structures (*jiegou* 結構).

As Jane Cauvel points out, these formations are precisely what make us "supra-biological" beings (Cauvel 1999, 158). It is the very concept of sedimentation that represents a crucial element of the artistic processes by which "primitive men" become "fully human." In this framework, tools that enable human species to transform its social and natural worlds in turn shape the human being (ibid., 156). This process is a dialectical and reciprocal one.[13]

> As the process of designing and applying tools became more complex, habits of body and mind developed into mental forms or sedimentations; in fact, all biological, historical, social, and psychological influences shape these mental forms. (ibid.)

In Li's account of sedimentation, the emergence of the production of tools, use of fire, and dwelling construction over long periods are followed by the appearance of symbolic behavior in the form of personal decoration and rock and cave carvings. Material technological production predates and is the driving force behind the development of the cultural-psychological dimensions (Chandler 2016, 156). Li also points out that this process is connected with the concept of causality, which was the result of the discovery of cause and effect over the long history of making and using tools.

> All *a priori* intuitions, concepts, and principles are the psychological forms of the "sedimentation" of this primary practice, which lasted millions of years. They are beyond the experience of any individual, group, or society, but not beyond the experience of humankind as a whole, not "absolutely independent of all experience," as Kant claimed. (Li Zehou 1999e)

It is precisely this historical process of enculturation that differentiates humans from other animals. The long history of making and applying tools, along with specific forms of social organization, stimulated the process of the development of the unique human psychical functions. This led to the aforementioned cultural-psychological formation in which the "animal mentality and the cultural achievement are sedimented or stored up, along with sociality (rationality and culturalness) and individuality (sensibility and animalness)" (Wang, Keping 2007, 250). Li describes this unification as a dynamic, correlative, and complementary process. He emphasizes that

> [h]umaneness should be the mutual integration and penetration of emotional and rational, naturalness and sociality. This unity is not a simple addition, improvised unification, or a chaotic mixture. It is not "half angel, half devil." In fact, it consists of sensibility (naturalness) as an integral part of rationality (socialness), or of an internalization of rationality within the sensibility. Through agglomeration and sedimentation, both parts are united to form a coherent wholeness.
>
> 人性應該是感性與理性的互滲，自然性與社會性的融合，這種統一不是二者的相加、湊合或混合，不是「一半天使，一半惡魔」，而應是感性（自然性）中有理性（社會性），或理性在感性中的內化、凝聚和積澱，使二者合二而一，融為整體。 (Li Zehou 1994, 461)

What makes human psyche different from that of animals is the sum of the symbolic activities of the collective consciousness, i.e., the great self (*da wo*). Applying human language or making decorative objects requires imagination and abstract, symbolic cognition. Li claims that symbolic activity developed out of the music and dance of primitive shamanistic rituals (Chandler 2016, 136). The act of singing and chanting makes it easier to coordinate group work. Similarly, the emotional power of music and rhythm in shamanistic dances was important in transforming and humanizing our emotions and desires. Dancing and other rituals had a powerful impact on early humans since they created intense feelings of belonging within a community, manifesting itself in respect, love, and loyalty. These feelings, in turn, have settled into the emotional, moral, and aesthetic psychological structures necessary for human communities to evolve (ibid.). Li writes:

> Just as in the case of material production I insist that without activities of the collective social consciousness, i.e., without primitive shamanist ritual activities and without linguistic and symbolic activities, the formation of a human psyche that is different from that of the animals would not have been possible.
>
> 與物質生產一樣，我仍然堅持，如果沒有集體的社會意識的活動型態，即如果沒有原始的巫術禮儀活動，沒有語言和符號活動，也就不可能有區別於動物的人的心理。 (Li Zehou 1990, 191–92)

Early humans participated in collective dancing and other shamanistic rituals and thus experienced the intense emotional ecstasy of being part of the community (*da wo* or great self). At this stage, particular psychic formations or the individual ego (*xiao wo* or small self), was almost not sedimented at all. Individuals had little sense of themselves, "certainly not in the way we have had since the Enlightenment" (Chandler 2016, 149). Li firmly believes that the collective consciousness exists historically prior to the individual self and that members of a community were united in "one being," possessing one set of intentions, desires, and goals (ibid.). He sees humanity as the amalgamation of reason (*sociability*) into sense experience (*naturality*). Through this process reason is internalized, condensed, accumulated, and sedimented into the sense experience, integrating the two different aspects into one harmonious unity (Gu, Xin 1996, 213). Li explains this process of unification in the following way:

> If we say that the epistemological and ethical structures of the subject still have some external, one-sided, and abstractly rational characteristics, only in humanized nature and in an aesthetic sense can society and nature, history and reality, and humankind and individuals really achieve an internal, concrete, and comprehensive integration and unity. If we say that the former two structures are still characterized by reason, which has been internalized or condensed within the sense experience, the latter, i.e., the aesthetic structure is characterized by the sensuality in which reason was sedimented. If we say that the former two still manifest themselves in the unity of humans and nature, which springs out of the power of sensibility, action, and will, the latter exhibits itself in the unity of humankind and nature, which manifests itself in the needs, enjoyments, and desires of our senses. This kind of unity is the highest unity.
>
> 如果說，認識論和倫理學的主體結構還具有某種外在的、片面的、抽象的理性性質，那麼，只有在美學的人化自然中，社會與自然，理性與感性，歷史與現實，人類與個體，才得到真正內在的、具體的、全面的交融合一。如果說，前二者還是感性中內化的或凝聚的理性，那後者則是積澱了理性的感性；如果說，前二者還只是表現在感性的能力、行為、意志中的人與自然的統一，那麼後者則表現在感性的需要、享受和響往中的人與自然的統一。這種統一是最高的統一。 (Li Zehou 1994, 473)

In Li's philosophy, it becomes clear that the concept of humaneness and morality is one of his main concerns. Li states that the stage of elementary sedimentation has had wide ethical implications: the collective psychological formations created by this primary mode of sedimentation provide the foundation for human empathy, which in Chinese culture, manifests itself in the crucial Confucian virtue of (*co*)humaneness (*ren*).[14]

As Marthe Chandler (2016, 169) points out, Li's theory of sedimentation can successfully explain how *Homo sapiens* developed empathy without recourse to ad hoc claims about "imagination" and "analogy" (Chandler 2016, 169). Chandler grounds her interpretation on the theories penned by Michael Tomasello and Steven Mithen, who pinpointed the origins of language in human cognitive skill, which is reflected in the individual ability of recognizing that other humans are the same as oneself (Tomasello 1999, 15; Mithen 2006, 117). However, it is equally plausible to assume that human brains constituted this recognition the other way around, namely, that a human being first recognized herself as an individual separated from other human beings (or the community as the elementary entity of self-identification), because she perceived herself as being "just like the others." Much of Western anthropological theory is still (consciously or unconsciously) grounded in the primary position of individual self-awareness. Li does not claim that social awareness is predominant but merely points to the correlative and complementary relation between the individual self and the community or the social environment where they live (Li Zehou 2007, 186–87). Several contemporary studies on neurology also corroborate this correlativity. There is clearly a chicken-or-egg problem concerning the question which evolved first. However, most of scholars agree that "the main point is that the two coevolved, mutually enriching each other to create the mature representation of self that characterizes modern humans" (Ramachandran 2009, 2). Therefore, Li's theory is not only consistent with contemporary scientific evidence, but "provides a perspective from which to remedy some of the individualistic assumptions of much contemporary social science" (ibid.).

Sedimentation as an Aesthetic Concept

The concept of sedimentation is also tightly linked to the general stance of Li's aesthetics. The unfolding of Li's "theory of sedimentation" reveals the historic, transformative, and psychological relevance of arts for the humanity, accounting for the evolution of humankind. Indeed, awareness of the primary laws of beauty is the product of elementary sedimentation.

> Where do the order and the laws of beauty come from? When we speak about the origin of beauty, we must emphasize that, through their productive activities, early humans already possessed a sense of order, forms, and laws of nature. They were familiar with them and could master them. Because of the effects of elementary sedimentation, their transformations (of nature) developed in a certain direction and followed certain laws.

> 這些美的秩序、規則從何而來呢? 如講美的根源時所強調指出這是因為原始人類在生產活動中對自然秩序、形式規律已經有某種感受、熟悉和掌握的緣故。它所以在變化中要朝著某種方向, 遵循某種規律, 就因為原始積澱在起作用。(Li Zehou 2014a, 1)

A most important element in this process was its social nature. For Li, the forms of beauty could only be created through the social activities of joint productive labor. "The subjective emotions and modes of perception that corresponded with these objective forms of beauty were the first (manifestations of the) sense of beauty" (ibid., 5).

The sense of beauty as such is also a product of sedimentation.

> As we can see, the earliest aesthetic structures in human psychology were already formed in this elementary sedimentation. Through their primitive productive practices the active subjects could obtain a sense of the unity of their state of mind with external nature (not with the concrete natural objects, but rather with the general formal laws of nature). Thus the sense of pleasure was born. From this, we can conclude that aesthetics preceded art.

> 可見, 在這種原始的積澱中, 已在開始形成審美的心理結構, 即人們在原始生產實踐的主體能動活動中感到了自己的心意狀態與外在自然 (不是具體的自然對象, 而是自然界的普遍形式規律) 的合一, 產生審美愉快。由此應得出一個結論——審美先於藝術。(Li Zehou 2014a, 6)

The transformation of the social atmosphere into aesthetic works offers human beings the awareness of the meaning and significance of life. Simultaneously, it gives them aesthetic appeal, and according to Li, this means life has sedimented into art. As it does, new paths are created and new images emerge that refresh, expand, and renovate the original sedimentations through incorporations of new atmospheres in societies and new forms of life (Cauvel 1999, 165). In this context, Li repeatedly stresses the concept of social practice that unfolds in history by gradually (re)shaping human capacity for perceiving beauty—its origin is the pleasure human beings feel when interacting successfully with their environment. This feeling of pleasure is sedimented in certain mental forms that correspond to certain objects we find beautiful because they arouse in us a feeling of pleasure. The beauty that we perceive in form is a sedimentation of the pleasure "that our earliest ancestors felt about a concrete content, but in the course of history this concrete content became unconscious" (Chong 1999, 128).

Through his interpretation of the notion of sedimentation, Li attempted to achieve a dialectical solution to the contrariety of content and form in aesthetics. In his theory, content is sedimented into forms in the process of the historical development of art. Once art was established as formal beauty, the forms of sedimentation would be cracked, so new contents could be placed into these forms. Sedimentation is not a linear, one-way process of accumulation, but rather a process defined by a dialectical triad: sedimenting, cracking, and resedimenting. From sedimenting to the cracking, the process can be seen as one of negation: the stage of resedimenting is the process of the negation of the negation (Gu, Xin 1996, 215). The human aesthetic capacity is necessarily the result of such a historical dialectical process.

Sedimentation is also a process in which historical, rational, and social factors are brought about and accumulated in the individual psyche. Accordingly, it manages to link each individual in a conscious/unconscious way to the broader community of the human species. This process is a vital part of the larger goals behind the humanization of nature, in that humans evolve from their animalistic status to being truly human through their practice of systematically and continuously making and using tools.

As an important part of Li's aesthetic theory, sedimentation also influences the ways human beings judge aesthetic objects or artistic products. These judgements or evaluations are based upon sedimented forms of reciprocal interactions and mutual influences between humans and their environments. People are aware of the beauty that permeates the cosmic, natural, and social patterns that surround them. They communicate and interact with these patterns or structural principles and create living environments that "reflect their needs, desires, hopes, and aspirations" (Cauvel 1999, 158). They cultivate land, build houses, construct bridges, organize communities, and so on, and all these active modifications to their natural surroundings are necessarily linked to some forms of artistic design, that in turn shape the specific nature of the aesthetic sensibilities of the people living and working in these surroundings. These specific features do not completely or absolutely define the aesthetic feelings or aesthetic sensibilities of an individual, their mode of perception is still linked to a specific mode of object recognition that is to a large extent determined by culturally determined layers of mental sedimentations. In different surroundings defined by different modes of socialization and education, the differences in cultural and historical sedimentation that manifest themselves in "individual particularities" become even more obvious and effective (Li Zehou 2016, 154).

Since no one (including artists) can truly escape the social and cultural sedimentations that have shaped them, a Chinese scholar viewing a Chinese painting will view it very differently from a Western scholar from a different "cultural-psychological" background. They will perceive many things in common because they both belong to the human species, the Chinese scholar will still view "different levels of 'reading' in terms of worldview, symbols, and cultural attitudes and preferences that will not be apparent to a Western beholder" (Cauvel 1999, 160).[15]

Because of these limitations (or, we might say, different options of perception and aesthetic imagination), the very stage or level of the humanization of nature as such is of utmost significance for the development of humanity.[16] This is also one of the main reasons that no human being can be reduced to a single universal perspective that are manifested in common human features, characteristics, and tendencies. Humans are always historical, cultural, and personal beings.

For Li, aesthetics represents the highest realm in the development of the human mind. Aesthetics supersedes the ordinary internalization or condensation of reason, grounded in its sedimentation, that the particular is no longer overshadowed by the universal. In this realm, in the sedimented incorporation of both reason and sense, only the highest potentials of all individuals be entirely cultivated. This being the case, aesthetics facilitates the refinement of seven human emotions that include joy, anger, sorrow, fear, love, hate, and desire and "the delight in heaven-and-human oneness" (Wang, Keping 2007, 251). Moreover, the aesthetic level is also the realm of the highest freedom as it enables humans to think and act morally in accordance with their free will. To Li, this aesthetic sedimentation represents the summit of all human mental formations.

> Aesthetic sensibility is, precisely, the manifestation of the "sedimentation" of society in nature, and the "sedimentation" of humankind as a species in the individual, as Jane Cauvel rightly points out. The animal structure and quality of

psychology here have been transformed into something that has a human nature, in which sensation and rationality are dissolved and combined. The sense organs, with their animal origin, have become "humanized." Works of art now become the symbols of this "humanized nature"; they are the deepest expressions of human "cultural-psychological formation." (Li, Zehou 1999e, 181–82)

Thus, aesthetic sensibility is the most important of all human faculties. Aesthetic sensibility, a result of the long-lasting process of psycho-cultural sedimentation, transforms the way we see, feel, and communicate with the world, such that even our most mundane practices take on aesthetic qualities: mating becomes love, eating becomes dining, and so on (Li Zehou 2016, 175). In this process, humans become truly free, for they liberate themselves from any form of estrangement (Bruya 2003, 138). This process of humanizing nature becomes the essence of beauty. Just as the essence of humanity is not simply a product of evolution or a result of some divine purposes but the product of human practice. The essence of beauty also primarily symbolizes its changing effect on the world.

> Beauty as a form of freedom is a unification of law and purpose; it is the humanization of external nature or a humanized nature. Aesthetics is a psychological structure that corresponds with this free form. It is a blending unity of sensibility and reason, a humanization of the inner nature of humanity, or the humanization of nature. It is the highest stage of human subjectality and the clearest expression of human nature. In this realm, everything that is human (the entirety of history) is sedimented into one; everything that belongs to reason is sedimented into sensibility and everything that is social is sedimented into nature.
>
> 美作為自由的形式，是合規律和合目的性的統一，是外在的自然的人化或人化的自然。審美作為與這自由形式相對應的心理結構，是感性與理性的交融統一，是人類內在的自然的人化或人化的自然。它是人的主體性的最終成果，是人性最鮮明突出的表現。在這裡，人類（歷史總體）的東西積澱為个體的，理性的東西積澱為感性的，社會的東西積澱為自然的。 (Li Zehou 1994, 472)

Subjectality

Li Zehou's notion of *subjectality* is also of paramount importance for his philosophical system. Like sedimentation, it belongs to the central concepts in his theoretical framework, around which his entire philosophical system is constructed (Rošker 2018, 1–10). Subjectality is one of the key concepts of contemporary Chinese intellectual discourse (Lin, Min 1992, 977). In elaborating on this concept, Li expands the problem of the self in post-revolutionary modernism. Similar to his concept of sedimentation, Li's notion of subjectality, which implies a radical reconception of the subject, also achieved wide scholarly attention with the publication of *Critique of Critical Philosophy* (*Pipan zhexuede pipan* 《批判哲學的批判, 康德書評》).

The political urgency of this revolutionary upgrading of the traditional notion of subject was not silenced after the massacre at Tiananmen Square in 1989. Even throughout the 1990s, this interpretation of human agency as something relatively independent of the material world, but simultaneously always acting upon it, became more and more important in China and abroad. Subjectality was formed by sedimentation, although it contains a great deal more than individual consciousness, appearing to include all aspects of humanity—the natural, social, biological, historical, communal, individual, rational, and sensual. Hence, as Chandler emphasizes, subjectality also includes our material practices, social circumstances, and evolutionary development (Chandler 2016, 131).

While the term continues to be translated as "subjectivity" in most English editions of Li's work and in the English secondary material, Li himself has repeatedly declared this translation to be misleading (see for instance Li, Zehou 1999e, 174 and Li Zehou 1985a, 14). He points out the fundamental distinction between the Chinese notions of *zhuguanxing* 主觀性 and *zhutixing* 主體性. In his view, the first is an epistemological term, while the second is ontological. Their diverse semantic connotations imply significant differences in meaning. Rendering both terms as "subjectivity" can lead to misunderstandings or, at the very least, reduces the precision of his thought.[17] To solve this problem, Li proposes translating the notion *zhutixing* with a term of his own coining, *subjectality*.

As a historically evolved, dynamic form of humanness, subjectality consists of two double dimensions. First, it has two ontological structures: the techno-social or instrumental substance (*gongju benti* 工具本體) within the techno-social formation and the psychological substance (*xinli benti* 心理本體) within a cultural-psychological structure. Second, it involves human collectivities, such as societies, nations, classes, and organizations (*da wo*) as well as individuals (*xiao wo*). These four factors are interrelated and they interact, although the first two are conditioning the latter two, and are thus of primary nature. Each offers a multifaceted and complex structure through which we can investigate the development of humanity as well as of individuals (Li Zehou 1999b, 30).

Subjectality is also closely linked to that of human practice, which Li Zehou understands differently from the original Marxist notion. While he agrees with Marx's emphasis on the primary importance of objective conditions, productive forces, and the material base; he diverges from orthodox Marxism in his conviction that the objective content of human practice cannot be separated from all those factors that constitute human beings as autonomous subjects, especially in terms of their creativity, innovativeness, and the willingness to act. Li Zehou has tried to fix this inconsistency with the help of the Kantian philosophy in order to provide a link between Marx's idea of a "humanized nature" on the one hand, and Kant's understanding of the subject on the other.[18]

> The work that I now needed to do was to provide a link between Marx's idea of a "humanized nature" and the philosophy of Kant. That is the reason I associated "subjectality" with subjectivity, giving "a priori" subjectivity a materialistic "subjectality" foundation. (Li, Zehou 1999e, 179)

However, it would be wrong to reduce Li to a mere derivation of these two important European thinkers. On the contrary, while he uses Marx as his starting point in order to reexamine issues first proposed by Kant, he then seeks to resolve the problems that derive from theoretical approaches of the latter (Ding 2002, 247). With his theoretical reinterpretation of subjectality, Li aims to overcome Kant's idealist impasse and to restore Kantian rationality by placing it into a materialist and historical framework.[19] By expanding Marx through Kant and, in turn, by upgrading Kant through Marx, Li attempts to reinvent and enrich the traditional historical materialist concept of practice.

Li placed his notion of subjectality into the framework of a pragmatic (or practical) philosophy of subjectality (*zhutixing shijian zhexue* 主體性實踐哲學). His crucial aim was to formulate a philosophy that would address the question about what constitutes the essence of humankind and what constitutes the notion of the subject (*zhuti* 主體). To Li, the answer to this question revolved around the central concepts of practice (*shijian* 實踐).

Social Practice and Human Autonomy

Human action is a driving force for the humanization of nature. It consists of two inherent ontological formations. The first is biological-technical in nature. Li calls this *gongju benti* (the techno-social or instrumental substance). The second formation is culturally determined, *xinli benti* (the psychological substance). Li's concept of subjectality as an objective human existential feature is by no means limited to the level of individuals (including their ability to establish interactive relations with their environment), but rather refers to various kinds of human communities (societies, nations, classes, organizations). Li also identifies two kinds of subjectality: the first refers to each individual's identity, the second to the humankind as a whole. The latter precedes and is a presupposition of the former. The humankind creates for itself a structure of subjectality through the material practice of making and using tools. This structure is super-biological and is rooted in a universal necessity (Li, Zehou 1986, 136). Because without the tools, which represent a kind of prolonged human limbs, human beings would not be able to survive.

The objective and elementary dimension of subjectality can be found in the social realization of material reality. It manifests itself in the structural connections between technology and society, but also in social existence. It appears through the social realization of material reality—through the process of production.

In addition to this basic and objective level, the concept of subjectality also embraces the subjective level of social consciousness that are manifested in culturally conditioned mental structures. However, in addition to this basic and objective level, the concept of subjectality also embraces the subjective level of social consciousness, which manifests itself in culturally conditioned mental structures. Following this paradigm, the mental formations of subjectality are basically different from the subjective awareness of individuals, but mainly refer to the products of human history that manifest themselves in formations of spiritual and intellectual culture, as well as in structures of ethical and aesthetic consciousness (Li Zehou 2001, 43). In Li's view, Marx (especially the early Marx) was still interested in sociality, whereas post-Marxist theories focused more and more on the individually conditioned type of subjectality. To Li this was the main common flaw of most "fashionable" contemporary streams of thought emerging in the Euro-American region throughout the twentieth century.

> Analytical philosophy, structuralism, and many other streams of the contemporary capitalist world (for instance, philosophical methodology or epistemology) are cold philosophies, which overlook the substance of subjectality. In addition, Sartre's existentialism, the philosophies of the Frankfurt School and other fashionable currents (like the philosophy of rebellion or the philosophy of emotion) on the other hand, are blindly propagating the individual subjectality. They have nothing to do with the practical philosophy of subjectality.
>
> 目前資本主義世界中的分析哲學結構主義等等，可說是無視主體性本體的冷哲學（方法哲學、知性哲學），而沙特的存在主義，法蘭克福學派等，則可說是盲目誇張个體主體性的熱哲學（造反哲學、情緒哲學），它們都應為主體性實踐哲學所揚棄掉。 (Li Zehou 1985a, 21)

Because of this emphasis on the social nature of subjectality, some scholars (e.g., Wang, Jing 1996, 21) criticize the philosopher, pointing out that this kind of subjectality could "hardly be associated with any sense of autonomy, since it is conceived first and foremost as an end product of socialization" (ibid.). They overlook the fact that, for Li, social practice, education, and other crucial dimensions of the socialization process were anything but absolutely determining, for they included the component of free will.

Li also clearly asserts why his concept of the subjectality is different from that of Sartre and other existentialists. Li states explicitly that Sartre's concept clearly refers to the individual, whereas his is rooted in the notion of human community (*renlei qunti* 人類群體). Li claims that "while Sartre's subjectality emphasizes the freedom of choice, my own (published in Li's *Outline*[20]) primarily deals with the productive practice" (Li Zehou 1985a, 15).

To Li subjectality not only consists of the action, rooted in free will, but also involves particular structural laws and objective principles. Subjectality is not only a simple reflection of human sense-experience—

it proceeds from the elementary activity of making tools and applying them in the continuous process of social production. Individuals cannot be defined solely in terms of their biological existence, without any reference to the role of the concrete historical process of social practice (Lin, Min 1992, 979). Here, it is very important to note that, for Li, the humanness—the human nature or the essence of that which characterizes or defines human beings—cannot be equated with social nature in the mere sense of group nature, because the latter is also typical for other animals. Li points out that in many kinds of animals one can find certain models of organization and divisions of labor, and even a kind of moral behavior or certain types of altruism—individual sacrifice for the preservation of the group or the kind (Li, Zehou 1986, 135). As a historical materialist, Li repeatedly emphasizes that human beings must ensure their existence before they occupy themselves with other issues. However, cultural-psychological aspects that manifest themselves in various social, communal, ritual and linguistic dimensions are what separate humans from other animals. In Li's view, this difference arises precisely because humans—through their engagement in the practice of making and using tools—possess subjectality.

The stress Li places upon the autonomous nature of this subjectality also reflects Kant's influence. Although Li finds Kant helpful in understanding the psychological-spiritual development of humanity, he criticizes him for focusing exclusively on the intellectual aspects of subjectivity, without taking into consideration the historical, evolutionary development of our humankind. Li's theory remedies this error by providing an interpretation of Kant consistent with Darwin (Chandler 2016, 131).

Ultimately, Li wanted to elaborate a theory of modernization that took into account Chinese traditional elements, while attempting to find solutions to the issues of the modern Chinese era—alienation and exploitation. Li understood the Marxist notion of estranged labor defined in *Marx's Economic and Philosophic Manuscripts of 1844*.

> The object which labour produces—labour's product—confronts it as *something alien*, as a *power independent* of the producer. The product of labour is labour which has been embodied in an object, which has become material: it is the *objectification* of labour. Labour's realization is its objectification. Under these economic conditions this realization of labour appears as *loss of realization* for the workers; objectification as

loss of the object and bondage to it; appropriation as *estrangement*, as *alienation*. (Marx 2007, 29)[21]

Estranged labor is a state in that the human being (worker) is related to the *product of their labor* as to an alien object.[22] Li believed that the basic or essential characteristics of humanity were seriously alienated in class society. It is this estrangement that makes humanness (or human nature) appear similar to animal nature.[23]

> As Marx pointed out in his *Economic and Philosophical Manuscripts of 1844*, the alienation of labor has caused men to feel free only in such activities of an animal nature like eating and drinking. Although there is a connection between freedom and human nature, this sort of animal freedom has nothing to do with human nature. (Li Zehou 1986, 135)

According to Woei Lien Chong, it was precisely Li's desire to formulate a new philosophy of humanness (*ren xing*) in post-Mao China that prompted him to combine Marx and Kant (Woei Lien Chong 1999, 121).[24] While Marx focused on the aspects of the capacity of the collective human subject to engage in economic production by means of tools (technology), Kant provided Li with the theoretical model that enabled him to reflect on the mental and ideal aspects of human nature, that is, the faculties of knowledge, ethics, and aesthetics. While Marx focused upon the material basis of human existence, Kant elaborated on its spiritual super-structure: "The fact that Li turned to Kant was significant in itself: he thereby opened a philosophical road to a treatment of intellectual and spiritual phenomena that reduced them neither to class, as in the Mao period, nor to the epiphenomena of matter, as in vulgar materialism" (ibid.). Li named this philosophical system the "ontology of human subjectivity" (*renlei zhutide bentilun* 人類主體的本體論), or "anthropology of human practice" (*shijianlunde renleixue* 實踐論的人類學). Li placed great emphasis on the constitutive character of practice, defined as material production and practice of tool-making, rather than "praxis" (Li Zehou 2008, 4),[25] used in Western Marxist writings to include "theoretical and cultural productions" (Liu, Kang 1992, 123). Following Engels, Li characterized systematic toolmaking as the quintessential characteristic of human beings that separates them from nature and forms their subjectality, self-reflection, and autonomy.

Following Kant's three Critiques, Li also tried to explain his notion of subjectality through the epistemological, the ethical, and the aesthetical dimension.

Epistemology, Ethics, and Aesthetics

Li's concept of subjectality is not treated as an exclusively epistemological term, and it is not defined in contrast to objectivity.[26] It is not merely an epistemological category. It also includes ontological configurations, with three interrelated dimensions: the subjective level (*zhuguan cengmian* 主觀層面), the objective structure (*keguan jiegou* 客觀結構), and the historical process of subject-object unification (Lin, Min 1992, 977). Regarding its cognitive dimension, subjectality is still—inter alia—also tightly linked to epistemology, ethics, and aesthetics. It also includes the human intention to understand (and to change) the world, as well as our longing for goodness and the love of beauty.

Kant's transcendental philosophy and his theory of mental forms were very important for Li Zehou's concept of subjectality (*zhutixing*). Li aimed to place this theory on a material basis, and thus transform the *a priori* nature of these forms into one that is determined by empirical and historical features. To Li, these forms originate in the material practice of making and using tools. According to him, the motoric organs had to be humanized before the sensory organs—sight or hearing or the humanized speech organs, and also before language and thought. To Li the origin of human perceiving and understanding the world are not the sense-data or the structure of language, but the material practice of making and using tools (Li Zehou 1994, 465). This is the foundation of the human subject of recognition, completely different from everything in the animal world. If we expose this problem from a philosophical point of view, it becomes very relevant for the theory of science, and also for child psychology and educational sciences. Li is convinced that the human learning process is incomparable to that of animals. From childhood on, human cognitive structure is completely different from the animal. Conditional learning discovered by Pavlov has nothing to do with the human learning process, the ability of abstraction and symbolic operation. Symbols are, of course, something completely different from the "signals of signals" which are, after all, still (merely) signals. Human learning is rooted in material practice, but, on the other hand, it also includes rational intuition, which is nondeductive and noninductive. Li denotes this ability as "free intuition" (ibid.).

Mathematics, for instance, is a specifically human tool of recognition and comprehension. However, the question of its origin is still a philosophical riddle. Li discloses that Kant connected mathematics with his transcendental theory and that in his *Categories*, he (in contrast to Hegel) placed quantity before quality (ibid., 466). Li also believes that the mastering of quantitative aspects of the objective world through mathematical abstraction clearly reflects the specifically human process of recognition and comprehension, which is defined by subjectality. Hence, mathematics also belongs to the most important distinctive markers that separate human and animal epistemology.

Even in this epistemological context, the concept of human practice is still of utmost importance. The unification of knowledge and action (*zhixing heyi* 知行合一) belongs to the most characteristic epistemological paradigms of Chinese ideational tradition. Li points out that in this tradition, the thinking subject cannot be separated from the acting subject, and consciousness cannot be separated from human material (bodily) existence. "Hence, knowledge cannot be separated from power (action), scholarship cannot be separated from ideology (dominating power), and epistemology from ethics and religion" (Li, Zehou 1999, 180).

Even when reduced to its psychological and cognitive dimensions subjectality is still a highly complex notion. Its multilayered implications cannot be limited in order to be treated within one single, narrow theoretical discipline, like epistemology or scientific methodology. A coherent philosophy of mind must "also include the ideals, intentions and sense of responsibilities of the subjects, as well as their subjectality, which has been constituted through ethics and human free will (Li Zehou 1994, 469).[27]

Li believes that Kant's greatest contribution was that he demanded that individuals establish free will and to follow it in their actions and decisions, that individuals have to subdue themselves to a duty and a responsibility for all humanity (ibid., 471). Kant understood these forms as *a priori*, independent of any kind of experience. According to Li, however, they only seem to be completely free from the impact of any social, historical, cultural or national circumstances or interests, because their transformation and their (re)shaping is much too slow to be perceived by human beings. In reality, these forms are still products of history and social development. The same applies for the continuous succession of the structure of free will. This structure is the agglomeration of human reason, which causes a fusion of individual and the entire humanity. Thus, it also seems to be surpassing all individual and collective interests and causal laws and obtains an incomparable sublime quality. That which is transferred through thousands of generations, however, has nothing to do with moral or ethical contents, for these are culturally determined and can differ—or even contradict each other—from area to area and from generation to generation. What is being passed on is the form of the free will that can only be realized within and by an autonomous human subject. Li also describes the process in which this kind of autonomous subjectality was formed, and he explains how it manifested itself in his own tradition.

> In China, we say that "virtue is established at the highest level." This kind of uniqueness of each individual existence shows here its incomparable brilliance. Such existence can only become possible through conscious and self-aware rational construction, which takes place in the framework of constructing subjectality. This construction implies practice, behavior, and action, but also emotions, desires, and other sensations, which agglomerate in human reason (similar as in epistemology, in which reason is internalized into sensuous intuition). This is the real free will.
>
> 中國古話說，「太上立德」，個體存在的這種一次性，這這裏顯示出它的無比光輝。而這卻只有通過人的自覺有意識的理性建構才存在。這屬於建立人的主體性的範圍。這是在人的實踐、行為、活動、情感、願欲等感性中的理性凝聚（如同在認識論的感性直觀中有理性內化一樣），這才是真正的自由意志。 (Li Zehou 1994, 469)

Li regards human beings as rational animals. Their cognitive ability as such is not opposed to its animal origins (Lynch 2016, 714), and the human psychology has an emotio-rational structure, where reason is melded into animal sensibility. All kinds of knowledge and forms of natural laws are first preserved and accumulated through human practical activity, which constitutes their subjectality (Li Zehou 1994, 461). Through the process of human development they are gradually turned into information systems of languages, symbols, and cultures, and are finally sedimented in the structure of the human mind. In this context, Li emphasizes again that the link between humans and the world of nature is not provided by language, but by the practice of making and using tools. This practice transforms natural laws and natural struggles into the forms of human society, humanness, and even the human brain: "In this way there emerged a human subjectality of cognition, which enables humans to know the world in their super-biological modes" (Li Zehou in Lynch 2016, 713). As we have seen in the chapter on sedimentation, Li believes that human psychology, just like humanness or "human nature," is not fixed or given, but is rather something characterized by changing developmental forms of human pragmatic reason. This process determines the subjectality of cognition. Human reason is formed over millions of years and it is still continuously accumulating and changing (ibid.). However, reason alone is by no means something that would separate humans from their sensuality and thus from other animals. The difference between human beings and other animals primarily occurs somewhere else, namely in the very realm of specifically human social existence, which is defined by subjectality and includes specific human values.

> We have to note that, as a kind of animal, the human individual does not possess any value, meaning, uniqueness, or richness. All these are nothing but assets and products of human history. Hence, philosophical ethics does not deal with this animalistic individual, but precisely with such an individual, who is a part of social communitarian existence, including its various psychological structures. The universal mental forms are also rooted in the totality of human history.
>
> 應該說作為動物，人的個體存在的價值、意義、獨特性、豐富性並不存在，所有這些恰恰是人類歷史的財富和產物。因此，哲學——倫理學所講的個體主體性不是那種動物性的個體，而剛好是作為社會群體的存在一員的個體。包括他的各種心理建構也如此。普遍心理形式也仍然來自人類歷史的總體。 (Li Zehou 1994, 470)

Li points out that only human beings possess the capacity of self-awareness regarding their own rational sensitivity: "Their ethical behavior and their rational sensitivity are completely different from instincts that can cause particular animals to sacrifice themselves in order to protect the group of their own species (Li Zehou 1994, 469).

Although in the field of social ethics, subjectality directly occurs on the communal level in the form of ritual institutions and moral rules and is thus outwardly focused, human needs and preferences have both personal and social aspects. Among other things Li's concept of subjectality is rooted in traditional Chinese axiology, in which ethics and morality are interwoven, for they are based on the inseparable connection of individual and social levels of existence. The traditional Chinese axiological notion of "completing oneself" (*cheng ji* 成己), for instance, is a form of conscious self-reflection, for it involves looking inward in order to recognize the complex nature of the inner self, including its social constitution.[28] Such traditional ideas internally affirm the social aspects of morality. They also imply that "confirming one's moral subjectivity also affirms one's inherent moral intersubjectivity—that is, an ethical connection to other people" (ibid.).

In his fundamental conceptual assumptions, Li rigidly distinguishes between ethics and morality. Ethics refers to external factors (political systems, customs, norms, regulations) and morality refers to internal factors (will or intentions, views, senses, feelings, and emotions). In spite of their mutual correlativity and complementarity, Li emphasizes that the external (ethics) is absolute primary and basic. Morality, which is inherent and individualized, is inter alia conditioned by an internalization of ethics (2015a, 6).[29] The question of how this morality has been transferred and transmitted from the preceding to subsequent generations, Li argues that in this process the continuation of morality is not based upon a development of its concrete contents. These are culturally conditioned and linked to the specific social, ethnical, political and economic circumstances of the time and space. This succession cannot be reduced to the external forms of language. It does not mean that what has been carried forward are merely moral words and concepts.

> That which has really been transmitted must be the internal forms of human mental structures (or the agglomeration of reason). Although the (concrete) contents (included in these forms) are different according to specific societies, periods of time, nations, or classes, the substance of human ethics is being developed and accumulated precisely through these formal principles.
>
> 實際上繼承的應是這種人類心理結構（理性凝聚）的內形式。盡管內容可以是歷史具體地決定於社會、時代、民族、階級，但正是這種形式原則卻構成不斷發展、累積的人類的倫理學本體。 (Li Zehou 2015a, 20)

In the realm of axiology, Li highlights the primary and fundamental value of human beings: each individual life within our species is meaningful because it is human. In this respect, Li emphasizes the significance of Kant's categorical imperative (Li Zehou 1994, 468). He connects this notion to his own interpretation of the structure of human moral psychology, which consists of three basic elements: will, ideas, and emotions or sensitivity. The first two belong to human reason, in which ideas form its content and will constitutes its form. Li points out that this form of mental structure is absolute and can thus be equated with Kant's categorical imperative. It is nothing but free will and represents "the universal and necessary absoluteness that has been formed through historical sedimentation from the relative ideas that formed the contents (Li Zehou 2015a, 6). Li also highlights the semantic and conceptual difference, as well as the inherent mutual complementarity of beauty and aesthetics.

> Beauty is thus the form of freedom. It is the unification of rules and purposes. It is the external humanization of nature or humanized nature. Aesthetics, which constitutes a mental structure that corresponds with this form of freedom, is a fusion and unification of sensitivity and reason. It is the inherently human humanization of nature or humanized nature.[30] It is the ultimate product of subjectality and the clearest, most visible manifestation of human nature.
>
> 美作為自由的形式，是合規律和合目的性的統一，是外在的自然的人化或人化的自然。審美作為與這自由形式相對應的心理結構，是感性與理性的交融統一，是人類內在的自然的人化或人化的自然。它是人的主體性的最終成果，是人性最鮮明突出的表現。(Li Zehou 1994, 472)

But when exploring the notions of beauty and aesthetics in the framework of Li's philosophy of subjectality, we also have to pay attention to the fact that there are two different Chinese notions that are both translated with the term *aesthetics* into English, although they cannot be completely equated. While the term *shenmei* 審美 refers to concepts, ideas, and values that tend to be linked to the specific features of the Chinese ideational tradition, the term *meixue* 美學 denotes aesthetics as the (originally Western) academic discipline (Zhao Wenhe 2016, 1), focused upon mechanisms of perception and criteria of judgements.[31]

In Chinese, the word *meixue* was derived from Japanese, where it was originally coined as an equivalent for the Western *aesthetics*. Li also pointed out that "in Chinese, a more exact translation of aesthetic should be *shenmeixue* 審美學, which means the study of the process of recognizing and perceiving beauty" (Li and Cauvel 2006, 19).[32] In his thoughts on aestheticism, Kant argues that it is our faculty of judgment that enables us to have experience of beauty and grasp those experiences as part of an ordered, natural world with purpose. Although proceeding from materialistic grounds, Li reconciles with Kant by generally agreeing to his supposition, according to which aesthetic judgement has a close similarity to the moral judgement (Burnham 2016, 1).

Li's elaboration of this similarity is ultimately different, for it is rooted in the traditional Chinese concept of the unity of nature and humans *tian ren heyi*, or, in Li's own words, in the "one world view" (Li, Zehou 1999e, 179).

When explaining his notion of subjectality in the field of aesthetics, Li first disclosed Kant's notion of aesthetic pleasure, which is not a passive reception or reflection of what was perceived by the sense organs, and neither a rational, abstract or logical comprehension. It is rather a result of many subjective elements, including desires and intentions. Kant denoted the result of this process "aesthetic judgement." According to Li, aesthetic judgement constituted the subject of the humanized nature in relation to the objective world (Li Zehou 1994, 475). Beauty is the ultimate result of the subjectivity, and it is the clearest and most transparent expression of humanness.

To Li, Kant's greatest contribution to the philosophy of subjectality is primarily found in Kant's reflections upon the complex formation of human rationality (Liu, Kang 1992, 122). Following Kant, Li claims that in both the epistemological and ethical arenas even such unity between the individual and the social spheres (the fusion of "great" (*da wo*) and "small" selves (*xiao wo*) is still reduced to the agencies of abstract cognitive reason and moral codes or norms. However, in the realm of aesthetics, or through human aesthetic appreciation, human beings are able to develop in their mind a higher stage of synthesis in that their social nature accumulates in the inherent psychological structure of the human beings as individuals (ibid., 984). In this sense, Li argues that "the characteristic feature of aesthetics is the fusion of history and human mind, of society and individual, of reason and sensibility in the human self (Li Zehou 1985a, 20).

Li's aesthetics of practice (*shijian meixue*) is an important part of his theory of subjectivity and the culmination of his philosophical system. In beauty, Li tried to unify epistemology and ethics, truth and goodness.[33] Following Hegel's quest for an all-embracing identity and relying heavily on Kant (Gu, Xin 1996, 216), Li argues that the laws of nature can be understood as truth and the essence of the subjective practice of humankind as goodness. In Li's view, the purposiveness of subjective goodness and the lawfulness of objective truth can be integrated and united when people who hold certain subjective purposes act in accordance with objective laws and achieve desired results. For Li, the unity of truth and goodness, as well as lawfulness and purposiveness, is precisely the essence and origin of beauty (Li Zehou 1984, 465). Hence, "the free aesthetic could become the key to free intuition (cognition) and free will (morality). Thus the sedimentation of reason, the free, aesthetic feeling becomes the summit of human structure" (Li Zehou 1985a, 20).

Li also argues that such a fusion of beauty and goodness could be achieved in Chinese intellectual history because

> [in] the Chinese tradition religion was replaced by aesthetics[34] in order to create this highest realm of human life. This highest, latently existing realm of aesthetic substance, which surpassed morality, offered humans the possibility of free choice and moral action. This was called the realization of goodness through beauty.
>
> 中國傳統是通過審美代替宗教，以建立這種人生最高境界的。正是這個潛在的超道德的審美本體境界，儲備了能超越生死不計利害的自由選擇和道德實現的可能性，這就叫「以美儲善」。(Li Zehou 1985a, 20)

Therefore, the main and most important foundation of Li's system of subjectivity is not to be found in ethics, but in aesthetics.

The human subject constitutes him or herself in continuity with his or her environment through material practice, through which he or she becomes aesthetically sensitive. For Li, aesthetic sensibility is the most important human faculty. The realm of beauty is the very area in which human subjectality can overcome alienation. As described earlier, Li followed early Marx in arguing that estrangement, which occurs because of forced labor, is equal to the animalization of humans.[35] It is a state in which humans are deprived of their right to be human. For Li the essence of being human lies precisely in the free activity of production—especially in the production of art. In this process, humans become capable of achieving the free unification of their cognitive powers as described by Kant. Yet, in Li's historic, materialistic view, such production, grounded in subjectality, is not rootless. It is not merely a "soul," or a mind, detached from the body: "Rather, sensibility is made possible only through humanized nature, . . . which has the capacity to view the world in a manner that unifies the purely rational, the practical, and the aesthetic" (Bruya 2003, 137). For Li, the highest stage of subjectality is to be found in the realm of aesthetics that cannot be reduced to the spirit. Li considers aesthetics to be the ultimate fruit of human subjectivity, and the most striking and prominent manifestation of humanity (Gu, Xin 1996, 216). His view is that all historical dilemmas will finally be reconciled in this realm. It is therefore only natural that the aesthetic category of beauty acquires an ontological dimension; as such, it belongs to the crucial notions shaping Li Zehou's philosophical system.

Li also follows Kant in dividing the aesthetic pleasure from sensory pleasure and conceptual cognition. The former cannot be seen as a passive perception of the external world through the sensory organs, but rather as a subjective and universal necessity, derived only after an object has first been judged beautiful. In Li's philosophy of subjectality,

> this aesthetic experience is the result of the activity of many different psychological functions, including sense, perception, imagination, emotion, intention, and understanding all mixed together. The historical origin of this kind of pleasure is also rooted in the primary practice—the activity of making and using tools—the consequence of which is the quality of beauty in the objective world and aesthetic sensibility in the subjective world (psychological) world. (Li, Zehou 1999, 177)

Aesthetic sensibility therefore belongs to the fundamental characteristics of subjectality and to the basic features that distinguish human beings from the animal world. Li's interpretation of the subject follows the *Economic and Philosophic Manuscripts of 1844*.[36] Marx clearly states:

> An animal forms only in accordance with the standard and the need of the species to which it belongs, whilst man knows how to produce in accordance with the standard of every

species, and knows how to apply everywhere the inherent standard to the object. Man therefore also forms objects in accordance with the laws of beauty. (Marx 2007, 32)

Hence, subjectality is the "internal standard of human civilization, especially in aesthetics and art" (Li, Zehou 1999e, 181). Marx did not directly address aesthetics as such, but he presupposed that, through their social practice, human beings became capable of molding nature into objects for themselves, thereby transforming it into their own reality (Bruya 2003, 135). In his elaborations, Li interprets Marx "as a remedy for Kant, introducing his own specialized vocabulary and offering a synthesis of Kant and Marx through a notion of aesthetic freedom that presupposes political freedom" (ibid., 134). As we shall see below, the latter notion also belong to the basic characteristics of Li Zehou's subjectality.

Political Implications

In his attempts to expand the idealistic framework of Kantian epistemology by examining the subjective psychological structure of human subjectality in terms of a three-dimensional inquiry into epistemology, ethics, and aesthetics, Li has—*inter alia*—aimed to rejuvenate Chinese Marxism (Li Zehou 1994, 474). If China wants to catch up with the latest developments in science and democracy, Li believes, the orthodox Marxist "mirror" theory of knowledge[37] must be expanded, if not completely eliminated.

His theory of subjectality is, on the other hand, a philosophy that treats humankind (as well as the individual human) as a subject. On such grounds he strove to revive the traditional Chinese concept of humaneness (Li Zehou 1980a: 89), which he saw as a specifically Chinese form of humanism.

> From "rituality," Confucianism has proceeded to "humaneness." This is a method that proceeds from people to the spirits, from the "human Way" to the "Way of Nature." To summarize this issue: It is man who provides mind to heaven and earth, and not vice versa.
>
> 孔門由「禮」歸「仁」，以「仁」為體，這是一條由人而神，由「人道」現「天道」，從「人心」建「天心」的路。從而，是人為天地立「心」，而非天地為人立「心」。(Li Zehou 2016, 180)

Li applied and reinterpreted this traditional notion on the foundation of the Western idea of humanism, which was a child of the European Enlightenment processes and which also formed a core element of (especially early) Marxism. The idea of humanism was of utmost significance in the social and political arena of the 1980s in China, especially considering the then recent, excruciatingly dehumanizing experience of the Cultural Revolution. Living in the atmosphere of gradual (though primarily economic) liberalization, Chinese intellectuals, particularly young university students, were especially eager to search for a "theoretical key by which the problem of dehumanization in Chinese society could be solved for good and for all" (Gu, Xin 1996, 210).

Li's aesthetic thought and his idea of human subjectality doubtless contain important humanistic values.[38] He argues that the classical notion of humanism was theoretically weak, for emotions, sentiment, cognition, and moral valuation by far cannot sufficiently explain the extremely complex developmental process of the relations between the individual and the societal (Gu, Xin 1996, 982). During the first years of post-Mao China the notion of individual freedom, which was largely suppressed in the previous decades, acquired wide popularity. However, Li thoroughly warned against its exaggerated idealization.

> Individual subjectivity manifests itself in the outcries of modern Western thought currents and also in contemporary Chinese humanism. They all are just revolts and rebellions against different forms of alienation, and cannot lead to any truly substantial results.
>
> 個體主體性表現在近現代西方思潮和當代中國的人道主義吶喊中，它們大都只是對各種異化的抗議和反抗，並無真正檢視的理論成果。(Li Zehou 2016, 125)

For Li, these forms of ideology corrupted the idea of humaneness (or, in Li's conceptualization, of humanness or "human nature") and had nothing to do with his concept of subjectality, which to him, is the basis of everything that is truly human.

> I think that only if we understand "humanness" on such a basis, can we distinguish it from other theories of human nature and from humanism. Only on such basis can we establish a

practical philosophy of anthropological ontology, namely the
practical philosophy of subjectality.

我以為只有在這種基礎上來講「人性」，才能與其他的人性論、
人道主義區別開來，才是我叫它為人類學本體論的實踐哲學，也
就是本體性的實踐哲學。(ibid., 170)

Just as he opposed Rousseau's or Sartre's predominantly individualistic kind of humanism, he also opposed the upsurge of subjectivist forms of Western Marxism and, analogous, the so-called socialist humanism that became fashionable in the prevailing Chinese ideologies at the time.[39]

He argued that in spite of these trendy ideational waves, "it is the very ideal of making our material and spiritual existence increasingly humanized that defines our humanity" (Chong 1999, 141). Hence, Li's humanism of subjectality similarly cannot be compared with the present predominant, ideologically undermined notion of romantic, allegedly "traditional Chinese" humanism, which is based on a concept of harmony that has been deprived of its genuine meaning and grounded on a simple ideology of blind obedience and disciplined conflict-avoidance.[40]

Li Zehou also criticized the neoconservative intellectuals and their critique of humanism for their lack of fundamental understanding and knowledge of the real social and historical background underlying its theory. Even though in their elaborations these scholars often quoted Marxist classics in order to emphasize the importance of the collective against the individual, they tended to ignore the sociohistorical grounds of the concept of humanism in the context of modern Chinese society. In his framework of subjectality Li aimed to combine historical materialism with the moral and ethical interpretations of humanism in order to surpass the dichotomy between individual and social, between uniqueness and universality. Lin Min (1992, 984) argues that in this manner Li tried to bridge the ideological gap between the progressive and the conservative intellectuals.

Li proposed a new focus on research into Marxism. In his eyes, the prevailing interpretations of Marxist thought were reductionist in many different ways.

It is much too superficial to identify Marxism with humanism
and individualism, or to summarize it under these currents. On
the other hand, however, it is absurd to understand the view

of historical materialism merely in the sense of an immutable vulgar determinism or structuralism (i.e., as a theory that opposes humanism).

> 所以一方面，如果把馬克思主義等同和歸結為人道主義、個性主義，便是膚淺的；另一方面，如果把唯物史觀當作一成不變的庸俗決定論或結構主義 (反人道主義)，也是謬誤的。 (Li Zehou 2016, 173)

He did not ground the necessity of this change of focus directly and explicitly upon the lack of political freedom and he did not limit the problem he highlighted to China. Even though he proceeded in his argumentation from the universal, worldwide state of alienation, his proposal implies a radical questioning of the ideologically grounded methods of inquiry, hitherto prevailing in the PRC in social and political sciences as well as in the humanities. This was a call for a new humanism, which could, in his view, not only transform alienation into a real "human condition," a spiritual fulfilled society of autonomous individuals, but also fill up the prevailing "vacuum of values." This call for a new awareness was also significant in the context of political freedom. It can be understood as an implicit critique of the social liberation that is solely limited to the sphere of economy without including a genuine political liberation. In addition, it placed the urgent need to establish a theoretical solution for the establishment of integral and free personalities into the center of intellectual interests.

> In his time, Marx focused upon political economy in order to investigate the fundamental science of historical materialism. Nowadays, in societies with highly developed technology, the questions of culture and psychology become increasingly important. Today, the problems we face are not problems of economic poverty, but those of spiritual poverty, of loneliness, isolation, and dullness. All these will become the most severe problems of the future world.

> 政治經濟學是馬克思當年所著重研究的有關唯物史觀的基本學科。在現代科技高度發展的社會，文化心理問題卻愈來愈迫切而突出，不是經濟上的貧困，而是精神上的貧乏、寂寞、孤獨和無聊，將日益成為未來世界的嚴重課題。 (Li Zehou 1994, 474)

Therefore, it was by no means a coincidence that, in the China of that period, a shift of interest emerged within the research on Marxism from its analysis of capitalist economy to the idea of the person as a self-creative being (ibid.). In this sense, Li's philosophy of subjectality can be regarded as a pioneering contribution to a new, critical, and humanistic reinterpretation of Marxism. His concept of practical philosophy led to a vital reevaluation of the orthodox version of the Marxist theory of cognition by many Chinese scholars and his ideas on human subjectality directly affected the formation of subject-related theories in Chinese literature (Lin, Min 1992, 975).

Nevertheless, in this context Li also warned against voluntarist tendencies that could be found in both Confucian and Maoist discourses.[41]

> After victory in the 1949 revolution, Mao instigated many other revolutionary movements; among them, the economic revolution (the confiscation of private industrial and commercial property), the Great Leap Forward, the political revolution (the anti-rightist movement), and the "Great Proletarian Cultural Revolution" are the most famous. None of these revolutionary movements and class struggles were in fact necessary for social or economic development; they simply came out of Mao's utopian idealism, which the Chinese refer to by the terms "subjectivism" and "voluntarism." (Li, Zehou 1999e, 178)

Li placed great emphasis upon the fact that the human subject has no access to perfect knowledge and absolute supremacy, because both knowledge and action are constrained by the objective limitations of existing technology and the level of social and cultural development. "This is the position that Li defends against the voluntarisms of Mao and Fichte, which regard the objective world as the playground of a godlike ego" (Chong 1999, 140). Li believes that, in order to counter such tendencies, Kant's emphasis on the activity of the human subject must be revised on the basis of Marxist analyses of the function of social labor.[42]

Li strongly opposed all kinds of comparisons between his theory of subjectality and the philosophy of existentialism or that of the Frankfurt school because they placed too much emphasis upon the individual freedom and individual actions. However, particularly in the context of the political dimensions of Li's theory, his concept of social practice and his notion of human agency (*zhutide nengdongxing* 主體的能動性) show some similarities with Hannah Arendt's concept of human action, which also provides humanity with possibilities for a continuity between generations, for social memory and, thus, for historical development. According to Arendt, these possibilities cannot be achieved by individual actions, for a particular individual can survive in society without work, without any action, and without producing anything by themselves. While Arendt consigns labor and work to the social realm, she tends toward the human condition of action as the political that is both existential and aesthetic. Although she approaches the connection between the realms of ontology and aesthetics from a different angle, her main goal is comparable to Li's central concerns. Both of them are deeply committed to the search for a theoretical solution that could show humans the way out of the alienation as a product of forced labor (see for instance Li Zehou 2016, 315, or Arendt 1998, 253–54). Similar to Li's theoretical endeavors, the purpose of Arendt's theoretical analyses is to trace back the roots of the phenomenon of estrangement, leading to the common state of alienation that prevails in the modern world. These analyses aim to follow alienation in its twofold flight "from the earth into the universe and from the world into the self" (Arendt 1998, 6). Arendt tries to trail this flight to its very origins, "in order to arrive at an understanding of the nature of society as it had developed and presented itself at the very moment when it was overcome by the advent of a new and yet unknown age" (ibid.).

Regarding the political dimensions of their respective views on the subject, there are many striking similarities between Li Zehou and the late works of György Lukács, especially his book *The Ontology of Social Being*. In the late 1970s when Li wrote his crucial work *Critique of the Critical Philosophy*, he probably did not have the opportunity to read Lukács's book. However, some scholars argue that it is possible that the vessel by which the later Lukács influenced Li was his 1967 preface to the new edition of his earlier work *The History and Class Consciousness*, "which provides almost all the key components of the framework for Li to construct his theory" (Gu, Xin 1996, 222). Li confirmed this similarity, stating that his

> "practical philosophy of subjectality" was an "anthropological ontology" that is comparable to the concept of the "ontology of social being," as proposed by Lukács' in his later years. Both

systems are equally focused upon the human being as a subject (on both levels of humankind as well as of an individual) as the main object of inquiry.

我用的「主體性實踐哲學」相當於「人類學本體論」，也接近盧卡契晚年提出的「社會存在的本體論」概念，即以作為主體的人（人類和個體）為探究對象。(Li Zehou 1985a, 1)

However, Li did not explicitly affirm the direct influence of Lukács's work on his theory so we could also consider the possibility that both intellectuals created similar theories simply due to their shared *Zeitgeist*. To a certain extent, both systems could also be attributed to the general intellectual, ethical, and cultural atmosphere of the era that gradually led to the fall of the so-called communist regimes in Eastern Europe and the Soviet Union.[43]

In their elaborations, both Li and Lukács proceeded from the realm of aesthetics and crossed over to politics, relying on their common inheritance of the Enlightenment tradition (Lin, Min 1992, 974). Gu Xin even argued that, "in some sense, Li can be called the 'Chinese Lukács'" (Gu, Xin 1996, 234). Li himself, however, strongly opposed such classifications of his theoretical system, pointing out that even though his theory has been criticized and labelled "naive materialism," "essentialism," and "Hegelian Marxism" by some Chinese scholars who sometimes even call him "the Chinese Lukács," he would still stand by his theory (Li, Zehou 1999e, 179).

In the chapter on his concept of "proper measure," we shall see that especially in his later years, Li was a sharp critic of all violent and sudden social shifts. He utterly negated the importance of the concept of class struggle and permanent revolution (Li Zehou 1999e, 177–78). Instead, he proposed gradual, reasonable changes, and social progress based upon an evolution customized to free autonomous personalities and taking into account the integrity of human subjects. He even argued that Marxism should not merely be seen as a doctrine of revolution. In studying Marx, readers should focus upon Marx's constructive elements. Li emphasizes that Marxism is not only a philosophy of revolution. It is rather, and even more so, a constructive philosophy, a philosophy for constructing material and spiritual civilizations (Li Zehou 1994, 474).

With the political dimensions of his philosophy of subjectality, Li (consciously or unconsciously) doubtless played a role in preparing the theoretical grounds for the student demonstrations in 1986 and 1989. With subjectality, Li has, in addition to emphasizing the crucial role of social practice, also highlighted the significance of politically suspicious, if not openly dangerous concepts such as individuality (*getixing* 個體性), sensibility (*ganxing* 感性), creativity (*chuangzaoxing* 創造性), and free will (*ziyou yizhi* 自由意志). A serious challenge to the authorities was also posed by his theory regarding the implications of the May 4th movement, in that he argued that in the China of the early twentieth century the urgency of "national salvation" suppressed the fight for the realization of the Enlightenment ideals. This theory, which was mentioned in the introductory sections and which will be introduced more in detail later in the chapter on Chinese modernization, was tightly linked to another uncomfortable idea, namely the need for a new Enlightenment movement that should "establish the principles of democracy and science firmly in Chinese society" (Lin, Min 1992, 991). Even Li's Marxist reinterpretation of Kant can be seen as potentially subversive. As Brian Bruya (2003, 134) points out, the Marx that Li invoked was not the Marx who wrote the *Capital* or the *Communist Manifesto*, but a young, idealistic theoretician who was creating a radical theory of human emancipation. Freedom and its highest expression are what Li finds appealing in both Kant and Marx. According to Bruya, the arc of Li's aesthetic theory that can be followed throughout his elaborations on Kant and Marx clearly shows that Li's ultimate concern is articulating a philosophy of aesthetic freedom, and therefore, of political freedom.

Humanization of Nature and Naturalization of Humans

In the Footsteps of Early Marx

Li Zehou developed his concept of the humanization of nature from the classical Marxist view of "humanized nature." In his early work, *Economic and Philosophic Manuscripts of 1844*, which is among Li's most important influences, Karl Marx described this as a process in which "not only the five senses, but also the so-called mental senses, the practical senses (will, love, etc.), in a word, human sense, the human nature of the senses, comes to be by virtue of *its* object" (Marx 2007, 46). Several contemporary scholars (e.g., Wang, Jing 1999, 103) argue that this Marxist notion emphasizes the "increasing domination of human beings over nature as an indispensable process of the progressive emancipation of human society from the tyranny of natural necessity." In such a view, the "development of the forces of production goes hand in hand with the gradual conquest of nature" (ibid.). This is a rather simplified interpretation of the Marxist view of the relation between humans and nature, for in his *Manuscripts* Marx explicitly states that

> Nature is man's *inorganic body*—nature, that is, insofar as it is not itself a human body. Man *lives* on nature—means that nature is his *body*, with which he must remain in continuous interchange if he is not to die. That man's physical and spiritual life is linked to nature means simply that nature is linked to itself, for man is a part of nature. (Marx 2007, 31)

According to Marx, it is precisely estranged labor that separates humans from nature, and therefore from their species-being (*Gattungswesen*): "In estranging from man (1) nature, and (2) himself, his own active functions, his life activity, estranged labor estranges the *species* from man" (ibid.).

Following this Marxist notion, Li points out that people humanize their natural (and thus, also their social) environments by making them more suitable for our habitation. However, based on traditional Chinese philosophical approaches, he develops the idea and places it on a more complex foundation. Li explains that through this process our inwardness, in turn, also becomes increasingly human, since it allows us to improve and advance our "inner worlds of reason, understanding, attitudes, and feelings" (Cauvel 1999, 159).

> Marx's idea of . . . humanizing nature implies two levels. On the one hand, it implies the humanization of external nature, i.e., the humanization of mountains, rivers, and of the entire cosmos. . . . In the process of humanizing external nature, humanity created material civilizations. On the other hand, it is about the humanization of inherent nature, i.e., a humanization of the senses, perception, sensation, and desires. . . . In the process of humanizing inherent nature humankind created spiritual civilizations.
>
> 馬克思關於「自然的人化」思想就是如此 . . .「自然的人化」包括兩個方面。一方面是外在自然的人化，即山河大

地，日月星空的人化。人類在外在自然的人化中創造了物質文明 . . . 另一方面是內在自然的人化，即人的感官，感知和情感，慾望的人化 . . . 人類在內在自然的人化中創造了精神文明。(Li Zehou 2001, 39)

Woei Lien Chong echoes Li by stating that the humanization of nature is thus visible on two levels: civilization manifests itself on the external level, and the spiritual civilization on the internal one (Chong 1999, 124). In this context, Li, once again, points to the significance of the aesthetic level, claiming that "the highest achievement of this 'humanization of nature' . . . is in the field of aesthetic" (Li, Zehou 1999, 177). For Li, the realm of beauty as the ultimate unification and highest synthesis for human beings to pursue constitutes "the ideal unity between nature and human beings, and between the externalization of human life and the internalization of nature. This highest synthesis is the fulfilment of the ultimate ideal of one's life in the aesthetic process" (Lin, Min 1992, 989). As Li sees it, this is the realm in which both the external and internal nature of the human being is being comprehensively humanized. As Woei Lien Chong points out, aesthetic education plays an important role in this process, since it provides a realm of freedom that does not exist in everyday reality, but which is necessary for that flight of the imagination that elevates us above our particularistic concerns and interests. Moreover, it cultivates our sensitivity, increasing our capacity for empathy with other human beings (Chong 1999, 124). The origins of this idea can also already be found in Marx's *Manuscripts*. Li has doubtless greatly expanded and developed the importance of the aesthetic field for the very essence of humanity. Nevertheless, the notion of beauty as one of the central, specific features that distinguish humans from other animals was already (though more or less latently) present in early Marx.

> An animal forms only in accordance with the standard and the need of the species to which it belongs, whilst man knows how to produce in accordance with the standard of every species and knows how to apply everywhere the inherent standard to the object. Man therefore also forms objects in accordance with the laws of beauty. (Marx 2007, 32)

For both early Marx and Li, the sense of beauty is primarily a social notion, for it could not be evolved outside of human communities and external to human history. However, the basis of beauty is firmly rooted in the humanization of nature as a process of human social practice in that nature and human beings are historically unified. But Li further develops the early Marxist view of the subjective aspects of this socially determined concept.[44] He points out that human practical activities that express the creativity and richness of individual subjectivity are reflected or exhibited in the form of beauty. Beauty can be viewed as a measure of human social development that evolves historically (Lin, Min 1992, 984). In Li's philosophy this aesthetic concept thus becomes a central ontological category.

The humanization of internal and external nature is also important for the establishment of Li's concept of subjectality. The humanization of nature is viewed as a crucial condition for the evolution of the physical, historical human subject, who is actively involved in its practice.[45] Through the humanization of nature, human beings become increasingly able to surpass the objective restrictions of their own environment. Due to our capability to make and apply tools (technology) humans can progress in an enduring process of history, which is, in Li's view, directed towards an ideal developmental stage of socialism in that both the humanization of external and internal nature will be completed and in which humankind will ultimately become free. In this sense, Li sees socialism as the onset of a world of beauty—the ultimate and highest goal of human history. "Here, the link between Li's theory and Marx's idea of a communist millennium is too obvious to be ignored" (ibid.).

Naturalized Humans and Their Unity with the World

In order to create a new model of philosophy that could achieve a synthesis between Marxism and traditional Chinese philosophy, Li also views the humanization of nature through the lens of the classical Chinese paradigm, "unity of nature and human beings" (*tian ren heyi* 天人合一).[46] This refers to the traditional Chinese holistic cosmology, or, in Li's own terms, to the "one world view" (*yige shijie guan* 一個世界觀), as opposed to the "two worlds view" (*liangge shijie guan* 兩個世界觀), the dualistic perception of reality that prevailed in the history of Western philosophy (Li Zehou 1999b, 1). The ultimate realization of this unification can, as we have seen, can be achieved in the final realm of beauty. As such, it cannot be separated from the humanization of nature. According to Li, "this ultimate 'unification of nature and humans' is rooted in the humanization of nature in the sense of material reality that modifies the internal, as well as the external worlds" (Li Zehou 1985, 20).

However, since this integral unity is based on a complementary relation between nature and humans, the one-dimensional concept of humanized nature is not sufficient to reach this goal. In Li's view, the process of the humanization of nature must include the naturalization of humans: "The integration of humans and the cosmos includes both humanized nature and naturalized humans and reflects the Chinese aesthetic doctrine of reciprocity fundamental to Confucianism and Daoism" (Li and Cauvel 2006, 66). Li suggests that the notion of the naturalization of humans put forward by the Daoists (and especially by Zhuangzi) at once opposes and complements the idea of the humanization of nature emphasized by the Confucian tradition of rites and music (Li, Zehou 2010, 77). Thus, if we claim that Confucianism is concerned with the humanization of nature, then Zhuangzi's concern is with the naturalization of humans.

> The former contends that a person's true naturalness must be conformed and permeated with sociality in order to attain true humanity. The latter argues that to become truly human one must shed sociality, allowing one's naturalness to attain unity with nature. (ibid., 79)

Thus, the "unity of heaven (nature) and man" not only includes the "humanization of nature," but also implies the "naturalization of humans." According to Li, the specific spirit of Chinese aesthetics, based upon the complementarity of Confucianism and Daoism, can be found precisely in such a unity.[47]

> The theory of the unity of Heaven (Nature) and man is a theory of the transformation of humans and nature, since it embraces the humanization of nature, as well as the naturalization of humans. We thus have two different names for the same content.
>
> 天人合一論也即是自然人化論 (它包含自然的人化與人的自然化兩個方面)，一個內容兩個名詞而已。 (Li Zehou 2001, 87)

The unity of man and heaven (nature) appears in bipolar forms in both the Confucian "humanization of nature" and Daoist "naturalization of humans." Within the Confucian tradition it appears as an emphasis on the moral values of human society, while in Daoism it is expressed in an intimate value of personal freedom.

> When Confucians speak about the "unity of Heaven (Nature) and man," they often compare it to inter-human matters, postulates of adjustment, and obedience in relations. But according to Zhuangzi's view this "unity of Heaven (Nature) and man can be reached only through the radical negation of inter-human matters." The Confucians define the value of an individual according to their relations with others, while Zhuangzi seeks their value precisely in the absence of such relations.

> 儒家講「天人合一」常常是用自然來比擬人事, 遷就人事, 服從人事；莊子的『天人合一』, 則是要求徹底捨棄人事與自然合一。儒家從人際關係中來確定個體的價值, 莊子則從擺脫人際關係中來尋求個體的價值。 (Li Zehou 2003, 266)

This unification is expressed by establishing or denying an inherent formalized set of ethics. This qualitative divergence also influences the creation of specific aesthetic criteria: while Confucians based these upon immutable ritual forms, Daoist aesthetics were based on the transcendence of any absolute valuation.

> The Confucians were focused upon the humanization of inherent nature, which meant a socialization of human instinctive desires and sensual needs. Aesthetic forms, i.e., the aesthetic results (of their discourses) were pleasant to see, hear, or read. Still, Confucian aesthetics were limited and confined to the area of interpersonal relations and morals. The particularity of Daoist aesthetic lies precisely in their going beyond this area.

> 如果說, 儒家 . . . . . . 注重在人化內在的自然, 使自然性的生理欲求, 感官需要取得社會性的培育和性能, 從而它所達到的審美狀態和審美成果經常是悅耳悅目、悅心悅意, 大體限定或牽制在人際關係和道德領域中, 那麼 . . . . . . 道家特徵卻恰恰在於超越這一點。(ibid., 265)

As we can see, Zhuangzi went a step beyond the Confucian *Book of Changes*, which stressed the harmony of a unified structure. What Zhuangzi emphasizes here is a total dismissal of Self and the Other, of subject and object. This position no longer concerns the question of structural unification (which strives for the unification and harmonization of subject and object), but the question of "re-creation" (in which the boundary between subject and object no longer exists). . . . It belongs neither in the domain of psychological causalities, nor in the area of religious experiences. This is a purely aesthetic domain.

可見，從儒家周易所強調的同構吻合又進了一步，莊子這裡強調的是完全泯滅物、我、主、客，從而他已不只是同構問題，(在這裡主客體相吻合對應)，而是'物化'問題 (在這裡主客體已不可分) . . . . . . 它即非心理因果，又非邏輯認識，也非宗教經驗，只能屬於審美領域。(ibid., 269).

But then again, the negative propositions and mundane images of Daoism are transformed into positive Confucian propositions and independence of character. In this synthesis, the humanization of nature is complemented on a higher level (ibid., 105). In life and in human personality as a whole, nature becomes the highest ideal and the arena in which the naturalization of humans can achieve its fullest development. The result of this synthesis is a kind of a "deepened aesthetics," in that the very act of creation or the feeling of appreciation of a single grass stem or flower could express "a transcendent attitude of life" (ibid., 99). This attitude permeates everyday life with a sacred aura, bringing "refreshment to fevered office seekers and moralists, providing those enslaved and wrenched about by various forces a way back to what is natural for humans, to genuine sensuosity" (ibid.). However, Li also points out that this return to the senses should not be seen as a return to animalism. On the contrary, it represents a process of mental (or spiritual) development in that social restraints can be surpassed through transcending the experience of nature. Li also emphasizes that this transcendence of sensuosity "is not mere sociality or rationality, but a sedimented sensuosity that at once includes and transcends these things while attaining unity with the universe (ibid.)."

In addition, both processes are rooted in the elementary presumption that life is beauty. The vital energy, quality, power, and appearance that life naturally manifests in the human body, are beautiful (ibid., 115).

Therefore, the realm of aesthetics is, inter alia, the highest realm in which humanized nature and naturalized humans can be unified into one integral entity. If we consider Zhuangzi's thought as a form of aesthetic thought, it becomes clear that it incorporates the notion of naturalization of humans.[48] It encompasses everyday life, our attitudes toward life, the ideal human personality, and the realm of unconsciousness. Here, aesthetics becomes a question "of much more than just pleasure in the appreciation or creation of art. It becomes the great philosophical problem of attaining unity with nature and plumbing its secrets to build up the mind and the body of the subject" (ibid., 116).

The process of naturalization of humans primarily aims at human fulfillment or the integrity of human beings that can be reached through the cultivation of aesthetic feelings, appreciation, and creativity. Aesthetics as an axiological paradigm can replace religions and offer human beings a safe sanctuary in which we can embrace the meaning of life. Li explicitly states that since he is "thoroughly advocating a replacement of religions through aesthetics, the 'naturalization of humans' should replace concepts such as 'salvation' in Christianity and 'Nirvana' in Buddhism" (Li Zehou 1999b, 12).

Li stresses this notion, pointing out that it could help modern (and postmodern) humans discover their deepest self and liberate themselves from the yoke of external alienations and artificial limitations. In this context, the naturalization of humans, which is originally a Daoist notion, could—through its complementary relation and interaction with the humanization of nature—also help Confucianism develop and integrate certain values linked to the appreciation of individual integrity and uniqueness. Li repeatedly points out that he aims to

> unveil the search for the individual, the shaping of human nature, and "the second Renaissance" in order to comprehensively develop the unique potentials of individual human beings such as their wisdom, strength, temperament, and character through recognizing, taking care of, and realizing our own Selves. In this way we can find the meaning of our life. The purpose, the sustenance, and the inner spirit of our life can all find their place in this limited, yet endless sensual world and the feeling of life. I sincerely hope that the Confucian tradition can absorb such aspects of Christianity and other religions, because in this way, its "inner sage" could stride

towards a completely new "realm of heaven and earth" that can be reached through the "naturalization of humans."

> 從而，重提人的尋找、人性塑建和「第二次文藝復興」，以「認識自己」、「切自己」、「實現自己」，在深刻的情感聯繫中充分展開個體獨特的潛能、才智、力量、氣質、性格，作為人生意義。使人的生活目的、命運寄託、靈魂歸依置放在這個有限而無界的感性世界和情感生命中，企望儒學傳統在這方面吸取基督教神學等等營養，使它的「內聖」邁上一種嶄新的「人自然化」的「天地境界」。(Li Zehou 1999b, 12–13)

The concept is also tightly linked to the creation of art. The formal stratification of art that is grounded in primitive sedimentation, extends in two directions. In one direction, it "refers to the ever-changing objects, events, and relationships that reflect the trends of different times and societies" (Li and Cauvel 2006, 139). In the other,

> it reconciles, amalgamates, and unifies the rhythms of external (cosmic) nature with the body-mind nature of creators and viewers, which pertains to the above-mentioned so-called naturalization of humans. This process is not limited to various practices such as, for instance, Chinese *qigong*, longevity exercises, or *taiji*, but also manifests itself in the formal stratification of artworks, and in the above-mentioned concept of *qi* (vital potential), in the so-called bones or bone-strength, and so on. All these belong to this scope.

> 藝術作品的形式層，在原始積澱的基礎上，向兩個方向伸延，一個方面是通過創作者和欣賞者的身心自然向整個大自然 (宇宙) 的節律的接近、吻合和同構，即前講中講到的所謂「人的自然化」，這不但表現為如中國的氣功、養生術、太極拳之類，同時也呈現在藝術作品的形式層裡，前面講到的「氣」以及所謂「骨」、「骨力」等等，都屬此範疇。(Li Zehou 2014, 8)

In Li's view, natural humans are the complement to humanized nature. They are merely different aspects of the same historical process. In this view, the term "naturalized humans" implies three meanings. The first relates humans to their environments, as context for their living and working. This is manifested in a coexistent and harmonized interaction between humankind and nature that enables humans to perceive nature as a shelter in which to live and rest. The second regards nature as an object for appreciation. It occurs in the process of the humanization of nature, in which nature becomes beautiful. The third refers to humans integrating themselves with nature through various practices like *qigong*, *taiji*, *yoga*, and different forms of meditation, through which they begin to adjust their bodily rhythms to the all-encompassing rhythm of nature, thus attaining the heaven-and-human oneness. While humanized nature is the product of construction, the naturalized human is the product of psycho-emotional formation. All three aspects are connected with a certain state of mind or aesthetic feeling—reason merges with emotions, subject with object, and social consciousness with individual freedom. Li believes that these three meanings of the naturalized human, and the related traditional Chinese idea of the integration of humans and nature (as expressed in the notion *tian ren heyi*), are vital for contemporary societies (Li and Cauvel 2006, 74–75). Through the naturalization of humanity, people might turn back to nature and practice "dwelling poetically" in the world, and so emancipate themselves from the omnipresent "control of instrumental rationality, from alienation by material fetishism, and from enslavement by the system of power, knowledge, language, and so forth" (Wang, Keping 2007, 251). The process of naturalization enables human beings to achieve and enjoy freedom in an aesthetic and spiritual sense. In doing so, the original biological concepts pertaining to the human body are turned into aesthetic notions (Li, Zehou 2010, 114). The driving force behind this process is human creativity in that rationality is intertwined with a wide variety of emotions, modes of perception, and expressions. Li believes that the realm of aesthetics is superior to both the rational and ethical realms. It is thus neither limited to the internalization nor to condensation of reason, and so surpasses cognitive and ethical limitations. It can be seen as a sedimented incorporation of both reason and sense (Wang, Keping 2007, 251) that could accelerate the "reconciliation of seven human emotions" (*qi qing zheng* 七情正).[49] Although the naturalization of humans, which leads them to the realm of aesthetics and to the open spiritual enjoyment of beauty and freedom, does not imply the domination of rationality over sensibility, nor the shaping of the latter by the former, it is also important in the epistemological and axiological senses. It not only "illuminates the truth through beauty" (*yi mei qi zhen* 以美啟真), but also "preserves the good through beauty" (*yi mei chu shan* 以美儲善). The recognition of truth leads humans to genuine knowledge and wisdom and to the discovery of goodness to moral cultivation.

From Marx to Kant and Back

Through the naturalization of humans and its counterpart, the humanization of nature, Li aims to highlight the active role of the human subject in the ultimately mechanistic Hegelian and "orthodox Marxist" dialectics of historical development.[50] Both processes are driven by human creativity and are directed toward the highest realm, namely that of aesthetics. The basic presumptions that help Li avoid the danger of falling into the trap of determinist laws of purely materialist development can be found in Kant's aesthetics[51]—the promise that the universality of human freedom and create the conditions for the comprehensive humanization of nature and naturalization of humans.

> The work that I now needed to do was to provide a link between Marx's idea of a "humanized nature" and the philosophy of Kant. This is the reason I associated "subjectality" with subjectivity, giving "a priori" subjectivity a materialistic "subjectality" foundation. After I had settled on this foundation, I emphasized that the significance of subjectivity lies in "cultural-psychological formation" or "sedimentation" in human beings, because this is the defining characteristic of the human species (Li, Zehou 1999, 179)

Marx not only emphasized that humanized nature was established through human material practice, but also that it led towards the constitution of a fully developed subject. Li adopted this proposition and aimed to complete it—with the help of Kant's philosophy—by elaborating on the problem of bridging the gap between chiefly material laws and a comprehensive human subjectivity.[52] Li thus expands the Marxist notion of material practice through Kant's idea of subjectivity and simultaneously adds to Kant that which he considers to be the basic philosophical approach of early Marx—an historical materialism centered on a philosophy of practice and the idea of humanized nature (Lynch 2016, 708). He found the link connecting all these aspects of human advancement in the constitution and development of aesthetic pleasure.

> So-called sensory pleasure arises from feelings of joy derived from sensual perception, which leads people to see a certain

object as beautiful. But aesthetic pleasure (or sensibility), which is a product of specifically human enjoyment based upon universal subjective necessity, is of a different nature. It primarily proceeds from judging a certain object as beautiful, and feelings of pleasure arise only afterwards. This means that aesthetic pleasure is not a passive sensual perception, reception, or reflection. It also cannot be reduced to rational, abstract or logical recognition. It is a product of the active human subject, of various human psychological factors, functions, modes of perception, imaginations, emotions (including intentions, desires, etc.), and ways of understanding. Kant named it aesthetic judgement. The future task of research in the scientific field of aesthetic psychology lies in more mature and comprehensive investigations of the formal structure of such "judgements." However, from the viewpoint of philosophy, it is most important to see that it was precisely this aesthetic pleasure that shaped the subject of humanized nature in relation to a humanized nature pertaining to the world of objects.

所謂官能愉快，是由感官獲得愉快而判斷對象為美，審美愉快作為具有主觀普遍必然性的人類享受成果（感性）不是這種性質，它是先判斷對象為美，而後得到愉快。這就是說審美愉快不是感官被動的感知、接受、反映，也不是理智的抽象邏輯的認識。它是人類主體多種心理因素、功能、感知、想像、情感（包括意向、願欲等等）、理解、活動的結果。康德把它叫審美判斷。這種「判斷」的形式結構是將來應由更成熟的審美心理學來研究和發現的科學課題。從哲學角度說，這裡重要的是，它相對於客體世界的人化自然，形成了人化自然的主體。(Li Zehou 1994, 472)

According to Li, beauty is a form of freedom, integrating both laws and purposes. It is a humanization of external nature or humanized nature. The aesthetic appreciation as a mental structure that corresponds to this form of freedom is a unification of sensitivity and rationality.[53] It is the humanization of the inner nature of humans, representing the second aspect of humanized nature. In this context, both concepts are of primary importance. For Li, beauty is also the ultimate product of human subjectality and the clearest expression of human nature (or of all that is essentially, specifically and uniquely human). He also writes that here everything belonging to humankind (as a universal historical entity) is sedimented into individuals, everything rational into sensitivity, and everything social into natural. The originally animalistic nature of sensuality becomes humanized, while natural structures and qualities become parts of the specific essence of humankind.

在這裡，人類（歷史總體）的東西積澱為個體的，理性的東西積澱為感性的，社會的東西積澱為自然的。原來是動物性的感官自然人化了，自然的心理結構和素質化成為人類性的東西。(ibid.)

Kant's supposition that beauty is a symbol of morality takes on the utmost significance in this context. Li emphasizes that both Kant and Goethe pointed to the analogous relation between color and morality, which was a core of traditional Chinese moral analogy (ibid., 148). He describes the processes through which, in the Chinese aesthetic tradition, conceptual knowledge is interwoven with moral and ethical emotions and imaginations, primarily through the processes of emotional creation that are characterized by "integrity and purity of intention," as embodied in and developed by symbols. In ancient Chinese philosophy, nature and the universe were seen as vital, relational, and emotional. The imaginations that led to this nonconceptual mode of moral emotion had first to pass beyond the stages of primitive religion, and they also had to supersede the conceptual stages of moral analogies. In this way, he emphasizes, ancient Chinese tradition already succeeded in generating the notions of nonconceptual pleasure that Kant spoke of in his aesthetics.

As is widely known, Kant elaborated on the philosophical dimensions of aesthetics in the third and last of his *Critiques*. In *Critique of the Power of the Judgement*, he upgraded his epistemological notions regarding the so-called Copernican revolution, according to which the conditions for knowledge or recognition cannot be defined by the objective conditions of a purported world or being, but are rather in accord with cognitive conditions that are already given in the subject. What this means for the realm of aesthetics is that beauty does not lie in the world or its objects, but rather within subjects themselves. This supposition inspired Li to extend Marx through Kant. While the former was concentrating on the ability of the collective human subject to engage in economic production through "material practice," the latter provided a philosophical framework that enabled Li to reflect on the cognitive and ideational aspects of this process. In other words, while Marx remained largely limited to the material infrastructure of human existence, Kant dealt with its ideational superstructure. As such, Kant was important for Li, because he provided a philosophy that enabled him to treat the cognitive capacities of the human subject without limiting them to the function of secondary effects of matter, as in vulgar materialism (Chong 1999, 121). "Li felt attracted to the aesthetic philosophy from Kant to Schiller because it opened up a whole universe of spiritual and artistic freedom that was alien to both Mao and Marx" (ibid., 124).

Within the Kantian framework, the multilayered and complex impressions received by the human senses can be ordered and synthesized in our minds precisely because we possess forms and categories of understanding that are not derived from experience, but that are logically prior to it. Because they are common to all human beings, universally valid knowledge is possible. Li emphasizes that this universal necessity is inseparable from the particular objective social circumstances in which human subjects live (Li Zehou 2007, 72). Li's anthropological philosophy takes up Kant's elementary questions regarding necessity and freedom and elaborates on the answers, inter alia, by integrating into his system some basic paradigms from the classical Chinese philosophy, e.g., the concept of the mean or equilibrium (*zhong yong*). In Li's understanding, the balance between these extremes (or all oppositions determining our life) can be achieved by developing a sense of proper measure (*du* 度), comparable to Kant's power of judgement (Li Zehou 2007, 383). While in the limited space of this section we cannot deal with this concept more in detail, it is important to state that both equilibrium and proper measure can be cultivated by (aesthetic) education, which develops "the senses, the imagination and the intellect, allowing them to interact freely without any concern for orthodoxy or practical utility" (Chong 1999, 124). In this sense education, which is directed towards the unity of naturalization of humans and humanization of nature, is essential for human progress, because, as we have seen, individual subjectality is not boundless, but is subject to objective constraints. Progress rather relies on the capacity of the entire society to coordinate labor and promote the growth of knowledge in an increasingly effective manner. Therefore, Li argues, in order to counter voluntarism, Kant's emphasis on the activity of the human subject must be revised on the basis of Marx's analysis of the role of social labor (ibid., 125). Li's view of the human subject, which is defined by the humanization of internal and external nature, is thus free and active, but still limited by the objective boundaries of existing technology and the level of cultural development of its society. In this way, human beings can truly become "the ultimate goal of nature" (Li Zehou 2007, 418). Li writes:

> This is also the subjectivization (humanization) of natural objects and the objectification of human goals. It seems that, for Kant, the whole of nature achieves its meaning and value because of human beings. However, in reality, human agency is still realized within the necessity of natural causality, and only on this ground can it reach objectives and results that are external to nature. Such a mutual co-dependence, penetration and transformation of subject (human being) and object (nature), of aim and law can only be constructed on the basis of a long-lasting historical practice through which humankind is changing the world.
>
> 這也就是自然對象主體化（人化），人的目的對象化。康德所謂整個自然好像是為了人的存在才有意義和價值，實際仍是人利用整個自然的因果必然而實現，達到非自然的目的和成就。主體（人）和客體（自然）目的與規律這種彼此依存、滲透和轉化，是完全建築在人類改造世界的長期歷史實踐的基礎上的。(Li Zehou 2007, 430–31)

In this long-lasting process, humankind humanizes external and internal nature to open up both the cognitive or epistemological and the ethical or axiological realms. Li extends this process further and blended it with the naturalization of humanity in order to achieve the aesthetic realm (Wang, Keping 2007, 252). From such a multilayered perspective, by combining Marx, Kant and Chinese philosophy, Li proposes a new, modernized and enriched understanding of the traditional paradigm of *tian ren heyi* as a dynamic, historically interactive oneness of humans and nature.

The sum effect of this is that Li has enriched Kantian philosophy through Marxism and vice versa. However, on the basis of these discourses he has established his own, unique system, which is different from Marx and from Kant in many ways. These differences and innovations will be summarized and explained more clearly in the final chapter of this book.

3

Upgrading and Modernizing Traditional Chinese Philosophy

The central concepts that constitute the core of Li Zehou's philosophical system are rooted in the Chinese philosophical tradition. Even the fundamental paradigm that determines his entire historical ontology—the notion of humans as social beings—is by no means only an invention of Marx or Hegel. As Gu Xin stresses, this was also a central idea of the ancient Chinese worldview (Gu Xin 1996, 210). In the Confucian *Analects*, for instance, it is written: "We cannot associate with birds and beasts. If I don't associate with other members of the humankind, with whom can I then associate?" (鳥獸不可與同群, 吾非斯人之徒與而誰與?) (Lunyu 2009, Wei zi, 726).

Therefore, it is by no means coincidental that Li regarded classical Chinese philosophy as a theoretical and methodological basis of his own ideational system. Many of his important books and essays are based on traditional Chinese philosophical discourses, which he regarded as most significant. His wide and comprehensive knowledge in this field is clearly visible not only in his three monographs on the history of Chinese thought but also in many of his other works, even those in which Chinese philosophy is not the central theme or the main topic. In these elaborations he either introduces or explains particular specific features of the historical development of Chinese philosophical idea or tries to incorporate them into his own system of thought or into his syntheses with particular Western philosophical ideas.

The Winding Course of Chinese Intellectual History

In Li's view, the understanding and the study of traditional Chinese philosophy is most important for the Chinese people, especially the younger generation. He maintains that spreading the study of the classics is a kind of Enlightenment (Li Zehou 2006, 1), especially from elementary school until college, Chinese students are primarily preoccupied with the study of natural sciences and technology, because the educational system (like almost everywhere else) widely neglects the humanities. The Confucian ideational system makes up an important part of the Chinese intellectual tradition and at the same time a significant contribution to the universal humanism on the global level. Accordingly, Li often emphasizes that a widespread study of Confucian classics in China should be more actively promoted, especially given that there is one material civilization but multiple spiritual cultures. He points out that even though the material civilization in China can be nearly the same as in the Western world, it still has quite a different spiritual culture, which in turn has important impacts on the material civilization (Li Zehou 1999a, 1). This fact manifests itself in the "miracle" and the crisis of the East-Asian modernization and its economic development.

Confucianism is among the most important pieces in the mosaic of the Chinese people's cultural heritage. It cannot, therefore, be abandoned, for it implies the very core elements of the Chinese cultural identity.[1] Here, the relationship between material civilization (modernization) and spiritual culture (tradition) becomes a crucial point. Thus, Li believes it is necessary to return to the Chinese tradition in order to learn something from history, especially to return to the history of Confucianism that dominates Chinese tradition (ibid.).

However, Li is strongly opposed to ideologically rife Confucian reading circles for young people like those that were organized across the whole country by the most famous representative of contemporary political Confucianism, Jiang Qing 蔣慶. Li believes that such practices, through which the Confucian classics are idealized and presented unsystematically and superficially, are counterproductive and even harmful. If the May 4th Movement was a movement of Enlightenment, such contemporary endeavors of bringing into modern life an alleged "Confucian revival" were, in his eyes, just the opposite, namely "the return to the ignorance and unawareness after the Enlightenment" (Li Zehou 2006, 1).[2] In Li's eyes, such ideologically colored reading circles could impose upon people from a very young age a kind of "slave morality," similar to the ones that were needed in the most autocratic periods of the traditional Chinese political system (ibid., 2).

Li views such endeavors as abusing ancient Chinese teachings because Confucianism as a system of ideas is multifaceted and, as a philosophy, it is anything but doctrinal or dogmatic. On the contrary, openness, tolerance, mutability, and flexibility were the most striking features that characterized the development of almost all Confucian discourses. This openness was clearly visible already in the Confucian *Analects* (*Lunyu* 論语), which contains numerous passages reflecting this attitude. In one of them, which Li also quoted (ibid.), Confucius directly and unequivocally emphasizes that "to attack different viewpoints was harmful" (子曰: 攻乎異端, 斯害也已!) (Lunyu 2009, Wei zheng, 365).

This tolerance towards other schools of thought, other ideas, and thinking systems was clearly visible throughout the entire historical development of Confucianism, which lasted for more than two millennia. According to Li, this historical development can be divided into four stages, which he calls "The Four Periods of Confucianism" (*Ruxue siqi* 儒學四期).[3] As we shall see, it shows that in its multifaceted history Confucianism has often incorporated into its own system numerous elements that originally belonged to other philosophical schools and to different theoretical discourses.

All this implies that Confucianism cannot be understood as a static, linear, or unchangeable tradition. Precisely because in its long-lasting historical development it was continuously challenged, fleshed out, and enriched by the introductions and integrations of many elements that belonged primarily to other schools of thought. Li believes that the dynamic nature of traditional developments must be preserved and evolved further in present China.[4] A new, reborn and revised Confucianism must be forged from a synthesis of the most precious elements of its own traditional teachings on the one hand, and various Western ideational systems on the other.

> The "flexibility" of Confucianism is not just the principle of tolerance, it is the acceptance, absorption, and, in the end, assimilation of different and even opposite ideas. Today, in the modernization of people's material lives, just as it absorbed and assimilated the Yin-Yang school and Buddhism before, Confucianism will absorb and assimilate Marxism, liberalism,

and existentialism, and change its notions and forms again, take another development, and enter a new period. (Li Zehou 1999a, 3–4)

This flexibility and the immense potential of integrating originally alien modes and patterns of thought manifested themselves throughout the entire Chinese intellectual history in the specific features brought about by the developmental streams of the four periods of Confucianism, and by its fruitful interactions with other schools of thought, especially Daoism and Legalism. However, if we want to fully understand the role of these important elements within Li's thought process, we must first investigate the very foundation of specific modes of reasoning and acting that has prevailed in traditional China. As Li sees it, this foundation was formed in the process of "rationalized shamanism."

In the past, I have proposed concepts such as "pragmatic reason," "the culture of pleasure," "emotion-based substance," "Complementary relation between Confucianism and Daoism," "Reciprocal utilization of Confucianism and Legalism," etc., to describe Chinese culture and thought. Now, I intend to summarize them with the phrase "shamanistic historical tradition" because this is the very foundation of all above-mentioned characteristics and concepts defining the Chinese culture.

我以前曾提出「實用理性」、「樂感文化」、「情感本體」、「儒道互補」、「儒法互用」、「一個世界」等概念來話說中國文化思想, 今天則擬用「巫史傳統」一詞統攝之, 因為上述我以之來描述中國文化特徵的概念, 其根源在此處。 (Li Zehou 2015, 3)

From Shamanism to Confucian Rituality

Li views the shamanistic (*wu* 巫) culture as an important origin of Chinese tradition, an origin that has later been historicized and rationalized through Confucian discourses. Following the tradition, established by the Duke of Zhou, Confucius was hence a "transformative creator (*zhuanhuaxinde chuangzaozhe* 轉化性的創造者)"[5] who has significantly modified the long-lasting shamanistic tradition that prevailed in China at the edge of the Zhou Dynasty. As noted, it was in this process that shamanistic ceremonies were converted into Confucian rituality.

Li believes that "rituals were generated from emotionality" (*li sheng yu qing* 禮生於情), a presumption already found in the *Guodian bamboo slips* (*Guodian chu mu zhu jian* 郭店楚墓竹簡).[6] In this context, he emphasizes that from the viewpoint of history, shamanistic ceremonies that were rationalized and later transformed into Confucian rituals did not directly arise from individual emotions (Li Zehou 2015, 11). Instead, they were incubated in shamanistic ceremonial practices, which included powerful elements of communal emotions that far surpassed those of the individual's personal feelings. In Li's view, shamanistic ritual activities included numerous components of intense collective emotional engagement. These emotions chiefly originated in the existential conditions of community or group to which the people who participated in these practices belonged.

It is within this context that, "heaven, earth, and the myriad things all reside within specific and concrete circumstances of emotionally interactive relationality" (Li Zehou 2016, 1099–1100), which differs fundamentally from the emphasis on logos, reason, language, and logic that later defined the dominant streams of Western thought. Such an "interactive relationality," which remained preserved in the prevailing Chinese philosophical and cultural paradigms, is based on the human ability of emotional responsiveness (*gan* 感). This capacity enables people to act not only in resonance with the universe, but also in harmony with members of their own group. On such a basis, which is founded on the Chinese shamanistic historical tradition (*wushi chuantong* 巫史傳統), Confucius later managed to formulate his teachings as a kind of "emotional cosmology" (*you qing yuzhou guan* 有情宇宙觀).

Because shamanism in Li's view was an important part of the essential foundation of classical Chinese culture, he investigated a broad scope of archeological material, as well as the earliest Chinese written sources to shed light on the relation between shamanistic cultures and the evolution of early Chinese social and governmental institutions (Li Zehou 2015, 6). In several earlier publications and in *From Shamanism to Rituality: Explaining Rituality as a Return to the Humaneness*, in which he aimed to summarize his theories on the topic, Li revealed a basis for describing shamanism, its social functions, its relationships to humanness, and its deep evolutionary origins. He explains that the deeper evolutionary roots of shamanism can be found in the capacities for creating and performing rituals, which provide for the most important communication and integrative processes in primeval communities. The evolution of shamanism, which later led to Confucian rituality, can be deduced from these grounds. Li shows in a very detailed and accurate way how and why the Confucian ritual originated in the ceremonial practices of shamanism. Scholars such as the modern Confucian theoretician Xu Fuguan (1987, 649), believed that this was a result of the fusion of two different types of culture: an agrarian system typical of the defeated Shang (or Yin) Dynasty (1600–1066 BC), and the hunting and gathering culture of the nomadic ancestors of the Zhou Dynasty (Rošker 2016, 136).[7] This hypothesis is supported by a passage from the *Historical Notes* (*Shi Ji* 史記). In spite of the fact that the mythological founding ancestor of the Zhou Dynasty (2100–1600 BC), Hou Ji, was credited with greatly improving Xia agriculture. His son Buzhu, however, abandoned agriculture entirely, living a nomadic life in the manner of their Rong and Di "barbarian" neighbors (see Shi ji 2013; Zhou benji, 147). Hence, a mixing of agrarian and nomadic religious rituals was also among the consequences of this "intercultural" encounter. The Zhou Dynasty certainly arose from a mixture of different types of cultures and different modes of social production in which shamanistic elements, or at least the relics of shamanism, were still very much alive.

In the period of the dynastic transition from the Shang to the Zhou, which took place approximately in the eleventh century BC, the development and specialization of ancient shamanistic ceremonies, especially in the form of totemic dances, led to the formalization of rites and music that were henceforth seen as the formal representation of aristocratic political power. Its systematization was completed at around the time of the dynastic transition from the Shang to the Zhou Dynasty (roughly the eleventh century BC). The Zhou tradition, which claims that "the Duke of Zhou established the rites and music" (Zhou Gong zhi li zuo yue 周公制禮作樂) (Lun heng jiao zhu 2010; Shu jie, 556), has some historical foundation. The Duke of Zhou certainly established a set of institutions that integrated and systematized the previously existing rites and music. In his work on Shang and Zhou institutions, Wang Guowei 王國維 also highlights the importance of the transformations that occurred in this transition from the Shang to the Zhou Dynasty.

> Most important among these were the establishment by the Duke of Zhou of the patrilineal, feudal, and sacrificial systems as well as the systematization of rites and music. These devel-

opments were indeed of epoch-making significance in Chinese history. Many studies over the past three decades, however, have focused solely upon general social formation, ignoring the important historical phenomenon of the establishment of ritual institutions. The real reason that Confucius and his followers so extolled the Duke of Zhou, and that later generations would even regard the Duke of Zhou as Confucius's equal, is precisely his systematization of the rites and music that Confucius so staunchly upheld. (Li and Cauvel 2006, 11)

Li pushes the origins of Chinese culture further back than the majority of Chinese scholars by suggesting that Confucianism originated from the rationalized shamanism with the Duke of Zhou as its initiator. This is also one of the reasons Li advocates a return to the pre-Song way (Gu 2015, 20) of addressing Confucianism as the "School of Duke Zhou and Confucius" (*Zhou Kong zhi dao* 周孔之道); instead of the later, more common denotation "School of Confucius and Mencius" (*Kong Meng zhi dao* 孔孟之道).

To a certain extent, Li grounds his argument on the nature of shamanistic rituals in primitive societies on Mircea Eliade's famous book, *Shamanism: Archaic Techniques of Ecstasy*. However, as Marthe Chandler points out, the book has been severely criticized for making romantic over-generalizations and lacking overall archaeological evidence (Chandler 2015, 135). Although Eliade offers some very general (and sometimes rather bold) characterizations of shamans as people who entered a state of ecstasy to interact with spirits on behalf of their community, he also establishes many additional specific concepts regarding the shaman, while many later researchers neglect to address in their applications of this term (Winkelman 2011, 54). For Li, shamanism has its basis in the innate dimensions of human emotions, cognition, and sensuality. The shamanist cultures engaged the use of altered states of consciousness in order to incorporate information derived from several levels of the brain, producing visual symbolism demonstrated in visionary experiences (ibid.).

According to Li, the central practices of shamanism are linked to group engagement and have important social, psychological, and psycho-physiological effects. These effects reflect the human need for group coordination, deriving from an expansion of attachment bonds that evolved to maintain closeness between infants and caregivers and to provide a secure basis for the self by assuring feelings of protection provided by powerful figures. "Humans' evolutionary ancestry produced a neuropsychology for a social world, a need for emotional life that is wired into the human nervous system" (Winkelman 2011, 61). Social identity and personhood accordingly became a necessity, a reflection of social interdependency that produced a canalization and coordination of individual neurological, emotional, and psychological development in relations to other members of one's own group (ibid.).

Neolithic humans living in the land occupied by modern-day China were rather advanced and based their societies on small-scale agricultural production, in which communities were mainly constructed through kinship relationships. Against such a social and cultural background, the above-mentioned rationalization of the shamanistic tradition has led in turn to the incorporation of ideas linked to "relational selves,"[8] or, in Li's own words, to "relationalism"[9] (*guanxizhuyi* 關係主義) into a realm of a "traditional unconscious" (*chuantong wuyishi* 傳統無意識). The concrete collective social consciousness (*jiti shehui yishi* 集體社會意識) manifests itself in the condition of the relational individual, who was necessarily and existentially an organic part of a social group. Such consciousness reflected the manner in which individuals came to view themselves as a part of their group and in which patterns of commonality among individuals brought legible unity to interhuman relations. Such awareness was formed through shamanistic ceremonies (Li Zehou 1985a, 17). These early collective rites, especially those that include music and dance, had a powerful effect on early humans, creating "intense feelings of respect, love and loyalty, which sedimented into the emotional, moral and aesthetic psychological structures necessary for truly human communities to evolve" (Chandler 2016, 163). Li writes:

> Just as in the process of material production, I uphold that without activity on the part of the collective social consciousness—i.e., without primitive shamanist ritual activity and communal linguistic and symbolic activity—the formation of a human psyche that is different from that of the animals would never have been possible.
>
> 與物質生產一樣，我仍然堅持，如果沒有集體的社會意識的活動形態，即如果沒有原始的巫術禮儀活動，沒有群體性的語言和符號活動，也就不可能有區別於動物的人的心理。(Li Zehou 1985a, 15)

In these ceremonies, we can see the manifestation of the natural and animalistic aspects of the individual person, but at the same time, also the sprouts of their "humanization." In shamanistic ceremonies, reason and sociality merged with sensuousness and naturalness. Once these activities have developed into fixed ritual systems, this unification had to be carried on through music and rites (Li and Cauvel 2006, 17), which formed the earliest framework of the institutional structure of ancient China. With the infusion of a sociocultural dimension, animal consciousness was transformed into the human psyche. All kinds of uniquely human psychological functions such as imagination, cognition, comprehension, and other intellectual activities, sprouted and developed while preserving their connection to elementary animalistic mental functions such as perception and feeling. This occurs much more intensely and self-consciously than in the processes of direct material practices like hunting, gathering, and agrarian production. It is in this fashion that shamanistic totemic activities helped organize and structure the originally disparate processes and elements of actual material production and everyday life (Li and Cauvel 2006, 7). Hence, totemic dance and shamanistic ceremonies are the earliest forms of human spiritual civilization and symbolic production.

It is also important to note that although the development of shamanistic practices toward a rationalized Confucian rituality was rooted in emotions, it was by no means limited to them. In its psychological dimensions this development has been evolving within the emotiorational structure of the human mind.[10] Hence, it did not terminate in the specific, emotionally grounded forms of Confucian rituality, but also initiated a movement leading from ritual to reason. In light of this finding, the notion of reason has two major connotations: "the solidification of reason (will) and the construction of reason (knowledge, as conceptions of good and evil). The movement from ritual to reason cultivates these two aspects of individual reason" (ibid. 78). The Confucian notion of "ritual" (*li*) is also an expression of social morality. According to Li, ritualized social behaviors began in shamanistic ceremonies and gradually became generally accepted social norms (D'Ambrosio, Carleo, and Lambert 2016, 1063–64).

In Li's view, the collective shamanist feelings were transformed (and rationalized) into new forms of Confucian rituality. However, these rationalized forms did not remain an independently predominant element of Chinese tradition. Confucius has explained "ritual" (*li*) through "humaneness" (*ren*). There are various passages in the *Analects* that directly refer to the inseparable connection between this central Confucian virtue and Confucian rituality, for instance: "If a man does not possess humaneness, what has he to do with the rituals?" (人而不仁, 如禮何?) (Lunyu 2009; Ba Yi, 375).

Given that humaneness is essentially a form of social empathy, it cannot be reduced to reason, because it also involves emotions. In this sense, it is an important part of that basic paradigm of Chinese ideational tradition, which Li named as emotio-rational structure.

In its concrete reality, humaneness is rooted in the collective psychological formations or the Great Self, which represents the unification of the individual with their community. This type of awareness was created through primitive sedimentation and was shaped through shamanistic dances. For Li, however, the main question was how to explain, historically and concretely, the unification of different, originally incongruent elements of the human psyche, such as the sensuous and the rational, the natural and the social, or the individual and the collective. He believes that the earliest form of the intersections of these elements becomes most apparent in totemic dances. "Dancing around the group while drumming, rattling, and chanting, the shaman exhorted the spirits to come to the assistance of the members of the community" (Winkelman 2011, 54). Here, Li points to the holistic nature of the ideational world of shamanistic societies and accentuates.

> It is extremely important to see that (shamanist ceremonies) were based upon a unity of body and mind and by no means separated soul and flesh. They attached importance to the very process of activity and not to its objects.
>
> 特別重要的是, 他是身心一體而非靈肉兩分, 它重視的是活動過程而非客觀對象。 (Li Zehou 2015, 13)

In Li's view, "primitive totemic dance took disparate individual sensuous existences and sensory activities and knit them consciously together, melding them into a whole" (Li Zehou 2010, 6).

The symbolic activities of such collective consciousness, for instance the so-called Great Self (*da wo*) awareness, distinguished the human mind from animal consciousness. Using language and producing ornamental objects required symbolic and abstract reasoning and imagination. Li believes that such symbolic activities grew out of the music and dance of original shamanistic rituals. "Drumming, group vocalization, and other displays were the foundations from which the uniquely human mimetic capacity evolved and provided a basis for shamanism" (Winkelman 2011, 54). Rhythmic chanting was a tool for a better coordination of the work of larger groups and the sensuous force of music in shamanistic dances was most important for shaping and transmuting human desires, transferring instinctive feelings to more cultivated emotions, and thus making us increasingly human. This humanization of "inner nature" was the beginning of the process of rationalizing shamanism, which took place in the framework of the shaping of Confucian culture. Li places emphasis on the vast number of references to dance in various Confucian classics. In the chapter "The Overseer of Ritual Affairs in the Spring Offices" (*Chun guan zongbo* 春官宗伯) of the *Rites of Zhou* (*Zhou li* 周禮), there is the following passage:

> The sons of the state must be instructed in music and dance; they must be taught (different dance styles) such as the Yunmen Daquan, Daxian, Daqing, Daxia, Dahu, and Dawu. With the six pitch standards, six bronze pitch pipes, five pitches, eight kinds of instruments, and six kinds of dance, a great celebration is performed in order to call the spirits, to harmonize the states and the people, and to calm the sojourner. In this way distant tribes are soothed, and the phenomenal world can be brought to motion.
>
> 以樂舞教國子，舞《雲門》、《大卷》、《大咸》、《大韶》、《大夏》、《大濩》、《大武》。以六律、六同、五聲、八音、六舞大合樂，以致鬼神示，以和邦國，以諧萬民，以安賓客，以說遠人，以作動物。 (Zhou li 2014; Chun guan zongbo, 478)

Li points out that although texts such as the *Rites of Zhou* (*Zhou li* 周禮) are likely of relatively late provenance, what they record can reliably be taken as longstanding historical fact (Li Zehou 2010, 5).

Forms of dance are also recorded in *Master Lü's Spring and Autumn Annals* (*Lü shi Chunqiu* 呂氏春秋) in which we read that, "in former times, the people of the Getian clan would stamp their feet with oxtails in hand, singing eight stanzas" (昔葛天氏之樂，三人操牛尾，投足以歌八闋) (Lü shi Chunqiu yi zhu 2011; Gu yue, 118).

The *Book of Documents* (*Shang shu* 尚書 or *Shu jing* 書經) also contains similar statements: "When I hit the stone drum, or softly strike it, countless animals lead on one another to dance, and all the chiefs of the official departments are in harmony with each other" 予擊石拊石, 百獸率舞, 庶尹允諧。(Shang shu 2011; Yi Ji, 89). In this classical Confucian work, dancing was directly associated with shamanism: "People dared to constantly dance in palace halls, and sing in their chambers under the influence of drugs. This was called the 'shaman style'" 敢有恆舞於宮, 酣歌於室, 時謂巫風。(ibid., 1).

Li emphasizes that the crucial aims of these practices were of a strictly pragmatic nature.

> The "shamanistic ceremonies" were mainly performed with a direct connection to certain inter-human issues that arose in the community. Their goals were very concrete and realistic, and always linked to material benefits. They were not carried out merely because of some individual spiritual needs or soul comfort. All of them had to do with prayers for the rain, for extinction of enemies, or good fortune.
>
> 「巫術禮儀」主要是直接為群體的人間事物而活動的, 具有非常具體的現實目的和物質利益, 絕非僅為個體的精神需要或靈魂慰安之類而作。降雨、消滅、祈福等等均如此。 (Li Zehou 2015, 11)

Li points out that there are also many materials among the oracle bone inscriptions that are connected with prayers for rain (Li and Cauvel 2006, 4). In the *Rites of Zhou*, one passage refers directly to such practices: "When the country faced a severe drought, the master shaman was invited to perform a rain dance" (司巫: 掌群巫之政令。若國大旱, 則帥巫而舞雩。(Zhou li 2014; Chun guan zong bo, 545–46).

It is also important to note that it was precisely this primeval culture that allowed humankind to slowly develop self-consciousness and appreciate its uniqueness among the living beings of the natural world. With its ceremonies, which included totemic songs and dances focused on sacrificial ritual, the shamanistic culture constituted, structured, organized, and strengthened original communities, arousing and uniting human consciousness, intention, and will. These early rituals also gradually refined the individual skills and communal cooperation of early communities "by committing to memory and rehearsing their processes of subsistence and livelihood" (Li and Cauvel 2006, 3). Primeval culture as a result, increasingly regulated human behavior and endowed it with order, pattern, and direction.

In addition to shaping and nurturing the beginnings of a sense of the collective and of order in human action and thought, it also constitutes the normalization of individual emotions and thoughts. All of these are, in turn, related to the ordering of the postulated spiritual world through magical arts and religious imagination. In the human mind these patterns contain the sprouts of intellectual activity while simultaneously allowing the expression of feelings.

> To summarize: in this process of rationalization, all kinds of activities that originally only served as intermediaries or tools for performing shamanistic ceremonies became symbolic systems and operators. They were increasingly objectified, objectivized and recorded, but still contained strong emotions and beliefs like fear, respect, loyalty, and honesty.
>
> 總之，本在巫術禮儀中作為中介或工具的自然對象和各種活動，都在這一理性化的過程中演化而成為符號性的系統和系統操作。它日益對象化、客觀化、敘事化，卻又仍然包含有畏、敬、忠、誠等強烈情感和信仰於其中。 (Li Zehou 2015, 16–17)

These emotions and beliefs also represented the crucial foundations for the later Confucian moral virtues and values. Because the shamanistic ceremonies were a form of the unity of human beings with the spirits (*yu shen tongzai* 與神同在), they did not represent forms of worshipping objectified deities, but could be conceived as a sensual experience of the inherent and were inseparable from them. Li emphasizes (ibid. 23) that in such a unity, there was no room for the birth of any "transcendence," nor for any idea of an objectively existing God. In this process of rationalization, the shamans, who were originally spiritual or religious leaders, gradually also assumed ethical and political leadership. This is also the reason or the origin of the tripartite nature of Confucian rituality in that religion, ethics, and politics are amalgamated into a coherent and inseparable unity.[11]

The Four Periods of Confucianism and the Culture of Pleasure[12]

In Li Zehou's schema of the "Four periods of Confucianism" (*Ruxue si qi* 儒學四期) the fourth stage or period of development belongs to contemporary China but we can roughly speak of three main stages that determined the historical development of traditional Confucianism in ancient, medieval, and premodern China. In this sense, Confucianism passed through three main periods in imperial China.

As we have seen, Li claims that the original forms of classical Chinese philosophy (including Confucianism and Daoism) were formed on the basis of rationalized patterns derived from ancient shamanist cultures. In the period of the Eastern Zhou Dynasty (770–256 BC), the ancient religious concepts that were rooted in the earlier periods had almost completely disintegrated. This period marks an extraordinarily important historical and cultural shift, in which Chinese society entered what Karl Jaspers has called "the axial period."[13] In fact, as opposed to most other civilizations, China did not develop a theology, but separated itself from it (Yang Zebo 2007, 3). As Chen Lai 陳來 points out, instead of people recognizing their own limitations and turning towards some transcendent, infinite entity, or monotheistic religion, they recognized the limitations of deities and oriented themselves towards the real world and the ordering of society and inter-personal relations (Chen Lai 1996, 4). Thus, instead of a "breakthrough to transcendence," in China there was a "breakthrough to humanity" (Xu Fuguan 1987, 659). While other civilizations were moving towards "more developed" (mostly monotheist) religions during this same period, China turned towards a pragmatic search for an ideal social order.[14] According to Li, it was Confucius who (following the footsteps of the Duke of Zhou) made this breakthrough in the axial age around 500 BC, thereby shaping the foundation of Chinese philosophy (Li Zehou 2016, 159). He emphasizes humaneness and rituality to reinterpret and remold the ancient shamanistic rituals and mystic experiences, establishing at the same time the theoretical framework of "pragmatic rationality" that could replace a more advanced, or, in Li's own words, "real religion" (Li Zehou 1999a, 3). This period lasted approximately until the beginning of the Qin Dynasty (221–206 BC)—until the first unification of China under the rule of the emperor Qin Shi Huangdi. Its main representatives were Confucius, Mencius (Mengzi孟子), and Xunzi 荀子.

In Li's view, the second stage of Confucianism started around 100 BC (during the Han dynasty). The main characteristic of this stage lies in that, while absorbing the teachings of Daoism, Legalism, Moism, and the Yin-Yang school, Confucianism created a comprehensive system consisting of a "yin-yang and five phases" (*yinyang wuxing* 陰陽五行) cosmology. The latter is an all-encompassing scheme of the whole universe, including body and spirit, matter and idea, natural and social worlds, as well as politics and morals. Li points out that this cosmology in some degree still maintains its influence on common people in contemporary China (ibid.).

Here, we could add that this second phase of the development of Confucianism was also of utmost importance in the political sense, because in this period Confucianism gradually became the new state doctrine that was later reinforced by the introduction of the state examination system, which guaranteed successful candidates the achievement of political power. Until 1903, this system remained the main institutional pillar of Confucianism. In this second phase, which was marked by the work of Dong Zhongshu, the original Confucian teachings were also mostly interpreted through the work of Xunzi, who was one of the two most influential formal successors of Confucius, and who is often considered as a kind of a bridge connecting Confucianism and Legalism.

The third stage of Confucianism began around 1200 AD (during the Song Dynasty). At this stage, Confucianism accepted and assimilated many elements of Daoism, and, even more importantly, of the originally Indian Buddhism. In this period, the so-called Neo-Confucian school and its main proponent Zhu Xi constructed a complex system of moral metaphysics that had a great impact on the whole of society more than seven hundred years and that is still being developed further by the intellectual stream of Modern Confucianism (*Xin ruxue* 新儒學). In this third developmental phase, original Confucian teachings were mainly interpreted and explained through the lens of Mencius's elaborations.

The fourth stage of Confucianism is still ongoing in contemporary China. We now witness too its manifold approaches and often quite different discourses. The above delineated course of development belongs, as already mentioned, to Li's theory of the "Four periods of Confucianism" (*Ruxue si qi* 儒學四期), by which he opposed the view of the "Three periods of Confucianism" (*Ruxue san qi* 儒學三期), as was upheld by Modern Confucians such as Mou Zongsan (Tsung-san) 牟宗三 and his disciple Tu Wei-ming 杜維明.

I believe that the formal classification of the "theory of three periods" scheme contains two big flaws. Firstly, it lost a comprehensive view of this development by interpreting Confucianism through the lens of the moral ethics of the heart-mind and the inner-nature approach. Confucius very rarely mentioned the concepts of "heart-mind" and "inner nature"; they only occur twice in the entire *Analects*. Mencius discussed them a bit more, but for him neither was more important than issues pertaining to political philosophy. In the *Guodian Chu Slips* these two notions were mainly treated very concretely and were linked to the concept of "emotions," far from being seen as some abstract philosophical ideas. The fact that the "theory of three periods" placed the abstract moral theory of heart-mind and inner nature as the very foundation of Confucianism clearly shows that its proponents have ignored or even deviated from the original works of Confucius and Mencius. Secondly, precisely because of this, this theory simply eliminated Xunzi and even the whole Confucian discourse of the Han Dynasty together with its main representative Dong Zhongshu. According to them, the Han Confucians only dealt with the "unity of nature and humans," without considering the discourse of "heart-mind and inner nature" and therefore cannot be considered as the "essence" of "proper Confucianism." This view is not in concord with the factual history of thought.

我以為,「三期說」在表層上有兩大偏誤。一是以心性——道德理論來概括儒學,失之片面。孔子本人極少談「心」、「性」,「性」在《論語》全書中只出現兩次。孟子談了一些,但並不比談社會政治問題更為重要。郭店竹簡所談「心」「性」,大都聯繫「情」而非常具體,遠非抽象的哲學觀念。「三期說」以心性道德的抽象理論作為儒學根本,相當脫離甚至背離了孔孟原典。第二,正因為此,「三期說」抹殺荀學,特別抹殺以董仲舒為代表的漢代儒學。在他們看來,漢儒大談「天人」,不談「心性」,不屬儒學「道統」「神髓」。這一看法不符合思想史事實。 (Li Zehou 1999b, 1)

Thus, according to Mou and Tu, the first period was marked exclusively by the works of Confucius and Mencius. The second period did not start before the beginning of the Neo-Confucian discourses of the Song Dynasty, and even after that there was a "gaping void" of three hundred years, which means that they again completely ignored the entire period of the Qing Dynasty. According to them, a new developmental stage of Confucianism did not begin before the emergence of Xiong Shili and other pioneers of the Modern Confucian movement (Li Zehou 2006).

Li radically questions Mou Tsung-san's view, according to which Confucianism only represents the moral metaphysics of the heart-mind and inner nature. Li believes that this is how Mou reduced this ancient philosophy to a doctrine, limited to religious thought (Li Zehou 1999b, 1). In his *Reading the Analects Today*, he points out that Confucianism is neither a religion nor a philosophy, but is at the same time both a religion and a philosophy. To be more exact, he describes Confucianism as a "semi-religion" as well as a "semi-philosophy" (Gu 2015, 3).[15] Li firmly believes that Confucianism is a much richer discourse and that it cannot be limited to a form (though "unorthodox") of religion.[16] In his view, Confucianism can be upgraded and modernized by integrating many different modern ideas and theories. Li mentions the paradigm of the "unification of nature and humans," which has been treated by Modern Confucians solely through the lens of their moral metaphysics, although it has a much wider significance and a much deeper potential for development, since it can also be seen as a paradigm enriching modern discourses on ecology and on the unification of the natural and social spheres (Li Zehou 1999b, 1).

Li points out that in its historical development Confucianism thoroughly keeps its spirit or main specific feature of "pragmatic rationality," a concept profoundly different from Western speculative rationality or pure reason (Li 1999b, 3). It represents "a culture of pleasure" as opposed to the Western culture of sin (*zuigan wenhua* 罪感文化), or the Japanese culture of shame (*chigan wenhua* 恥感文化).[17] This traditional Chinese culture is based upon a "one-world view" (in contrast to the Western "two-worlds view" as elaborated throughout the development of Western philosophy from the Bible and through Plato and Kant). Its core is emotion-based substance (*qing benti*).

While we shall elaborate on this latter notion, and on the concepts of "pragmatic rationality" and the "one-world view" in more detail in later sections of this book, we will limit ourselves here merely to Li's explanation of the "culture of pleasure." This phrase has been variously translated as "culture of optimism," "culture of joy," "culture of happiness," and as "culture pervaded by delight," respectively. In his *Historical Ontology*, Li himself claims that this concept has a threefold semantic connotation. First, it denotes "a culture of worldly happiness," which is typical for Chinese tradition, for it centers on the material factuality of human life, which, in itself, is directed towards worldly happiness and relational harmony. Secondly, it implies "a culture of optimism," for it is focused upon opportunities for improving one's living environment from a humanistic and optimistic viewpoint despite history's progression through tragic and depressing events (Wang, Keping 2016, 188). Thirdly, it indicates "a culture of music and aesthetics,"[18] for it "helps facilitate the final accomplishment of human nature by virtue of musical appreciation and aesthetic feeling at its best" (ibid.). Characteristically, this culture does not identify cosmic order with any kind of moral order. In this framework, morality is by no means seen as the highest realm of human life. The culture of pleasure is not ruled or guided by any kind of supreme rationality, because its final purpose is the human being living in it. In this sense, it proceeds against social alienation and the sensitive, mental, and cognitive attitudes of the people living in it and is grounded on the emotion-based substance instead of a pure rational or a mere instinctive one (ibid.). The term *legan* 樂感 (pleasure) as such also indicates a kind of emotion. The nature of this "pleasure," however, also has metaphysical dimensions, for it implies religious elements (Li Zehou 2016, 195). The experience of this feeling of pleasure is namely the highest experience.[19] "Although it is individual, subjective and sensual, it represents the bodily recognition or the ultimate experience of the 'substance'." 它雖仍是個體的、感性的，卻是對「本體」的體認或最高經驗。(Li Zehou 2016, 195).

Li draws our attention to the fact that Confucius emphasizes the importance of such feelings of pleasure, for instance, by saying that "to know something is not as good as to like it, and to like something is not as good as to take pleasure in it" 知之者不如好之者，好之者不如樂之者。(Lunyu 2009; Yong Ye, 458).

In the Confucian discourse, this pleasure is a necessary precondition for the formation of the sense of (co)humaneness, which can arise precisely because of this unity (or identity) of human material and spiritual life (Li Zehou 2011, 61). Li also emphasizes that for the common Chinese people death is simply a continuation of the life in this world. As a result, the Chinese have always, from ancient times until the present day, presented all kinds of useful objects to their deceased at funerals or through burning, such as furniture, food, houses, and even fake banknotes that could be used in the "world beyond." This is because

> in the "culture of pleasure" the spirit cannot be separated from the body and there is a thorough affirmation of human existence in this world. Even in the darkest and most difficult times, people believe that it cannot get any worse, and that sooner or later, there must be a reversal towards the good. They firmly believe that their future is bright, and that it is not placed in any Heavenly kingdom, but rather in this very reality.
>
> 「樂感文化」重視靈肉不分離,肯定人在這個世界的生存和生活。即使在黑暗和災難年代, 也相信「否極泰採」, 前途光明, 這光明不在天國, 而在這個世界。 (Li Zehou 2016, 158)

The Chinese cultural-psychological formation does not direct people to strive for an external transcendent world, but rather to a wholesome affirmation of human life as a basic substance. This means that in the culture of pleasure the ideal or the most important goal of human life is to live happily and to enjoy (take pleasure in) the harmonious unity of body and mind (ibid.).

The culture of pleasure is permeated by the presence of an ultimate meaning, which directly arises from the concreteness, historicalness, and the social nature of human life. This meaning is the very origin of the culture of pleasure. Human life as such is originally coincidental and absurd, and human beings can decide where to search for its meaning. Instead of placing it in the sacred realm of external worlds and their transcendent deities, Chinese tradition seeks it in life itself (Li Zehou 2016, 192). In such life, no higher transcendental realm is needed in order to explain human life and guide human actions. In Li's view, the Chinese tradition contrasts with those traditions that derive their ethical and social codes and the significance of one's own existence from a divine creator or a transcendent supreme being. In a culture of pleasure, the search for existential meaning is confined to the human realm. This search is in accord with nature and is peaceful and calm. It is also "pleasurable," because it is completely unburdened by the necessity of sacrifice, self-negation, or the terrifying awareness of possible failing in the endeavor of reaching a more desirable realm or state (D'Ambrosio, Carleo, and Lambret 2016, 1059). There is no need for the creation of a metaphysical realm by which this world—the world in which we live—could be transcended. There is not even any necessity to establish another, separate kingdom of heaven, for the philosophical foundation of the culture of pleasure is, as we shall see later, the holistic paradigm of the one-world.

This culture is also characterized by pragmatic reason, a unique form of (moral) reasoning based in concrete, historical experience that Li asserts in contrast to Kantian forms of reason, especially practical reason. In its existential realness, concreteness, and because of its social, historical and material nature, the culture of pleasure is essentially an ontological notion. Li emphasizes that contemporary people could also strive to reconstruct their culture in a way that neither pursues a commercial culture of material desires nor restricts desires as a culture of guilt. People should promote a culture of pleasure by living harmonious relations and balancing their emotionality and rationality (Li Zehou 2016, 1143).

This framework unifies religion, politics, and ethics. The ethical order is therefore inseparable from the political system and both of them are permeated with sacred and religious elements. However,

> because of the relicts remaining from the shamanistic culture, which linked the spiritual world with the world of humans, the position of the latter was elevated to the extent that in traditional Chinese culture people could usually not fully comprehend the limitations and impermanence of human beings. This has been thoroughly reflected in both Chinese literature as well as Chinese philosophy, in the lacking of fear of the unknown and unknowable ultimate spiritual realm, and, hence, in the absence of the sense of guilt or shame. Chinese people were satisfied with the peaceful and harmonious pleasures provided by this unification of body and spirit. Because they didn't possess faith in an external supreme God, they had to find the meaning and the value of their lives by themselves, without the help of any external forces.

但也由於巫傳統，巫通天（神）人，人的地位相對高昂，使中國文明對人的有限性、過失性缺少深刻認識，從文藝到哲學缺乏對極端畏懼、極端神聖和罪惡感的深度探索。中國文化出不了以

不斷的靈魂拷問求精神純淨的陀思妥耶夫斯基。中國更滿足於
肉體和心靈的愉悅、平靜、健康、和諧。但由於沒有對上帝的
信仰，必需自求建立人生意義和生活價值，靠自力而不靠他力。
(Li Zehou 2016, 159)

Such a difficult and anguished task of transforming "absence" (*wu* 無) into "presence" (*you* 有) is by no means inferior to the task of projecting these needs to an external deity, which prevails in the Western tradition (ibid.). Li sees this as the very essence of the "culture of pleasure." His philosophical system places and elaborates upon this notion within the context of anthropological historical ontology, in which

> the substance is within the phenomena. It is being shaped precisely because of the phenomena and without a transcendent God or transcendental reason. All that exists is "humanity as a universal entity," which is a phenomenon, but simultaneously also a substance. Postulates forming the cultural psychological formation, as for instance the "categorical imperative" and so on, must accordingly be interconnected with experiences derived from the concrete conditions of particular time and space, on the basis of which this formation has been shaped and sedimented.

> 本體即在現象中，並由此現象而建立，沒有超越的上帝或先驗的理性，有的只是這個「人類總體」：它是現象，又是本體。從而「絕對律令」等等作為文化心理結構必須與特定時空條件下的經驗「現象界」相聯繫相貫通，並由之塑造、積澱而來。(Li Zehou 2016, 190–91)

The Complementary Relation between Confucianism and Daoism and the Reciprocal Utilization of Confucianism and Legalism

Chinese philosophy as a specific discourse was shaped during the Zhou Dynasty, especially in the last two periods of the Eastern Zhou, namely during the Spring and Autumn and the Warring States period (approximately from the sixth century until 221 BC). This "golden era of Chinese philosophy" was marked by the development of various schools of thought, the majority of which were not denoted and categorized before the Han Dynasty.[20] In the pre-Qin period only the Confucians and the

Moists were actually organized as schools with teachers and disciples. All the other "schools" were invented later according to scopes of content or groups of texts that expressed similar ideas, to edict and categorize multifarious thought currents flourishing in that period. There was no group of scholars describing themselves as "Legalists," and, similarly, the term "Daoist" was also invented as late as the Eastern Han Dynasty. Most of these schools are based on the same fundamental philosophical paradigms and share similar characteristics. This is a dynamic relational or structural mode of seeing and understanding the world.

Here, we shall mention the vibrant, organic, changeable, and binary-structured holism[21] that evolved in accordance with the binary categories and the principle of complementarity. The so-called binary categories (*duili fanchou* 對立範疇)—*yinyang* 陰陽 (sunny and shady), *benmo* 本末 (root and branch), *tiyong* 體用 (substance and function), *mingshi* 名实 (names or concepts and actualities), and so on—represents the bipolar opposition model that is inherent in every existing entity, and simultaneously the mode of reasoning of these entities. In contrast to the Cartesian model of dualism, the opposition of the two antipoles in the binary categories model is not a contradiction, for neither of the two poles exclude, but complement each other in a dynamic, mutually dependent correlation. Their interactive mutual relation is defined by the principle of complementarity.

A similar relation is seen between many currents of thought that were flourishing in pre-Qin China. Although on the surface, many of them mutually oppose or even exclude each other, if we investigate their thought on the deeper levels, they are often correlative or complementary.

Li has often pointed out that Confucianism as the crucial and pivotal stream of traditional Chinese thought, was expansively complemented by several other streams of thought, especially Daoism and Legalism. Even though Confucianism and Daoism are often diametrically opposed, they do not exclude each other but rather form a mutually harmonious whole. With its culture of pleasure, and with its emphasis upon the preciousness of interhuman relations, Confucianism embraces life and the world we inhabit. On the surface, Daoism forsakes the complicated social dimensions in which all these values are necessarily embedded, for it emphasizes the importance of the individual integrity and freedom. In reality, the two schools actually represent two sides of the same coin.

> This is true not only in the sense that later scholar-officials would regard the Confucian imperative to "aid all under

heaven" and the Daoist imperative to "do what is best for one's own body" as complementary ways of life. It is also true in the sense that the opposition between compassionate, generous public service and a spirit of enmity toward the world would become a normal element of the Chinese intellectual psyche as well as a common artistic convention. (Li and Cauvel 2006, 77)

The philosophy of the main representatives of the Daoist school was simultaneously opposing and complementing Confucianism. From the viewpoint of the ideational history, the chief representative of Daoism, Zhuangzi, can be seen as developer and extender of certain Confucian ideas (ibid.).[22] At the same time, Li also points out that this is not to deny that these two schools of thought were certainly quite different in their aesthetic consequences. Because of its strictly pragmatic framework, Confucians often enforced censures on aesthetic creation, sometimes impeding or even extinguishing its essence. The omnipresent and spontaneous Daoist imagination, along with the Daoist quest for the freedom and integrity of the individual, with its intensive emotional expression and the pursuit to preserve the unique human personality, has continually brought new and fresh incentives into Chinese art. Although Daoists reject the complexity of worldly affairs, regulations, and relations, by no means did they deny or reject natural life. On the contrary, they have always cherished and valued it. It follows that their philosophy and aesthetic attitude toward life influenced Chinese culture in a way that both complements and deepens Confucianism, and in fact—as Li points out—is Confucian (Li and Cauvel 2006, 77). In Li's view, there are two main aspects of this Confucian–Daoist complementarity (*rudao hubu* 儒道互補). The first one is political and adopts the Daoist worldly spirit, which affirms "timely adaptation" and "being all things to all people," in order to integrate it into the Confucian framework.[23] The second is artistic and can be found in traditional poetry as well as in landscape paintings. Both in real life and within the arts and aesthetics "the negative propositions and super-mundane images of Daoism are transformed into positive Confucian propositions and independence of character" (Li and Cauvel 2016, 105).

Li discusses the concept of the mutual complementarity of the two schools of thought in his early work, *The Path of Beauty*. He emphasizes that both Confucianism as well as Daoism arose out of the same ancient non-Dionysian cultural tradition.[24] Although Daoists opposed the rituals and "elegant music" (ya yue 雅樂), they never affirmed or endeavored sensuous indulgence or hedonism. Both schools also share the fundamental vision of an integral entity of humans and nature. Their mutually complementary orientation is also visible in that Confucianism always lays stress upon the humanization of (external and internal) nature, whereas Daoism emphasizes the importance of the naturalization of humans. Since both aspects are of immense importance for the evolution and completion of human beings and humankind, and since neither of them alone can achieve the actual synthesis of humans and nature, this complementarity is of crucial importance for the entire human culture. It is also visible in respective Confucian and Daoist understandings of the concept of harmony. Li writes: "In their mutual complementarity, Confucianism and Daoism are equally searching for a harmony of life" 儒道互補, 追求生活和諧。(Li Zehou 2010a, 27).

But while Confucians mostly emphasized its role in human relations, Daoist aesthetics *is* thoroughly focused upon the natural (or Heavenly) harmony, which manifests itself in one's harmonic unity with the Way (*dao* 道). Besides, it was most significant that both schools shared a common, strong affirmation for the primary position of the sensuous life. Although most representatives of Daoism were always criticizing and opposing the highly formalized Confucian rituality and its ethics, which was (in their view) based upon the "estranged" and "highly utilitarian" concepts of humaneness and righteousness (*renyi* 仁義), just like the Confucians they still strongly emphasized the importance of harmony, sensuosity, and the preservation of life.

> In this way, through opposition to Confucianism, Zhuangzi becomes its complement; for Confucianism and Daoism, or Confucius and Zhuangzi, share a fundamental affirmation of sensuous life. Therefore, as I have remarked elsewhere, Zhuangzi's philosophy is at bottom still very close to the Confucian spirit of "human participation in heaven and earth," while it is much further from Buddhism, religion in general, and modern-day existentialism. It is because of this commonality that Daoism and Confucianism were able to serve a mutually complementary function for the literati. (Li and Cauvel 2006, 90)[25]

This commonality of the two complementary schools, in which official service was not the only goal or proof of individual excellence, but which also allowed a high esteem of closeness to nature, has often provided a comfort to those scholars who failed in the official exams or became victims of political intrigues. Confucian-Daoist aesthetics thus also involved a transcendent attitude toward life, which made it easier for Chinese scholar-officials to attain a "certain psychological equilibrium, arising not only from an intimate relationship with nature in their lifestyle but also from an interpersonal transcendence in their personality, thought, and emotions" (ibid., 99).[26] This is how Daoist (especially Zhuangzi's) and Confucian aesthetic philosophy intermingled and blended with one another. Li Zehou also emphasizes that in this joint scheme, Confucianism actually retains control while absorbing Zhuangzi. He repeatedly stresses that because Confucianism was the leading ideology and the institutional backbone of traditional Chinese society, Daoism could never occupy more than a "supplementary and subordinate position." The Daoist discourses were "forever consigned to the role of spiritual comfort or therapy and could never become an independent force" (Li and Cauvel 2006, 89). In this Confucian–Daoist synthesis, Confucianism is the basis, and Daoism is incorporated into its ideational system.

In Li's view, Confucian teachings represent the central scope of fundamental ideas, based upon a skeptical and positivist worldview. This worldview is developed and upgraded in two different streams of thought. In the first one, which was mainly represented by Zhuangzi, it was—as we have seen above—transformed to a form of pantheistic and naturalistic philosophy, whereas in the second one, which was represented by the Confucian Xunzi (and later by some of the Legalist thinkers), it became a rational but optimistic form of atheism. We cannot forget that Xunzi is often seen as a bridge between Confucian and Legalist thought.[27] In the post-Qin development of Confucianism, Xunzi plays a much more important role than the one attributed to him by many historians and philosophers, especially the Modern Confucians.[28] Li faults them for their almost complete nullification of Xunzi and the entire second period of Confucianism. This significant period began with Dong Zhongshu's reform, into which he—beside many elements derived from the classical Chinese cosmology—integrated into the new teachings numerous aspects that originally pertained not only to Xunzi, but also to the Legalist school of thought.

> Here, the "emotion-based substance" was restricted under the framework of the cosmology of *yinyang* and the five elements, such as with Dong Zhongshu's assertion of humaneness as

the heart of "heaven" (or of the cosmos). This conception of cosmological emotionality supported the integration of Confucianism with Legalism during the Han dynasty and has bound China's political and religious institutions together for two millennia. (Li Zehou 2016, 1137–38)

This line in Confucianism was established during the Han Dynasty, which had inherited the enormous, centralized Legalist Qin state. Because ruling such a state required a centralized doctrine, and because the new rulers could not simply appropriate Legalism, which had represented the crucial ideology of the defeated Qin empire, the new state doctrine was based upon Dong Zhongshu's reinterpretation of the original Confucian teachings.[29] This reinterpretation was rooted primarily in Xunzi's elaboration of original Confucianism (Rošker 2016, 39). This new, reformed Confucianism, which comprised numerous cosmological and Legalist elements, gradually became the essential foundation of the official examination system. During almost the entire imperial era, until the beginning of the twentieth century, this system served as the main selection criteria for those who were worthy (and well educated) enough to achieve a position within the hierarchy of the state administration and thus, to attain both political as well as economic power.[30] In this examination system, and in the general system of governmental policies, Confucianism and legalism worked hand-in-hand throughout the entire history of imperial China, affirming the reciprocal utilization of Confucianism and Legalism (*Rufa huyong* 儒法互用). For Li, this reciprocal conception of Confucianism and Legalism also provides a basis for some new approaches to the discussion of the modernization of Chinese law, politics, and institutions (Ding Yun 2008, 6).

The multifarious mutual interactions between Confucianism, Daoism, and Legalism offered Li Zehou some well-grounded foundations for expanding upon his conceptual distinction of the two kinds of morality (to be discussed in greater detail in a separate section). For now, it suffices to say that religious morality was inherent and developed from Confucius through Mencian interpretations to the Song Dynasty Neo-Confucianism, while social or public morality was tightly connected to external (ethical regulations). It developed from Confucianism through Xunzi's elaborations, which were also converged with Daoism and the Yinyang cosmology, and contained numerous elements of Legalist rationality. It was this social or public ethics that dominated Chinese political history for two millennia (Gu, Mingdong 2015:, 10). Li also connects the former with the concept of the *inner sage* (*neisheng* 內聖) and the latter with the concept of the *external ruler* (*waiwang* 外王).

In this clear affirmation of the assimilative nature of Confucianism, Li's thought is rather unique, for most other Chinese scholars have predominantly focused on "pure" Confucianism—on its orthodox teachings, texts, and ideas. Only on a separate, subordinate level did they relate these texts to other schools like Daoism or Buddhism. Since Legalism has always been viewed as directly opposed to Confucian teachings and completely incompatible with Confucianism, most of them would not even touch the Legalist teachings (Gu, Mingdong 2015, 15). Li's broadening of their scope has immeasurable value and importance. According to Ming Dong Gu, Li's approach in this context has multiple implications (ibid.). First, it implies that Confucianism is not just one of the intellectual foundations of Chinese culture, but rather the primary foundation of Chinese culture with other schools of thought serving as its pillars (see Li Zehou 2016, 195). This broader approach also allows us to move out of the exclusive focus on orthodox Confucianism and to include other schools of thought, which enables us to gain a deeper insight into the genuine constitution of traditional Chinese philosophy and its social and political consequences. Li paves the way for further research to lead us to the establishment of new methodologies of investigating Chinese thought and acquiring new knowledge in this field. Such an approach suggests that Confucianism (in its assimilative potential) can become a foundation for a more general philosophy, for it may inspire scholars to reconstruct Confucianism as a thought system including universal values.[31]

Basic Paradigms and Approaches

The One-World-View and the Critique of Immanent Transcendence

Li describes the worldview that had prevailed in the Chinese tradition as a "one-world-view," which arose from and was developed on the foundation of rationalized shamanism. According to such understanding, there is only one world: the world we live in, the world we experience. In this world, the human mind is formed in accordance with the features and laws of this dynamic empirical world. There are no transcendental, preexisting forms of knowledge. There is neither a need for, nor a possibility of, transcending into higher, intangible realms, and there is also no necessity for a higher force or a personalized god. There is no need to establish another, separate world of a Heavenly kingdom. This holistic worldview is completely different from the so-called two-world view, which prevailed in the history of Western philosophy and which distinguishes the noumenon from phenomena, heaven from earth, and body from mind. Li explains it as follows:

> The main difference between the Chinese cultural tradition and the Judeo-Christian tradition, roughly speaking, is the difference between a "one-world view" and a "two-world view." The Bible, Plato, and Kant believe in two worlds: this world and the world beyond, this world and the world of ideas, phenomenon, and noumenon. But for the Chinese, there is just this world. Since nature, human society, and the gods are living in this same world, then anything in this world, including the gods, the emperors, even Heaven, must all follow and obey the same cosmic order of this world, which is called the "Way of Heaven" (*tiandao* 天道). The "Way of Heaven" is the same as the "Way of Humans" (*ren dao* 人道). This means that these two are interdependent and interrelated, and human beings can exercise power to such an extent in this world that they can have a significant impact on the cosmos. (Li, Zehou 1999e, 179)

The specifically Chinese paradigm of the unity of men and nature is, of course, possible only in the framework of such holistic worldview. This is the only realm that enables the complementary functioning of reason and emotion, of objective cognition and subjective judgement, of abstract analysis and emotional imagination. Li sees this as still latently inherent in the cultural-psychological constitution of modern Chinese people.

The one-world paradigm has not only epistemological and cognitive, but also ethical implications. In his *Response to Michael Sandel and Other Matters*, Li wrote: "I believe that the focus on the integration of emotion and reason rather than mere reason is the philosophical basis for the major divergence between Chinese ethics and Western ethics" (Li, Zehou 2016, 1069). For these reasons, the Chinese tradition contrasts with those that derive their ethical and social codes from some transcendent supernatural beings. In this one-world, people's search for existential meaning is confined to the human realm. It does not value sacrifice, self-abnegation, or the feeling of failure because of the impossibility of reaching a more desirable realm or state (D'Ambrosio, Carleo, and Lambert 2016, 1059). This is also the reason the one-world realm can produce the culture of pleasure, defined by the pragmatic (and not practical or even less speculative) reason, which is not separated from emotions (or intentions) and does not seek to disconnect human beings from the network of the relationships (*guanxi* 關係) to which they belong.[32] D'Ambrosio et al. write: "In a contemporary context this means that Confucianism, especially in terms of the attention it pays to the 'emotio-rational structure,' can function as a corrective to curb certain shortcomings of modern thought associated with liberalism, formal justice, abstract reason, and notions of the atomic individual" (ibid.). Precisely because of its one-world orientation, the Confucian tradition upholds the values of human life, concrete experience, and emotion, and discovers pleasure and meaning in the worldly life (Jung 2017, 108). Several other crucial approaches and concepts of Li Zehou's philosophy (for instance, historical ontology or emotion-based substance) are also grounded in this one-world view, for in such a view there is no separation between the phenomenal world and the world of substance, nor is there a clear and fixed distinction between the human and the transcendent world.

From this perspective, Li redefines the notions of ontology and noumenon in Chinese philosophy. He points out that precisely because this worldview was not dualistic, traditional Chinese theoretical discourse did not need to raise philosophical questions of being, or define various realms of phenomena and noumenon. He states:

> We translate noumenon as *benti* 本體, a word coined from *ben* 本 (root, origin) and *ti* 體 (stem, body). *Bentilun* 本體論 literally means a discussion, theory, study, or views of *benti*, and this compound was adopted to translate ontology in Chinese.[33] So instead of a study of being, *bentilun* is a study of *ben* (root, origin) and *ti* (stem, body) of things. (Li and Cauvel 2006, 40)

Li emphasizes that in the one-world view, the existence of everything is necessarily connected with the existence of human beings and as such any being cannot be separated from the existence of human beings.

Several contemporary Chinese theoreticians have undertaken this idea of a unified, single world, which is typical for classical Chinese philosophy, constructing their philosophical systems on similar, or even the same grounds. Yang Guorong, for instance, also presupposes that this view entails important ethical implications. He emphasizes that in such a Chinese philosophical "one world" the above-mentioned unity of beings also predicates the unity of facts and values. He emphasizes that because there is only this world, it could not exist in a state of separation or duplication. The entire relation between fact and value is determined by this basic point. At first glimpse, the reality world seems to be determined by diversity and not by oneness, but beings in a world of diversity do not exist in separate, discrete conditions. Yang also emphasizes that even though there is more than one dimension in every being and each dimension is different, every being succeeds in holding these dimensions together within itself (Yang 2008, 272). Beings that are in a state of diversity are simultaneously always involved with a various potential or actual values. The concrete world is characterized by the unity of fact and value and by the unity of a variety of features on the level of fact—this unity is rooted in this one world (ibid.).

Li maintains that the Chinese one-world view is a complicated feedback system in that the relation between heaven and humankind (or nature and human beings) is but a single element or moment of it. It becomes clear why there is almost no conception of pure truth or pure reason in Chinese philosophy. Because of such a worldview, Li emphasizes, the Chinese ideational tradition looks down on pure speculative reasoning, rather emphasizing the value of "pragmatic rationality."

> For the Chinese, "transcendental" or *a priori* cannot be the last word. The Chinese mind would ask why something is "transcendental," or where the *a priori* comes from. Because of this "one-world view," it would also be difficult to accept the idea of something "absolutely independent of all experience." This is also the reason that Chinese find it difficult to accept the formalism in Kant's ethics. On the contrary, filled with a sense of history, the Chinese mind always searches for some historical interpretation. Thus, the "transcendental" and the *a priori* must also have their roots in this world, in the movement of history. (Li Zehou 1999e, 180)

In such an understanding, the thinking subject cannot be separated from the acting subject, and human consciousness similarly cannot be separated from its physical or material (bodily) existence. Thus, in Chinese philosophy, epistemology is inseparably linked to ethics and religion, because knowledge cannot be separated from power nor can learning be disconnected from ideology, which again, is tightly linked to the dominating power.

At the same time, Li strongly opposed the Modern Confucian supposition that held the basic paradigm of the classical Chinese philosophy to be that of immanent transcendence because he believed it to be incompatible with his notion of the one-world view. Before we proceed to the main arguments of Li's critique, let us examine the reasons why the Modern Confucian philosophers (especially and most distinctively Mou Zongsan) have established this idea.

Modern Confucians focus on ontological questions because for them ontology can be seen as a key for the modernization of traditional Chinese philosophy. In their view, classical Confucianism saw Heaven (*tian* 天) as the ultimate noumenon. It was the elementary entity, creating and modifying all that exists. Heaven possessed ontological duality, for it was simultaneously transcendental and immanent. It endowed human beings with innate qualities of humanness that were essentially determined by the fundamental Confucian virtue of humaneness. This was a development of Mencius's understanding of the human "self," a view that was typical of the Neo-Confucian discourses in that Mencius was defined as the only proper follower of Confucius. However, in their explanations of classical schemes, the Modern Confucian philosophers went a step further. In their discourses, human innate qualities or humanness became the potential that not only formed the moral or spiritual Self, but also transcended the individual's empirical and physiological characteristics. By acting in accordance with humaneness, every individual could be united with Heaven and realize the genuine sense and value of existence.

These elementary features of the Modern Confucian concept of Heaven also help us understand their view of the difference between external (*waizai chaoyuexing* 外在超越性) and internal (or immanent) transcendence (*neizai chaoyuexing* 内在超越性), with the latter being one of the specific features of Confucianism and Chinese philosophy in general.

In interpreting traditional Confucian thought (especially the idea of Heavenly Dao or the Dao of Nature), the contemporary New Confucians[34] often made use of the concepts of "transcendence" or "immanence." They pointed out that the Confucian Dao of Nature, which is "transcendent and immanent," is diametrically opposed to the basic model of Western religions, which are "transcendent and external."

當代新儒家常借用「超越性」和「內在性」這兩個概念來詮釋傳統儒家思想 (特別是其天道思想),強調儒家的天道或基本精神是「超越而內在」,以與西方宗教中「超越而外在」的基本模式相對比。 (Lee Ming-Huei 2001, 118)

Immanent notions essential to defining Chinese philosophy are also necessary products of the holistic worldview. This explains why notions seen as transcendent in prevailing Western philosophical discourses and that are generally perceived as transcending one and proceeding into another (usually higher) sphere are immanent in most traditional Chinese philosophical works. Most theoreticians attribute to such notions of immanent transcendence the concepts of Heaven and of the Way. Mou Zongsan explained this double ontological nature of these classical notions as follows:

The Way of Heaven, as something "high above," connotes transcendence. When the Way of Heaven is installed in the individual and resides within them in the form of human nature, it is then immanent.

天道高高在上,有超越的意義。天道貫注於人身之時,又內在於人而為人的性。這時,天道又是內在的 (Immanent)。 (Mou Zongsan 1990, 26)

David Hall and Roger Ames criticize such understanding, observing that while Mou accentuates the inseparability of Heaven and humankind and proposes an immanent classification of the idea in question, at the same time he claims that it is transcendent "to the extent that it connotes independence," a definition that, in their view, "seems inappropriate" (Hall and Ames 1987, 205). They rather see the notion of transcendence as having been shaped and generally understood in Western culture, and can be defined as follows:

> A principle A is transcendent in respect to that B which it serves as principle if the meaning or import of B cannot be fully analyzed and explained without recourse to A, but the reverse is not true. (ibid., 13)

Their concern is that the usage of such notions might lead to still further misunderstandings in the already difficult interchange between Chinese and Western ideational traditions. They also take Mou to task for his distinctions concerning the connection of transcendence with the Decree of Heaven (*tian ming* 天命): "To have a sense of the Decree of Heaven, one must first have a sense of transcendence, which is possible only if one accepts the existence of such transcendence" (如果有「天命」的感覺, 首先要有超越感 [Sense of Transcendence], 承認一超越之存在, 然後可說。) (Mou Zongsan 1990, 21).

Hall and Ames believe that in such passages Mou is clearly trying to attribute a "strict transcendence" to early Chinese philosophy. For them, such an attitude seems to be problematic (Hall and Ames 1987, 205). For Lee Ming-huei, however, their criticism is the result of a misunderstanding.

> When Modern Confucians apply the concept of "immanent transcendence," they are adhering to the basic premise that "immanence" and "transcendence" are not in logical contradiction. This means that they never apply the concept of "transcendence" in the strict sense understood by Hall and Ames. Their critique is thus clearly based on a misunderstanding.[35]
>
> 當代新儒家在使用「內在超越」的概念時, 顯然認為,「內在性」與「超越性」這兩個概念在邏輯上並不矛盾, 這就證明他們並非依郝、安二人所認定的嚴格意義來使用「超越性」一詞。因此, 郝、安二人的批評顯然是基於誤解。(Lee Ming-huei 2002, 226–27)

Lee Ming-huei's main argument is that notions, especially those that are abstract, have a range of semantic connotations. Here, the term "transcendence" is no exception, as it has had several connotations throughout the history of Western philosophy. The notion of "immanent transcendence" denotes a *certain type* of transcendence. It certainly does not cover the entire spectrum of the possible semantic connotations of this concept, particularly not those connected to "independence" or to the "separation between creator and creation." For Modern Confucians, immanent notions do not constitute absolute principles, as in the theological idea of Divinity or the Ancient Greek idea of substance (Rošker 2016, 131–37).

To a certain extent, Li's critique of Mou Zongsan's definition of immanent transcendence is similar to that of Hall and Ames. In his argument, Li proceeds from the Modern Confucian classification of the Confucian philosophical tradition and strongly opposes their idea of "three periods of Confucianism." Modern Confucians have completely neglected the entire second period, marked by Dong Zhongshu's reform and his integration of cosmological and legalist elements into the framework of original Confucianism—reducing its development to the philosophy of moral metaphysics as elaborated by the Song Neo-Confucianism. Li maintains that such interpretations can only lead to developments of the narrow scope of Confucianism's religious aspects, whereas the Confucian teachings in their entirety could offer a much more complex foundation for the modernization of the Chinese ideational tradition (Li Zehou 1999b, 2–5). Li claims that this problem became even more severe because Mou tried to elaborate upon it within the Kantian framework. Mou describes his theory of immanent transcendence as a theory that is based upon Confucian tradition and that therefore necessarily negates the existence of an external god. Mou tries to establish moral imperative on the foundation of a unity of human and heavenly or on the unity of human and spiritual nature. He also aims to establish the noumenon based on inherent human morality and assumes the Western two-world view, which separates the divine and the worldly, the realm of ideas and the realm of physical reality, and that of noumenon from that of phenomena. In Mou's view, the human heart-mind and human nature (or humanness) were "transcendent." However, Li emphasizes that in this Western framework "transcendence" necessarily means a realm that surpasses experience and one in which the transcendent (god) determines and rules over human beings, who are confined to the realm of experience. Humans, on the other hand, cannot influence God, who is independent and absolute and who represents the ultimate origin of any existence. According to the two-world view, all that exists in the concrete reality is limited to the sphere of appearances, for substance or essence only pertain to transcendent existence. Li sees that such a paradigm can neither be combined with the traditional Chinese paradigm of the unity of heaven and humans nor with the view that holds substance and function to be inseparable (*tiyong bu er* 體用不二). In other words, the Western notion of transcendence can by no means fit into the Chinese one-world view. Consequently it is completely wrong to lay stress upon the traditional Chinese notions of the unity of heaven and people, and not explain the concepts that are originally confined to the sphere of sensuality and emotions such as humaneness or inborn knowledge (*liangzhi* 良知) as something immanently transcendent or transcendental. Li stresses that, precisely because of the one world-view, the social and ideational development in ancient China could have led to the culture of pleasure, because in this framework human beings have no tensious relation (*jinzhang guanxi* 緊張關係) towards external deities or fears of god. In this context, Li additionally explains:

> Zheng Jiadong discovered that Mou Zongsan has actually proceeded from the supposition of a mutual division of Heaven and human beings, which means that there cannot be any equation of humans and Heaven (in this way, he acknowledged the existence of some sort of external transcendent entity). Only afterwards did he gradually establish the union of human beings and Heaven by emphasizing that the "immanent transcendence," i.e., the human moral self, was actually grounded in the Way of Heaven. People were thus endowed with an "immanent transcendence," which means that god was already in their heart-minds. Why should they then have any "fear" of a transcendent, externally existing god?
>
> 鄭家棟發現，牟宗三是由某種「天人相分」即由講述「人不即是天」(承認有某種外在超越對象)，而逐漸轉到「即人即天」，即強調「內在超越」，人的「心性」即「天道」本身上來的。這樣一來，人既有此「內在的超越」、心中的上帝，也就不需要去「畏」那作為對象存在的超越的上帝? (Li Zehou 1999b, 9)

According to Li, these contradictions are rooted in the Song period's Neo-Confucianism. He believes that Modern Confucianism has not succeeded to create any genuinely new philosophical approaches or theoretical innovations that could serve as a foundation for future philosophical discoveries or new philosophical systems (ibid., 8).

> Thus, it is solely a modern "reflection" or a "distant echo" of the School of the structural principle (*Li xue* 理學) from the Song and Ming Dynasties, unable to construct a new period of philosophic investigation.
>
> 所以我說它只是宋明理學在現代的「迴光返照」、「隔世迴響」，構不成一個新的時期，「恐怕難得再有後來者能在這塊基地上開拓出多少真正哲學的新東西來了」，「如不改弦更張，只在原地踏步，看來已到窮途」。(ibid., 10).

Because of all these reasons, Li claims that Chinese philosophy is thoroughly immanent. It becomes clear that his one-world is exclusively the world of here and now, the concrete world in which we live. Some contemporary Chinese theoreticians are critical towards such a view. Chen Lai, for instance, agrees with Li in the conviction that, in contrast to the Western discourses, traditional Chinese ethics was never rooted in belief in supreme being. However, in contrast to Li, Chen sees the crucial difference between Chinese metaphysics and those of monotheistic religions in the nature of the relationship between the two worlds, and not in the lack of a transcendent realm D'Ambrosio, Carleo, and Lambert 2016, 1059). Chen Lai upholds that, although in Chinese tradition there is a distinction between the concrete and the metaphysical world, this distinction does not equal a separation. This is important to Chen because he believes that Li's assertion that Chinese thought is one-world impedes the existence of traditional Chinese metaphysics. Nevertheless, for both thinkers "the West sees a gap between this world and a transcendent, divine world of greater truth or reality whereas China remains focused on divinity occurring within this world" (ibid.). In this context, Chen Lai exposes the importance of Li's division between the narrow and broad senses of metaphysics. Carleo and D'Ambrosio explain that in this framework, metaphysics in the narrow sense is quintessentially Western and pertains to that of the analytical and rational tradition of thought that had developed in ancient Greece (Carleo and D'Ambrosio 2015, 14). This kind of thinking never prevailed in the Chinese tradition. Metaphysics in a broad sense implies the pursuit of values and the meaning of human life, which is central to traditional—and even contemporary—Chinese thought.

Immanent transcendence doubtless refers to the realm of the human inwardness, of the heart-mind, which is rooted and actualized in human consciousness.[36] In Confucian discourses, heaven is perceived as a great, infinite organism, of which all of us are parts. In this sense, a human being is separated, but simultaneously also united with it. From the viewpoint of each individual, Confucians do not strive not to be themselves or to be more than what they are. In so doing, the individual would be acting against his own humanness and hence against the Way of Heaven. Liu Shu-hsien writes that to promote complete humanism does not imply that human beings have to cut their connections with the transcendent (Liu Shu-hsien 1972, 48). Once they understand the creative sources within themselves, they can take part in the creative process of the universe and forget their troubles that are linked only to their "small selves." A human being who has no concerns other than those of the small self is not a wholly developed human being. Such a being is trapped in a feeling of anxiety and never feels free. Only if they widen their views and recognize that they are parts of the creative process in the universe can they completely overcome this feeling of anxiety. Then they will gladly accept their destiny without regret. What they achieve is not a kind of personal immortality, but a method to live according to the way and to join into the transforming and nourishing process of all that exists that will never cease, even if the universe no longer exists in the present form.

Although the individual human heart-mind is restricted by the physical limitations of the body, there is doubtless a deep connection between human consciousness and the infiniteness of the universe, which operates as the Way of Heaven, as is evident in numerous sections of the classics.

For example:

The duke inquired: "May I ask what it is that the nobleman values in the Way of Heaven?" Confucius answered: "He values its endlessness."

公曰:「敢問君子何貴乎天道也?」孔子對曰:「貴其『不已』」
(Li ji 2016; Ai Gong wen, 660)

The most important point regarding the question of immanence and transcendence in Chinese (and Li Zehou's) philosophy is that Li's holistic one-world view cannot be understood as a monistic worldview, as has been presupposed by some Chinese scholars (see for instance,

Chongbai Moluo's interpretation in Li Zehou 2016, 293).[37] As already discussed, Li believes that the biggest flaw in Mou's system can be found in that he tried to place the concept of immanent transcendence into the (albeit broadened) framework of Kant's transcendental philosophy. Li emphasizes that this notion is not in line with Kant.[38] Along with another central concept of Mou's philosophy, namely the concept of intellectual intuition (zhide zhijue 智的直覺), Li defines it as a kind of "mystical experience" (Li, Zehou 2016, 1139), which from the viewpoint of historical materialism, cannot be taken theoretically seriously.

Pragmatic Reason and Emotion-Based Substance

In Li's view, Chinese philosophy, as a one-world discourse, does not strictly distinguish between reason and emotion, because in its basic epistemological framework reason and emotion are mutually intermingled and cannot exist independently of each other in a pure and clearly defined form (Li Zehou 2008, 248). Because human beings are rational animals their rational capabilities are not opposed to their animal origins (Lynch 2016, 714). The human psyche is ordered in accordance with an emotio-rational structure, where reason is amalgamated into animal sensibility. Li lays stress upon the integrity and balanced nature of this formation, the core of which is an inventive combination of Kantian rationalism and Confucian philosophy, leading Jia Jinhua to observe that "Li admires Kant's rational ontology of ethics, but criticizes his exclusion of human emotion and desire" (Jia, Jinhua 2016, 757). In the course of traditional Western intellectual history, reason and emotion were mainly seen as being in mutual opposition or even in contradiction. However, in recent decades, this supposition has been criticized by numerous sociologists, psychologists, and philosophers, who argue that reason cannot be fully separated from emotions, and that emotions are not always private and subjective. In this view, the function of emotions within intellectual discernment and rational judgement is crucial. They proceed from an emotional-rational continuum, which has a striking similarity to Li's emotio-rational structure. Jia Jinhua further points out that "Li Zehou's study of the Confucian ethics of emotion started in the early 1980s and his theses of emotion-based substance and emotio-rational structure provide pioneering contributions to this new intellectual trend Jia (Jinhua 2016, 758)."

Pragmatic reason or rationality and emotion-based substance belong to the basic paradigms of Li's interpretation of classical Chinese, especially

Confucian philosophy. For Li, pragmatic reason can "primarily be defined as a kind of rational spirit or rational attitude" (Li Zehou 1980a, 89). Confucian teachings doubtless represent such an attitude:

> In accordance with the rise of atheism and skepticism of his time, Confucius has explained "ritual" through "humaneness," which was, in essence, very much congruent with this line of thought.
>
> 與當時無神論、懷疑論思想興起相一致, 孔子「對禮」作出「仁」的解釋, 在基本傾向上符合了這一思潮 (ibid.)

Emotion-based substance or situation-based substance represents the most basic features that define human beings, for it is something that surpasses the narrow and limited realm of experience (Liu Zaifu 2016, 2).[39]

The characteristic feature of this kind of reason was its pragmatic orientation towards the real, concrete world in which people live. It was by no means a cognitive, abstract, or purely theoretical kind of reason.[40] Mainstream ancient Chinese culture showed no affinity for such abstract rationality, because earliest Confucians were convinced that abstract reasoning without a direct connection to real life was pointless and redundant. Pragmatic reason means that the practical activities in this concrete world are guided by rationality and people's emotions and desires are cultivated by means of reasonable regulations. Li argues that in the beginning early human operational activities in the form of producing and using tools offered humans a means of controlling their environments. Over time, the accumulation of experience allowed our ancestors to surpass other animals and to form a specifically human pragmatic reason, which sedimented in the dynamic structures of our mind. Although this uniquely human quality was still rooted in animal nature, it also allowed people to transcend its physical limitations and to become "supra-biological" beings.

In the first edition of his essay "A Reevaluation of Confucius" (*Kongzi zai pingjia*), to express this notion, Li originally used the term *shijian lixing* 實踐理性 (Li Zehou 1980a, 77). However, in Chinese this term was already in use to translate Kant's "practical reason." In order to differentiate between his own concept and Kant's notion of practical reason Li later creates the term *shiyong lixing*, which can be translated as "pragmatic reason."[41] He explains that although they are by no means the same, there is still a certain similarity between Kant's and his own notion, especially regarding their tight connection to ethics—a crucial feature of both (Li Zehou 2008, 246). Here, Li points out that Confucianism has always emphasized ethical practice. Practical reason, however, is much more than ethical practice as it stands in contrast with patterns of (rational) reasoning (ibid.). Although there is no metaphysical or supernatural origin of human cognition, it cannot be seen as given simply in one-to-one correspondence by an empirical world (Lynch 2016, 718). In a certain sense, Li's theory of pragmatic reason is similar to John Dewey's pragmatism, for both philosophies regard usefulness as a criterion for determining the truth. However, there is a very important difference between them as well,[42] because—in contrast to pragmatism—pragmatic rationality or pragmatic reason

> accepts, honors, believes in and even emphasizes its congruence with objective principles, rules or orders which are, in a certain sense, independent from human thought or experience. These objective principles, rules or orders can be denoted as "the Way of Heaven" or the "decree of Heaven."
>
> 它承認、尊重、相信甚至強調去符合一個客觀的原則、規則或秩序, 此一原則、規則或秩序在某種意義上乃是獨立與人的思維和經驗的, 這就是天道, 或稱天命。 (Li Zehou 2008, 247)

For this reason, Li Zehou still believes that Confucianism contains some semireligious elements, although it is not based on the idea of an external (anthropomorphic) God. This central ideational system of traditional China is clearly defined by agnosticism. In the Confucian *Analects*, there are numerous passages in which the existence of deities is questioned, though not explicitly denied. Confucius unambiguously stressed that he does not talk about "strange powers and irrational deities" (子不語怪力亂神) (Lunyu 2009; Shu er, 490). He also emphasizes that if "we are not even capable of serving humans, so how could (or why should) we serve ghosts" (未能事人, 焉能事鬼); and, if "we even don't understand life, so how could we know anything about death" (未知生, 焉知死) (ibid.; Xian Jin, 569). In this context, the wisest thing one could do is to "keep a respectful distance from spirits and ghosts" (敬鬼神而遠之, 可謂知矣) (ibid.; Yong Ye, 459).

Li points out that such a theoretical foundation of this ancient Chinese agnosticism was philosophically quite mature because the existence of supernatural beings is very hard to affirm or to falsify in terms of scientific demonstration. In this sense, Confucian agnosticism is precisely a proof of the "clear rational spirit" inherent to the ideational system of humaneness (Li Zehou 1980a, 89). The rationalization of emotion, which took place in China in the process of transforming natural religions into ideational systems of humaneness, was by no means based upon restrictions of desires—in this process, humans were offered a regulated way of satisfying their needs and wishes.

> There was no need for an external God, whose orders, which were based upon irrational authority, had to be blindly followed. On the other hand, people still possessed hope of salvation (humanism) and self-fulfillment (individual sense of mission) without rejecting this world or humiliating themselves. . . . Everything could be left to the balanced measure and regulative function of the pragmatic reason.

> 不需要外在的上帝的命令，不盲目服從非理性的權威，卻仍然可以拯救世界 (人道主義) 和自我完成 (個體人格和使命感)；不厭棄人世，也不自我屈辱、. . . 一切都放在實用的理性天平上加以衡量和處理。(Li Zehou 1980a, 89)

Besides, pragmatic reason as one of the basic features of Confucianism and most other Chinese ideational traditions is similar to the concepts of sedimentation or cultural-psychological formation and is by no means a static or closed notion (Li Zehou 2008, 250). All these ideas actually refer to dynamic processes. The dialectical logic of pragmatic reason is not "fatalistically deterministic," but leaves enough room for potentials and contingencies as well as necessities, including the "potential and accidental elements of human choices and decisions" (Lynch 2016, 719). Li repeatedly highlights that in these processes people have the freedom to create, select, and regulate their own lives. The dialectically interactive, correlative development of necessity and eventuality, factuality, and potentiality, which arose from the concrete operational level, thus became the historical leitmotif of human life and existence.

Since for Li, material existence is fundamental, reason is not *a priori* or inherent. Rather, it is a quality that is attained through material practice and is therefore a product of such practice. Li sees the operative process (and the results) of work as providing the fundamental content of human experiences. Symbolic operations abstracted from this groundwork take on an independent character that can be separated from particular experiences. Logic, however, for instance, is not something with substance (Lynch 2016, 719). Reason cannot be hypostatized. It is merely a method of cognition or a means people use to deal with the objects by which they are surrounded. Li emphasizes that it is by no means the nature of things or objects inherent in themselves. Here we can see another important difference between Li's own understanding, which was closer to achievements of the second period (the more rationalistic tradition within the development) of Confucianism and the discourses of the Neo-Confucian School of the structural principle of the Song Dynasty, which belonged to the third period. In *On Classical Chinese Intellectual History* (*Zhongguo gudai sixiang shilun* 中國古代思想史論), Li points out that in this third period Confucian philosophy transformed the structural pattern *li* 理 (that can, to a certain degree, be compared to the Western notion of *ratio*) from its originally cosmologic notion to a concept that pertains to human inwardness that is permeated with ethical connotations (Li Zehou 1985, 220–22). At first glance, Zhu Xi's understanding of *li* 理, which is inherent in every object of the factual world, stands in sharp contrast with Li's belief that reason is something impeded or applied to objects from outside. However, recent investigations show that in the post-Han era, the Chinese notion *li* 理 gradually became (inter alia), the mutually compatible structure of the external word and the mind (Rošker 2012, 8). In the scope of Neo-Confucianism, the notion *li* 理 was understood both as a particular structural pattern as well as the all-embracing, overall structure. Cheng Hao concludes that "the basic structure of each single thing is also the basic structure of everything that exists" (一物之理即萬物之理) (Cheng Hao and Cheng Yi 1981, I, Yi shu, 13). As opposed to this traditional Chinese notion, the laws of reason in Western pragmatic philosophy represent external axioms that influence and determine things exclusively from outside. In contrast to such a view, Li's pragmatic reason was a dynamic and correlative notion, although he emphasized the gradual internalization of rationality that was imposed onto human consciousness from outside, through rites and scopes of ethical regulations (Li Zehou 1980a, 85), Li's pragmatic rationality was not something fixed, purely abstract, or unchangeable.

The same holds true for the central Confucian endeavor of "shaping and constructing human emotions and sensitivity" that are being gradually cultivated and being made the norm by (proper) music and rituals, which makes possible the incorporation of reason into emotions (Li Zehou 2014, 3). In this context, Li points to the Confucian highlighting of "pleasure derived from music" (*yezhe yue ye* 樂者樂也) (Li ji s.d.; Yue ji, 32), while he simultaneously demonstrates that Confucians also emphasize the need to regulate this pleasure (and, hence, to control the emotions involved). This can be achieved through proper, i.e., (rationally) regulation of music and rituals (ibid., 9).[43] For the Confucians, people can "find pleasure in regulated rites and music" (*le jie liyue* 樂節禮樂) (Lunyu 2009; Ji shi, 690). By such proper, sensitive regulation, people's natural emotions were molded into a rational form, and this allowed for a fusion of emotion and reason (Li Zehou 2008, 251).[44]

Besides this integration of reason into emotions, Confucianism also stressed the assimilation of emotions into reason. In the ancient Chinese worldview, nature, heaven, and earth were permeated with positive feelings that affirmed the value, the goodness, and the beauty of life. In its very essence, this attitude was by no means scientific, nor cognitive or philosophical, but purely emotional and aesthetic. Therefore, Confucianism is much more than merely ethical teaching. Although it cannot be regarded as a religion, it still far surpassed the scope of ethical regulations and thereby achieved the highest realm of the unity of Heaven (nature) and humans, which is comparable to a religious experience. According to Li, this is the realm of the aesthetic.

Pragmatic reason allowed for a sensible fusion of emotion and rationality. In contrast to religion it makes this unification possible without any external dogmas, and therefore allows people to remain open to new insights and to accept new things. Besides, it encourages people to better assume historical experiences and adapt them in a way such that they could best serve the interests of their contemporary societies.

As an example, Li describes the fate of science and technology in China. Although the mainstream of traditional Chinese intellectual history never developed abstract cognition, logic, or any other foundations of scientific thought to a noteworthy extent, the Chinese people nonetheless quickly (and most efficiently) adopted all these modes of reasoning as soon as they experienced their pragmatic value after Western thought was introduced to China. Thus, Li concludes:

> Representing the structural principle of the cultural psychological activities of the Chinese people, pragmatic reason is by no means a static, unchangeable formation. What it values is

precisely the change, expansion, renewal, and development. Hence, Chinese tradition, Confucianism, and pragmatic reason cannot be seen as obstacles to modernization.

> 實用理性作為中國人文化心理活動的結構原則，並非靜止的、一成不變的形式，它重視的正是變化、擴展、更新和發展。從而，中國傳統、儒學和實用理性不會對現代化構成障礙。(Li Zehou 2008, 251–52)

Although Li mentioned the concept of emotion-based substance several times in his early works (Li Zehou and Liu Xuyuan 2011, 9), he provided a deeper theoretical explanation of this notion for the first time in *Pragmatic Reason and a Culture of Pleasure* (*Shiyong lixing yu legan wenhua* 實用理性與樂感文化). Emotion-based substance is the core of Li's notion of the culture of pleasure. He uses the concept of substance (*benti*) not as a noumenon that is (in the Kantian sense) different or separated from the sphere of phenomena, but simply as the "root" (*bengen* 本根), "basis" (*genben* 根本), or the "ultimate reality" (*zui hou shizai* 最後實在) of everything concretely existing in the material world. This means that emotion is also the very foundation of human life (Li Zehou 2008, 54) and is something that pertains to the empirical world (Li Zehou and Liu Xuyuan 2011, 27).

It is important to note that in Chinese, the term *qing* 情 does not only refer to emotions (*qinggan* 情感), but also to situations and (different) contexts or atmospheres (*qingjing* 情境). In ancient Chinese philosophy, especially in the classical Confucian framework, *qing* was regarded as the ontological groundwork of existence, which did not refer solely to human life, but also to the entire universe. But during the later course of post-Han intellectual history, the concept became more and more separated from the notion of nature or inborn qualities (*xing* 性).

During the Neo-Confucian reform, which took place during the Song and Ming dynasties, emotion, which also included intentions, wishes, and desires, was seen as something negative, something that had to be eliminated or fought against.[45] Only in the beginning of the seventeenth century, and especially in the scope of the May 4th Movement (1919), emotion was rehabilitated, since human desires were also an important driving force of scientific progress. Emotion preserved its positive connotation until it was oppressed once again by the moral philosophies of contemporary Modern Confucians. In a longer subchapter of *Pragmatic*

Reason and a Culture of Pleasure, Li posits that inborn moral qualities are the ontological basis of humans.[46] Li concludes that similar to their predecessors—the Neo-Confucians of the Song and Ming dynasties—modern Confucians failed in constructing a genuine and coherent moral metaphysics precisely because they did not pay attention to a crucial difference between the cultural-psychological formations of religious and shamanistic cultures. While the former were rooted in spiritual tradition and construed human life upon this basis, the latter developed in an exactly opposite way, namely proceeding from humanity and creating human spiritual life on the basis of its physical, material foundation. Li explained this supposition, which he developed on the firm grounds of historical ontology, in the following way:

> Because in historical ontology morality and religion are not the most important or final point of reference, and because it rather emphasizes that it is rooted in the "free feelings" that belong to human sensibility, it does not stop at ethical morality (resulting) from the "agglomeration of reason." According to historical ontology, the real ultimate reality of human substance lies in "sedimented reason (in a narrow sense)," which encompasses and simultaneously transcends ethics and morality. This means that the substance of human beings is not reason, but rather a sensitivity to the fusion of reason and emotion. This is also an important reason why I have replaced the term "practical reason" with "pragmatic reason." Although from the viewpoint of the universe, human beings arose from nature, while simultaneously also transcending it, we cannot claim the same from the viewpoint of humans. From this viewpoint, we cannot remain in this sphere of transcendence. You and me, he or she, we all still exist in nature. Hence, our seeking the "ultimate goal" has necessarily returned to this realm of concrete, sensual life.
>
> 由於歷史本體論不以道德－宗教作為歸宿點，而強調歸宿在人的感性的「自由感受」中，從而它便不止步於「理性凝聚」的倫理道德，而認為包容它又超越它的「理性積澱（窄意）」，才是人的本體所在。即是說人的本體不是理性而是情理交融的感性。這正是當年棄「實踐理性」(practical reason) 而用「實用理性」(pragmatic reason) 一詞重要原因。儘管從自然說，出現文化－道

德的人是由自然而超出自然, 但作為人, 卻不能停留在這超自然的目標和境地中。你、我、他（她）仍然是自然的存在物, 所謂「最終目的」仍然要回到這個感性生命中來。(Li Zehou 2008, 68)

In his essay "A Reevaluation of Confucius," Li points out that Confucius plays a crucial role in developing the emotio-rational structure of the people in his times away from the worship of external deities to inter-human emotional bounding that was rooted in kinship relations (Li Zehou 1980a, 85). Several crucial elements of religions—feelings and rituality—were thus melted and incorporated into the all-embracing, unified system of sacral ethics and everyday psychology. This meant that there was no need to establish any other institutions of theological faith.

It is by no means a coincidence that the central Confucian virtue of humaneness belongs to the most important concerns within his discourse of emotion-based substance.[47] Li recognizes this virtue as Confucius's crucial notion and interprets it as encompassing four central levels or characteristic features determining traditional Chinese society, namely:

1. foundation of blood (kinship) relations,

2. psychological principles,

3. humanism,

4. ideal personality.

These four levels are interwoven and correlative. In their dynamic interaction, they construct the organic ideational entirety that is guided and permeated by pragmatic reason. However, in this context, the most important element that makes up the very foundation of all these levels is the psychological principle of emotions. Through the mutual interaction of these levels, Confucius uses humaneness to interpret and (even more importantly) to preserve rituality, and in this way internalizes external ethical regulations in order to transform them into a vital part of individual inwardness. This internalization is the most important cornerstone of the Chinese cultural-psychological formation (Li Zehou 1985, 16).

Such a worldview cherished secular life and saw emotions as the main source in experiencing and perceiving the world. This view held that emotions were understood as the very foundation on which people lived their lives and sustained their mutual relations. "Every day, every moment, people experience emotions stimulated from their various relations within their family and community: parent–child, lord–subject, brothers, husband–wife, and friends" (Jia, Jinhua 2016, 775). Interpersonally, socially, and ethically-defined emotions were tightly interwoven into the concrete substance of human life in communities. Thus the "emotional energy" that was based in the central virtue of humaneness became "the main motivating force in social life" (ibid.). Such emotions that were permeated by moral values manifest themselves in proper actions and consequently in a harmonious life.[48] Confucian emotion-based substance has had wide ethical implications. Wang Yunping, for instance, emphasizes that the "Confucian understanding of emotions and their ethical importance confirms and exemplifies the contemporary Western renewed understanding of the nature of emotions" (Wang Yunping 2008, 352). In such a view, ethical life is always emotional and virtues are therefore inclinational. To Wang, "the reason for the ethical significance is both that emotions are heavenly endowed and that there exists a union of emotions and reason in Confucian ethics" (ibid.). Such a view poses a challenge to the predominant Western theories of ethics, that have commonly dealt with a search for confirming abstract and normative moral rules.

Wang Jing questions the concept of emotion-based substance by emphasizing that in Li's view, it is not primarily defined in terms of "subjective consciousness, emotions, and desires of the individual," but rather in collective terms of "social consciousness" and "cultural-psychological formation" (Wang Jing 1996, 104). In Wang's understanding, this implies the subjugation of the individual to the community. In Li's philosophical framework the ethical implications of the emotion-based substance concept should be viewed through the lens of the role ethics as it was developed by Henry Rosemont and Roger T. Ames (Ames 2011; Rosemont and Ames 2009). Rosemont and Ames coined "role ethics" because Confucian relational ethics (or, in Li's words, "relationalism") does not fit well in any of the existing Western categories of ethical models. In contrast to the Western image of the individual, entering into particular social relations as an independent, isolated self, the Confucian role-constituted person does not play a particular set of roles, but lives them. Hence, in this framework, people are the roles that they live, because they cannot be abstracted from their relations with other fellow humans. This understanding has been placed into Ames's concept of process ontology, in that there are no substances that bear property or essence; every existence is dynamic and relational (Elstein 2015, 242). Such an understanding is completely natural. The community exists before the individual, for the latter is constituted through social relations and cannot exist without them.

Li further elaborated upon the emotion-based to establish his theory of the emotio-rational structure (or formation).[49] He tried within this context to combine Confucian ethics, which he sees as being rooted in the pragmatic reason, with certain elements of Kantian rationality. He hoped that with this kind of renewed or transformed reinterpretation of Confucianism he could provide a new form of public reason, suitable for modern global societies. In his view, such Confucian ethics of cherishing human existence, emotions, and harmonious inter-human relations "can become a general ideality and universal values that contribute to the remedy of the critical conditions of contemporary times and the new construction of humanity and world cultural order" (Jia, Jinhua 2016, 787). Proceeding from such a basic supposition, as we shall see later, Li promotes a return to ancient, original Confucianism as a kind of a "second Renaissance."

> While the Renaissance humanism emancipated humans from the control of God, Li Zehou expects that the second Renaissance will aim at the emancipation of humans from the control of both material and social machines, as well as going beyond the limitations of Enlightenment rationality to reach a balance of reason and emotion in both psychological and cultural-institutional domains, in order to inspire fruitful actions for the sustainable development of the human race." (ibid.)

Two Kinds of Morality and Proper Measure

Li believes that the idea of the unity of reason and emotion—rather than the concept of sheer reason—is the philosophical foundation that enables us to see the key differences between Chinese and Western ethics (Li Zehou 2014i, 2). In his long essay "Response to Michael Sandel and Other Matters" (*Huiying Sangde'er ji qita* 回應桑德爾及其他), he points to the implications and consequences of this difference for the understanding of the contemporary human being, i.e., the *homo marketus*. In Li's view, the idea of emotio-rational structure, which is a paradigmatic basis of the specifically Chinese cultural-psychological formation, is tightly connected to the traditional Chinese understanding of human beings.

> This also belongs to the Chinese philosophical tradition, which understands humans as a kind of rational animal, but, on the other hand, also as organisms with instincts, desires, and natural needs. All these can be by no means simply eliminated through rational principles. The market economies in contemporary societies are opening this Pandora's Box of instincts and desires. They effectively satisfy various human wishes and even produce new ones, even to the point of generating a surplus of material desires. This problem cannot be solved only by virtue of rational principles and moral guidelines. It simply cannot be cracked without considering people's emotio-rational structure. Freud revealed the suppression of the id by the superego, and the doctrines of many religions and dogmatic ideologies suppress emotions and desires with rational regulations.
>
> 這也是中國哲學傳統，既重視人是理性動物，同時重視人是具有本能欲求和自然需要的生物體，不能用某種道德的理性理念將它們抹殺。今天的市場經濟打開了這個本能慾望的魔盒，有效地、充分地滿足並製造出人的各種慾望，以至"物慾橫流"。光用理性原則和道德律令，不講情理結構，不能解決問題。Freud 發現了超我對本我的壓制。各種宗教教義和各種主義教條以理性律令來壓制情慾。八個樣板戲裡無愛情，但今天重來，恐怕行不通了。(Li Zehou 2014i, 3)

Li maintains that the problems addressed by Michael Sandel—questions connected with the moral or ethical limits of the free market—can be solved through the perspective of his "theory of the two kinds of morality" (*liangde lun* 兩德論) (ibid., 1). Li denotes the two types as religious (*zongjiaoxing daode* 宗教性道德) and social morality (*shehuixing daode* 社會性道德). The former refers to the religious nature of private virtues (*zongjiaoxing side* 宗教性私德) that are rooted in individual values that arise from subjective emotions and mature through innate cultivation and faith. The latter form of morality pertains to internalized public social virtues (*shehuixing gongde* 社會性公德) that are the result of external regulations, ethical principles, laws, and systems (Li Zehou 2008b, 6). In general, ethics pertains to external rules of conduct, while morality is based upon individuals, internal values, and beliefs. Li Zehou largely assumes this differentiation. According to his *General Scheme of Ethics* (*Lunlixue zong lanbiao* 倫理學總覽表; see appendix), ethics refers to external axiological contents of social life—humanistic values and values dependent upon the actual society or period of time. Morality, on the other hand, is internal and thus refers to individual psychological forms. However, in Li's view, this inner domain is further subdivided into an internal and an external sphere. While the former consists of purely psychological or mental factors (e.g., will, ideas, and emotions), the latter includes the two kinds of morality (religious and social) in question. In this external realm of the inner individual moral world—in the realm that belongs to cultural-historical formations and is therefore socially determined and historically shaped—Li makes a distinction between religious morality (associated with emotions, goodness, and beliefs) from social morality (linked to justice, equality, reason, independence, and human rights): "Religious morality stems from social morality" (Li Zehou 2016b, 35).

In China, religious morality originated from the shamanistic ceremonies of the clan-based societies of the Neolithic era. These ceremonies were

> systemized by Duke Zhou, spiritualized by Kongzi, and philosophized by the School of the Structural Principle of the Song and Ming Dynasties, but they always preserved the original shamanistic sacredness. Over thousands of years they shaped the traditional Chinese codes of conduct and modes of life, i.e., the so-called ritual ethics. People were convinced and truly believed that this "ritual ethics" had a "universal nature, which surpasses time and space"; it became the "religious morality" of the Chinese people.
>
> 它來源於遠古至上古（夏商周）的氏族群體的巫術禮儀，經周公而製度化，經孔子而心靈化，經宋明理學而哲學化，但始終保存了原始巫術的神聖性，成為數千年來中國傳統社會的行為準則、生活規範，即所謂「禮教」。「禮教」正是被論證和被相信為「放之四海而皆準，歷時古今而不變的」中國人的「宗教性道德」。 (Li Zehou 2016b, 35)

In essence, these two kinds of morality are "often intermingled and difficult to separate" (Li Zehou 2016b, 34). In traditional societies, the division between them was originally embryonic. A clear demarcation line between the two axiological categories was actually drawn at the age of Enlightenment and can thus be seen as a product of modernity. Therefore, it is by no means a coincidence that Li Zehou sometimes denotes the second kind of morality as "modern social morality" (*xiandai shehuixing daode* 現代社會性道德). Li defines it as follows:

> So-called modern social morality mainly refers to the principles and criteria that people in modern societies consciously follow in their individual and group interactions. Because the scope of its implementation is extremely wide, for it reaches from the political system and everyday life to the inner emotions and feelings of individuals, it is a topic that has been jointly investigated by many different scientific disciplines (e.g., sociology, psychology and especially by political sciences and various professional ethics).

> 所謂「現代社會性道德」主要是指在現代社會的人際關係和人群交往中，個人在行為活動中所應遵循的自覺原則和標準。由於涉及面積廣闊，從政治體制和日常生活，到個人的內心情感、信仰，它是多種學科 (社會學、心理學特別是政治哲學和各種職業倫理學) 所共同研究的課題。 (Li Zehou 2016b, 39)

D'Ambrosio, Carleo, and Lambert (2016, 1062) point out that for Li, "religious moralities" are grounded in different traditions and therefore imply different values, serving as foundations of moral virtues and as crucial elements of moral education. In the Western world, however, modern values grew to prevalence as the "traditional religious morals associated with Christianity weakened—for example, with Kant's notion of pure reason replacing the Church's interpretation of the word of God" (ibid.). Traditional religious moralities were overshadowed in this framework by new concepts such as (pure) reason, justice, autonomy, or equality. All these gave rise to a positive evaluation of individualism and liberalism. Li sees people following these values primarily because they are supported by economic powers.

> These economic forces have taken abstractly conceived concepts like "the atomic individual" and "natural human rights" and seemingly actualized them, making the independent individual, the social contract, and public reason increasingly part of the institutional order, behavioral norms, and moral

> standards. This modern economy of free trade, fair exchange, commodity production, and the market, especially the free trade of labor that Marx discusses, serves as the foundation and origin of actuality. (Li Zehou 2016, 1085)

As we all know, these foundations continue to develop and spread globally. Thus, for Li, it is completely clear that liberalism will continue to expand the world over. Li acknowledges that in spite of these problematic dimensions inherent to rational principles, these principles are still to be considered as great contributions of European Enlightenment. The fact that these ideals continues to be carried forward and expanded upon results from specific trends and patterns of our modern life. Therefore, it is difficult to resist their omnipresent influence.

Li understands social morality as the necessary grounds of any modern society. He was never against the ideals of the Enlightenment movement. In his view, the current postmodern antirationalism is harmful. He believes that radical individualism and absolute rationality require modification and regulation through certain aspects of religious morality and so he proposes "emotion-based substance" and "the emotio-rational structure" as a helpful way of clarifying questions linked to the psychology of contemporary humans. He believes that such concepts, which draw on traditional Chinese thought, could obtain universal significance. This led him to propose a Confucian "alternative," that the Confucian relational ethics could provide certain valuable elements to the religious moral content of modern societies. When reasonably applied, these elements could help globalized societies balance, correct, and may even replace those aspects of social morality that are potentially harmful or dangerous. Concepts such as relationalism or proper measure, for instance, could serve as alternatives to the absolute rule of normative and fixed laws, abstract and therefore empty principles of equal rights, or of a mechanistically constructed concept of justice. Li proposes that societies should be guided "through virtue rather than utilitarian benefit, free choice, and the market" (ibid.). He stresses that he values harmony more than justice, arguing that "'justice' is primarily a 'rational structure,' while 'harmony' comprises both, emotion and reason" (Li Zehou 2014i, 2).[50] Li claims that harmony between people, between body and mind, and between people and nature is to be found in the "regulation and proper constitution" of (modern) social morals by means of human emotio-rational structure and the system of relationalism. For Li, this is the highest level of preserving the elementary "common good" and "good life." Li also believes that this level is "higher than, though not a replacement for, fair and reasonable notions of justice and their distinction of right from wrong" (Li Zehou 2016, 60). His idea of social harmony, which involves transforming humans through education and cultivation, is established upon justice. It merely represents a "regulative and properly constitutive" standard and can by no means be applied as an ultimate criterium determining or guiding "justice."

Similarly, his concept of relationalism, which must be channeled by proper measure, is not a negation or a complete oppression of modern individualism—it is nothing more than the negation of its absolute supremacy. In China the proper measure, which is based upon the emotio-rational structure, could be applied as a part of traditional religious morals and function as a regulative principle for the individualism inherent in modern social morals.

In "Response," Li also deals extensively with the question of the relation between emotions and desires. First, he reproaches Sandel for not paying attention to the fact that emotions cannot be bought monetarily. Although Sandel states many different examples of what money could not (or should not) buy, he simply did not see the significant role of emotions in this whole discourse. This is the context in which Li indicates that Sandel "elaborates at length on questions of surrogate pregnancy but does not discuss its close relationship with or intense complications of and damage to emotions" (Li Zehou 2016, 1075). Proceeding from Sandel's basic problem, namely, from the question of how to limit the freedom of economy and its marketing principles through ethics, considering the fact that desires can be fulfilled (and manipulated) with money, he emphasizes that the same does not hold true for emotions, even though there is certainly a close connection between the two aspects of human inwardness. While (the fulfillment of) desires can be bought, sold, or exchanged, we cannot purchase, sell, or exchange emotions. Li acknowledges that this problem must be treated more carefully and more in depth by contemporary ethics and philosophy.

> Nevertheless, emotions and desires are generally intertwined and can be difficult to fully distinguish from one another. But on the other hand, emotions in some aspects transcend individual biological desires. . . . The extremely complicated intertwinement of emotions and desires must be carefully

investigated by the philosophy of mind and analytical philosophy and can only be discussed generally here. In sum, what kind of relationships emotions, desires, and money have and should have are issues worth investigating. This is, moreover, exactly the type of problem that contemporary ethics should focus on. (Li Zehou 2016, 1075)

Here, we might consider that desires can be seen as only a part of emotions. Emotions can be seen as an umbrella-category. Desires are a kind of emotion, but emotions cannot be reduced to desires (or to any other part of itself, for instance, to joy or fear). While the market economy can sell, buy, exchange, and manipulate (create, reduce, multiply, or generate) many emotions in this particular sense, it cannot directly influence human emotions as such. This distinction is clearly visible in traditional Chinese thought, which treats emotion as a highly situationalized or contextualized notion, for it also implies the semantic connotation of "situation." Emotion has often been seen as an umbrella term comprising seven particular feelings or situations (*qi qing* 七情), *including* desires (*yu* 欲).[51] Li states that the demarcation line between what can and cannot be exchanged in terms of market economy lies in emotions. If we now take into consideration that moral feelings—even though a part of the emotio-rational structure—are understood as a part of religious morality, then they must necessarily also be subordinated under the emotion. It becomes clear that the whole discourse should be centered upon the problem of religious morality. We cannot forget that Li considers free will to be the core of human capacity. In spite of his conviction that reason is the prior element of human historical development because it makes us human through its amalgamation into our animal sensibility, he also emphasizes that: "Both logically and practically speaking, ethics and morals have priority in relation to cognition" (Li Zehou 2016, 1107). In contrast to Kant, Li believes that no human capacities are inherent or *a priori* and should thus rather be seen as results of history and education.

Li further explains that the criteria for this demarcation line, which limits the free market, cannot be set on a normative or universal but rather on a case-to-case basis. He claims that

> we ought to promote economic development in so far as it improves people's lives, and yet at the same time we should remain emotionally aware of the suffering that remains in

the world and retain a sense of benevolence toward others in order to allow historical tragedy and moral emotion to guide our grasping and establishment of "proper measure." This is what I call "the art of governing," which allows for "conforming to emotions as well as reason." We cannot simply adopt strict utilitarian or liberal principles of justice. (Li, Zehou 2016, 1091)

In "Theory of the Two Kinds of Morality," Li states that the elementary axiological basis of modern societies is social morality, which is primary and must be rooted in public reason, a contemporary legal system, and formally determinable justice. Religious morality in this framework only functions as a (though very important) regulative principle. Modern social morality should also remain paramount in public education. This forms the basis for Li to believe that individuals can still freely decide on the beliefs of their "private virtue (religious morals) and find meaning and values for their lives in the teachings of Buddhism, Christianity, Islam, Confucianism, and even Communism (as a political religion)" (ibid., 1127). Such a complementary function of religious morality and private virtues that are rooted in the emotion-based substance is nevertheless significant, for it can fill up the emotional vacuum that prevails among members of alienated contemporary societies. Li argues that this not only offers people a way to harmonize with each other, but also "alleviate(s) the emotional vapidity and coldness of human relationships brought by mechanistic public reason, formal justice, the market economy, fair trade, and the atomic individual" (ibid., 1134). On such an emotio-reasonable foundation, relationalism would not function as a set of fixed traditional rules, but rather as an interhuman instrument that is able to decrease the social gap between rich and poor and between fixed social classes.

Here, Li's synthesis of Kant and Confucianism becomes, once again, clearly visible. While his highlighting of the importance of individual rights of modern social morality is directly linked to Kant, his concentration on the emotio-rational structure of religious morals doubtless originates in classical Confucianism.

In his theoretical proposal, Li describes the role of this complementary function, assumed by religious morality, relationalism, and private virtue, with terminology that he borrowed from Kant, as "regulative and constitutive." Li's "Theory of the Two Kinds of Morality" presents the relationship between these two features (the regulative and the constitutive) as always historically concrete, for at any particular stage of development, and in any culture, they always include elements of "historicism, idealism and emotionality" (ibid.). He subsequently emphasizes that history is a dynamic and circumstantial process that always depends on particular social, political, cultural, and economic contexts. Ethics and social morality are always shaped by concrete historical conditions and cannot be viewed as something *a priori*. Besides, as we have already seen in the chapter on sedimentation, Li views history as progressive and accumulative. The sedimentation of particular common axiological outsets, together with matching emotions, continuously develops through education. In our increasingly globalized times, this will sooner or later lead to a world in which humankind will possess common ethical standards and moral criteria. Li argues for a relativity in ethics, but warns against ethical relativism, in the framework of which relativity becomes a kind of holly or absolute truth.

He also compares the two kinds of morality to the ancient Chinese concepts of inner sage and external ruler (*neisheng waiwang* 內聖外王).[52] In this framework, the "inner sage" can be identified with religious morality and help human beings through philosophy, religion, art, and literature in their search for significance and the spiritual realms of life. The "external king," or external ruler, (social morality and public virtues) is important as a basis of reasonable, fair, and democratic political systems. Li attempts to modernize this traditional category by promoting a "new way of the internal sage and external king" (Li, Zehou 2016, 1137). In Chinese tradition there was always a strong focus on individual cultivation, the "inner sageness" was never able to translate or develop directly into "outer kingliness." However, in the postmodern, globalized world, which is governed by instrumental rationality, the external ruler could be complemented by traditional Chinese model of self-cultivation that is based on emotion-based substance and relationalism.[53] In general, Li believes that modern China should develop the restoration of rationality, by which he—in contrast to Modern Confucian philosophers like Mou Zongsan 牟宗三—did not imply that it should reconstruct any kind of "transcendental" but rather a pragmatic reason. Only this way, through the revival of certain paradigmatic cultural values, will it become capable of preventing the rise of a market society, a commercialized culture, completely dominated by material desires. This prevention could take place without dogmatically restricting human desires through religions or ideologies of guilt. Li finds it necessary that the Chinese people (and especially the scholars of humanities) remember why it is important to reinvent the ancient Chinese culture of pleasure with its balanced complementarity of emotionality and reason. For Li, such an ethical investigation into a "Chinese path" could integrate individual and social components into the aforementioned "new way of the inner sage and external king" (ibid., 198).

This quest for a balanced way, where two polar opposites could be unified in a correlative mutual complementarity, has found vivid manifestation in yet another notion. Based on his profound knowledge of traditional Chinese philosophical discourses, Li sought to modify and develop the static frameworks of post-Copernican theories through his newly coined but originally traditional concept of (proper) measure, which is rooted in the material-technological formation and constitutes a dynamic basis for historical ontology, governed by the human subjectality (Li Zehou 2002c, 1–4), 7). The (proper) measure is the ever-changeable, flexible, undeterminable criteria of human (but also animal) adaptability that enables living beings to exist and develop (Li 2002c, 9, 1). *Du* is necessarily changeable, dynamic, and different in every moment because the conditions of human life are also continuously changing (Li 2002c, 3).

This view of human development is manifestly rooted in classical Chinese philosophy. Lien Chong Woei argues that in both his social theory and philosophy, Li wants to hold fast to the mean, which he designates with the classic Confucian term *zhong yong* 中庸 (Lien Chong Woei 1999, 124). Choosing the mean entails developing a sense of the proper measure: "Since ancient times, Chinese thought has always stressed the 'Mean' (*zhong* 中) and 'harmony' (*he* 和), which are nothing other than the objectification of '*du*' (ibid., 3)."

Du, which is not a transcendent external force, a concrete object, or a pure abstraction, but a human creation and product, is also closely linked to the concept of subjectality (ibid., 2). It is also a means for Li's quest for controlling human wishes and desires, but without seeking to minimize or eliminate them. The "state of equilibrium or the mean" is thus of paramount importance, for it makes us aware of our limitations, while also encouraging us to see and explore the unlimited space within this limited framework (Li Zehou 1985, 298). This is another common thread that connects Li's work to the Modern Neo-Confucian theorists, for whom (and for very similar reasons) the concept of *zhong yong* is also of fundamental importance (see Rošker 2016, ch. 7.4).

This search for a middle way, for a balance between human desires and the actual limitations of our life that presupposes negotiating with reality and trying to adapt to it without losing one's own creativity and uniqueness, is also reflected in Li Zehou's political philosophy. Throughout his writings, he advocates gradual adaptations instead of explosive changes, sensible reforms instead of sudden shifts, evolution instead of revolution.[54]

Tradition and Modernity

Chinese Modernization and Its Theoretical Reflection in Twentieth-Century China

Li's exploration of traditional Chinese thought is inextricably interwoven into the problems of Chinese modernity. He believes that classical Chinese philosophy was the first step in the transformation of the traditional into the modern and therefore, a profound understanding of this thought is a sine qua non for any realistic solution to the contradictions between the old and the new (Li Zehou 1996, 230). He consequently devotes a lot of his time and energy to the systematic investigation of traditional Chinese thought. Through his coining of several new concepts, Li tries to bring this ancient philosophy closer to the understanding of modern human beings and to establish a systematic network of the various interrelated paradigms that underlie this ideational system. For him, the fulfillment of such tasks is a crucial and necessary step on the path to establishing a theoretical system that could serve as a theoretical or ideational basis of specifically Chinese modernization. The very problem of Chinese modernization as such and the role of Chinese intellectual and cultural tradition within this process occupies an important part of Li's thought. However, before introducing and evaluating his theoretical contributions in this field, we shall take a brief look into the specific historical, social, and cultural characteristics that condition the particular development of Chinese (or East Asian) modernization.

When dealing with the modern and contemporary endeavors of establishing a "specifically Chinese" philosophical foundation for modernization, we must consider the concept of "invented traditions" (Hobsbawm and Ranger, 1995). We must consider to what degree past philosophical and intellectual traditions are based on historic expectations and to what degree they are only a product of ideological and political requirements of their contemporary time. The revitalization of traditional Chinese thought, especially Confucianism, belongs to the most important components within present-day East Asian modernization ideologies. We must also investigate the crucial factors that made possible the incorporation of traditional Chinese values, ideas, and principles into the network of prevailing global ideologies and axiological contexts. We must not forget that many indigenous cultural and philosophical (re) sources have survived in China until the present day, even if they can no longer be counted as the dominant ideologies. We witnessed in the twentieth century various cultural, historical, and theoretical revivals in China, although these relics of the past were obviously invented in order to satisfy certain ideological demands of the contemporary era.[55] We cannot understand them as a negation of modernity because they all happened under its banner.

Most traditional Western modernization theories were rooted in the presumption that Chinese tradition would have to be eliminated if China were to develop a modern dynamic society. The traditional Western modernization theorists, including Marx and Engels, presumed that traditional Chinese culture was impermeable and unfavorable to modernization. Max Weber wrote at length on Asia, particularly on India and China, concluding that their cultural, philosophical, and religious traditions were not appropriate to serve as ideologies required to start the modernization process. His famous theory, that Protestant ethic was instrumental for the rise and spread of modernization, stands in sharp contrast with the recent East Asian idea that societies grounded in the Confucian ethic may, in many ways, not only be equal but even superior to the West in achieving industrialization, affluence, and modernization. This idea, which has gradually developed and spread in many East Asian regions in recent decades, is known as the "post-Confucian hypothesis" (see Berger 1988, 7).

In this context, we have to understand that the Eurocentric discourses of the dominant Western social sciences still focus on Western paradigms of social development. These discourses conclude that China would never produce an industrial revolution on its own due to its inadequate technological development. However, as the research of the well-known theory of the "germs of capitalism in China" (*Zhongguo zibenzhuyi mengya* 中國資本主義萌芽) clearly showed, China—as early as in the twelfth century—already possessed the technological means that could have booted up an industrial revolution. The fact that this revolution did not occur can be explained by the inability of the traditional Chinese political and economic system to bring about such a transformation, as well as due to the fact that China, unlike Europe, did not face an economic crisis in that period (Rošker 2016, 226–27).

We cannot forget that modernization is a complex process of social transitions that cannot be limited only to universal elements that are equally valid everywhere, but also necessarily includes culturally conditioned factors. China had already experienced a transitional situation at the end of the nineteenth century, when the two-thousand-year rule of Confucian state doctrine gradually lost its prevailing and dominant role in society—when Confucian state doctrine began to lose its institutional background. After the Opium Wars (1842–44), it became quite clear that the traditional philosophies and ideologies were outdated and could no longer meet the requirements of the new era. An era that was defined by both the economic and political superiority of the Western colonial powers and the clash with Western scientific and philosophical ideas. The first results of these contacts with Euro-American thought began to show by the middle of the nineteenth century, when Chinese intellectuals began treating modernization as a means for transformation and departure from the traditional axiological, economic, and political standards that had hitherto determined the social reality of the ancient Middle Kingdom (ibid., 19). An analysis of this process, based on the general theoretical premises of modernity, and the central paradigms of Euro-American sociological, philosophical, and cultural discourses, must begin with the traditional definition first formulated by Hegel, and then developed in the theoretical works of Marx, Weber, and the early Lukács, as well as by other representatives of the Frankfurt school.[56] These theories were based on an absolutist critique of reason and they eventually led to a self-referential cul-de-sac. In the twentieth century we find various alternative theories that proposed self-critical foundations of modernity grounded in a linguistically determined consideration of the term "reason." This linguistic shift led to two different approaches towards the understanding of modernity. The first manifested itself in the postmodern surpassing of the normative understanding of this notion, while the second involved the intersubjective transformation of its traditional definition (Habermas 1998, 195). The dominant Western definition did not remain focused on its analyses of a specific social situation, which was usually expressed in the form of critique of reason but moved its weight to the terminological range of modernity that includes the connotations of the "conscious discontinuity of the new from the old" or the "modern" from the "traditional" (ibid., 15).

In observing modernization processes in China, we should be aware that it manifests itself as a series of consecutive phases. Each of these periods lasted for a few decades and was connected in its own way either to the specific features of the Chinese tradition, or to the problems of accepting and transforming non-Chinese forms of production, reproduction, and lifestyles. In investigating the process of Chinese modernization, we must take into account the following characteristics (see ibid., 16).

1. In China, modernization in the sense of an all-encompassing political, economic, and cultural process and its theoretical discourses was always influenced by the invasion of Western military and technological supremacy; as a logical outcome of this situation, Western technology, political systems, and culture became a referential frame for the modernization of China. (Geist 1996, 13)

2. Any theoretical discourse has thus always equated tradition with Chinese and modernization with Western culture.

3. Historically, the debate on modernization in China took place within the framework of classical Chinese discursive methodology, which is defined by traditional binary categories. With respect to modernization, nineteenth- and early twentieth-century Chinese intellectuals tried to clarify the relation between modernity (the West) and tradition (China) through the binary categories of "substance" and "function." In the nineteenth century, Zhang Zhidong's slogan advocating "the preservation of the Chinese Substance and the application of Western Function" (*Zhongxue wei ti, Xixue wei yong* 中學為體, 西學為用) was widely shared by Chinese intellectuals (Rošker 2008, 96).[57] This approach sought to preserve the Chinese tradition in the face of modernization that was understood as being limited to assimilating Western technology and administration. In the twentieth century,

Li Zehou inverted this binary opposition by defining modernization as the transformation of the substance, in the sense of general social consciousness, production, and lifestyles.⁵⁸

4. The inner logic of traditional Chinese society was intrasystemic (Moritz 1993, 60) in the sense that guaranteeing stability through a centralized and cohesive society was its chief aim. The past was not only the main reference for reflecting on the present, but also served as a signpost for the future. (ibid. 61)

5. Enlightenment in the sense of spreading the ideological domination of reason, seen as essential to modernization, did not find its dynamic potential for change in the indigenous (Chinese) philosophical tradition, but rather in the adaptation of Western currents of rationality.

Defined in these relations, the Chinese modernization process cannot be understood as a natural one, nor as a process that could be reduced to the inherent forces of some "autochthonous advance" of society (Luo Rongqu 2008, 1). In the mid-nineteenth century, profound alternations of the existing economic and political systems seemed essential, particularly given the inability of those systems to satisfy the requirements of the modern era. We must also consider that modernization processes in China were defined by conflicts with foreign powers—they were largely defined by European colonialism. China of the eighteenth and nineteenth centuries also had to deal with a bottomless internal crisis. This crisis was much greater and reached far deeper into the traditional structures of society and the state than the recurrent periods of chaos and turmoil brought about by the rise and fall of dynasties. A radical transformation of social values, means of production, and the political and economic system in general would have been unavoidable even without the hurtful encounter with the European supremacies.⁵⁹ Clearly, such a reform would not have looked like the Western-type of modernization. We can only wonder what China would look like today if it had started a reform on its own—drawing only on its own economic, political, and philosophical funds and capabilities (Rošker 2016, 17).

The Chinese philosophy of the first half of the twentieth century was still determined by the decline of the Chinese New Age. Almost all theorists of this period were forced to deal with the ideas and contradictions imposed by the incomparably more technologically advanced Western countries. While the radical pro-Western intellectuals (*Quanpan xihua pai* 全盤西化派) engaged in the iconoclastic repudiation of all traditional culture and sought to resolve China's crisis through the complete Westernization of Chinese society, the conservative intellectuals (*fugu pai* 復古派) argued for a modernization of ancient, especially Confucian, thought. They believed it provided the only possible spiritual basis to reestablish an independent and sovereign Chinese state. Ultimately the majority of the intelligentsia preferred to follow a middle way, focusing their efforts on a possible synthesis of both traditions. Based on their command of Western philosophy, they reinterpret their own tradition through the most appropriate methods for integrating Western systems of thought into the framework of traditional Chinese discourses. In the context of the theoretical reflection of modernity, which necessarily included the confrontation with Western thought and its values, Chinese philosophy was distinguished by the following three main currents:[60]

1. The first was characterized by having faith in progress and in the redemptive potential of reason and the natural sciences. In social terms, it manifested itself in a wide range of liberal ideologies, while philosophically it tended toward the neorealistic and pragmatic discourses of the more recent American philosophical schools.

2. The second current was distinguished by a comprehensive attempt to revitalize traditional (particularly Confucian and Neo-Confucian) thought by means of new influences borrowed or derived from Western systems. In this search for synthesis the spirit of German idealism was especially important, while certain approaches of the Viennese circle also attracted a number of exponents of this current. During the first twenty-five years of the People's Republic this current, at least officially, was reduced to silence, However, their main concerns continued to be developed by Taiwanese theorists and, to a certain extent, by those from

Hong Kong. They followed the tendency to revitalize traditional thought through elaborating on the philosophies of the Song and Ming Dynasty Neo-Confucianism. They were generally known as Modern New Confucianism (*Xiandai Xin Ruxue* 現代新儒學).

3. Over the past three decades, with the explosive economic liberalization of the People's Republic of China, a similar current occurred on the mainland under the name, New National Studies (*Xin Guoxue* 新國學). All these tendencies of a revitalized tradition and its reinterpretation through the lens of modern and contemporary thought continues to form one of the main streams of contemporary Chinese theory.

Following his own path and trying to resolve the problems linked to Chinese modernization from a broader, more comprehensive view, Li did not completely fit into any of these mainstream currents. Well aware of these differences, he pointed out: "My view differs from modern Western Marxism, from the new Confucianism of Hong Kong and Taiwan, and also from the mainland New National studies" (Li Zehou 2016, 87).

The decade from 1978 to 1988, the period in which Li became popular and his works became increasingly influential, was a time of great political, economic, and cultural transformation. The pragmatically oriented economic liberalization and relatively comfortable political approaches resulted in a less dogmatic and less rigid atmosphere and offered a more liberal platform for intellectual and cultural agendas. In comparison with the previous periods, the role and functions of intellectuals who lived and worked in the PRC between 1978 and 1988 became increasingly complex within a rapidly changing social context (Lin, Min 1992, 969). However, the new market economy reform did not result in a lasting mass movement that could, at least, offer the illusion that it was based on Enlightenment ideas—that it met certain theoretical assumptions concerning modernization. This is hardly surprising if we consider that the economic liberalization led by Deng Xiaoping in the last two decades of the twentieth century (after the death of Mao Zedong) was enacted primarily by government decree, which meant that it already differed considerably from the classic (Western) modernization model. However, a spontaneous, albeit short-lived mass movement demanding parallel political "democratization" did occur during the gradual economic liberalization. This movement, which was primarily led by and comprised students, was as naive as the May 4th Movement and ended with the infamous massacre on Tiananmen Square on June 4, 1989. This period of economic reform was reflected at many different levels throughout Chinese society and political criticism often manifested itself in the search for new forms of cultural expression (Rošker 2016, 22).[61]

In this period, Chinese thinkers engaged in a theoretical revival, which came to be known as the New Enlightenment. Li writes about two crucial movements.

> After the death of Mao Zedong and the downfall of the "Gang of Four" there arose two waves of intellectual movements in theory, research, and culture. Both of them were reminiscent of the May 4th Movement. The first manifested itself in the outcries and controversies on Enlightenment, Humanism, and Humaneness. The second one occurred over the past two years in the so-called Cultural Fever regarding the comparison between China and the West.
>
> 在毛澤東逝世和「四人幫」垮台後, 理論、學術文化界所掀起的兩次思想浪潮, 都使人回想起「五四」一次是關於啟蒙人道人性的吶喊和爭論, 一次是最近兩年關於中西比較的所謂「文化熱」討論。(Li Zehou 2016c, 333)

These movements formed the crucial theoretical reflection on contemporary Chinese social reality.[62] However, since government institutions managed to discharge intellectuals' critical potential not only through repressive measures, but also, and especially, through the professionalization of the theory, this reflection could never become a part of mass movements. In the post-1989 period, Chinese academics (including Li, who was forced to leave the country because of his critical influence on young intellectuals) were therefore compelled to rethink their historical experiences.

This state of affairs gave rise to the increasing dispersion of intellectuals and their alienation from the state and its policymaking institutions. "In fact, in today's China, intellectuals no longer constitute a homogenous social group" (Wang Hui 2000, 16). Thus, according to numerous contemporary critical thinkers, the theoretical production of the New Enlightenment has clearly served as the fundamental ideology for China's economic reform (ibid.).[63]

Against the background of these theoretical approaches we shall now explore Li's view on Chinese modernization and its connection to China's traditional discourses. As we will see, it is a rather complex one.

Li Zehou's View on Modernity

Li's views on Chinese modernization cannot be separated from his general philosophy, which is, as we already know, based upon the method of anthropological ontology. Regarding the necessary social and cultural transformations that it brings about, he remains faithful to his principle of proper measure and advocates the middle way.

> Changes and transformations do not imply that we completely continue our tradition, but they do not mean we should completely abolish it either. It means that we must infiltrate traditional sediments and cultural-psychological formations based on the new substance of our social existence and by virtue of our awareness of this new substance.
>
> 改變、轉換既不是全盤繼承傳統，也不是全盤扔棄。而是在新的社會存在的本體基礎上，用新的本體意識來對傳統積澱或文化心理結構進行滲透。 (Li Zehou 2016c, 361)

Li argues that Chinese modernization passed through three interconnected phases between the mid-nineteenth century and the May 4th movement, a view that endows the modernization process with a significant historical dimension. The first phase, or the so-called Westernization movement (*Yangwu yundong* 洋務運動 or *Ziqiang yundong* 自強運動), which took place approximately in the years from 1861 until 1895, concentrated primarily on modern Western technology and science. The second phase was marked by the so-called Hundred-Days Reform (*Wuxu bianfa* 戊戌變法), which was put into place from June 11 to September 21 1898, and by the Xinhai revolution (*Xinhai geming* 辛亥革命), which ended the Chinese empire in 1911. In this second phase, the focus was shifted onto Western political institutions. Li considers the May 4th Movement, historically known as the New Culture Movement (*Xin wenhua yundong* 新文化運動) and generally seen as the very origin of Chinese Enlightenment, merely as the third phase of Chinese modernization, whose representatives dealt with the transformation of value systems and cultural traditions (Li Zehou 2016c, 334).

In Li's reading, the modernization (or Enlightenment) process had already come to a premature end in the nineteenth century when it was supplanted by the urgent nationalistic priority of saving the country from foreign aggression (*jiuwang* 救亡) (Chong 1999, 120). He declares: "In my view, the Enlightenment suffocated under the weight of saving the nation. This is a historical fact that cannot be changed" (Li Zehou 1996, 568).

Li also sees this as the reason why the history of Chinese modernization—including the necessity of the occurrence of an Enlightenment movement—did not succeed in the first half of the twentieth century and thus had to repeat itself on the threshold of the 1980s. The two preliminary phases ended in a similar way, and the fact that the country's salvation suffocated the Enlightenment (*Jiuwang yadao qimeng* 救亡壓倒啟蒙) became even more visible during the expansive blossoming of the new culture in the scope of the May 4th Movement.

From its very beginning, the movement included patriotic and nationalist elements while simultaneously harshly criticizing or even completely rejecting Chinese tradition, especially the Confucian state doctrine.

Li points out that, despite their apparently conflicting agendas, the two components were actually complementary at the start (see Li Zehou 1996, 568; 2016c: 1–21). He concludes that the enlightenment tradition of the May 4th Movement gradually disintegrated in the turmoil of this period, which required the mobilization of all physical, economic, and intellectual resources in order to resist foreign aggression and preserve the sovereignty of China, while at the same time laying the groundwork for an internal revolution (ibid., 21–39). Socialist centralism prevailed, in that minorities submitted to the majority and the lower strata of society were led by their superiors (ibid.). According to Li, this principle represented a revolutionary heritage, which was founded, promoted, and mediated at great length, until it gained a general social status and became part of the general social awareness (Li Zehou 1996, 568).

Although Li's analysis is widely accepted among contemporary scholars, some historians have questioned as to whether the reason for the Enlightenment's failure is to be attributed solely to the political situation of that time. Liu Huiru 刘慧儒, for instance, argues that the failure of the movement's modernization potential, inter alia in philosophical terms, cannot be attributed chiefly to external factors, given that the May 4th Movement was never an enlightenment movement to begin with. In Liu's view, the "incongruence between 'what is said' and 'what is actually meant'" that was consciously applied by the "New intellectuals" of the May 4th Movement, originated in Confucian pragmatism and was a tried-and-true strategy in the Chinese tradition (Liu Huiru 1993, 48). Their public proclamations repudiating this tradition, which had ostensibly been sentenced to death, were thus actually intended to hinder its transformation. While challenging a previously unquestionable sacred authority was, in itself, a form of enlightenment, the May 4th activists did not make a sufficient effort to establish a generally binding "instance of reason" that could go beyond the declarative level in order to create a truly new discourse. Not surprisingly, this much-lauded cultural reformation movement, which sought primarily to create awareness about the effects and reality of modernity, was considered by many thinkers as incapable of producing a new philosophical approach or system (ibid., 49). Such an approach would not merely require a new methodology that would help it offer new ways of analyzing the past through considering the future, but should also offer a new and creative reflection on reality (Rošker 2016, 27).[64]

The basic elaborations of such a reflection in China began in the 1980s, when a new search for modernity emerged. It seemed that it has unified all three of the phases into a coherent process, albeit with a stronger focus upon the cultural-psychological aspect and a relatively cautious approach to political-economic reforms (ibid.). Both of these major areas are central to Li Zehou's own thought.

With respect to the central issue that defined modern Chinese philosophical discourses, what position to assume towards Western thought, Li inverted the famous slogan "(preserving) Chinese substance and (applying) Western functions," proposing that China should rather "(assume) Western substance and (apply) Chinese functions."[65] We will examine this position in detail in the next section. We can note here that Li's view does not differ essentially from those many thinkers who advocated the appropriation of Western technology and the preservation of Chinese institutions, ideologies, and value systems (Li Zehou 1998, 174–77). The latter, the function, is of immense importance, for it determines the concrete circumstances of people's lives. This led Li, among other initiatives, to modify Lin Yusheng's 林毓生 proposal for the creative transformation of tradition to its transformative creation. Li intends for this reversal to underscore the innovative elements that were autonomously created in this process (Li Zehou 2016c, 380). According to Li, in the context of modernization, China should create its own transformation and not just "creatively transform" (or Sinicize) certain Western elements (Li Zehou 2016, 89). In the context of the transformative process that led from mystical shamanism to historical Confucian culture, Li wants in the same way to highlight the creativeness that was inherent to the Confucian shift (Li Zehou 2015, 4); and to express that such social or cultural shifts are linked to reformation processes and not to revolutionary ones (Li Zehou 2016, 95).

Li understood Lin Yusheng's original phrase to imply that China's tradition should be transformed in accordance with Western paradigms (Chan 2003, 111). For his part, he believed that:

> We must not necessarily imitate and appropriate the already achieved form of the Western model as the object of our aspirations for "transformation." Instead, we should create new forms and models in accordance with the specific conditions of Chinese history and contemporary Chinese reality. . . . The basic emphasis should be on the *creation* of new, and not on the *transformation* of already existing Western forms. *Creation*, of course, is much more difficult than *transformation*, since it implies many more attempts and possible mistakes, with many more necessary changes and urgent corrections. However, I still believe this effort is worthwhile, for it is the only way to discover the model and form that correspond in factual terms to specific Chinese circumstances.
>
> 不一定要以西方現成的模式作為模仿、追求、『轉化』的對象。可以根據中國自己的歷史情況和現實情況創造出一些新的形式、模態來⋯⋯但強調『創造』新形式,而不是『轉化』到西方的既定形式這一基本思路。當然,『創造』比『轉化』會需要更多的嘗試錯誤,需要更多的修補改正,但我以為,付出這些代價是值得的,因為它是在能夠尋找一些最適合中國情況的模態和形式。(Li Zehou 1998, 178)

Li aims to expand a more intelligible theory of Chinese modernization that takes into consideration traditional elements, while simultaneously offering solutions to the more general problems of the globalized post-industrial era, such as those linked to ecology or to new forms of alienation and exploitation. He also emphasizes that he is strongly against cultural relativism (in the sense that all cultures are equal or equally valuable) while he wholeheartedly supports cultural pluralism (Li Zehou 2016b, 6).

From Zhongti Xiyong to Xiti Zhongyong

Li believed that all the above-mentioned modern Chinese streams of thought, especially the radical progressivists and the nationalistic conservatives, were much too dogmatic in their views on what position to assume vis-à-vis Western culture and thought. He dedicated himself to the task of finding a sensible, suitable way of harmonizing past and present, tradition and modernity, China and the West (Rošker 2016b). His synthesis is to be found in the reversed slogan regarding the relation between substance and function.

> From the May 4th Movement on, all the promoters of Westernization, from Yan Fu to Hu Shi and Chen Duxiu, emphasized universality. The conservative nationalists from Zhang Taiyan to Liang Shuming, on the other hand, constantly laid stress on specificities. The former advocated a complete Westernizationbut the others wanted to preserve Chinese substance and apply Western technology (*Zhongti Xiyong*). But the truth can be only found if we eliminate the one-sidedness and the prejudices of each of them. This is precisely what I mean by Western substance and Chinese function (*Xiti Zhongyong*).
>
> 自「五四」以來，西化派從嚴復到胡適、陳獨秀，強調的是普遍性；國粹派從章太炎到梁漱溟強調的是特殊性。一派追求「全盤西化」，一派強調「中體西用」，但只有去掉兩者各自的片面性，真理才能顯露，這也就是「西體中用」。 (Li Zehou 2016c, 364–65)

Li's inversion of the slogan, *Zhongti Xiyong* to *Xiti Zhongyong*, was generally seen either as a provocation (Li Zehou 1998, 168–69) and the expression of a radically anti-traditional, pro-Western stance (Chan

2003, 110–11) or as a confused proposition lacking any theoretical foundation (Lin Daoqun and Li Zhihua 1991, 258–59). His revised slogan was immediately attacked and harshly criticized, indicating that he had touched a sore spot for many contemporary Chinese intellectuals.[66] In my view, these attacks derive from the fact that most twentieth-century intellectuals did not understand this bipolar opposition as a complementary binary category. It is a traditional Chinese model of opposites, with simultaneously correlative dualities, in the sense of idealistic or materialistic dualism, in which the concept of substance clearly predominated over that of function. Logically, this meant that in Li's model China played a subordinate role with respect to the West. But Li never meant to imply anything of the sort. Due to the many criticisms he received, he was forced to explain his intentions repeatedly, and in various ways (see for example Li Zehou 1998, 168–200; Lin Daoqun and Li Zhihua 1991, 258–59; Li Zehou 1990, 252–56).

Li's dictum of *Xiti Zhongyong* is not as antitraditional as Chinese authorities made it out to be. Even in the heady days of the antitraditional fever of the early 1980s, Li never endorsed the fashionable idea of "wholesale Westernization" and consistently made a balanced assessment of Confucianism in his three intellectual histories (Chan 2003, 110–11).

In his most complete elucidation, he begins by defining both oppositional terms, defining *ti* as "body, substance, principle" (*benti* 本體、 *shizhi* 實質、 *yuanze* 原則) and *yong* as "use, function, application" (*yunyong* 運用、 *gongneng* 功能、 *shiyong* 使用).[67] He points out that *Xiti Zhongyong* must be understood within the historical context in which it was first formulated, where it appears as a response both to neoconservative traditionalist currents, as well as to iconoclastic advocates of radical Westernization (Li Zehou 1998, 169). In order to demonstrate the mutability of semantic connotations with respect to the various contextual frameworks in which they appear, he summarizes the changing political contexts of the original slogan, *Zhongti Xiyong*.

When it was first formulated in the mid-nineteenth century, *Zhongti Xiyong* was a progressive expression that was directed against the conservative Confucian government, and only under the administration of Zhang Zhidong 張之洞 (1884–89) did the slogan assume a neoconservative connotation.[68] While the emphasis was originally on "Western function" or the need to apply Western technology and know-how, under Zhang it shifted to "Chinese substance," as a catchword signifying the necessity of preserving the Chinese tradition at all costs. This is the meaning against which Li directed his own modified slogan. At the same time, Li was also criticizing the radically pro-Western currents (*quanpan xihua*) that strove to abandon tradition, which they saw as the main obstacle to Chinese modernization, completely and without room for appeal. Indeed, at first glance, Li's inversion appears essentially as a question of terminology.

> I understand the word "substance" (*ti*) differently from others. In my opinion, it primarily expresses social substance. . . . I have always stressed the fact that social existence represents the substance of society, and that "substance" (*ti*) for me means social existence, which for the most part was not defined by ideology.
>
> 我用的「體」一詞與別人不同，它首先指的是社會本體......我曾經強調社會存在是社會本體，把「體」說成是社會存在，這就主要不是意識形態。(Li Zehou 2002b, 155)

The correct interpretation of the new slogan hinges on the understanding of the concept *ti*, or substance, which the proponents of the original motto viewed as the "substance of tradition," while Li instead saw it in Marxist terms as the material basis of society.

> The main flaw of the (slogan) "Chinese substance and Western applications" is to be found in the assumption that technology is application and not substance. But the exact opposite is true: technology is substance, because technology is connected with social existence, as well as with productive forces and the modes of production.
>
> 中體西用論的最大的錯誤就在於認為科技是用而不是體，其實科技恰恰是體，因為科技理論是與社會存在，與生產力、生產方式聯繫在一起的。(Li Zehou 1996, 253)

Here, we must bear in mind that in Marxism, which is founded on historical materialism, the material base is paramount and absolute. Li tries to attenuate this absoluteness by incorporating many elements of cultural-psychological formation into his version of Marxism. Li sees a return to original Marxism, the "original historical materialism," in order to revive the "constructive aspects" of Marx's philosophy (Li Zehou

1998, 176). By emphasizing the class struggle and revolution, instead of developing a constructive political, economic, and cultural theory, Li believes that Marxism had become essentially destructive, and that the ideational, cultural, and artistic aspects of society could only be developed on a material-technological foundation. This interpretation of *ti* is in accordance with both original Marxism and original Confucianism (ibid., 177). In this regard, Li explains that he understood *Western substance* primarily as modernization, which cannot be equated with Westernization, even though modernization undoubtedly began in the West (ibid., 156). Hence, the concept *yong*, or function understood to be specific and culturally determined mode of production, reproduction, and life styles, assumes a crucial significance for Li, for it defines the concrete circumstances of individuals in society. To illustrate this concept, Li replaces the traditional terms of substance and function with the more contemporary terms *hardware* and *software*.

> Even though the hardware of material life (refrigerators, air-conditioners, televisions, etc.) are in unlimited use throughout the world, the software of human life (economic organization, political systems, customs, behavioral patterns, worldviews, value systems, particularities of thought, etc.) differ with respect to diverse political and cultural traditions.[69]
>
> 因為儘管物質生活上的硬件 (冰箱、空調、電視機等等) 世界通用, 並無國界; 但人們的生活軟件 (經濟組織、政治體制、生活習慣、行為模式、人生態度、價值觀念、思維特徵等等), 卻因不同政治, 文化傳統而不相同。 (Li Zehou 2002b: 383)

Because Li believes that identifying with one's own tradition is a prerequisite for the development of any society or individual, the methods of modernization that correspond to specifically Chinese social conditions (or Chinese function), is fundamental to the future of the Chinese state, society, and culture. Function is immensely important, in fact, it is crucial (Li Zehou 2016c, 379). It is precisely the kind of "transforming creation" that defines the mode of transition towards a modern society, thus making this transition easier and more rational (Li Zehou 2002b, 385).

Li is clearly following the basic principles of materialistic philosophical approaches, on which Marxism is also founded. In his effort to merge Marxism with traditional Chinese philosophy, he was confronted with several problems. Li believes that this new explanation of substance leads back to classical Confucianism as well as to classical Marxism and claims that "[t]he question of how to connect these two 'classics' is the problem I want to elaborate on" (Li Zehou 2016c, 379).

In Li's view, these two discourses could already be linked since they are both materialistic philosophies. He considers the pragmatically oriented Confucian philosophy to be in essence materialistic as it was founded upon the (almost exclusive) treatment of the concrete, material conditions of human life. However, his view of Confucianism as a materialistic system is somehow difficult to substantiate (Li Zehou 1998, 175–77). While it is true that Confucianism (especially in the original teachings) is defined by a pragmatic and very secular philosophy, and that it generally does not deal with issues of metaphysics or transcendent religion, this still does not make it a materialistic philosophy in the ontological sense. In Marxism, materialistic philosophy is based on an absolute materialistic conceptualization of history (denoted as historical materialism). According to this view, material conditions (the particular developmental stages of the means of production) determine the mode of social production (the unification of the productive capacity and the productive relations) or the manner of producing and reproducing the means of human existence. These material conditions essentially and categorically define the development and organization of societies, determining and reflecting a particular society's political structures, ideologies, and ways of thinking. The Confucian classics, on the contrary, never suggest that the means of production condition social development. Rather, they stress the important role of ideational and axiological elements such as rituality, relational ethics, the virtues of humaneness and justice, and the crucial role of education as a basic means of cultivating and improving (inborn) humanity and achieving human progress and development in any society. Likewise, Li Zehou's claim that the neo-Confucianism of the Song and Ming Dynasties is a purely idealistic philosophy is difficult to prove (Li Zehou 2016c, 378). Here, we can also point to the problematic nature of Li Zehou's equation between his own "Philosophy of Eating" (*Chi fan zhexue* 吃飯哲學) and materialistic philosophy, noting that the awareness of the crucial importance of the material and physical conditions of life for human (or any) existence is not sufficient to confirm a materialist worldview (Li Zehou 1998, 142, 176–77).

The problem underlying these conceptualizations is simply a problem of intercultural or comparative philosophy. For example, materialism and idealism are categorizations and demarcations belonging primarily to Western philosophical thought. Therefore, these categorizations cannot be applied as designations of specific Chinese categories, which are grounded upon concepts and paradigms that are more dynamic, changeable, contextual, and relational.

Many scholars believe that Li's model attempts to modify the so-called orthodox Marxist system by expanding the material base and incorporating certain elements that originally belonged to the ideational superstructure without actually defining in concrete terms the scope of this new base (Li and Liu 1999, 331–32; see also Lin and Galikowski 1999, 50).[70] Li's theoretical system—the *ti* and *yong* categories—cannot be equated to the Western base and superstructure even as he tried to underplay the class struggle and the revolutionary imperative in order to make Marxism less destructive and more constructive, and thus more suited to the "pragmatically optimistic" nature of the traditional Chinese (especially Confucian) worldview (Li Zehou 1985, 36–37).

However coherent Li's efforts may appear, it is doubtful whether this synthesis of traditional Chinese thought and early Marxism still corresponds to that worldwide influential theory and one of the leading discourses of the twentieth century known as Marxism. Li's relativization of his Marxist orientation by designating it a return to "original-Marxism" only begs the question (Li Zehou 1998, 176).

As a theoretical system, Marxism is rooted in Hegelian dialectics. But because Hegel's system was established upon ideational foundations, Marx and Engels combined it with Feuerbach's materialistic system and transformed the latter from a contemplative materialism into a more practical and humanistic one.[71] Marxism is thus a theory that applies a materialistic interpretation of historical development and a dialectical view of social transformation. These working theses became the basic instruments for the critique and analysis of capitalism as a phase of dialectical development, in which the concept of class struggle, together with the concept of revolution, play a crucial role. The former concept represents the contradictory negation (of the thesis by its antithesis) and the latter the sublation (*Aufhebung*) that leads to synthesis. Both concepts are crucial elements in the theoretical model of the Marxist dialectics.

In this materialistic developmental model, each stage of society is determined by the contradiction between the class that owns the means of production (technology) and the class that provides the necessary labor. At a certain stage of development, the material productive forces of society come into conflict with the existing relations of production.

This conflict manifests itself in a class struggle, that leads to an era of social revolution, that results in a qualitatively new stage of society. Social change occurs because of a struggle between two different social classes that are in contradiction with each other. In the Marxist dialectical model, the two contradictory classes represent the abstract categories of thesis and antithesis. Like in any other dominant European theoretical model, this abstraction is static and, as such, it cannot be made to conform to any aspect of real life.

This was the issue that most troubled Li in his evaluation of Marxism, even if he never explicitly criticized this aspect of its theory. His criticisms were instead directed against specific elements within the Marxist system (its tendency towards destruction, determinism, and so on) but not against the conceptual framework that defined the theoretical model of Marxist dialectics. His many attempts to incorporate a dynamic component into the system of Marxist dialectic certainly indicate his dissatisfaction with the limitations of this framework.[72] Given that his modifications altered or even eliminated some of the essential elements that define the Marxist model, it is doubtful whether this new system can still be called Marxist, or even Neo-Marxist.[73] It is clearly evident that traditional Western concepts and categories cannot simply be transferred and applied in order to explain Chinese philosophical systems that are based upon completely different referential frameworks.

The complex (and complicated) relation between matter and idea (especially in Western, particularly Marxist discourses), heavily occupies Li Zehou's thought. This was probably the reason because of which Li originally emphasized that his slogan could merely be understood as a reversion of the (abbreviated) phrase "Chinese substance and Western application." It could by no means be connected with the entire original slogan, which reads "Chinese learning for substance (fundamental principles) and Western learning for function (practical application)."

It is the complex relation between matter and idea (in Western, Marxist discourses) that Li's "Chinese substance and Western application" could not be connected with the original, "Chinese learning for substance (fundamental principles) and Western learning for function (practical application). He explains:

> Already in 1986, I pointed out in one of my articles that "learning" (i.e., education, knowledge, culture, ideology) cannot represent a "substance"; "substance" refers to the

"substance of the social existence," namely basic necessities and the everyday life of the people's masses. "Learning" is only thoughts, theories, or ideologies that spring out from this fundamental basis.

> 我在 1986 年的文章中就指出,「學」(學問、知識、文化、意識形態) 不能夠作為「體」。「體」應該指「社會存在的本體」, 即人民大眾的衣食住行、日常生活。「學」不過是在這個根本基礎上生長出來的思想、學說或意識形態。 (Li Zehou 2016c, 376–77)

Regarding the relationship between substance and ideology, Li also writes:

> If I say that substance (ti 體) means social existence, this cannot be reduced to ideology (lit.: it does not comprise only ideologies), it is more than just "learning." Social existence is the social mode of production and everyday life. From the viewpoint of historical materialism, the real substance is the foundation of human existence.

> 把「體」說成是社會存在, 這就不只包括了意識形態, 不只是「學」。社會存在是社會生產方式和日常生活。這是從唯物史觀來看的真正的本體, 是人存在的根據。 (Li Zehou 1987a, 24)

Substance, here equated with social existence includes ideologies (albeit a minor part). Although Li emphasizes that such view is based upon historical materialism, this Marxist discourse differs from his model of how the two regard the relation between matter and idea. According to Marxist historical materialism, social existence pertains to the (material) basis, whereas ideologies (as a part of human consciousness) belong to the ideal superstructure (Marx 1859, 5). The former conditions the latter. Marx clearly writes: "It is not the consciousness of men that determines their existence, but their social existence that determines their consciousness" (ibid.).[74] This means that the superstructure, which includes ideologies, cannot represent an (albeit small) part of the basis that conditions it and is, in this scheme, separated from it. In the Marxist model, the material basis cannot mix with the ideal superstructure, for, in the dualistic logic of dialectics based on the mutually contradictory relation between thesis (matter) and antithesis (idea), these two categories are mutually exclusive.

Li distances himself from any kind of economic determinism. He does not believe that social existence determines social ideologies (in politics and culture), nor does he believe that the establishment of a market economy leads automatically to the establishment of a democratic system. He still believes that a market economy is a necessary condition for the establishment of a democratic system (Li Zehou 2016c, 387).

With his inversion of the slogan, Li tried to attenuate the ultimately mechanistic and deterministic nature of Marxist theory. Proceeding partly from traditional Chinese thought, which is based on a correlative relation between matter and idea (and all the other binary oppositional notions resulting from this basic dichotomy, like subject and object or body and mind), Li understood that such absolute and static distinctions can only be drawn in formal theory, whereas in real life, matter and idea always appear as interconnected and inseparable from each other. Later, Li somewhat revised his earlier exclusion of the notion of "learning (xue 學)" as a part of the "substance (ti 體)."[75]

> Today, however, the productive forces (i.e., the bases of the substance of the social existence) are tightly connected to scientific technology, which is, of course, also a kind of "learning." In the curriculums of contemporary elementary schools, high schools, and universities, mathematics, physics, chemistry, and subjects other than science and technology occupy the most important positions. Are we not spending the greatest part of our time and energy on studying and applying these technologies? Science has already permeated our everyday life and our basic necessities. It has become an indispensable element. In this sense, we can certainly speak about "Western learning as substance."

> 可是今天與生產力 (社會存在本體的基礎) 密切攸關的科學技術，恰恰也是一種「學」，科學。今天，在大、中、小學的課堂上，數理化等科技課程不佔著主要位置嗎? 我們大部分或主要的時間和精力不都花在學習和運用科技上面嗎? 科學已進入現代日常生活和衣食住行之中，成了不可或缺的要素。所以，在這個意義上，說「西學為體」又是可以的。 (Li Zehou 2016c, 393–94)

Hs elaboration of the relation between tradition and modernization, between physically determined social existence and the ideational conditions of social life, becomes much clearer and theoretically much better comprehensible. Li is strongly aware that these dichotomies are dynamic, continuously changeable parts of the complex social and ideational networks, which define contemporary social pluralities. His conviction that "societies are systems of organic structures," emphasizes that in the process of modernization, the understanding of Chinese tradition is of utmost importance (Li Zehou 2016b, 359).

> Modern societies are based on pluralism and include numerous diversities, modern "Western learning" is the same way. Because of this the processes by which they are introduced, imported, and assumed will include certain decisions, selections, corrections, and renovations. "Chinese function" is precisely a product of such decisions, selections, corrections, and renovations. It includes questions of how to adapt and apply it within various particular situations and practical activities. Originally "substance" and "function" cannot be separated; Chinese tradition understands them as a unit, not as two separate things. There can be no "substance" without "function," and "substance" is always contained within "function." Hence, the question about how to "apply" "Western substance" in China is a very difficult and also a very creative one, for it is linked to the process of social evolution. For instance, everyone knows that we must adopt Western "science" and "democracy." But as soon as we try to apply them in China, we immediately stumble upon a range of barriers connected to the transformation of "substance" and "function" that we were not aware of. This is because we have insufficient knowledge about specific Chinese circumstances or tradition.

> 現代社會是一個多元化和多樣化的社會，現代的「西學」亦然。因之，在全面了解、介紹、輸入、引進過程中，自然會發生一個判斷、選擇、修正、改造的問題。在這判斷、選擇、修正、改造中產生了「中用」——即如何適應、運用在中國的各種實際情況和實踐活動中。「實體 (Substance)」與功能即「用」(Function) 本不可分，中國傳統也講「體用不二」：沒有離「用」的「體」，「體」即在「用」中。因此，如何把「西體」「用」到中國，是一個非常艱難的創造性的歷史進程。例如大家都早知道要去取西方的「科學」、「民主」，但在中國用起來，卻由於沒有意識到「體」、「用」轉化的艱難性而遇到了重重阻礙。這就是由於對自己的國情和傳統不夠了解的緣故。 (Li Zehou 2016c, 360)

Following the unorthodox often somewhat headstrong path and very much aware of the problems linked to the creation of intercultural theoretical syntheses, Li began to fashion a new, interculturally consistent theoretical model of social and human development. In creating this model, he drew upon elements from Marxist (or Hegelian) dialectics but remained faithful to aspects of the traditional Chinese correlativity of binary categories, without being identifiable to either. An initial schematic summary of this model is presented in the last chapter.

4

Exploring the Beauty of Humanity

Aesthetics: The Unity of Contradictions, Fusion of Being, and Belonging

Aesthetics is the field were Li Zehou's intellectual contributions to modern and contemporary Chinese philosophy are most visible and were he reached the highest peaks of his intellectual endeavors. In Li's view, aesthetics represents the ultimate realm of philosophical thought and human existence, a realm of genuine freedom and humanity. He believes that aesthetics is "the first (or primary) philosophy" (Li Zehou 2016b, 234).

Li singled out four types or discourses that define his assessments on specifically Chinese aesthetics. He prescribes an elementary importance to the concept of music or joy (*yue* or *le* 樂), which occupies an essential position in Chinese culture. He often points out its "humanizing" or "civilizing influence."

> [Li] finds the roots of the Chinese aesthetic psyche in the nonhedonist but nonetheless strongly sensuous cultural tradition that grew out of primitive totemic ritual and dance. The life-affirming, this-worldly character of the Chinese aesthetic tradition has its basis in this pre-Confucian foundation. (Samei 2010, xi)

Music promotes togetherness, mediates the rhythms of nature to human inwardness, and establishes a sense of harmony. It pours through time and expresses feelings and emotions in the most direct way. This flow of music leads in its linearity to the second central characteristic of Chinese aesthetics, namely, the central role of the "line" in Chinese traditional visual art.[1]

> Correspondingly, the "line" is time unfolded in space. Whether in calligraphy, painting, poetry, prose, sculpture, landscape gardening, or architecture, the flow of emotion-filled time is apparent in the music and evident in the dance of the line moving continuously on paper, cloth, or other objects. This movement produces rhythm and rhyme, figures and scenes, stories, ornaments, themes, and so on, all of which flow and change as they move forward, be it ponderously or with ease. The line is free yet regular, abandoned yet controlled. At once external (sensuous) and internal, it expresses a transcendence that breaks through finitude yet is at the same time contained within this emotionalized time. (Li, Zehou 1994, 57)

Li has also emphasized, reinterpreted, and revived numerous other characteristic features of Chinese aesthetics and art. He studied the crucial roles played by rhythms, flavors, as well as rhymes and other metrical means of expression. Like his general philosophy, Li emphasizes the importance of the fusion of reason and emotion in aesthetics, pointing out that imaginative reality is more important than pure, sensible reality. Artistic and aesthetic expression are contained in the elementary spirit of Chinese philosophy. Aesthetic culture is the ultimate realm of human freedom as well as a domain in which we can understand ourselves and return to the never-ending unification of humans and nature (or heaven).

From a very young age Li had been exceedingly interested in this field. In his later years, he admitted:

> I liked aesthetics even before the beginning of the "Great debate on aesthetics." As early as in the first grade of university, I had started to read books on aesthetics in English by myself. In junior high school, I enjoyed literature; later, I developed an interest in philosophy, and I also liked psychology. In aesthetics, all these fields were united.
>
> 在美學討論之前，我就喜歡美學了。大一就自己讀英文美學書。在初中時就是文藝愛好者，以後，對哲學有興趣，也喜歡心理學，而在美學裡，這三方面結合在一起。 (Li Zehou in Yang Bin 2015, 14)

According to Wu Ji, Li's aesthetic thought can be divided into three periods. In the 1950s (first period) his theory was based upon the materialist aesthetic of reflection (or mirroring). In the 1960s (second period) it was denoted as a practical approach to aesthetics. And in the 1970s and 1980s it was the aesthetics of anthropological ontology (Wu Ji, 2016, 276).

There have been, as we have seen, two very influential movements regarding aesthetics as a philosophical discipline and field of investigation in the People's Republic of China. The first occurred within a few years after the establishment of the new socialist state, the second at the beginning of the 1980s. According to Li, the fundamental difference between these two waves of aesthetic debates was that the first one was guided by governmental ideologists and was thus conducted top-down towards the bottom of society, whereas the second was initiated by the intellectuals and therefore spread from the bottom towards the top (Li Zehou 2008d, 1).

The first debate arose under the label "The Great Debate on Aesthetics" (*Meixue da taolun*) in the 1950s and was conducted under the unquestionable banner of Marxism. It mainly focused on the relation between subjectivity and objectivity, in which Marx's *Economic and Philosophic Manuscripts of 1844* was particularly important, given its relatively detailed elaboration on sensual experiences and alienation. This debate served as part of a broader project of bringing Marxist philosophy to a higher level of attention, comprehension, and application. The main goal of the campaign was to clarify the question of how to unite the Marxist theory of social economy, which was grounded on a material base, with the domain of culture and art, which was part of the superstructure.

The controversies that arose from conflicting interpretations of art, aesthetic feelings, and beauty resulted in what has come to be known as the "Four Currents" (*Si pai* 四派) of aesthetics. The main figures of these schools were Gao Ertai 高爾泰, Cai Yi 蔡儀, Zhu Guangqian 朱光潛, and Li Zehou. While the former two currents (represented by Cai Yi and Gao Ertai) advocated subjectivity and objectivity. The latter two (guided by Zhu Guangqian and Li Zehou) cannot be placed so easily into either of these two, relatively limited epistemological categories. Rather, each in its own way, they aimed to create the possibility of resolution or unification of both oppositional epistemological notions. Li defines their central guidelines in the following way:

1. Gao Ertai's theory of subjectivity (高爾泰的主觀論),[2]

2. Cai Yi's theory of objectivity (蔡儀的客觀論),

3. Zhu Guangqian's theory of the unity of subjectivity and objectivity (朱光潛的主客觀統一論),[3]

4. My own theory of the unity of objectivity and sociality (自己的客觀性和社會性統一論). (Li Zehou 2014k, 1–2)

The second public movement arose in the 1980s under the label "Aesthetic Fever." The younger generation of intellectuals, especially students and young scholars, were quite intimately involved in this second movement, investing in it their most profound, intense, and passionate emotions. This was not a surprise, for the Chinese youth of that period belonged to a generation that was born and raised within the two decades of the immutable and tedious greyness that was omnipresent and prevalent at all levels of society, from politics to art, from fashion to literature and philosophy. This was a generation that had longed for beauty and freedom, for new and challenging experiences, to make their life more intense, more autonomous, and more meaningful.

In this period Li, who had just entered the fifth decade of his life, was standing at the threshold of philosophical maturity. On the one hand, he had already gained deep insight into the complex relations connecting theory and practice, form and content, ethics and politics. On the other, he had not forgotten his own youth with its struggles, dilemmas, fears, and desires. It was also impossible for him to forget the important, provocative, and confrontational essay on aesthetics[4] that he had published back in his twenties, which, due to the many unorthodox and innovative views it comprised, had raised a series of passionate controversies, not only at the time it was published, but even several decades later.[5] All these may have been reasons that made him understand the 1980s generation better than most other scholars of his age. He often stated that he understood and respected their feelings of frustration and dissatisfaction with the state of society, as well as their anger (Li Zehou 2008d, 2). It is even more understandable that he soon became one of the most charismatic role models for the Chinese youth. However, the roots of this charisma were hidden on a much deeper level, namely in the very personality of Li as a young author who had already written an important theoretical essay on aesthetics in his twenties.

Two Wise Old Men and Two Passionate Youngsters

Li Zehou penned the fundamental approaches of his aesthetic theory as early as 1956, when his essay was published in the renowned *Philosophy*

Research.[6] Despite having written it at such a young age, the content was significantly supplemented, reworked, and upgraded during Li's later years, as he outlined his ambitious project of combining and complementing Kant's aesthetics with that of Georg Wilhelm Friedrich Hegel, and especially, with that of early Marx. In this elementary theoretic foundation, we find an exciting summit of four extremely interesting thinkers—three Germans and one Chinese—whose lives were separated by hundreds of years and thousands of miles, but who nevertheless shared similar interests and continuously explored similar questions.

Li's aesthetic thought was strongly influenced by Kant's *Critique of Judgement*, which was the last important work written by this great philosopher having passed away at the beginning of the nineteenth century. He also drew a lot of inspiration from Hegel, who died almost exactly one century before Li's birth and who himself was influenced by Kant's charming ideas about the inherent link between beauty, aesthetic feeling, and freedom. Almost four decades after Kant's and more than a dozen years after Hegel's death, a young 26-year old German intellectual was writing one of his first theoretical works, *Economic and Philosophic Manuscripts from 1844*. In this small book, Marx dealt with questions that were somewhat similar or related to problems that once occupied the minds of his two great compatriots. These were questions of sense-perception, which in his eyes, ought to become "the basis of all science" (Marx 2007, 47).[7]

A little more than a hundred years later, and many thousand miles away, another young man of exactly the same age was enthusiastically reading this early work of Marx and trying to combine it with the ideas of his two aforementioned predecessors, Kant and Hegel. In May 1956 the result of this enthusiastic work, Li's "On Aesthetic Feeling, Beauty and Art," published in *Philosophy Research*, was the first time that an important official Chinese academic journal had published a theory that was based upon the viewpoints of early Marx, which was printed in his *Economic and Philosophic Manuscripts from 1844* (Yang Bin 2015, 19).

Early Marxist thought differs in many ways from mature Marxist theory. Apart from some basic concepts of Marxist political-economic theory, explained in earlier chapters, the most important ideas elaborated in the *Manuscripts* pertained to the scope of epistemology. Marx proceeded from the problem of human estrangement, which he saw as a product of the forced labor that restrains the formation of a direct relationship between the worker and the product of their work (Marx 2007, 30). He sought to elaborate an epistemology of liberation, which could serve as a scientific basis for a theory of human development that would lead us back to the unalienated state of existence and freedom. Half a century before that, Immanuel Kant had already developed the idea that the epistemological realm of ultimate freedom and self-awareness is to be found in the realm of aesthetics (Kant 1987, 46, 185), superseding mere general epistemology. Kant is generally believed to have had the most profound impact of any (Western) theoretician of modern time. It was Kant's philosophy that formed the basis on which the elementary structure of Marxist theoretical system was built, although it was mainly rooted in those developmental directions of Kant's thought that were further elaborated upon and upgraded by Hegel. But Marx never directly mentions Kant's influence. On the contrary, he often explicitly distanced himself from this "idealistic philosopher."[8] With Hegel, the story is different. Marx basically assumed his view of historic materialism from Hegel's model of dialectic development, although he shifted it (via Ludwig Feuerbach) from an idealistic to a materialistic foundation. It is important to note that even Hegel's dialectical method, on which the young Marx built his theoretical system, was actually an extension and elaboration of the method of cognition by "antinomies" that was originally already applied by Kant (Li Zehou 2007, 278).

In his early years, Li was profoundly influenced by Kant, Hegel, and the young Marx. Many of the impacts upon Li that are usually ascribed to Karl Marx were actually drawn through Georgi Plekhanov's interpretation (and, even more importantly, through his elaboration and systematization of Marx's ideas).[9] Plekhanov was the first socialist theoretician to systematically apply the principles of historical materialism to art. For Plekhanov, art was a form of social consciousness that was subordinated to the mechanisms of sociohistorical development. He reinterpreted the origin and the genesis of aesthetic feeling and art in the framework of historical materialism. In Plekhanov's view, a utilitarian attitude to reality precedes the aesthetic relation. Labor precedes beauty and establishes it. Socioeconomic formations are also placed in the foreground (Swiderski 1979, 63) in his aesthetics. While these formations might have later inspired Li to flesh out the Marxist theory by coining his concept of cultural-psychological formation, elements of many of Plekhanov's ideas are clearly visible in Li's first attempts at constructing a modern, materialistic aesthetic theory.

In "On Aesthetic Feeling, Beauty, and Art," Li mentioned all three German thinkers from whom his elaborations were drawn. Early Marx and his *Manuscripts* were certainly given precedence in the essay, but (in contrast to young Marx himself) the young Li acknowledged that his dialectics was based upon the Hegelian model and that his aesthetics was strongly influenced by Kant.

Perhaps the most intriguing ideas that Li introduced in this essay were "duality of aesthetic feeling" (*meigan liangchongxing* 美感兩重性) and "specific features of image-thinking" (*xingxiang siwei tezheng* 形象思維特徵) (Yang Bin 2015, 18). Written in the relatively narrow referential and conceptual framework of the then prevailing Soviet-style Marxist theory,[10] it definitely contains the incipient stages of many crucial ideas that define Li Zehou's theoretical system, including the concept of sedimentation (ibid.).[11] After the essay was published, Li became well known in Chinese philosophical circles as a Chinese pioneer of "practical aesthetics" (ibid., 19). His growing importance among those working on this theory became visible less than a year later, when his elaboration of his discourse on the duality of aesthetic feeling and its connection to the concept of beauty was published in China's prominent official newspaper, the *People's Daily* (*Renmin ribao* 人民日報).[12]

A summary of the essay that follows provides an insight into the essentials of Li Zehou's aesthetics. In its barest form, it contains a lot of elements or building blocks from which his later, much more complex philosophical system was constructed. On the basis of this essay, we shall first try to clarify his central notion of "image-thinking."

The Duality of Aesthetic Feeling and the Primary Role of Its Objective Sociality

The essay opens with the presumption that the basic philosophical questions of aesthetics as science[13] are tightly linked to epistemology.[14] Li argues that aesthetic feeling was precisely the crucial link that connected the two fields or disciplines (Li Zehou 1956, 44). It is the starting point or the crucial approach for analyzing the dialectic of human perception (or comprehension) of beauty. It is also a necessary tool for solving (or clarifying) the question of the relation between subjectivity and objectivity, or between being and consciousness. In the first part of the essay, it becomes clear that Li was approaching the subject from Kant's aesthetics and that he tries to connect it with Marxist materialism. Although Kant was an idealist philosopher, he was dealing with the concept of aesthetics important for the development of Li's interpretation of aesthetics, which he aimed to combine with early Marx.

For this purpose, and in order to save the political correctness of the notion of aesthetic feeling, Li had to clarify that mental or spiritual phenomena can, in spite of their abstract or ideal nature, still be elaborated upon by materialist philosophies. He questions Zhu Guangqian's self-criticism, into which this important modern Chinese aesthetician was forced after the establishment of Communist rule. Li's disapproval did not come from a radical leftist (or radical materialist) angle but rather a result of a different consideration.

In his self-critique, Zhu admits that in his earlier works his research into aesthetic feeling concealed the fact that literature and art belong to the superstructure and that they reflect reality. His research was an "ideological expression of idealism" (Li Zehou 1956, 44). Although he agrees, Li points out that Zhu went too far in his self-criticism. In his eagerness to rehabilitate himself, he lumped together everything he had written before and negated it in an overgeneralized way. He reduces any kinds of explorations of the concept of aesthetic feeling to idealist ideologies. In Li's eyes, the problem of aesthetic feeling still (even in the materialistic theory of perception) remained a very important question and one that undoubtedly deserved attention. According to Li, Zhu raised the right question but he raised it in the wrong way, because aesthetic feeling must not necessarily be viewed solely as something pertaining to subjective individual mental activities (ibid.). Since Zhu reduced it to this individual realm, he necessarily limited his investigation into aesthetic feeling. While the problem was by no means wrong, what was wrong was Zhu's previous approach towards investigating the concept. In other words, what was wrong was his idealistic methodology. To illustrate, Li notes that both materialists as well as idealists can equally raise the question of the relation between consciousness and existence but the results they obtain will be different or even in mutual opposition. The idealists have, in Li's view, manipulated Kant's notion of aesthetic feeling that transcends utilitarianism and any direct purposes.

> This characteristic of the aesthetic feeling was first discovered and proposed by Kant. Later on, numerous idealists caught it with a strong grip and began to write many articles in which they misrepresented its reality in a distorted way.
>
> 美感的這種性質和特色是由康德發現和提出的，以後許多唯心主義者就盡量抓住這一點，大作其歪曲事實的文章。 (ibid., 45)

The idealists treated the experience of aesthetic feeling as a purely individual issue. The materialists, however, connected it with society and culture. Li emphasizes that we can understand aesthetic feeling as an objective and necessary product of our social, educational, and cultural environments if we examine it in a scientific way (ibid.).

Here, Li elaborates on a quite important differentiation in the notions of materialism and idealism. In China, because of the profoundly different traditional ideational background, these notions were somewhat difficult to understand. He shows very clearly that it is not the problem or the content we investigate that defines our approach (or the question of whether this approach is idealistic or materialistic). Through the concept of aesthetic feeling (or of the experience of aesthetic feeling), he shows that difference between these two philosophical (or epistemological) currents lies in their respective methodologies, or in the referential framework[15] within which a concept is explored.[16]

Li then proceeds to the duality of aesthetic feeling. He starts by recalling that Marxism always deals with contradictions in a dialectic way. In a Marxist framework, the dual contradiction of the experience of aesthetic feeling *is* the basic contradiction of aesthetics. The danger and the unscientific nature of idealism manifest themselves in that they treat aesthetic feeling as an isolated phenomenon instead of seeing it as a unity of dual contradictions. To clarify the origin of this concept, he points to the relational nature of reality and consequently, of our recognizing and comprehending this reality. This leads him to Hegel's *Shorter Logic*,[17] in which the German philosopher emphasizes that we cannot separate the existential reflections of phenomena and things in themselves (ibid., 46).[18] Li holds that aesthetic feeling consists of two parts in mutual contradiction. The first is made up of individual mental activities that are of a subjective and intuitive nature (a product of individual's subjective direct perception) (*zhijue* 直覺), while the second part involves social life, which is of a general and objective nature. To Li, this is the basic contradiction of aesthetics. After safely positing this contradictive distinction within aesthetic feeling, which manifests itself in the difference between subjective intuitivism and objective utilitarianism, he tries to construct a bridge leading to the unification of both mutually contradictory parts, pointing out their mutual interdependency and inseparability in order to resolve their contradiction (ibid., 45). His solution differs from Hegel's *Aufhebung*, which is followed by a synthesis, a unity of harmonization in which both parts continue to exist and constantly exchange with each other in mutually fruitful opposition. In his redefinition of the duality of aesthetic feeling, Li has—probably unconsciously—applied the traditional Chinese principle of correlative complementarity. An analysis and interpretation of this part of the text and its theoretical solution can be found in the following chapter on Li's theoretical system.

For Li, the objective and social nature of aesthetic feeling is the primary, most important part of its inherent contradiction (ibid. 49). The same holds true for intuition. At its basic, most superficial level, intuition is an act of direct perception completely without purpose, this primitive and purely sensual form of intuition has nothing to do with aesthetic feeling (ibid., 48). At a higher level, this direct perception is merged with aesthetic feeling into aesthetic intuition, which is in essence (in contrast with the pure intuition) social and is linked to education, socialization, and cultivation.

> While the research on common intuition belongs to the fields of physiological or psychological sciences . . . aesthetic intuition is much more highly developed and much more complex. It is not simply a biological or psychological concept, but rather a symbol of the developmental history of mankind and of individual cultivation, respectively.
>
> 如果說,一般的直覺的研究主要還屬於生理科學心理科學的範圍,那麼......美感直覺比這種直覺是遠為高級複雜的東西。它不是簡單的生理學或心理學上的概念,而是人類文化發展歷史和個人文化修養的精神標誌。 (ibid., 48)

He concludes that it is significant to see the deeper but more important, primary part of aesthetic feeling's dual nature in order to comprehend that "aesthetic feeling objectively and necessarily encompasses social utilitarianism (美感是有客觀必然的社會功利性的)" (ibid., 52).

It is no different from science or logical thought. All of these serve humanity, since they reveal the necessary connections between things by disclosing their relational essence. Aesthetic feeling also has specific features that distinguish it from science or logic, features seen in its intuitive quality, which is an essential part of the aesthetic feeling. Without it, there would be no qualitative difference between aesthetic feeling and other epistemological modes of comprehension. This is why in Li's view the duality of aesthetic feeling is a unified entity and why it is wrong and dangerous to ignore or neglect any part of it.

The fact that beauty exists objectively is an important reason to hold that aesthetic feeling objectively and necessarily encompasses social utilitarianism. It does not depend on our subjective consciousness. It is beauty that determines and defines aesthetic feeling and not vice-versa (ibid., 55). Li emphasizes that this objective nature of beauty cannot be seen as an inherent quality of objects because the criteria for such inherent qualities are still created by humans. They are usually seen as being derived from a higher, supernatural, metaphysical order.[19] This opinion is therefore also based upon an old, outdated idealist worldview, even though according to it, beauty could also exist independently from human consciousness and thus be objective.[20] This distinction is important, because as we have seen, the majority of Chinese theoreticians of that time (and the theoretical shortcuts they created) were accustomed to assuming that every type of objectivism was automatically materialistic and that every form of subjectivism was necessarily idealistic. Even the hard-core objectivists like Cai Yi, could not be counted among the genuine, metaphysical, outdated, materialists.

In this first controversy Li, rejects not only Gao Ertai's subjectivism, but also Cai Yi's objectivism. Zhu Qianzhi's dialectic view also lacks some important and essential elements and could not be seen as a sensible contribution to the further development of aesthetics as a part of the socially-determined, historical-materialistic framework. Li is critical of Zhu's shift to subjectivity for the origin of beauty as he tries to develop an aesthetics that assimilates early- and later-Marxist positions with his own view of the subject-object relationship (Man 2001, 51).

Li holds that the only method that could solve the problem of the objective existence of beauty was dialectical materialism (ibid., 57). Beauty is objective because it does not depend on individual consciousness and is not rooted in some metaphysical supernatural order. It is a quality of humankind. Li compares it with relations of production. Beauty in Li's eyes is a general, collective matter, created by and through socialization. Li draws our attention in this essay to the early Marxist concept of the humanization of nature and explains that beauty can only arise when humans recognize in nature. According to early Marx, the objectivization of themselves, is the richness of their own essence and is possible only through the humanization of nature. To emphasize the social, collective component of this process, Li uses the phrase "socialization of nature" instead of "humanization" (ibid., 57). Li exemplifies this by comparing a landscape painting of a certain natural scene on the one hand, and a scientific diagrammatic sketch of the same scene. Although they depict the same environment, the painting induces an aesthetic feeling in observers, while the diagram does not. Although the application of certain generally acknowledged principles is visible in both. The reason for this difference lies in the fact that the painting reflects or expresses sociality, while the diagram is merely a reflection of some features of the nature being depicted. The sociality of beauty therefore objectively exists. It is dependent on human society, but not on an individual human mind: "Beauty is a category of social existence and not one of social consciousness. That which belongs to the latter category is aesthetic feeling and not beauty" (ibid., 58).

Beauty and Image

The social nature of beauty is also the reason people can enjoy the beauty of nature and experience pleasure by observing it. Human beings can transfer their own feelings onto an object, with the result that in this natural object they can directly recognize the alienation of their own essential power and the social nature of beauty. The beauty of nature is, in fact, nothing more than a distinct form of the beauty of social life (or the beauty of reality). The nature of beauty is objective and social. Beauty is determined by objective sociality (*keguande shehuixing* 客觀的社會性). Beauty is the objective foundation and the reason for the transfer of feelings, which, are also social phenomena (and by no means an inborn subjective mental ability). This objective and social nature of beauty manifests itself in its infinite, limitless contents that are related to and connected with each other. Li's view of objective social existence is essentially relational and structural. Beauty as a social phenomenon simply has to be objective since social beings are defined by structures of mutual relationships that are not directly a part of their awareness and emotions. It is "physically intangible and imperceptible but objectively existent" (Liu Kang 2000, 129). In some aspects, this understanding of objective social existence as a dynamic and reciprocal structure, is similar with the theory of Louis Althusser. Althusser views history as a structural totality, as an objective external cause, which bears a certain resemblance to Li's understanding of social being as objective existence. Liu Kang emphasizes that there was no actual contact between the two theoreticians at the time they both reflected on these questions, even though Althusser had read Mao's work and had great interest in Chinese Marxist cultural theory (ibid.). Besides, Althusser became known in China only in the 1980s.

To the young Li, the beauty he saw was a living image, a figurative expression of being that bears in itself the most complex levels of sociality and reveals the meaning of human existence (ibid., 60). Because such images or figures are concrete, they are rooted in natural characteristics of the object they depict or reflect. Li emphasizes that although the inherent properties of things are not the absolute criteria for determining beauty (as the idealists propose), they are still often a very important condition for the construction of beauty (ibid., 61).

Beauty divulges the meaning of life. It can also be seen as an image of truth. Li recalls Hegel's understanding of the notion "idea" that also expresses a form of beauty resulting from direct images or figures derived from the sense organs. To fulfill the essential requirements of historical materialism, Li proposes replacing Hegel's term "idea" with the notion "the essence of social life." He also highlights an important additional difference between his own and Hegel's understanding of beauty. Hegel's idea belongs to the realm of transcendent substance, whereas Li's essence of social life is concrete and rooted in human existence (ibid., 60). In fact, it is life itself and therefore it cannot exist separately from life, let alone transcend it.

It follows from the previous that the nature of beauty is not only social and objective, but also concrete and figurative. This second specific feature of beauty, namely, its concrete figurativeness (*jutide xingxiangxing* 具體的形象性) in the sense that it exists through concrete images, implies that it manifests itself in limited and finite forms.[21] They can be both social and natural. Both aspects of beauty (objective sociality, which is endless, and concrete figurativeness, which is terminable) form a basic contradiction inherent within the comprehensive whole of beauty. While they reflect the duality of aesthetic feeling. At the same time they "establish the central artistic link between the figurativeness (or image-nature) of art and its typical representations."[22]

To Li the endless, unlimited social content of beauty is a primary and dominant aspect of the opposition for it cannot be fully expressed or reflected by the limited and transitive form of images (or of the pure figurativeness). Similarly, artistic beauty is only a reflection or mimicry of the beauty of reality. In exquisite art both aspects of the contradiction—its form and its content—are united in the entireness of beauty. Investigating the beauty of reality involves investigations into the problems of artistic beauty (ibid., 62). These investigations and "analyses of art should always proceed from figurativeness (from the image-nature) and from the aesthetic feelings it evokes (ibid., 72). In spite of its limited and concrete nature, art is namely the synthesis of the dialectical development of beauty and aesthetic feeling, for Li concludes: "Beauty is the negation of the aesthetic feeling, and art is the negation of negation (ibid., 62)."

Li's first important theoretical article already contains most of his unique and innovative ideas, even though merely in rudimentary form. In the gradual later process of his personal and intellectual maturation, he certainly essentially systematized, expanded, deepened, and completed these first sprouts of his philosophical and aesthetic thought. Some of the notions that appear here in this emergent thought were later renamed, because the original term was too dubious or too limited to express Li's particular idea. In my opinion, this is also the case with his notion of "image-thinking" (*xingxiang siwei*), because in a certain sense it can be interpreted as an early form of his later idea of emotion-based substance with which we are already familiar from earlier sections of this book.[23]

In the essay, Li proceeded from the presumption that image is the central issue of art, because without images, there would be no art. The social nature of beauty, on the other hand, necessarily requires a typification or exemplification (*dianxinghua* 典型化) of images (ibid., 64). The problem of typicality can in turn only be treated adequately through image-thinking.

> The basic aesthetic question of art is about the relation between art and reality. The concrete manifestation of this question is the problem of artistic images and artistic typicality, because art reflects reality through images and types. In artistic creation, this question is expressed through image-thinking, because it is precisely this kind of thinking through which art creates images and types and through which it reflects reality.
>
> 藝術的根本美學問題是藝術與現實的關係問題。這一問題的具體化，就是藝術形象與典型的問題，因為藝術是通過形象和典型來反映現實的。這一問題表現在創作力，就是形象思維的問題，因為藝術是通過形象思維來創造形象和典型，從而去反映現實的。(ibid., 62)

The very idea of image or image-thinking gained even more popularity in the aesthetic debates of the 1960s. In these discussions, the focus shifted from the question of the essence of beauty to image-thinking. In the fifth issue of the 1966 volume of the official journal "Red Flag" (*Hongqi* 紅旗), the concept of image-thinking was criticized as being an idealistic notion that stands in sharp opposition to the Marxist epistemology. No one (including Li) dared to further elaborate on this concept until after the Cultural Revolution when times loosened up again. On December 31, 1977, the *People's Daily* printed a letter on literature written by Mao Zedong to his old friend Chen Yi, in which the idea of image-thinking was mentioned and praised (Gao Jianping in Zhao Shilin 2012, 212). This was an official sign that the debate on image-thinking could be carried on. Immediately after, most of the aestheticians, including Li Zehou, Zhu Guangqian, and Cai Yi, grasped at the opportunity to elaborate upon the topic at length.[24] It was during these years that Li Zehou wrote the following important advice for the researchers involved in this discussion.

> Let us proceed from image to image; we shall not part from the images, but at the same time, however, we shall fully preserve all our emotions. Staying with images and simultaneously being filled with emotions is a profound refinement of the images as such.
>
> 從形像到形象，不脫離形象，但是充滿著情感，不脫離形象，是形象本身的一種提煉。 (Li Zehou in ibid.)

In the following years, the focus of the aesthetic debates shifted once again from image-thinking back to questions linked to the essence of beauty. This important shift, however, is already a subject belonging to the wild years of the "aesthetic fever."

Aesthetic Fever of the 1980s

The era that began with China's opening to the foreign world and domestic economic liberalization was simultaneously an era of new reflections of the Chinese intellectual tradition. It was a period of critical evaluation regarding the prevailing currents of Euro-American thought. These ideas were reflected in the field where seeds of contemporary ideologies were created. Aesthetics functioned as a concealed, latent, and subtle rebellion against the dominant, ideologically determined social rationality, and simultaneously it served as an unequivocal formula that articulated the endeavor for beauty in the sense of emotional liberation. Aesthetics and beauty should be alternatively rehabilitated and dealienated. They should no more be forced to serve exclusively ideology like before. The Maoist government instrumentalized and politicized the aesthetic, ignoring and even eradicating its function as an affective and subjective realm of culture. Its essential nature of freedom was neglected in discourses of hegemonic power, which caused a dispersion of its values (Liu, Kang 1992, 116). In addition, it assisted the intellectuals as a discourse tightly linked to the politics and to the possibility of reinterpretation or elaboration of Marxist theories (Sernelj 2010, 91).

One of Li's most influential contributions to the Aesthetic Fever was his article "The Subject and the Scope of Aesthetics" (*Meixuede duixiang yu fanwei* 美學的對象與範圍), which was published in 1980 at the threshold of new debates on aestheticism (Yu Chuanqin 2016, 249). He points out that contemporary aesthetics was an amalgamation of the philosophy of art, aesthetic psychology, and the sociology of art. In fact, this was already an important pillar of his aesthetic theoretical system, with which he made an imperative imprint on the aesthetic consciousness of the contemporary Chinese intelligentsia.

> At that time, this article greatly broadened the common perspective. It eliminated the long-lasting prejudice that has led people to reduce aesthetics only to the narrow field of the philosophy of art. Thus, it played an immensely important and catalytic role in boosting the movement of the Aesthetic Fever.

> 在當時，他的這篇文章極大地開闊了人們的視野，打破了長期以來人們把美學僅僅局限於美的哲學的觀念，也打破了我國美學界僅僅討論美的本質問題的局限，對80 年代那場影響廣泛的美學熱起了很大的推動作用。(ibid.)

Li's central book on aesthetics, *The Path of Beauty*, published in 1982 came out as a kind of manifesto for the aesthetic fever that burst out in the beginning of the 1980s. His *Critique of Critical Philosophy* (1979), is a significant prelude to the movement. It became clear that the rebirth of modern Chinese aesthetic thought was firmly grounded not only in the Soviet theories of orthodox Marxism, nor in classical

Chinese philosophies, but also in the philosophies of German Idealism, and especially in the epistemology and aesthetics of its most important predecessor and pioneer, Immanuel Kant.

The Aesthetic Fever movement came into life soon after the end of the Cultural Revolution and lasted for approximately five years. Chinese intellectuals, in particular students and scholars as well as some of the ordinary, not highly educated people, became deeply interested in aesthetics. "Courses in aesthetics were in demand at schools and universities, even engineering schools. Public lectures attracted thousands of students and even common workers" (Li and Cauvel 2006, 22). Various printed collections and other works on aesthetics became bestsellers. They could be found in the bookstore departments that were reserved for books from the field of philosophy and humanities. At the same time, one could hardly find any books on epistemology, ethics, or political philosophy on those shelves (ibid.). Zhou Xiaoyi writes that numerous academic works from the West not regarded as belonging to the gambit of aesthetics (for instance, studies of semiotics) were published in China as works of aesthetics. Roland Barthes's *The Elements of Semiology* (1964), for example, was published in Chinese translation as *Fuhaoxue meixue* 符號學美學 (*Aesthetics of Semiotics*). Zhou remarks that "[a]t that time, this general aestheticizing tendency turned into a vogue among academics, and aesthetics became the leading discipline of humanities" (ibid.).

This controversy regarding the nature, function, and significance of aesthetics arose as a part of (or a prelude to) the broader, more general "cultural fever,"[25] that spread among Chinese intellectuals in the mid-eighties and lasted until the June 4th tragedy.[26]

In the political sense, this new aesthetic movement resulted from the intense desire for a return to a classical, more humanistic Marxist theory and consequently, from the questioning of certain omnipresent, but hitherto taboo, social phenomena like that of the "socialist alienation" (Wang, Jing 1996, 12). People revitalized the repressed memory of the early history of Marxism and they recalled the humanist epistemology of the young Marx. Immediately after the downfall of ultra-leftism, they longed for a rehabilitation, not simply a rehabilitation of the so-called individual victims of the Revolution, but also of young Marx himself. They wanted to revive the philosophical Marx, who remained buried in a historical past and whose outcry against estrangement now provided disheartened Party ideologists a new possibility to reinvent Chinese Marxism (ibid., 10).

The question of the "socialist alienation" was raised together (or in a broader context) with the question of "socialist humanism." These intellectual movements came into life a few years after the so-called Discussion of the Criteria of Truth (*Zhenli biaozhun da taolun* 真理標準大討論), which took place in 1978, marking an initial step in the emancipation of independent and critical individual thought. The debates on humanism and alienation took place from 1980–84 and were mainly triggered by questions such as whether human nature (humanness, *xing*) has an independent existence outside the class nature of human beings. Whether alienation exists in socialist society. And, how humanism and the theory of alienation should be related in Marxism (Lin, Rosemont, Ames 1995, 732). This rebirth of humanism (in reminiscence of the traditional Confucian notion of *ren* or humaneness), was most passionately proclaimed by Wang Ruoshui 王若水, who yearned for a new form of "Marxist Humanism." The main ideas of his well-known article "In Defense of Humanism" (*Wei rendaozhuyi bianhu* 為人道主義辯護), are based on the conviction that every individual human being and their life *is* the ultimate goal. The most profound significance and the highest essence of humanity. The highest value people can embrace is humaneness, freedom, and self-fulfillment. Wang opens "In Defense of Humanism" with a powerful paraphrase of the famous beginning of Marx's Communist Manifesto: "A specter stalks among the intellectuals of China—the specter of humanism" (Wang Ruoshui 1986, 217). He believes that the personal cult of Mao Zedong was a form of alienation (ibid., 190), which had to be surpassed and overcome if the Chinese people wanted to discover their inner and outer freedom and the genuine meaning of their life.

Li did not agree with Wang's critique, claiming that it was much too superficial and that it manipulated people's emotions. Even though the authorities requested from him twice to write an official critique of Wang's "politically uncomfortable" essays, he consistently firmly rejected these requests (Yang Bin 2015, 83).

The Aesthetic Fever of the 1980s—also often called the "aesthetic craze"—was made possible by the political thaw after the detention of the so-called Gang of Four. After a decade of disaster and chaos, which occurred due to radical Maoist policies, the Chinese government under the leadership of the Communist party gradually turned away from ideological slogans such as class struggle and introduced the fairly consequential slogan: "Practice is the only criterion for finding truth" (*Shijian shi jianyan zhenlide weiyi biaozhun* 實踐是檢驗真理的唯一標準). A short while later the slogan became popular in an abbreviated form as Deng Xiaoping's famous slogan "Seeking the truth in the facts" (*Shishi qiushi* 實事求是).[27] Here, Li Zehou's central notion of practice added much innovativeness to this new explorative atmosphere in the field of aesthetics. His creation of many other notions—sedimentation, cultural-psychological formation, proper measure—significantly enriched the aesthetic debate of this time (Pohl 2009, 95).[28]

This striving for individual and social emancipation and autonomy, which had, as Li Zehou often pointed out, the characteristics of a new Enlightenment movement, also manifested itself in the debates on aesthetics, although in a slightly different discourse. Besides Li and theoreticians Zhu Guangqian, Cai Yi, and Gao Ertai, who together represented the four most influential streams within aesthetic thought, others like Zong Baihua 宗白華, Liu Gangji 劉綱紀, Ye Lang 葉朗, Min Ze 敏澤 and Li's former student, Gao Jianping 高建平, also entered the debate. Li, who is "widely recognized as being one of the most important thinkers in the post-Mao China," was definitely "the leader of the Chinese Enlightenment of the 1980s" (Chong in Li and Cauvel 2006, 12). Karl Heinz Pohl deemed him "the towering figure of this period" (Pohl 2009, 94). His role in this crucial period has yet to be fully accessed and evaluated but one thing is already very clear, his writings will "figure prominently in any account of the intellectual life of that time, in view of their tremendous impact" (Chong 1999a, 200). Most Chinese scholars also believe that in that period Li was a theoretician with the "highest and deepest insight," and that he was the "most systematic and by far most influential" of all Chinese scholars who shaped this important transitional period (see Xu Youyu, in Zhao Shilin 2012, 207). Li describes the characteristic features of this intellectual movement.

> The Aesthetic Fever arose during this period of ideological liberation, a time free of the ideological constraints that had controlled the Chinese people for four decades and a time when different theories and opinions were debated. These serious scholarly debates were ones in which resolutions were always open to renewed challenges. In contrast to the sensitive political, ethical, and social ideas at that special time, issues of aesthetics were safe to debate; to gain new perspectives, scholars began studying the traditional Chinese scholarship that preceded the 1949 revolution. (Li and Cauvel 2006, 23)

On a popular level, especially among the Chinese youth, there was a clear sense of liberation from the restrictions of revolutionary asceticism: "They explored new ways of decorating their homes, coloring and cutting hair, and trying various fashions of dress" (Li and Cauvel 2006, 23). Scholars began to focus upon the Chinese art theory and tried to systemize it. This led several theoreticians to lay out a concise groundwork for the well-organized establishment of transparent and well-ordered classical Chinese aesthetic thought. Meanwhile there was a demand for history books on Chinese aesthetics written not only by Li Zehou, but also by Liu Gangji, Ye Lang, Min Ze, and others. Although in these works, there were still traces of theoretical and ideational appropriation, one could clearly sense a new view of their contents and modes of arguments. These discourses implied a clear semantic transfer and a conceptual shift in Chinese aesthetics. They were all embedded in Chinese traditional thought and they described and explained the history of Chinese aesthetics and its uniqueness (Wang, Keping 2006, 119).

One of the main slogans in the forefront of these discussions was the "aesthetization of the everyday life," which was based upon an originally Western, but subsequently Sinicized concept. Such an aesthetization was understood as a form of emancipation, as an everyday space of freedom, a space that cannot be intruded upon by official politics with its principles of ideological functionality. This emancipation was rooted in a rebellion against the world of a strict political hierarchy and unconditional authority within it.

A subjective negation of politics that represent the core of the Aesthetic Fever from the 1980s was in fact completely charged with the political character of civil society. The apparent ivory tower of aesthetics was constructed in the very core of politics. These controversies did not deal with hierarchic power relations or with the questioning of the *a priori* unquestionable authorities, but with politics in the original meaning of the term—with a politics of human being as an *a priori* political creature (*Zoon politikon*). The Aesthetic Fever that dominated China in the 1980s originated from the tendency to realize such subjective political freedom. However, the reality of the June 4th tragedy and especially the reality of the explosive changes in Chinese society and its economic liberalization soon surpassed all such ideals, which sadly drowned in the floods of the new, commercialized aesthetics that characterizes all globalized capitalistic societies. It became clear that the theories that were flourishing at the time of Aesthetic Fever were no longer appropriate for the conditions of increasingly rapidly changing Chinese social reality. By the end of the 1980s, the role of aesthetics in China had transformed. During this period, aesthetics as an academic discipline quickly (and for many people unexpectedly) lost its revolutionary and emancipatory function. By the middle of the 1990s, only a few years after the "fever," aesthetics discourses (as something defining the central scopes of public interest) and aesthetics as an academic discipline sharply decreased in public as well as theoretical circles. By the end of the millennia, it was reduced to a marginal scope of studies that were dealing only with theoretical problems in the ivory tower at the margins of Chinese social reality (Sernelj 2010, 98–99). Gao Jianping denotes this period as the age of the "Aesthetic Cold" (ibid.). Even though in the 1980s, aesthetics was hot in China, it cooled down shortly afterwards. Gao remembers the experience of the "aesthetic cold." No one read books on aesthetics, and no bookstores sold them. The authors who wrote these books were unable to find readership. In 1997, Gao went to the Taofen center of the Sanlien publishing house. There, all he could find were two books on aesthetics, both written by Zhu Di. "One of them was *Contemporary Western Aesthetics* and the other was *Contemporary Western Philosophy of Art*. There was not one other book on aesthetics" (Gao Jianping 2014, 15).

Nevertheless, Gao trusts that there is currently a recovery and a new development of aesthetics in China. He believes that "from 1998 to the present, we have been witnessing new signs of the revival of aesthetics, or the 'Renaissance of Aesthetics (*Meixuede fuxing* 美學的復興),'" which is much less burdened by politics than the first and the second period of aesthetic debates (Gao, Jianping 2006, 110–12; 2014, 15). If this is true, then this new Renaissance of Chinese twenty-first century aesthetics already has a substantial base to rely on. Li Zehou's contributions to this field will doubtlessly remain an important, fundamental, and continuously challenging part of the intellectual heritage of twentieth-century Chinese aesthetics.

This heritage is a result of Li's long-lasting hard and conscientious work, which he has often carried out under almost unbearable conditions. Li reached the first peak of his theoretical development immediately after the Cultural Revolution. During the turbulent phase of this social chaos Li did not publish any serious theoretical work (which was then impossible), but he worked secretly and continuously on the two books that came out immediately after the pandemonium subsided. In these first years after 1976—the period that already felt like a prologue to the Aesthetic Fever—he published some of his most important essays and articles, in which he either delineated or additionally explained his theoretical system that comprise his most important books.

In this period, and during many years that followed, he upgraded and often remarkably modified the concepts he was applying in his twenties. He successfully combined two important Western thinkers and essentially enriched them by incorporating into them crucial aspects or paradigms of classical Chinese thought. Last, while following this innovative path of combinations, he created some of his own unique concepts. Let us take a closer look at the process of his intellectual progress through the lens of his own transformative creation.

Refinement, Systematization, and Development of Concepts

During the period of the aesthetic fever, Li was already a very mature thinker—the views, opinions and hypotheses he proclaimed were obviously derived from a very complex and comprehensible theoretical system.

The process of his theoretical ripening becomes visible if we compare his first theoretical essays from the mid-1950s with his later works on the same topic published two or three decades later.[29] Tu Wei-ming describes this process by pointing out that the framework of Li's thought was constructed very early, when he was still very young (Zhao Shilin 2012, 205). Through a process of transformative creation, he consciously revised and reconstructed it by taking into account the criticism of other people, as well as its own academic development. Tu emphasizes that this is very rare in Chinese philosophical circles.

Here we will delineate Li's intellectual development through the lens of some central concepts that are characteristic of his philosophy. We have already introduced his central philosophical, anthropological, or psychological concepts that constitute the essential framework of his aesthetic thought. Some of them were already present in his early works, even though in sprouting form. One concept is sedimentation, which was not yet clearly defined or directly formulated in *On Aesthetic Feeling, Beauty, and Art*. One senses in several passages, that Li was at that time already thinking about the processes and functions of mental layering, although he had not yet found a suitable term to describe such processes and to define its principles and laws. Already at that time, he was borrowing from geological terminology and comparing the historical development of people's social and cultural life with the gradual layering of silt that accumulates along riverbanks.

Therefore, social life is like a long river. Slowly and endlessly it flows towards new depths and vast, faraway places. It is always moving and ever-changing. Yet, tracing it to its very source, we see that its nature is to irrigate life. And in its endless changing there are also motionless and accumulations of firm forms and standards.

所以，社會生活是一條長河，它滔滔不絕地流向更深更大的遠方，它是變動的；但是，追本溯源，生活又有著它的續承性，變中逐漸積緊著不變的規範、准規。 (Li Zehou 1956, 71)

In his *Critique* on Kant's epistemology, which Li finished in an earthquake tent in 1976, the concept of sedimentation is already clearly explained and distinguished from mere internalization.

Time and space are not concepts. Reason also differs from the pure passive sensitivity by which we perceive, for instance, colors, tastes, scents, or temperatures. In such sensual intuition, there are sedimentations of social reason. Hence, for the individual, they seem to belong to the *a priori* forms of perception without any origin. However, from the viewpoint of all of humankind, they are still the results of social practice. These results cannot be reduced to formal logic, which is only an "internalization" of operating activities and which transforms practical external activities to inner rational structures; in addition, they are sedimentations, accumulated deposits of social rationality in sensual perception.

時空不是概念、理性，也不同於被動的純感覺如色味香暖之類，而在於這種感性直觀中積澱有社會理性，因之對個體來說，它們似乎是先驗的直觀形式，無所由來；然而從人類整體說，他們仍然是社會實踐的成果。這種成果便不同於如形式邏輯那樣，只是操作活動的「內化」，即外在實踐活動轉化為內在理性結構，而更是積澱，即社會理性積累沉澱在感性知覺中。 (Li Zehou 2007, 115–16)

As mentioned earlier, it is plausible to believe that the young Li Zehou's interpretation of the (originally Russian) concept of image-thinking (*xingxiang siwei*) was—at least to a certain degree—an early form of his notion of emotion-based substance. After his first description of his view of this concept, which he published in the essay "On the Aesthetic Feeling,

Beauty and Art," he wrote an even clearer explanation of it in "On Image-Thinking" (*Shilun xingxiang siwei* 試論形象思維) published in 1959.[30] In "On Image-Thinking," Li was combatting the manifold prejudices directed against the concept, mostly by people who did not really understand it and who tried to shove it into the narrow framework of direct perception, too insignificant to be considered by serious materialistic philosophy. Li shows that, similar to logical thinking, image-thinking is a rational method of comprehension (Li Zehou 1959, 104). He points out that the two different modes of cognition (presentative and conceptual) had already been scientifically proven by psychology. Both methods of cognition already belong to the stage of comprehension, where external impressions have been elaborated through rational principles. Image-thinking is a higher and much more complex stage within the human process of understanding of the external world than the first stage of direct perception. There is also a significant difference between logical and imaginative thinking. While logical thinking, eliminates all emotional (or axiological) elements, imaginative thinking always retains its tight connection to feelings and sensuality. The second difference is that the logical thinking method is oriented towards formalization and generalization of received data, while imaginative thinking expresses them on an increasingly concrete level. Image-thinking is also a process of typification. Li believes that image-thinking is a necessary precondition for any kind of artistic creation. He points out that there is nothing mystical or supernatural about it.

> There is nothing mysterious about this phenomenon. It is simply a fact: the artists are good in sensible observation of images and their meaning and, because of this, they can start creating.
>
> 這現象並不神秘但卻是事實: 藝術家善於敏銳地感受生活形象的意義而開始創作。 (Li Zehou 1959, 104)

Li also explains that the second special feature of image thinking is its inseparable connection with the emotions that surface in aesthetic feeling.

> In this process of image-thinking the artist completely expresses their emotional attitude and aesthetic feeling; furthermore, they concretely embody this attitude in their artistic work.

在整個形象思維過程中，藝術家每一步都表現著自己的美感或情感態度，並把這種態度凝結體現在作品裡。(ibid., 107)

This close, inseparable connection between image-thinking and aesthetic feeling is of utmost importance, for it separates human beings from other animals. In the procedure of mental or cognitive processing of the myriad information, data, and impressions we perceive from the external world through our sense organs, and in the process of the transformation of this information into rationalized entities, image thinking based on aesthetic feeling is of utmost importance. The very fact of its complex nature makes it clear to Li that it must be grounded in logical reasoning.

> Actually, the reason artistic image-thinking is different from pure biologic animal sensuality, and also from ordinary people's representations or imaginative illusions and fantasies, lies precisely in the fact that it includes certain special features of aesthetic feeling. These features have been constructed upon a basis of a long-lasting process of firm and solid logical reasoning, judgements, and inferences, and its principles were formed, guided, and controlled in accordance with the principles of logical reasoning. Aesthetic feeling is both objective reality reflection as well as subjective judgment. It does not merely include perception and sensibility, but also certain epistemological elements. Its mirroring and judging reality cannot be reduced to mere direct sensual reaction but includes all life experiences, positions, views, and the highly complex reflections connected to culture and education. Hence, the shaping of aesthetic feeling is based upon the process of logical and rational recognition.

> 事實上，藝術家的形象思維之所以不但不同於動物性的純生理自然的感性，而且還不同於人們的一般的表象活動和形象幻想，就正是因為它作為一種具有美感特性的東西，是必須建築在十分堅固結實的長期邏輯思考、判斷、推理的基礎之上，它的規律是被它的基礎（邏輯思維）的規律所決定、制約和支配著的。美感是對現實的一種客觀反映，又是對現實的一種主觀判斷。它不但包含知覺、感情的因素，而且也包含認識的因素。它對現實的反映和判斷不是一般感性活動的直接反應，而是表現其整個生活經

歷、立場、觀點、文化教育的複雜的高級的反映。美感的形成是
以長期的邏輯理智認識為基礎。(ibid., 110)

But the mere fact that logical reasoning is the basis of image-thinking does by no means imply that logical thinking could replace any part of imaginative thinking (ibid., 112).

At the end of "On Image-Thinking," Li explains that it was written as a challenge to raise further debate. In Li's later essays on this topic, we see that the concept was indeed subjected to severe critiques in the following years, because his sensual connotation with feelings and emotions was automatically marked as a form of idealism or sensualism.

To the entire debate: Throughout the 1950s and the beginning of the 1960s, the broader context of all the debates was related to questions ranging from of the essence of beauty to the problem of the image-thinking. The underlying problem, however, was linked to the question of who was the real Marxist: Li Zehou, Zhu Guangqian, or Cai Yi? As previously noted, the journal *"Red Flag"* published in 1966 an article in which image-thinking was condemned as idealism and as standing in great contradiction to Marxist epistemology, after which no one dared discuss it anymore (Gao Jianping in Zhao Shilin 2012, 212). Only after the end of the Cultural Revolution and after the publishing of Mao's letter in the *People's Daily*, which was understood as a signal for the rehabilitation of the notion, could the debate be carried out on an academic level and in the framework of modern Chinese aesthetics. Li Zehou wrote three explanatory essays in the beginning of these controversial discussions, which formed an important part of the entire Aesthetic Fever movement. The first of these three essays, was published in January 1978, only a few days after the publishing of Mao's letter, which was published on December 31, 1977.[31] It is therefore plausible to think that the article was written much earlier and that Li kept it hidden in a drawer, where it secretly waited for the next opportunity to see the light of the day. In 1980, during the first phase of the Aesthetic Fever, he wrote another important essay on the concept.[32]

In this second phase of the aesthetic debates regarding image-thinking, writes that in the past it was often criticized as a method of mere visual perception, in that people's minds merely moved "from one image to another" (Li Zehou 1978, 102). In those iron times, Li was sharply criticized for propagating a concept that centered on emotions.

There was a very strange phenomenon, which lasted for many years: not only did our literary theory pay no attention to and failed to investigate emotions, [the theoreticians] seemed to be afraid of even talking about them. After I pointed out in my article "On Image-Thinking" that image thinking has to "include emotions," comrade Zheng Jiqiao accused me of being a sensualist. But in fact, art without emotions is not art. We always only say that the main characteristic of art is its image-nature. But in fact, for art, its emotiveness is even more important than its image nature (or figurativeness).

多年來，一個很奇怪的現象，就是我們的文藝理論不但對文藝和文藝創作中的情感問題研究注意極為不夠，而且似乎特別害怕談情感。我在《試論形象思維》中提出形象思維必須「包含情感」，就被鄭季翹同志斥為唯心論。其實，藝術如果沒有情感，就不成其為藝術。我們只講藝術的特徵是形象性，其實，情感性比形象性對藝術來說更為重要。 (Li Zehou 1980b, 33)

Another subversive element in Li's interpretations of image-thinking lies in his barely hidden admiration for artists and their special talents, which manifests itself especially clearly in their image-thinking, because the image-thinking of an artist leads—in contrast to that of "ordinary people"—to aesthetic artistic creation. Especially in the period of the Cultural Revolution, a period of artificial but universally repeated ideology that took as given the absolute inborn equality of all people, such an elitist point of view could hardly find acceptance in the Chinese state and society.

In his following works, Li increasingly focused on elaborating on more complex aesthetic notions and, consequently, he wrote about image-thinking only sporadically during the following years.[33] In any event, Aesthetic Fever lost its attraction for the broader public. As pointed out by Gao Jianping's and Zhao Shilin's essay, the "Great Debate on Aesthetics," which took place in the 1950s and 1960s, proceeded from the question of the essence of beauty towards the question of image-thinking (Gao, Zhao 2012, 213). In the 1980s, the debate continued in the opposite direction (from the image thinking to the essence of beauty). Because of this, image-thinking fell out of fashion.

But this aesthetic notion, which occupied Li's mind in his early years, had wide-reaching implications. Li's connecting image-thinking with the double nature of aesthetic feeling was already an innovative step toward a new aesthetic theory. In addition, his elaborations on the concept of image-thinking and its close connection to emotions might be instrumental for the shaping of his later pioneering notion of emotion-based substance. If we consider that Li—especially in his later essays—always stressed his belief that inextricable continuous unity with emotions is the core characteristic of the image-thinking, we might agree with You Xilin, who claims that Li's essential issue regarding image-thinking "was the issue of emotions, which is linked to the concept of emotion-based substance." Therefore, in his theory, image-thinking is, "in fact, a very early expression of emotion-based substance" (You Xilin in Zhao Shilin 2012, 214). In my opinion, image-thinking cannot exactly be seen as an early form of the idea of emotion-based substance simply because the former is an epistemological notion and the latter an ontological one. Nevertheless, it can be safely presupposed that his specific understanding of the notion of image-thinking led him to further elaborate upon the problem of emotions and, finally, to outline the concept of emotion-based substance.

It is also clear that in his first essay, due to his young age, Li was not yet a completely accomplished thinker. At that early age he seems to be able to understand most of the complex ideas and sophisticated theories much better than the majority of his contemporaries. It still seems as though he did not properly understand some of the notions, systems, or concepts he was dealing with. For instance, the concept of estrangement, which, at that early point, he seems to have equated with the concept of objectification. He writes: "Beautiful nature is the result of the socialization of nature, and it is also the result of the objectification (estrangement) of human essence" (Li Zehou 1956, 57).

If we read Marx's *Manuscripts* carefully, it becomes quickly clear that he denotes as "objectification" every result of human labor—every embodiment of it (in an object). The objectification of labor becomes, and can be equated to, estrangement only under the conditions of forced labor (Marx 2007, 29). In this context, Marx explicitly refers to class society, a society where only two classes remain.[34]

Private property is also a very important condition for the occurrence of estrangement or alienation. While objectification, which is in fact the visible, tangible, and concretized manifestation of human labor can certainly be seen as something positive (as a possible origin of aesthetic feeling and, consequently, the origin of beauty), alienation is a negative term that distances a human being from their essence, and which can only appear under conditions in which human labor becomes a kind of commodity and can thus be sold (Marx 2007, 10). Li did not yet see the difference between objectification and estrangement or alienation.

In a certain sense, the young Li here finds himself in contradiction with the elder Li, who held that aesthetic feeling and the feeling of pleasure people can obtain from beauty (including natural beauty) is something through which estrangement can be surpassed and eliminated and something through which human beings can trace a path back to unity with their own essence (see Li, Zehou 1986, 135; Li Zehou 2016, 195; or Wang, Keping 2007, 251). Some sections in this earliest essay are in sharp contrast to his later works because sometimes the young Li actually equates beauty with estrangement.

> Human beings can enjoy the beauty of nature; they can "project" their own feelings onto an object and this means that through their intuition they can actually recognize the estrangement of their essential power in the objects, and hence, they can recognize the social nature of beauty. . . . In fact, the beauty of nature is a special form of existence of the beauty of social life (or the beauty of reality)—it is the form of existence of estrangement.
>
> 人能夠欣賞自然美，人能夠把自己的感情「移」到對象裡去，實際上，這就是說，人能夠在自然對象裡直覺地認識自己本質的力量的異化，認識美的社會性......自然美就只是社會生活的美 (現實美) 的一種特殊的存在形式，是一種「異化」的存在形式。(Li Zehou 1956, 59)

Later, in the revised *The Chinese Aesthetic Tradition* (2010), a translated, revised, and complemented version of his Chinese book *The Chinese Aesthetic Tradition* (2001a), the concept of alienation is clearly seen as something negative, something that must be and can be exceeded by art.

> Similarly, beginning in the Wei-Jin period, many spatial images (natural objects) become infused with a humanistic nostalgia and with deep temporal emotions. This is a very important point. Even if, because of this, the feeling and imagination of Chinese arts and literature might be confined forever to a

closed, harmonious system of space and time, it was also for this reason that natural images lost the alienating, mystifying, or terrifying character with which they could be endowed and were able in their later development to gradually blend with a variety of human emotions in order, in the end, to result in the creation of one of the fundamental categories of Chinese art: the artistic conception, or *yijing* 意境. (Li, Zehou 2010, 152)

The mature Li Zehou often points out that the humanizing of nature becomes "the essence of beauty, and what are activities of humanized nature but those that are free, that are liberated from kinds of alienation?" (Bruya 2003, 138).[35]

Despite such minor (and entirely understandable) inconsistencies, Li's earliest essay contains the important foundational elements of Li's later philosophical system. The young scholar already firmly states the very basis of his aesthetic theory. It is a discourse that should be viewed through the lens of social practice, through which it came into life, but also comprehended through sensitivity and feeling. While the first approach manifests itself in Li's early definition of the double nature of aesthetic feeling, the second becomes vividly clear through his unique reinterpretation of the (originally Soviet) concept of image-thinking.

The Meaning of Life and the Highest Domain of Human Existence

We can assert with much certainty that Li Zehou's emphasis on the social dimensions of aesthetics can be traced back to two main sources. In a more general sense, this idea was unquestionably linked to the framework of Marxist historical materialism. In a narrower sense, however, his reasoning was certainly also the result of Plekhanov's influence. Even though in this first theoretical essay Li mentions Plekhanov only once,[36] it is nevertheless clear that he was very familiar with the aesthetic work of this Russian theoretician, who is considered to be the first "genuinely Marxist" aesthetician (Swiderski 1979, 60).[37]

Beside these influences, it is also worth paying attention to the original and distinctively specific elements of his initial theoretical experiments. Considering both above-mentioned central elements of his first important theoretical essay, namely the dual nature of aesthetic feeling and image-thinking, we can easily see that what he actually wanted to establish and elaborate upon was a combination of sociality and emotiveness. This emphasis on the socioemotional nature of aesthetics is connected to his conviction that beauty (and consequently also aesthetic judgement) are necessarily objective. It is important to emphasize that Li's aesthetic (or epistemological) objectivism is not determined by pure natural laws or (even less) by any supernatural or mystical conditions. It is tightly connected with human beings. He holds that beauty is objective, but not in the sense of a quality inherent to things. The objective existence of beauty is comparable (or analogous) to the objective existence of human society and its historical development. Beauty does not exist per se, but only for and through human beings, because they are the only ones that can comprehend and appreciate or create it. The criteria for aesthetic judgements, however, are not arbitrary, coincidental, or dependent upon individual subjective decisions. These criteria are social, and at a certain level generally valid and objective. In this broader sense, emotions are not also seen (as is usually the case) as an entirely subjective factor, but rather as the necessary installation for the human appreciation of beauty. This combination of objectivism, feelings, and sociality (or, in a more narrow and concrete sense, social practice) is rather unique and cannot be found in the frameworks of previous theoreticians. Although Li's system is inspired by Kant and early Marx, it also greatly differs from them. For Kant the primary and compulsory precondition of any judgment of taste was that it must be *subjective*. For Marx *emotions are entirely and absolutely dependent* upon mechanistic external laws and social circumstances. Later, Li deepened and broadened this fusion of sociality and emotiveness by increasingly drawing inspiration from classical Confucian thought.

Li's immense contribution to the establishment of Chinese aesthetics as a theoretical academic discipline is clearly visible in his profound and exhaustive analyses of the Chinese aesthetic tradition, which before him was hardly subjected to a thoroughly modern analysis. Most of his own concepts were formed and developed in the context of these analyses. This led him to explain and reinterpret numerous important existing concepts that were misunderstood or misused due to their complexity or ambiguity. The notion of aesthetic realm[38] (*jingjie* 境界), which was also central to Wang Guowei's (1877–1927) aesthetics.[39] Wang defined the concept as:

> The "realm" does not only refer to a landscape or scene. The emotions of joy and sorrow, anger, and pleasure also constitute a sort of aesthetic realm in the human heart. So if a poem captures in words a real scene or a real emotion, it can be said to convey an aesthetic realm.
>
> 境非獨謂景物也。喜怒哀樂, 亦人心中之一境界。故能寫真景物、真感情者, 謂之有境界。 (Wang Guowei 2013, 18)

Li emphasizes that a realm created in the emotional experience derived from concrete life is then transformed into an artistic subject: "What Wang is referring to here is the objectification of psychological emotion in order to construct an artistic noumenon that manifests something about human life" (Li, Zehou 2010, 210). Although Wang's theoretical framework was strongly influenced by Western philosophy (especially by Arthur Schopenhauer and Friedrich Nietzsche), Li defines it as the "revelation of life through the relationship between feeling and scene, and the objectified realm of the artistic subject" (Li Zehou in Samei 2010, xvi). Li also emphasizes that aesthetic realm cannot be reduced to mere integration of feeling and scene, nor to the feeling, sensibility, or motivation of the artist who creates it. This important and typically Chinese aesthetic notion in Li's treatment is a hermeneutic means that can help us understand artistic creations through the lens of various manifestations of the realm of human life. The *jingjie*-sphere can only be experienced in art but not described in language or imagined in conceptual thought.[40] Li points out the noumenal dimension of Wang Guowei's aesthetic realm—idea. He also highlights the importance of Wang's synthesis between such traditional notions and Western philosophies of aesthetics. Wang's aesthetic realm, which implies eliminating the difference between self and the others, transcends all utilitarian purposiveness without having to negate the will, desire, and life itself.

Another specifically Chinese notion that was transformed and re-created by Li is the so-called artistic conception. This notion is an imaginary domain, which similar to the aesthetic realm, is based upon a fusion of emotion and scene or situation (*qingjing jiaorong* 情景交融). What the artistic conception implies is more centered upon the mindful awareness of the here and now, which is conveyed by artistic creation. In his writings about artistic conception, Li highlights that precisely because of this fusion or the unity it implies it is completely useless and redundant to seek comprehension through any kind of conceptual medium between feeling and object.

The genuinely new aesthetic ideas that Li created and developed in the course of his intellectual development are embedded within the general system of his Chinese aesthetic theory and art history, which functions as a synthesis of the entire developmental course of Chinese aesthetic thought, from the earliest eras through the premodern and modern periods. Li integrated his theory pre-Confucian and Confucian concepts with Daoist and Buddhist (especially Chan Buddhist) philosophies, also integrated the later impact of Western thought. As an authority on Marxist social theories and Kant's ethics, epistemology, and aesthetics, and as a theoretician who is not only well equipped with knowledge of the development of both Chinese and Western thought, Li is qualified to make the specific features of the Chinese aesthetic tradition intelligible to Western readers (Samei 2010, ix).

As we have seen, Li's theory is always based on belief in the objective nature of reality. It is important to see that this objectivity is only significant with regard to humankind, because without humans, reality has no meaning. In Li's theory, human existence is based upon the paradigm of objective sociality (Li Zehou 2016, 153). This amalgamation of feeling and objectivity, this unity of human togetherness and intimacy, was an innovative idea. Although it was certainly, either consciously or unconsciously, inspired by Chinese ideational tradition, especially by Confucian philosophies, it could not be found in the works of any other Chinese aestheticians of his time. This comprehensive and dynamic unity also resonates, in a somehow distant and antiquarian form, from the well-known interdependent and correlative interaction of the small and the great Self, a pattern often used by Li himself, but going back in its origins to premodern history. Li's system comes to us in a new and multidimensional appearance. A system in that the realities of beauty and human beings and their inwardness, shaped by emotio-rational structures, obtain ontological dimensions and form a noumenal basis for Li's concept of anthropological ontology.[41] Li's ideational system is a reflection of this deeply human ontology that is embedded in the dynamic unity of material social practice, on the one hand, and aesthetic sensibility on the other.

This unity naturally strives toward harmony, which is not a state but a dynamic process. Beauty pertaining to such a concept of harmony can be achieved through the dynamic realization of the ever-changing configuration of that which Li denotes as a "proper measure," another important notion of his philosophical system. Proper measure is an elementary category of Li's anthropo-historical ontology, but it also plays a crucial role in aesthetics and artistic creation. The active realization of proper measure is also tightly linked to his axiological ideas of "preserving the good through beauty" (Yi mei chu shan 以美儲善) and "illuminating the truth through beauty" (Yi mei qi zhen 以美啟真) (Li Zehou 2016b, 234).

Such an example of beauty linked to the consolidation of a dynamic harmony is timeless in terms of flowing moments and limitless regarding its forms. It is highly subtle, ever changing, and never complete. Classical Chinese notion of beauty is something comparable to the notion of the sublime in the Western aesthetic discourses.[42] In Kant's aesthetics, for instance, beauty is also an indefinite concept. At the same time, it is necessarily confined to boundaries, for it is connected to the form of an object (Kant 1987, 98). The notion of the sublime, on the other hand, rather pertains to formless objects and is represented by boundlessness (ibid.).[43],[44] In Chinese aesthetics, beauty is similar to the Western concept of the sublime. It can never be captured in rigid structures of vibrant and unswerving expressiveness.

> Among all peoples the sublime is superior to beauty. In China, since such negative factors as guilt, suffering, tragedy, mystery, and so on were excluded at the outset, works of art and literature always avoided the extreme cruelty and pain of realistic conflict, preferring to appease, lull, or even deceive the suffering spirit by ending in the spirit of a happy reunion. Thus deprived of realistic or psychological bloodshed, what remains is simply to put a good face on everything, as the modern writer Lu Xun so incisively exposed in his stories. (Li, Zehou 2010, 74)

This aesthetic feature, which is typical for the specific Chinese tradition, is connected to the fact that in China aesthetics it assumes the comforting role played by religion(s) in the Western world.

But, Li's notion of the sublime also differs from Kant's. In essence, sublime is the greatness of humankind It manifests itself especially vividly in struggles against forces of nature or social enemies: "The struggle of frontwar warriors and the people in their millions, marching forward courageously, advancing wave upon wave, unyielding, valiantly sacrificing themselves" (Chong 1999a, 190). In Western art, works that depict the giant and uncontrollable natural power are often interpreted as expressions of human emotions. And in fact, the perception of the sublime in nature is actually a feeling of respect towards ourselves, our collective human power, and the power of our subjectality and imagination (Li Zehou 2007, 399). Li often wrote about the concept of the sublime as a social notion, and investigated the idea of the "social sublime (*shehui chonggao* 社會崇高)," which does not lie in nature and neither in subjective spirit.

Li draws our attention to the fact that in the Chinese tradition, aesthetic sensibility and aesthetic appreciation were always cherished and highly valued, for they belonged to those specifically human features, through and by which both the transmission of metaphysical reflection and the pursuit of transcendence became possible. In this context, transcendence is not understood as transcending the sensual world, time and space—this is a transcendence that is not hidden in an inaccessible future or divine heaven, nor within a transparent noumenon without any sensuosity. Rather, it can be achieved within this sensuous mortal world. In this view, time adopts a specific meaning in human consciousness. It becomes something like a special inner sense, but not in Kant's epistemological conception. In the Chinese ideational tradition, time becomes an aesthetic category, a historically and socially realized noumenal emotion. Through the course of history, time accumulates emotional implications. In the Chinese aesthetic discourse, time is not merely a cognitive faculty in the extensive objectivity of space. It occurs as an aesthetically perceived mood; deeply interwoven in feelings of nostalgia or homesickness; in the yearning for love and compassion; in the attachment to existence, people, and life; but also in the desperate awareness of its transitory nature.

In Li Zehou's one-world view there is transcendence within this concrete perceptual realm, within these worldly spatial and temporal measurements. In these immanent dimensions the surpassing of mundane and entry into the sublime occurs in the ontology of human life, which is, in Li's own words, "not Being, but rather Becoming" (Li, Zehou 2010, 52). Although in Li's opinion his view differs from the Modern New Confucian paradigm of immanent transcendence. Both conceptualizations are grounded in a similar tendency towards a complementary unification of binary oppositions, represented by concrete, worldly, and everyday human life on the one side, and the highest realms of spiritual experience on the other. In contrast to monotheistic religions, which are based upon having faith in external Gods, and which seek to achieve the highest echelon of transcendent insight into the mysteries of life and death through humble submission and respect towards them, religion in China was substituted by aesthetics (Li Zehou 2016c, 362).[45] Chinese ideational tradition held that the aesthetic attitude permeated human life, which was therefore elevated to the level of metaphysical transcendence, to a "supra-ethical and supra-moral, quasi-religious level, where it was able to supplant religion" (Li, Zehou 2010, 188). Li explains this replacement of religion through aesthetics.

> In the Chinese tradition aesthetics takes the place of religion as the means of establishing this highest realm of human existence. It is this potential supramoral and aesthetic noumenal realm that makes possible such uncalculated free choice and the kind of moral realization that transcends life and death. The postulation of this aesthetic realm can be said to constitute the high point of Confucian philosophy and the Chinese aesthetic tradition. (ibid., 189)

Li highlights the cathartic role of aesthetics in the Chinese tradition, emphasizing that for traditional intellectuals the aesthetic realm or the artistic world was the noumenon. It offered intellectuals an imaginary domain to which they could (temporarily) escape from the pain caused by unfulfilled desires and sufferings. Because they lacked religious faith it was only in art that they could experience meaning and comfort embedded in the phenomenal world. Chinese tradition never founded a supramoral religion centered around a divine noumenon. Instead, it created a supramoral aesthetics with a human psycho-emotional noumenon. Chinese tradition never taught people to pray for salvation from God, but rather to seek emotional consolation in the human world.

In Li's ontology of human life, aesthetic sensibility enables people to experience spiritual realization and freedom. This sensibility is preserved and simultaneously continuously reshaped in the long lasting dynamic developmental course, in that "human wisdom and virtuous behavior are sedimented and transformed into a psychological noumenon that transcends the foundation of wisdom and morality upon which it is built" (Li, Zehou 2010, 52). As described in previous chapters, sedimentation and its dynamic shaping of human cultural-psychological formations, which occurs in the process of the humanization of nature, plays a crucial role not only in the general path of human development but also in terms of the incorporation of specific aesthetic values. During the accumulation of material cultural experiences, which starts with the making and using of tools, and during the accretion of aesthetic value into ceremonies, begins the long, continuing process of shaping the cultural and mental structures that will come to define *humanity* (Samei 2010, x). Each new development in aesthetic thought adds a new level of sediment to this process.

In the domain of aesthetics, the process of sedimentation is most important because of three reasons. First, sedimented forms are significant for different culturally and socially determined evolvements of specific notions of beauty. Second, because it preserves the appearance of the rational in the sensuous. And, third it enables humans to convey the "social atmosphere" of any concrete period of time into its artistic productions. It is especially important in the process of the humanization of human inner nature. In these developments, sedimentation manifests itself in the shaping of aesthetic psychological structures. At the same time, its expression is also visible in the humanization of external nature. It manifests itself in aesthetic objects—that which actually modifies the very relation between human beings and nature is, according to Li, precisely the creation of the aesthetic. The aesthetic sedimentation preserves in the cultural-psychological formations such social entities like values, ideals, meanings, and attitudes, and conveys them from previous to subsequent generations. In this regard, the accumulation of emotions and sensory cognition is of particular significance. Pure aesthetics has nothing more to do with ordinary sensuous pleasure, which is below moral valuations, for it is obtained through direct perception and mediated to us through receptive organs. It belongs to something Li denotes as the "perfect pleasure," which transcends morality, since it is a sedimented form of the infinite universe. This infinity cannot, of course, be expressed or comprehended in language or conceptual thought. Rather, it must be seen as a sedimented sensuosity that forms—together with its object, the beauty of the illimitable—the core of human noumenal existence. Li points out that the last stage of this giant imaginative enterprise, which has passed through primitive magic religions, moral analogies and conceptual knowledge, corresponds to the nonconceptual pleasure Kant speaks of in his aesthetics (Li, Zehou 2010, 148).

Sedimentation is also important in the process of artistic creation. For the unconscious is also attained through the sedimentation of consciousness, because sedimentation has its own innate logic and regularity that is connected to consciousness.

> In this sense, the unconscious does not refer to "dormant" animal instinct, but to a kind of nonconscious condensation or sedimentation achieved through conscious human effort. If we say that the aesthetic attitude discussed above is the psychological result of that sedimentation, then what is described here is the process by which that sedimentation takes place. (Li, Zehou 2010, 110)

That which is exhibited at the level of individual unconscious is itself a product of long lasting historical accumulation and sedimentation. The rational structure of aesthetics, which is also very important, is formed by sedimentation of different forms of imagination (including conceptual and truly emotional forms), which forms a "humanistic matrix" sedimented in tradition and expressed in art. All these factors influence the formation of culturally determined diversities in art and aesthetics. They are also the reason why Chinese art, for instance, emphasizes imaginary reality instead of sensory reality.

Li sees the root of this basic specificity in that in the Chinese Confucian tradition, rituals were seen as basic to the development of the central virtue of humaneness. The Confucians always stressed the importance of the relationship between rituality and human inwardness because they saw the latter as the foundation and basis of the former. At its very core, humaneness (ren) is the conscious awareness of one's own humanness (ren xing), which has a double dimension. Being human means possessing biologically animalistic characteristics, as expressed, for instance, in the parent-child relation. It also comprises features that surpass this animal nature, as expressed in the realization of filial respect and love (xiao 孝). In Li's understanding, these form the ultimate reality of humankind and the very essence of what it means to be human (ibid., 40). In spite of all the novelties Li has displayed in his aesthetic theory, he likes to emphasize that his theory of art and aesthetics are "Confucian-based." Through the lens of these ancient, deeply humanistic teachings, Li hopes to elucidate the significance of being human and show that this significance is most clearly expressed in the domain in which it was first formed and from which it springs up over and over again—namely in the realm of beauty. In this sense, beauty is humankind itself.

The Dynamic Nature of Life and Reality: God Is Dead, but People Are Alive

As discussed, Li's aesthetic theories and his revival of the classical Chinese discourses cannot be reduced to one single discipline. Li finds the basic meaning of the universe in the existence of human beings. It is by no means coincidental that the central starting point (and the necessary precondition) for his entire opus is the fact that "the human being is alive" (*ren huozhe* 人活著). In Li's view, the primary driving force for human evolvement was first and foremost our survival instinct. It is unsurprising that he calls his theory as the "philosophy of eating."[46] He sees current postmodern Western philosophy as a discourse that became lost in a cul-de-sac of meaningless, empty existence. He points out to the fact that "its" human being is not alive anymore.

> Not only was God declared to be dead (by Nietzsche), the human being was equally pronounced as deceased (by Foucault). So reason is a prison, language has no meaning, history is false, and knowledge has been sold to power and does not exist anymore. Hence, philosophy should also be eliminated. . . .
>
> 不僅上帝死了（尼采），而且人也死了（福柯）。理性是監獄，語言無意義，歷史為虛假，知識乃權力廣本質，不存在，哲學應消亡 . . . . . . (Li Zehou 2016, 114)

Li is not at all in favor of such a nihilistic spirit. His goal is to enrich global philosophy with the power of his homemade, Chinese discourses, deriving from his "culture of pleasure," in which the human being is— very much so—still alive.

> In my view, negating, criticizing, and revolting alone cannot be the sole goals of humankind. Hence, I say that even though God is dead, the human being is still alive and people (the entire humankind and each individual) must still rely on their own strength in order to advance. There is no point

in calling out for a new God (or something like Heidegger's "*Sein*"), nor in producing a new "Superman." There is no use in creating a new, dull, red utopia. We still have to stand on our own, common, and ordinary ground, grounds on which our real subjectality can be developed. Then, we can decide upon our own way.

在我看來，就人類總體說，否定、批判、革命並非目的自身。所以我說上帝死了，人還活著，人（人類和個體）還得依靠自己的力量，繼續前行。不是再去重新呼喚上帝（如海德格爾的「在」），不是去企冀「超人」，也不是另造單調的紅色烏托邦，而仍然應該是立足在普普通通平平凡凡的每個個人的基礎上，立足在作為真正現實的人的主體性的基礎上，來決定自己的道路。(ibid.)

These free and autonomous decisions about one's own life, this faithful following of one's own way, the starting point of which is always the plain fact of bare human existence, is the central implication of Li's complex notion of subjectality. Li sees life as evolving, about the progression (individual and collective) of human beings who develop their surrounding (and are simultaneously being developed themselves) through material practice, while being entrenched in social relations and contextualized through different situations and different feelings, from mere passive perception all along through more active comprehension and then further, towards aesthetic awareness, which is, in itself, the ultimate meaning of life.

Li's system has this progress rooted in emotions, which, as we have seen, have obtained a noumenal dimension in his philosophy. It has also been driven by the pure and cold mechanistic law of dialectic development. His theory is grounded in the ontological paradigm determined by a specifically human model of historical development. Li named this basic paradigm "The Anthropo-historical Ontology."

Anthropo-historical Ontology

Anthropo-historical ontology is central to Li's research method and also the basic paradigm of his philosophical system—the practical philosophy of subjectality. A shorter form of the phrase—and also the subject and title of one of his major works—is *Historical Ontology*.[47] In his later works, Li notes that he shortened the name at the beginning of the new century but without changing the meaning of the phrase, which is still the same (Li Zehou 2008e, 318).

Anthropo-historical ontology is different from most traditional philosophical approaches, which usually proceed from feeling toward reason, in that it applies the opposite approach. It proceeds from reason, which manifests itself in humankind and its history, and in the laws of necessity. Ultimately, it explores the final stage of human evolution, namely emotion, expressed through and reflected in individuals, contingencies, and human psychology (Li Zehou 2016b, 401).

The phrase "anthropo-historical ontology" denotes this vision of human existence, comprising morals, as the result of human development seen through the lens of historical materialism. Following the basic Marxist structure of (economic and material) basis and ideational or spiritual superstructure, Li places concrete human values, as well as different, culturally determined systems of concepts, ideas, moral standards, ethical norms, and aesthetic preferences, into a dual framework. He sees them as something that manifests itself particularly in individuals, and also as something that originates and is grounded in the general material existence of the whole of humankind. In Li's system, anthropology is the primary approach to comprehending what makes human beings human. Li strongly opposes not only analytical philosophical explanations, but also all interpretations of human life from a strictly biological point of view.

While the material conditions of human existence are formative factors of human psychology and existence, humans are unique in their ability to act in accordance with rational principles, and thus in helping to shape these conditions by themselves. Both the human mind and the material conditions of human existence are cumulatively affected by social interaction and social practice. This leads Li to the notion of "historical ontology," in which human freewill and its active manifestation of subjectality play a central role. Historical ontology's emphasis on the concrete actuality of human existence as the origin and grounds of moral principles also serves to assert the importance of historically specific circumstances in moral judgment, since a concrete circumstance, takes precedence to any supposedly *a priori* principles.

Traditionally, since in its own specific philosophy China has never formed a metaphysical ontology, Li denotes his newly created "anthropo-historical ontology" as a "post-philosophical" (*hou zhexue* 後哲學) ontology (Li Zehou 2016b, 377). Immanuel Kant tried to summarize his theory in three basic questions, namely "What can I know?" (epistemology),

"What should I do?" (ethics), and "What can I hope for?" (theology). Li points out that, towards the end of his life, Kant added to these a forth question that pertains to anthropology: "What is the human being?" Li emphasizes that, in contrast to Kant, his own anthropo-historical ontology begins with Kant's fourth question by proposing as its central tenet that humans are alive. This assumption serves as the starting point and the most basic approach for the exploration of three different questions that highlight the most important expositions of Li's philosophy. In his view, the anthropo-historical ontology provides answers to the following problems:

1. How is it that human beings are alive? (*Ren ruhe huo* 人如何活?)

2. Why (or for what reason) do human beings live? (*Ren wei shenme huo* 人為什麼活?)

3. How do human beings live? (*Ren huode zenmeyang* 人活得怎麼樣?)

While the starting point for all three questions is the same, for they are all rooted in the simple fact that humans are alive, each of them represents a particular and unique discourse. We could say that the first question pertains to epistemology, the second to ethics, and the third to aesthetics. While the first question explores the subjectality of humankind, the second tackles issues belonging to individual subjectality. The third question is linked to axiology and deals with the aesthetic realm of human life, and its ultimate meaning.

In exploring the first question, it becomes obvious that there is a tight connection between the bare fact of concrete physical human life and questions of the reasons for this existence. To illuminate the difference between the abstract Western and the pragmatically concrete Chinese replies to this question, Li reminds us of Heidegger, who proclaimed that only by knowing death can one know life (see Heidegger 1967, 231–67). He saw this claim as being in a sharp contrast with Confucius's belief that we cannot know death, and should thus focus upon life.[48] In Li's view, such orientation can help us solve the riddle expressed by the first question, which could also be formulated as "How is humankind possible (人類如何可能?)" (Li Zehou 2016b, 384). However, it can also help us understand the broader context or the metaphysical level of the second and third questions. The essential point here is the fact that the meaning of human life is not derived from death, but from the life itself. This life depends on our ability to use and apply tools and to develop technology. In contrast to Kant, Li believes that the basic forms of human perception and comprehension are not *a priori*, but shaped and developed through and by practice. In Xunzi, who emphasized that life (of a gentleman) is tightly linked to his ability to apply material technology, Li finds the essential elements of the Marxist materialist paradigm, which emphasizes the primary nature of the material basis as a necessary and indispensable condition, for the consolidation and development of any element belonging to the ideal superstructure (Xunzi 2002; Quan xue, 4). Li emphasizes that even the Confucian philosophers, who value morality and personal cultivation above everything, have clearly seen that such cultivation is only possible on the basis of a material infrastructure that enables us to live and to evolve as human beings. The essential reason for the existence of humankind is its universal necessity and ability to systematically produce and apply tools. This ability, however, is not only the most important and indispensable driving force of human history, it is also essential in terms of the relationship between politics and morality, and between society and the individual. In terms of traditional Chinese understanding, this means that the historical dialectics of the "inner sage and external ruler" is only possible on the grounds of the instrumental substance.

Although human life is the ultimate reason for our existence, we still know that we are going to die. This certainty that we are alive and that we will be dead opens another question: Whether or not life is worth living at all. Because of the Chinese one-world view this second question cannot be completely separated from the previous one, since in such a view epistemology is intermingled with ethics and vice versa (Li Zehou 2016b, 392).

However, the question is significant and it ultimately affects every human being. We all trying to solve the riddle of why we are alive, or what we are living for. There are many possible answers: some people live for God; others for their children and grandchildren; some live for money, glory, or fame; and still others live for their community. All these decisions can be substantiated by various theories and pieces of evidence, but, eventually, we are still responsible for our own lives.

> Ultimately, everybody has to find out, to choose, and to decide upon the purpose of their life by themselves. . . . This is "free

will." Every human being decides consciously and freely upon his or her actions and attitudes. In this regard, nobody is limited or restricted by the causal laws of the phenomenal world.

究竟為什麼活，仍然需要自己去發現、去選擇、去決定......這也就是「自由意志」：每個人自覺地自由地做出自己的行為決定，而不為現象世界的因果規律所約束、限制。
(Li Zehou 2016b, 389)

Freewill is linked to Kant's categorical imperative and his concept of practical reason—that human behavior is only moral if it is based upon universal necessity. Here we see one of the crucial differences between Li's and Kant's view of human inwardness. While practical reason for Kant belongs to human *a priori* forms, Li's understanding of human morality is based upon pragmatic reasoning, which works in the human psyche through the emotio-rational structure and is inseparably linked to the emotion-based substance. The crucial point of these elements is that they do not directly belong to human inborn capacities, but are rather results of a dynamic, socially determined sedimentation process. We shall elaborate upon this issue in more detail in the section on Li's ethics. Here we point out that Li's answer to this second question: "why (or what for) are human beings alive" is closely connected to the interactions and relations between religious and social morality, absolute and relative ethics, the individual and society, and the great and the small self. Li's view of the moral and ethical meaning of human life follows the paths of all these multifarious proportions of humanness. He is continuously probing their grounds in order to find the proper measure that can always lead us to the harmonious middle way between the Confucian emotional view of the universe on the one hand, and the Daoist impassive rational laws of dialectical development (*wu qing bianzheng fa* 無情辯證法) on the other.

By treading this dynamic, winding, and often difficult and steep road to a mature (cultivated) moral human being—a road that is paved with the weight of individual responsibilities and the obligation of making one's own decisions—we are finally confronted with Li's third question. At this point we need to find the aesthetic realm of our life and understand our most intimate inner world. In the specifically Chinese one-world and one-life worldview, such spiritual, (almost) religiously imbued ultimate concerns and ideals can be summarized in this third question and defined by the search for our most intimate genuine aesthetic experience, for the beauty of our own. While the first two questions mainly refer to the internalization or solidification of reason, the third one concerns the melting of reason into emotion. While the first two questions concern problems pertaining to the collective soul, the third question concerns the individual heart-mind. While the first two questions can still be expressed by conceptual language, the third one refers to a realm that supersedes language, meaning, and rational cognition. It is a state of art in which even time is disclosed from spatial objectivity and becomes part of subjective feeling. The accumulative continuousness of the three questions depicts, step-by-step, development from technological to psychological substance. In this fleeting transitoriness of human life the only permanence is art. Li strives to establish possibilities for elevated forms of creativity, forms in which art would not remain trapped in "works of art," but could become life itself (Li Zehou 2016b, 401).[49]

Such an approach is deeply rooted in a strong awareness of one's inseparable connection or identity with all of humanity as well as in the awareness of one's own transitoriness surpassed only by our potential to love. For it is precisely this potential that brings us closer to an eternity that can be deeply felt in the fleeting moments we experience when absorbing the beauty of a solitary mountain, or in passing flashes of nostalgic submersion in memories.

> Christian love is ordered by God—it is God who tells you to love. In Christianity to love means to obey the commands of God. And, besides, one has to love God in the first place. But the Chinese people primarily love their parents and children. Parents show their children loving care and children are filial to their parents. Why is that so? These are completely natural feelings. Even animals have such feelings. However, in China these natural feelings were elevated in a rational way. This rationalization means that they were imbued with morality and ethics. But the emotions that prevailed in the Western world arise from obeying the requirements and commands of the external reason.
>
> 基督教的愛是上帝叫你去愛，是接受上帝那裡來的命令，並且首先要愛上帝。中國人首先是愛父母愛子女，講父慈子孝，為什麼？它這是一種自然性的本能情感。動物也有這樣的自然性的情感。

中國把他從自然本能情感理性化地提升上來，把它理性化即道德化和倫理化。而上述西方人的情是服從外在理性的要求和命令。
(Li Zehou 2016b, 627)

This rationalization of feelings witnessed in Chinese history and during the formation of Chinese culture cannot be reduced to epistemology (in the sense of the construction of reason). It was a dynamic process of sedimentation that lead to the solidification and the melting of reason. While the rationalization of feelings manifested itself in various forms of morality, the melting of reason belonged to aesthetic categories, in which the amalgamation of reason and emotions has led to the formation of emotio-rational structures. Recall that Li's anthropo-historical ontology is based upon the Marxist differentiation between the material basis (which is primary) and ideational superstructure (which is secondary). Li also assumes Marx's emphasis on the crucial role of social practice. However, he opposes the Marxist view of class struggle and violent revolutions as the main driving force of social development. He also eliminates the Marxist notion of abstract or theoretical praxis from the primary role of social practice, which was, for him, a purely material activity. He explains:

> Proceeding from "abstract labor," which is a notion that cannot be validly established, Karl Marx tried to deduce a communist "transcendental illusion." Although he emphasized that the basic life necessities constitute the foundation of human existence, he overlooked something that is very important, namely the fact that producing and applying tools has shaped humanness. The dominant theoretic field dealing with humanness (or human nature) and human spirit still belongs to transcendentalism and idealism. Historical ontology has absorbed and digested Kant, and, by applying the Chinese wisdom of survival and the strong consciousness of history, it also absorbed and digested Marx. It has thus enriched its own tradition. The "philosophy of eating," for instance, is even stronger in highlighting individual reality than the viewpoint of historical materialism.
>
> Karl Marx ⋯⋯ 由「抽象勞動」這個並不能成立的抽象概念推引出共產主義的「先驗幻想」。雖然注意食衣住行乃人類生存基礎，卻忽略了由製造——使用工具而塑建人性這一巨大問題。

人性以及心靈的理論領域仍然為先驗主義，唯心主義佔據著。如同吸納消化 Kant 一樣，歷史本體論以中國的生存智慧，歷史意識吸納消化 Marx，而豐富自己的傳統，例如「吃飯哲學」比唯物史觀更突出了個體實在。(ibid., 648–49)

In this sense, anthropo-historical ontology is an elaboration of the Chinese intellectual tradition. It is clear to Li that "after God dies, Chinese philosophy will appear on the stage" (ibid.).

Epistemology

As we have seen, Li was preoccupied with aestheticism for many years. It was his greatest intellectual passion. Li always emphasized that aesthetics cannot be reduced to epistemology. He aimed to overturn the traditional view that held that "philosophy was primarily epistemology," because he believed that the foundation and the starting point of any philosophy is human existence, and that epistemology is also submitted to this basic groundwork (Li Zehou 2012b, 1). He believed that epistemology as a philosophical discipline reached its end with Wittgenstein and that in the future it would become a discipline belonging entirely to the cognitive sciences (ibid., 2).

He often notes that as a theoretic discipline aesthetics is still grounded in epistemological discourses (Li Zehou 2002a, 2). He explains that even as he started to study aesthetics, he valued Kant's work immensely. He came to appreciate Kant's first two *Critiques* (i.e., his books on epistemology and ethics) through Kant's third book on aesthetic judgment (Li Zehou 2008e, 318). Li's epistemological thought is based upon his critique of Kant's transcendental philosophy, i.e., on a questioning and upgrading of Kant's famous investigations on the conditions of possibilities (or forms) of knowledge.

In his *Critique of Critical Philosophy*, Li refutes the generally prevailing presumption according to which Marx largely inherited Kantian subjectivism. Such interpretations of Marx were a deviation from Marx's actual philosophy (Li Zehou 1996b, 466). Instead, Li places great emphasis upon the Marxist notion of practice, a core tenet of his historical ontology. Li's theory of social practice as the crucial trigger of the development of humankind was tightly linked to the tool-making theory, which, in his eyes, was the true core of Marxists theory and the most complete explanation of human evolution. The clarification of these differences was another reason for his decision to reinterpret and modify Kant's epistemology. Besides, he believed that the question of how Marxism could have deteriorated into subjectivism had to be investigated by reviewing the inherent structure of Kant's idealistic philosophy.

Li was well aware of the fact that Kant's philosophical thought had a remarkable impact on modern cultures and contemporary science. He points out that Marxism should be enriched and improved by integrating Kant's reconceptualization of the natural sciences and of Kant's notion of free, autonomous, and active subject. Kant's static formal approach could also be enriched by the Hegelian and Marxist historical worldview. This synthesis should be developed to a higher level, one that is suitable for the contemporary era. In later explanations, Li describes the theoretical connection between Hegel, Marx, and Kant in the following way.

> The reason we must study Kant's philosophy . . . lies precisely in his contribution to the establishment of the subjective structure of subjectality, just like Hegel was important because of his great sense of history, which could be linked to the external, objective historical process of human evolution. Marx has established a new paradigm by transforming Hegel through sublation (Aufhebung), and now it is our turn to do the same work on Kant.
>
> 之所以聯繫康德哲學 . . . . . . ，則是由於正像黑格爾的宏偉歷史感與人類外在客觀歷史進程有關一樣，康德的貢獻主要是在主體性主觀結構方面。馬克思對黑格爾作出了揚棄改造的範例，今天似乎該輪到我們對康德做工作了。 (1985a: 15)

Precisely through this synthesis Li hopes to eliminate one of the greatest flaws of traditional Chinese philosophy, namely, the fact that it always fails to firmly link its ethics and philosophy with the basic paradigms of science and democracy. Li believes that it was necessary to reconcile the autonomy of human freedom with the autonomy of science, which was possible only by avoiding and eliminating subjectivism (and along with it, voluntarism) as well as determinism.[50] He aims to transform Kantian epistemology by replacing Kant's subjective and idealist approach, in which the problem of knowledge was dealt with only from the side of subjective intellect, by the Marxist viewpoint that all epistemology should start from humankind's interaction with the environment (Chong 1999a,

112). Li points out that so-called universal necessity is linked to the given levels of social practice in a certain time, highlighting that "in a certain sense, universal necessity is the manifestation of the objective sociality" (普遍必然性在一定的意義上是客觀社會性的表現) (Li Zehou 1996b, 13).

In investigating the essence and the development of knowledge, we should proceed from social practice and take into consideration the given developmental level of technology instead of limiting our explorations to perception and language.

Li's *Critique of the Critical Philosophy: A New Approach to Kant*, was based not only on Kant's first *Critique*, but also on the second and the third one. By far the largest part of it pertains to epistemology and therefore mainly refers to the *Critique of Pure Reason*.[51] Many scholars believe that it is Li's most important book. In *Critique of the Critical Philosophy*, Li followed the presumption that a proper understanding of dialectical mechanisms of Marxist epistemology could be found in Marx' early work *Economic and Philosophic Manuscripts of 1844*. He focused especially upon Marx's debate on estranged labor, which leads to alienation. Li completed this theory through his modern reading of Kant's three *Critiques* and his definition of subjectality, freewill, and morality.[52]

Li saw the most significant advantage of Kant's *Critique of Pure Reason* in the idea that human recognition was a result of an interaction between feelings or sensual perception and rational understanding, or between transcendental aesthetics and transcendental logic (Kant 2000, 78). According to Kant, there are two sources of human cognition, which perhaps spring from a common root that is yet unknown. Li proposed that this common root might consist of sensibility and intellect. Sensibility makes objects available to human cognition, but they are pondered and thought about via intellect.

Because sensibility might contain *a priori* representations that form the conditions under which objects are given to us, it belongs to transcendental philosophy. Sensibility precedes cognition, because the mere conditions under which objects are given to us necessarily precede those under which they are thought about (ibid., 107). Li believes that such a common root could be found in the crucial human practice of producing and continuously employing tools that turns members of the human species into subjects who possess transcendental aesthetics and simultaneously the ability of analyzing the external world. According to Li, both faculties are results of the cultural-psychologic formations. These formations represent a dynamic inner mental structure that is—in distinctive variations—common to all people and that simultaneously form the very foundation of all human cognitive activities. Li thus—through early Marx and his emphasize upon human nature in the sense of *homo faber*—placed Kant on material foundations.[53]

However, Li also went a step further. He established an epistemology of pragmatic reason, the logic of which was rooted in the toolmaking and -using habits of human beings. The starting point and the fundamental approach of this entire discourse is the paradigm of proper measure, which enables people to implement their practical activities in a way that allows them to obtain the knowledge (and wisdom) necessary for their survival.[54] The concept of proper measure can be seen as the "epistemic representation of human survival" (人類生存認識上的呈現) (Li Zehou 2012b, 2). Its logic, which is operational rather than transcendental, can be expressed by the form $A \neq A\pm$, which is different from $A = A$, but also from $A \neq \bar{A}$. It can neither be equated by any form of dialectical logic, based upon oppositions like "being–nonbeing," "quality–quantity," "substance-phenomena," and so on. Last, it is not based upon any form of existence, rationality, God, or matter.

Li replies to Kant's question of how recognition (or synthetic *a priori* judgment) is possible with another question: How is humankind possible. He argues that the social activities of human material production are the essence and the basis of any recognition or knowledge. In his view, the epistemology of humankind can only be explained through its integration into the ontology of humankind (Li Zehou 2008e, 318). This central supposition provides him with a solid foundation for the establishment of his sedimentation concept.[55,56] Thus if we look at sedimentation through the lens of epistemology, we can see it as a three-dimensionally structured process, deeply rooted in a dynamic interaction between universally human, culturally, and/or environmentally determined and individual factors. In this framework, knowledge (or recognition) represents the integration of reason. Li believes that Kant's view of the essence of mathematical thought, which includes synthetic and *a priori* judgments, is a good example for the flexibility and the dynamic nature of human comprehension. Li goes a step further and concludes that the primeval foundation of mathematics must have been the internalization of human operational activities (Li Zehou 2007, 82–84). In a later explanation, he summarizes this presumption as follows:

> Similar to formal logic, we still don't know what the foundation or the starting point of mathematics is. I can only state

my opinion from the viewpoint of philosophy. I believe that
it must be connected with the operational activities of primitive labor. Logic is the abstracted development of the laws (or
demands) inherent to the operational activities as such and
a great part of mathematics is the abstracted development of
the relation between operational activities and their spatial
environment.

與形式邏輯一樣, 數學的原點或根據是什麼呢? 至今並沒有解答。
我只是從哲學上認為它與人的原始勞動操作活動相關。邏輯是操
作自身規律 (要求) 的抽象化發展, 數學很大一部分是操作與空間
環境相互關係的抽象化發展。 (Li Zehou 2012b, 2)

In the course of this development, the distance between these forms of knowledge and cognition and material operational practice became increasingly large to the point where they were no longer in any kind of mutual relation. They became symbolic systems without any relations to material practice and reality. These systems, became frameworks of symbolic operational activities that were based upon numbers.

Similar to the tools that were rooted in human sensitivity and were the results of labor and material operational activities, numbers became tools of rational operations, which is extremely important for the sustainable preservation of human existence. Therefore, for Li, "'proper measure' is the first, and 'number' the second category" (『度』是認識論的第一範疇, 『數』是第二範疇) (ibid., 2–3).

Since this dynamic, ever changeable category of proper measure is "wisdom," ensuring sustainable human existence, it also ensures that "possibilities," which are contained in reality, can factually be realized. But numbers, are only a logical possibility. "Although 'numbers' were results of the survival wisdom of the 'proper measure,' they developed into logical possibilities and hence became independent from the 'proper measure'" (ibid., 3).

According to Li, the flexible and dynamic nature of the forms of knowledge becomes visible when we study Kant through the lens of the Marxist theory of practice. Through this theory, we gain a more reliable insight into the formal structures of human cognition.

In explaining Kant's transcendental perception theory, Li once again highlights the importance of the given level of technology and of social practice for the formation of Kant's hypothesis of the universal and necessary nature of time and space perception. He believes that Kant's attempts to provide mathematical proof for the existence of transcendental forms for temporal and spatial perception were "crazy" (*kuangran* 狂然) (Li Zehou 1996b, 119). He counters them with several examples from human history, through which he aims to show that notions of time and space, as well as conceptions of numbers, always evolved out of the need to master certain given social or economic situations in a respective concrete time and space. This drives his emphasis that not only concepts or thought patterns, but even logic, represents the forms and the laws of these patterns, is also grounded in human operational activities (Li Zehou 2012b, 2).[57] In this context, Li also points to a very important epistemological problem that was highlighted by Kant, but was mostly overlooked or ignored by his readers and interpreters (ibid., 4). Li points out that Kant's conviction that it is extremely important to differentiate between logical and real possibilities (or possibilities that exist in concrete reality) and criticizes them from this view the dialectic of Hegel and Marx.[58] Yet, he was certainly aware of the importance of logical discourse, highlighting that "this (critique) does by no means reject or diminish the importance of logical inferences or logical possibilities, although they are separated from experiences" (ibid., 3).

Using his proper measure paradigm, Li accuses Kant's view of human perceptional structure as much too rigid. He emphasizes that such forms are not universal in the sense of absolute and unchangeable entities. Rather, they are continuously evolving, progressing, and being modified—through the internalization of reason and through sedimentation—along with the changing level of human technology. The social practice of making and using tools has, in the form of specific human labor, broken through the narrow and deterministic framework of animal life activities and created numerous highly differentiated causal relations in the objective reality. Li also views this as the real beginning of the concept of causality and of mental categories (1996b, 175).

Li identifies the theoretical basis of this idealism. Although Kant admits that cognition cannot be separated from sensibility, he still presupposes that the former controls and guides the latter. In Li's view, this is the main flaw of the given state of the natural sciences, which also exaggeratedly emphasizes the primary role of reason. The problem of causality in Li's claims reflect a crucial philosophical question of contemporary quantum mechanics.

He also highlights the question of human consciousness of self (apperception), noting that this was one of the most important and most difficult problems within Kant's epistemology (ibid., 179). In Li's view, this is precisely the question that reflects the flexibility and dynamics of human comprehension in a most vivid and concentrated way. The objectivity of knowledge is not directly derived from sensual perception, but results from the dynamic character of consciousness. But while Kant strictly opposed any form of spiritual substance (ibid., 200ff), underscoring that apperception is not substance or being but merely form and function, Fichte and Hegel in this context drastically radicalized Kant's idealism, claiming that the dynamic character of our cognition does not only influence the mode of our comprehension, but also creates our reality (ibid., 205). In this context, Li explains the Marxist critique of such extreme idealistic subjectivism—the individual, subjective self, who was at the center of German idealist epistemology—is replaced by the vital role of social practice and material production of humankind as an entirety. Li points out that this is an important development of both traditional materialism, which proceeded from the individual perception of reality, and Kant's and Hegel's approaches, which were rooted in universal nature of human consciousness. He then proceeds to Kant's theory of antinomies and Hegel's elevation of this basic paradigm into a dialectical view of reality (ibid., 253). Here Li singles out the importance of Hegel's notion of sublation or "Aufhebung" (yangqi 揚棄) as a core element of his dialectics, which is a basis for a historical worldview.

At the end of this epistemological part, which makes up the largest part of *Critique of Critical Philosophy*, Li treats Kant's notion of the "thing-in-itself" (wu zi ti 物自體) in its function as a link from epistemology to ethics (ibid., 288). Although Li agrees with Kant in the basic presumption that there is a close connection between ethics and epistemology, he rejects Kant's idea of the thing-in-itself as a noumenon that is unknowable, but that simultaneously represents the highest moral substance (Li Zehou 2012b, 1). There is only knowledge of life and the world in which we live, created and derived by the collective human subject through social practice, especially material production. That which empowers human beings (as parts of humankind) to find a synthesis between their knowledge of natural laws and freewill and morality, is precisely this social practice or material production. Li agrees with the Kantian postulate of the categorical imperative, but, unlike Kant, Li believes that this imperative is not rooted in the unknowable divine and morally permeated nature of the noumenon but is rather a product of socialization. To Li, both the concrete existence of the objective reality and Kant's moral imperative itself are equally products of human collective, social activities. This means that the subjective consciousness is not primarily *a priori*, as defined by Kant, because the faculties of perception, comprehension, and cognition are created through practice in a long-lasting process of continuous social evolution.

However, the process of such evolution always includes transformations of both spirit and matter: "These processes continuously interact but cannot be reduced to each other. This is why both idealism and materialism in their pure form are one-sided and unsatisfactory" (Chong 1999a, 120). In his *Critique*, Li often criticizes the old, pre-Marxist, mechanistic materialism, holding that objective reality is much more than a predetermined external world that functions in accordance with unchangeable natural laws and that it is, as such, mechanically reflected in a passive human brain. The logical conclusion of this, is that science and freewill do not contradict one another. Without free thought and without the creative human mind, science would not be possible. This spurs Li to emphasize that the deterministic laws of Newtonian mechanics are outdated and simply wrong. But in the very structure of Kant's first *Critique*, Li detects a tendency towards an outbreak of the limitations of this complex system of thought, which, in the end, is still a deterministic and static dualism.

> Actually, Kant's way of seeing the "thing-in-itself," which originates from the sensibility and leads through the limitations of comprehension and conceptual reason to finally arrive at the path leading towards the moral substance, is objectively directed towards Fichte and Hegel, although Kant himself never gave up his dualism. But the real solution to the problem of Kant's thing-in-itself could only be found on practical foundations, and only after Marx's radical critique of Hegel's idealistic unification of recognition and practice, logics and history, nature and society.
>
> 其實，康德的「物自體」由感性來源到認識界限到理念理性，最終邁入道德實體，這條道路客觀上是指向費希特、黑格爾的方向的，儘管康德自己始終並不願放棄他的二元論。只有黑格爾唯心主義地把認識與實踐、邏輯與歷史、自然與社會統一起來，並遭到馬克思主義的徹底批判之後，康德的物自體問題才可能在實踐論的基礎上得到真正的解答。(Li Zehou 1978a, 52)

In his epistemology, Li therefore tries to find a way to reformulate different forms of Kant's *a priori* knowledge in terms of a dynamically evolving and continuously changing process of acquiring, preserving, and developing knowledge, transforming it into wisdom.

Ethics and Political Philosophy

Li expands a summarized version of his ethical thought in *An Outline of Ethics*, which was later, in a slightly reworked form, republished as a part of his book, *An Outline of Philosophy*. It was again republished in 2016 in the newest version of his *Anthropo-Historical Ontology*. Li also published an important recent work in this field. *A Response to Sandel and other Writings* was published in Beijing in 2014.[59] He has also elaborated upon ethical questions in numerous articles, essays, and interviews.[60] Li's inspiration comes from Chinese tradition, particularly from classical Chinese ethical thought. Although ethics is an important part of Western philosophy in China it has been far more emphasized and received much greater attention both theoretically and philosophically. In his ethical discourse, Li advances from the basic approaches that were created in the cradle of his own tradition, creatively transforming it to a new modernized axiological framework suitable for the globalized humankind of the twenty-first century.

Immanuel Kant's ethics was also an important source of his inspiration.[61] In Li's synthesis between Kantian and Confucian ethics, Confucian ethics plays the primary role. Kantian ethics is a mere supplement (Li Zehou 2016b, 212). Li devotes only two chapters of *Critique of Critical Philosophy* to Kant's *Critique of Practical Reason*.

Li admires Kant's concept of the categorical imperative and agrees with him in the presumption that human beings are always the ultimate goal and never merely the means of achieving something external to them. Although ethical relativism can also be viewed as one of the results of the Kantian emphasis on the role of the subject in constructing reality, Li strongly opposes this concept. He acknowledges that in politics this view can provide some support to the protection of minorities and other marginalized and/or oppressed social groups; however, he believes the idea is theoretically shallow, for it fails to convey that all forms of ethics share the same universal forms, which are passed further from one generation to another. Li consequently claims that ethical relativism neglects the role of subjective activity and free choice (Chong 1999a, 165).

Li also deeply appreciates the awakening of reason in Kant's philosophy of Enlightenment. However, in contrast to Kant, he sees this reason as a product of the dawn of modern times, and not as a universal transcendental principle.

> In fact, it is not at all "pure," but is rather a powerful reaction to the demands and tendencies of its era. It reflects the crucial themes and echoes the voices of the French Revolution. Under the banner of this "human being," who is equipped with the pure reason, Kant was actually the voice that demanded "independence," "equality," and "freedom" from feudalism.
>
> 它實際上並不「純粹」，而是強烈地提出了一定社會時代的要求和動向，反映了法國革命時代的課題和呼聲。康德打出這個純粹理性的、作為目的的「人」的旗號，實際上是向封建主義要求「獨立」、「自由」、「平等」的呼聲。 (Li Zehou 2007, 302)

Li also firmly rejects the absoluteness of values, which was a logical consequence of Kant's transcendental reason (Li Zehou 2016b, 215). He rejects the static, unchangeable *a priori* forms of knowledge because their inner essence is rooted in universal necessity that can never be transformed or modified. These forms are nothing but abstract formulas, motionlessly frozen and forever trapped in the intangible world of transcendental mysteries (Li Zehou 2007, 316). As a result, he rejects the idealist framework of Kant's ethical thought. In short, the Chinese philosopher criticizes Kant's idea of practical reason, because due to its transcendental nature it surpasses humankind and all individual human beings. It has nothing to do with human sensitivity, and even much less with concrete human lives.

Confucian pragmatic reason is formed and functions within the emotio-rational structure that is deeply rooted in the human world. It is based on actual human conditions and arises from human social emotionality, transforming these culturally integrated general communal emotions through rites in the process of "condensation of reason" (*lixing ningju* 理性凝聚) into rational concepts of right and wrong, good and evil. The rationality of these concepts governs subjective personal feelings of each member of a community. In the concrete social life, these rational concepts can nevertheless dissolve through the process of the "melting of reason" (*lixing ronghua* 理性融化) in the heart-minds of people and thus become an integral part of individual emotions.

Li's Confucian-inspired ethics accordingly proceeds from more realistic and more earthly human foundations. In his *Critique of Critical Philosophy*, Li brings this issue to the very point: "Kant's 'universal necessity' should be replaced by 'objective sociality'. It should be emphasized that humankind, as well as humanness, are both products of history" (ibid., 215–16).

Such an approach is a logically coherent part of his system, for Li explored all ethical questions—like all the other philosophical problems he was elaborating upon—through the lens of his anthropo-historical ontology, proceeding from the specific elements that make human beings human.

Li often emphasizes the necessity of drawing a clear and unambiguous demarcation line between ethics and morality. While ethics pertains to interhuman relationships and regulates human action in the concrete network of their relations with other human beings, morality belongs to the internal psychological forms and values of particular individuals. Li's view is that morality can also be divided in two parts: the external, which manifests itself in the traditional religious and modern social moralities; and the internal, which consists of inherent capabilities as will, emotions, and ideas or concepts (Li Zehou 2016b, 17).[62] Table 4.1 gives a general overview of Li's understanding of ethics and morals, which principally involves rituals being generated from general social or collective emotionality and reason governing emotion (Li, Zehou 2016, 1079).[63]

Table 4.1. Li's Ethical Thought

Ethics	→	Morals
(external, cultural activities, the content of social historical period)		(internal, human psychology or nature, individual psychological forms)
History	Education	Governance
Emotionality →	Ritual Regulations →	Reason → Emotion
(the circumstances of communal existence)	(customs, norms, ← institutions, social order, laws)	(the will and conceptual thought)	(individual emotions and desires, conduct)
Political Philosophy		Moral Psychology

From this schematic presentation, Li understands human reason as consisting of two parts: conceptual thought or comprehension and the will. "While the will is the form of reason, conceptual thought represents the content of the ideas of good and evil" (Li Zehou 2016b, 210).

Li explains:

> Human will is our awareness, consciousness, rational control, and domination of reason over our feelings. This is the psychological power of the form of reason. But what is the concrete content of this reason? These are the concepts of good and evil, right and wrong.
>
> 意志是人的自覺、有意識的理性對感性的支配、主宰的能力，這是心理的理性形式力量，但這理性的具體內容是什麼，便是善惡、是非觀念。(ibid.)

As we have discussed, Li does not follow Kant in his supposition that practical reason belongs to our inborn *a priori* forms. In his view reason is a historical concept, formed through the pragmatic necessities and requirements of human social life.

> From the viewpoint of anthropo-historical ontology, this apparent "*a priori*" is still rooted in the preservation and the evolution of the sustainable survival of humankind as an entirety (not of any particular community in any concrete time and space). As soon as an individual is born, they received the following "obligation": without being able to choose, you were born into a long river of human history (into a situation and an environment, which provides you with all basic necessities for your life). The civilization and the culture that are legacies of this "entirety of humankind" will nurture you and raise you, and therefore you are indebted to them. At all times you have to be completely committed to them, even to sacrifice yourself, if necessary. There are no other special reasons for this: one must absolutely follow and obey this "categorical imperative" and this "practical reason."
>
> 依人類學歷史本體論看，這個所謂「先驗」仍然來自維護人類作為總體 (不是任何特定時、空中的群體) 的生存和延續。個體一

> 出生，即有此道德「義務」：你出生在一個沒法選擇的人類總體的歷史長河 (衣食住行的既定狀況和環境) 之中，是這個「人類總體」所遺留下來的文明，文化將你撫養成人，從而你就欠債，就得準備隨時獻身為它，包括犧牲自己。這就是沒有什麼道理可說，只有絕對服從堅決執行的「絕對律令」和「實踐理性」的來由。
> (Li Zehou 2016, 315)

This view could be posited in contrast to the idea of the social contract. From the standpoint of the individual, both approaches are similar, for the social contract also proceeds from the fact that all people (likewise without being able to choose otherwise) are born into a society that provides them with the basic infrastructure for their existence. In Western discourse, each individual's moral and political responsibilities are dependent upon a fictitious agreement among citizens to shape the society in which they live in the best possible way. While this Western notion is largely based upon normative regulations and contractual law, Li's argument is rooted in each person's emotional comprehension of interhuman relationships. It is similar to the contemporary feminist critique, which argues that understanding interhuman relations merely in contractual terms constitutes a very limited model of human aspirations (see for instance Held 2006, 81). The crucial flaw of the social contract idea is that it unable to reflect or represent the richness and the multidimensional nature of human motivations and psychology, suggesting alternative types of interhuman relationships while searching for new insights into morality. These new models of ethics that focused on gender equality in moral development began with Carol Gilligan's book *In a Different Voice: Psychological Theory and Women's Development*, published in 1982 and often denoted as "the book that started a (gender) revolution." Sara Ruddick (1989) and Virginia Held (2006), propose the example of the mother-child relationship to replace the prevailing paradigm of individual agents who are guided by pure self-interest while negotiating with each other through normative contracts. They argue that such a model is more appropriate for it reflects numerous genuinely moral experiences of most people—particularly women—more realistically.

Li does not fully approve of this approach, viewing this kind of ethics as propagating a dangerous return to premodern times.

> This line of contemporary feminist theory is rooted in postmodernism, which is defined by anti-rationalist and

anti-Enlightenment features[64]. I have always promoted Enlightenment and even proposed surpassing it. . . . This was clear when I was explaining the emotion-based substance as (a part of) the emotio-rational structure. And I am certainly against a retro-sentimental ethics, based upon empathy or sympathy.

當前這股女性主義潮流，與後現代主義相關。後現代主義的特色之一是反理性、反啟蒙。而我一直強調的是「提倡啟蒙，超越啟蒙」......我以情理結構講情本體，就包含這一點，而並不贊成以同情、移情為基礎的新老情感主義倫理學。 (Li Zehou 2016b, 173)

It is not coincidental that modern care ethics, which is to a great extent an upshot of such feminist discourses, is often compared to Confucian role or relational ethics, which also forms a basis of Li's understanding of human relations.[65]

"Humaneness" is the main axis that is rooted in the loving emotions between parents and children (filial piety and gentle compassion). However, when radiating outwards, it gains a spiritual dimension and becomes a universal denotation for interhuman psychology, rooted in love.

「仁」是以親子情 (孝慈) 為主軸，輻射開來卻具有神聖性質的以愛為核心的人際心理的概括總稱。 (Li Zehou 2015, 117)

The central Confucian virtue of humaneness is also crucial in the framework of Li's emotion-based substance, which represents the sedimented form of a specifically Chinese (or East Asian) cultural-psychological formation, tightly linked to the corresponding view of human nature or humanness. Li explains:

Up [until] today, I am still insisting that "humaneness" is a structure which incorporates four aspects. It is a structure of human nature (humanness), which is composed of "the kinship basis, psychological principles, humanism and the individual personality." As I have pointed out in my work *Reading the Analects Today*, it can be equated with the so-called emotio-rational structure or the emotion-based substance. It implies a mutual interaction between reason and emotion, which makes us different from animals and also from rational machines. This is the core notion of my theory of humanness, which I have not changed for several decades.

> 我至今仍然堅持「仁」是這個四方面的結構體,即由「血緣基礎、心理原則、人道主義和個體人格」所形成的人性結構,也就是我後來「論語今讀」所提出的「情理結構」(emotio-rational structure) 即「情本體」(emotion-based substance), 其中的情理交融既區別於禽獸動物,也區別於理性機器,這是我數十年沒有變動的人性論的觀點圓心。 (Li Zehou 2015, 118)

It is important to note that in the interactive correlative oppositional pair of emotion and reason, which make up the basis of the emotio-rational structure, reason is the primary and decisive, controlling, and guiding element. This entire structure, which is implanted in the ontology of emotion-based substance, is not limited to the sphere of ethics, but is also tightly linked to political philosophy. The emotion-based substance not only pertains to the inherent experiences or to the actions and behaviors of an individual person. Since it is rooted in the Confucian ethics, in which "the Way (*Dao*) begins at emotionality" and "rites arise from emotionality," it is also a social, historical, and political substance (see Guodian chu mu zhu jian 1989; Yu cong II: 179). This incorporation of emotion into politics corresponds to Li's proposal regarding the two kinds of morality, according to which the religious morality should "guide by example and appropriately construct" the social morality (*fandao he shidang goujian* 範導和適當構建).

Especially concerning ethics and political philosophy, Li does not agree with the normative regularity of Western Enlightenment models (Li Zehou 2012c, 15). While the intention of the emotion-based substance (*qing bentide neitui* 情本體的內推) pertains to religious philosophy, in whose context religion should be replaced by aesthetics, its extension (*qing bentide waitui* 情本體的外推) is an emotion-based political philosophy that holds that "music is integrated into the governance" (*yue yu zheng tong* 樂與政通) and that "harmony is higher than justice" (*hexie gaoyu Zhengyi* 和諧高于正義). This last statement is rather controversial, for it can easily be misunderstood especially by Western readers who are unfamiliar with the essence or the complex scope of the traditional Chinese notion of harmony.[66] Li explains it several times, highlighting that justice and harmony are rooted in completely different social, political, and ideational referential frameworks. While justice arose in a tradition of universality, which emphasizes the equality of all humans, harmony highlights concrete situational, relational, social, and axiological contexts in that people in the given state of affairs were embedded. While the basic criterion for the regulation of human interactions and relations of justice was normative law, harmony was rooted in rites. Li tries to illustrate the basic differences between the two models in a contrastive analysis containing seven crucial differences (see table 4.2) (Li Zehou 2012c, 16).

Table 4.2. Ritual and Law

Ritual (li)	*Law (fa 法)*
1. Unwritten regulations and principles (based on the "Classics")	Written formal norms
2. Emphasis on situations and conditions, specificities, and differences; greater flexibility; individual rights and responsibilities are linked to emotionality	Emphasis on universality and determination (definition); striving for equality and consistency
3. Demands individual consciousness, awareness, and activity	Demands obedience and respect
4. Composed of two aspects, namely public morality (public behavior) and private morality (internal cultivation)	Only considers public morality, which should be respected and reflected in behavior, without taking into account private (internal, personal) morality
5. Considers public opinion, its sanctions, and condemnation	Sanctions are issued exclusively by governmental institutions
6. Incorporates purposiveness (it is a purpose in itself)	Incorporates instrumentality (it is, in itself, a tool or a means)
7. Is connected to emotiveness (it is a result of the humaneness)	Is not linked to emotions (and neither to humaneness)

Li reminds us that in China, a normative law-based Legalism (*fa jia* 法家) only dominated for a brief period of fifteen years during the short-lived Qin Dynasty (221–206 BC). Its successor, the Han Dynasty (206 BC–AD 220), however, was still confronted with the question of how to rule over a giant unified superpower-state. In addressing this problem, the court ideologist Dong Zhongshu took (hitherto already widely forgotten) Confucianism as a basis for the new social and political doctrine. In Dong's system, Confucian rituality complemented the legalist concept of law. This integration of numerous legalist elements into the framework of original Confucianism led to the "blending of ritual and law" (*li fa jiaorong* 禮法交融) and to the "reciprocal utilization of Confucianism and Legalism. In Li's view, this synthesis was extremely important for the further development of the Chinese state and society. He emphasizes that in working out this combination, Dong achieved a "transformative creation." He also thinks that in the present, which is also marked by transitional elements (similar to the Han Dynasty period), it is time to search for a new transformative creation. The two kinds of morality, which forms the very foundation of his ethics and political philosophy, highlights the need for contemporary China to enact and adhere to a strict division between state and religion.

> This is why I advocate a strict distinction and relation of "public social morality" and "private religious morality." This is important in order to deconstruct the traditional "trinity of politics, ethics, and religion." Actually, this "trinity" is nothing else but the traditional "rule of one man."
>
> 所以我提出「社會性公德」與「宗教性私德」的區分和關係，以解構傳統禮教的「政治、倫理、宗教三合一」，這「三合一」其實就是傳統的「人治」。 (Li Zehou 2012c, 16)

In Li's opinion, it is extremely important not to allow a blurring of the dividing line between reason and emotion, because this could lead to favoritism and to the despotism of so-called human feelings (*ren qing* 人情)—these days a notion that is only used to cover up private interests or a greedy desire for power. The Chinese people must not allow these distortions or negative aspects of their own tradition destroy the legal system. Only on the basis of a clear distinction between the two kinds of morality—and only if public social morality is firmly established in the sense of Rawls' "overlapping consensus," but with an emphasis on and on the basis of a well-developed modern economy—can it be allowed that traditional "private religious morality" would "guide by example and appropriately construct . . . public social morality." In such an ideal case, private religious morality could unfold its genuine essence as a morality of cosmic sentiment and human warmth. Such a private religious morality is an aesthetic power that can, in fact, be identified with the emotion-based substance.

The concept of justice as it is widely understood in modern liberalist societies is, in Li's view, much too ahistorical, for it is, in essence, rooted in Kant's transcendental ethics.

> In the utilitarianism of Sandel's discussions, the rightist liberalism of egalitarian liberals, and the leftist liberalism of libertarians, as well as Kant and Rawls, justice is always defined through abstract rational principles (for instance, as the greatest happiness for the greatest number of people, individual freedom of choice, the categorical imperative, or equality). But why does the communal life of humankind need the rational principle of justice? This is something they discuss very little. Of course, ideas of cooperative agreement for the sake of personal safety and benefit have been discussed, but questions remain as to how such agreement is possible. Without reference to historical factors, there is very little to say in this regard, and we can only come to suppositional rational postulations. (Li, Zehou 2016, 1076)

Li's Chinese alternative to modern Western concepts of liberalism and individualism is also based on his theory of the integration of emotion and reason in psychological formations, for these allow people to more or less smoothly live with the members of their families, but also function well within their groups and communities, for all of these are defined by the paradigm of relationalism. He brings up this notion in contrast to individualism, which, in his view, stresses independency, which includes separateness. Modern Western political thinkers place their theories within the framework of the Aristotelian virtue ethics, which is based on the concept of individuality. In Li's view traditional Chinese ethics also belong to a wider conception of virtue ethics. Euro-American ethical thought was initially shaped in the ancient Greek idea of a free civil society of equal individuals. Later, it was profoundly influenced by Judeo-Christian concepts of final judgment before God in which all individuals are also equal. In China, on the contrary, communities were formed according to the principle of kinship relations, in which the group members were anything but equal.

> China's high level of development in the Neolithic period, based on small agricultural production and social ties of kinship, gave rise to a system of tribal clans and the rationalization of the shamanistic tradition that led in turn to the transformation of the idea of "people as relationships" "into a "traditional unconscious" (*chuantong wuyishi*).[67] (Li, Zehou 2016, 1079)

Due to the prevailing ideologies described above, such "traditional unconscious" was determined by the notion of individualism in the Western world. The distinction between the emphasis on relationalism and individualism respectively is a fundamental dissimilarity between the two types of ethics, correspondingly prevailed in the Chinese and in the Euro-American cultural milieus.

Li is also critical of the Western notion of communitarianism, an idea that is highly prized and considered an alternative to absolute individualism by many contemporary Western and Chinese scholars. In contrast, he believes that it is a "product of developed countries with long traditions of liberalism" (Li, Zehou 2016, 1086). Hence, it has in his theory, a "referential value, but if directly or indiscriminately adopted in other societies [it] can be quite dangerous" (ibid.).

Li does not totally and completely oppose liberalism. Nonetheless, he endorses a different idea of liberalism, which he basically sees as a system in which the society exists for the individual, and in which individual rights are of primary importance.

> Liberalism stresses that all people are ends in themselves and should not be used as instruments or means. It emphasizes individuals' freedom to choose and make decisions for themselves. This hugely elevates the position and value of the individual, as well as respect for personal character, and thereby liberates the individual from various forms of enslavement by the past's political and economic systems, traditional customs, and ideologies. (Li, Zehou 2016, 1084)

He notes that his idea of a "modern social morality" (*xiandai shehuixing daode* 現代社會性道德) in many ways also resembles liberalism. It equally embraces freedom, equality, independence, human rights, democracy, and tolerance, but also cooperation, mutual respect, neutrality of values, and other elements. For Li—in contrast to the opinions of many advocates of Western liberal ideologies—all these are moral values and are formed on the basis of the public reason prevailing in modern societies. To him it is also important to separate them from any kind of religious moralities that are marked by emotional faith.

The variation of liberalism he advocates is much more dynamic and historical than the existing one (ibid., 1136). Ultimately, this means that it might not be the best possible arrangement. Li holds that liberalism is by no means the best possible system, eternally and universally applicable, but rather a transitory system.

> It is a requirement or product of the historical development of a certain period or stage. Liberalism is thus part of historicism, and history does not end with capitalist society and liberalism. This both emphasize justice as well as take the "emotional cosmology" of the idea that "harmony is higher than justice" as regulative in order to move toward a more ideal future. This transcends liberalism. (ibid.)

Li is fully aware that, historically, theories of liberalism and individualism appear and spread after the emergence and growth of capitalism. Since he claims that his theories are based upon early Marxism, we could assume that he opposes a capitalist system. He advocates a transcending or a surpassing of capitalism, which for him is by no means the last (or the best possible) stage of history. However, he does not see the capitalist period as an unbearable one. On the contrary, he is quite fond of the numerous material advantages and the high level of technological development it brought. Hence, he also rejects any violent attempts to destroy it. It is quite understandable in this sense that Li eliminates from Marxism the concepts of class struggle and revolution. Although these two elements are doubtless the essential driving forces behind the Marxist historical model of dialectical materialism. In light of this, we might ask ourselves whether Li's philosophy could still be associated with the immensely influential political-economic theory—one of the most dominant discourses of the twentieth century, widely known and associated with Marxism.

Li claims that the basis of his theoretical paradigms is dialectical materialism and that he attempts to complement Kant through the dialectical historical worldview as represented by Hegel and Marx. Nevertheless, since he eliminated the concept of class struggle from his theories of human progress, the dialectics of human progress he advocates is one that is not necessarily grounded in contradictions leading to syntheses through mutual sublations.[68] Instead of fighting his way through reciprocally conflicting oppositions towards the revolutionary salvation, he strives for the realization of social progress by means of proper measure and harmony. It is obvious that his theoretical model of a dialectically progressive historical development must necessarily be rooted in completely different theoretical paradigms. We shall deal with this issue in the section about Li Zehou's theoretical system.[69]

Considering his aversion to violent solutions of social conflicts, it is not surprising that Li bade goodbye to the Marxist concept of revolution in his thirties. If we consider the political situation in the PRC in the 1960s (when Li was in his thirties), such a decision was not an easy task and required quite a bit of courage. Based on her meticulous analytic work, Woei-Lien Chong points out that Li avoided violent upheavals as a trigger for social changes as early as 1964. She notes that even though Li's thought always remained dialectical and teleological, his post-1964 writings no longer contain gnostic-apocalyptic elements that were so prominent in his early works. Although he continued to use particular positions associated with the gnostic-apocalyptic scheme, he cleansed them of their revolutionary implications. This shows that Li said goodbye to revolution before the launching of the Cultural Revolution (Chong 1999a, 295).

In 1997, Li published *Farewell to Revolution* together with Liu Zaifu.[70] Through all these years and through the present day, Li has thoroughly advocated that humankind should rather pursue progress through sensible reforms instead of violent revolutions. Once again, he draws inspiration from the traditional Chinese notions of harmony and the middle way. Together with the implementation of his concept of the right proportions, in his eyes they should replace the numerous violent solutions of social and national conflicts in our globalized world.

5

General Evaluation and Impact

Theoretical System:
Models and Networks, Continuity and Change

In his own anthropo-historical philosophy, Li Zehou profoundly modified the systems of all classical Western philosophers from whom he drew inspiration. He not only complemented Kant with Marx and Marx with Kant but he further posited both of them in a dynamic and changeable configuration, borrowed from traditional Chinese philosophies. He redefined and completely transformed the static forms derived from the various systems of Euro-American philosophy in terms of development, especially human development.[1] In so doing, he proceeded from a materialist worldview and thoroughly applied the method of historical materialism (Chong 1999a, 171).

Network of Relations

Li Zehou's theory, which can—in contrast to particular methods or approaches that are only parts of it—be tested for consistency and can therefore either be verified or falsified in terms of a coherent system, is the theory of anthropo-historical ontology. This ontology, to begin with, is much more than only a theory of being, for it is—in the classical Chinese tradition—primarily also a theory of becoming.

Li often mentions in his works that because of the specific historical conditions and developmental patterns, Chinese culture is defined by the phenomenon of *relationalism*. This notion refers to the social significance of relationships between people, which in Chinese culture were shaped by the historical importance of family clan systems. In this socio-historical paradigm, relation—not only as a set of ordered pairs, but also as a basic element of a wider systematic network—has an instrumental function.

Analogously, relation also forms the foundation of Li's theoretical system. As previously discussed, the basic structure of this system also has a relational nature. The same as most of the prevailing streams in traditional Chinese philosophy, Li's own system cannot be strictly divided into or neatly ordered according to mutually separated disciplines or academic branches. Most of the central concepts forming the core groundwork of his philosophy are interconnected, interdependent, and continuously under the influence of one another. Each of them plays different, but significant roles in various particular areas of his theory. Accordingly, they occur as pivotal notions, shaping a relational network in which various contents are connected by one and the same structural relational paradigm. Li himself described his system as consisting of interconnected relations, pointing out that in his scheme, "everything is mutually interlocked" (Li Zehou and Liu Yuedi 2014, 195).

As we have seen, in his theory of human genesis and evolution, the concept of proper measure is of crucial importance, for it has a defining value in the shaping and development of humankind. At the same time, however, it is also essential in Li's ethics, political philosophy, epistemology, and aesthetics.

Sedimentation, on the other hand, is an indispensable concept in the framework of Li's anthropology, cultural studies, psychology and epistemology, but simultaneously strongly influencing the development of his aesthetic, ethical, and political thought. Something similar could be claimed for most of his other ideas, especially for the notion of subjectality, but to a certain degree also for concepts like the techno-social or the cultural-psychological formation, the collective social consciousness, the two kinds of morality, the psychological and the instrumental substance, and for many others.

The methods he developed such as the one of transformative creation or the one of dynamic correlative interaction, the processes of condensation and amalgamation of reason and so forth, are all likewise defined by strong correlative interconnections.

Even most of the notions he coined to describe certain specific features of Chinese culture, such as the emotion-based substance, the emotio-rational structure, or pragmatic reason, are intertwined and interweaved into various discourses, from ethics to epistemology and psychology, and can also be easily applied to universal human qualities. Hence, several attributes of the social structure belonging to the so-called culture of pleasure could—despite the fact that this culture was developed in the specific and unique scope of ritualized shamanism—in principle serve as an alternative mode and method of social existence in any human society. In Li's view, such a culture is rooted in the universal characteristics of human inwardness, in an un-alienated, immanently oriented human mind. It is therefore not surprising that Li believes in the positive force of his own cultural heritage, which could, in his view, enhance and enrich the future development of global philosophy. In its modernized form, after assimilating analytical reason and establishing a basis for contemporary legal thought, Chinese philosophy could serve as an alternative model of reflecting upon and changing societies.

In this light, Li points out that this possibility is grounded in the relational nature of its system, which forms a valuable foundation not only for new modes of thought or new patterns of interpreting reality, but also for the shaping of a new axiology.

> The Chinese people have no devout faith in gods. For them, heaven or nature and human beings are equally parts of one and the same correlative system of actions and reactions. Heaven is also nothing more than a part or an important element of this system, which, as such, is the real, the ultimate and highest, the unchangeable god.
>
> 中國人沒有對上帝的虔誠信仰，天與人同處一個宇宙反饋系統中相互作用，天也只是這個系統的一個部分或要素，只有這個系統本身才是至高無上不會改變的上帝。(Li Zehou 2016, 158)

It is precisely this relational nature of human existence that could provide a new hope for the further development of humanism and global ethics. In Li's view, Western liberal ideologies believe in individual rights and place individuals in the absolute foreground of their ethics.[2] To him this means that their starting point is an "atomized individual," which is actually an empty construct, for no human being can exist completely separated from human communities and their relational networks (Li Zehou 2016, 197).

In investigating the complexity of Li theoretical system, it soon becomes clear that it is almost impossible to confine his thought system into the narrow framework of one single discipline or even to squeeze it into one field of research. Many of Li's newly coined notions, categories, and concepts actually pertain to different fields, but are nonetheless mutually interconnected, intermingled, and interdependent. They cannot be coherently treated or comprehended in isolation from each other. However, it seems that there is a common thread that runs through his entire opus. To evaluate the coherence of his theoretical system, it is advisable to proceed from the central and most important methodological foundation that outlines every theoretical model. This is the referential framework that provides the defining structure that underlies every systematic and comprehensive theory.[3]

Referential Framework

When following this line of thought and analyzing Li's critical interpretations of modern Western philosophies, it soon becomes evident that Kant's theoretical system was rooted in a different referential framework than Li's (or Confucius's, for that matter). Although at first sight Marx and Hegel both seem to come closer to a deformalized and more dynamic, modifiable, and historicized approach, the evolving course of their theories in fact still remains largely fixed. Their historical approach is still abstractly formalized and trapped within patterns of static dualistic contradictions, in which binary oppositions are neatly separated from each other by the sublime divide that was firmly and unchangeable set up by the triple law of classical Western logical thought.

To obtain insight into the coherence of Li's philosophical system, we must first understand why his works cannot be seen merely as an upgrade or elaboration of Kant, Hegel, and Marx, as suggested by most of the Western interpreters of his work. Furthermore, his role cannot be reduced to that of a contemporary Chinese scholar who enriched and refined certain modern Western theories (or even made them "exotic") by imparting into them certain elements of somehow distant and peculiar ideas from ancient Confucian thought. Li can be seen as the creator of an independent, specific, and unique system, based upon his substantial mastering of both his own ideational tradition and the history of Western thought.

His theory must be seen as a philosophical system in itself and one that is rooted in a different referential framework based upon differently constructed and dissimilar paradigms than the ones contained in most of the dominant and influential theories in the Western world. It can be seen as a modernized evolvement and an upgrade of certain basic elements of classical Confucian philosophies or as a new theory based on classical Chinese philosophical paradigms.

To understand the innovative nature of Li's thought we will first compare its framework of reference with the one that is Confucian. After all Li himself has often implied that in his amalgamation of the Kantian, German idealist, Marxist, and Confucian discourses, the latter played the primary and dominant role, while the former three were merely seen as a supplement or an inspiration (see for instance Li Zehou 2016b, 212). We will also contrast it with the main characteristics of the framework of reference that was essentially common to the three aforementioned modern European philosophers who each influenced Li's philosophy in a most significant way. The following illuminates in a very rough and schematic way, the basic differences between the latter (A) and the former (B) framework.[4,5]

The basic setting of framework A is static, while framework B functions in a dynamic and changeable way. This basic setting influences not only the entire theoretical system integrated in the particular framework, but also each individual part composing these systems, as well as the relations between all these parts. The same holds true for the respective fundamental paradigms of the two contrasting frames, for their central thought patterns as well as their epistemological and interpretative methods.

The inner logic of argumentation and the central modes of processing the content are, to a great degree, abstractly formalized in framework A whereas in framework B, they function in accordance with variable semantic and axiological connotations.

The formal logic behind framework A is tightly linked to normative analyses of fixed and stable objects of investigation—of precisely defined objects excluded from the variable continuum of time and space. Whereas the semantic logic applied by framework B is highly contextual and relational—focused upon relations rather than upon individual isolated objects—the objects of inquiry are continuously modified. One of the central methods applied in this framework is the method of semantically conditioned analogies.[6]

Concepts contained in framework A are chiefly based on the *notion of absoluteness* (or the presumption of the absolute truth). Whereas in B they are rather relational, implying a relativity of reality and suggesting its relativistic understanding.

While categories are often applied in dual oppositions in both of the two frameworks, the basic structures and modes of interaction of these binary oppositions are fundamentally different.[7]

While in framework A, the mutually oppositional objects are (due to their following of the three classical laws of Western logical thought) mutually exclusive, in framework B they appear in the form of binary categories that function in correlative, interdependent, and complementary interaction.[8]

This dissimilarity is also reflected in the respective models of dialectical thought that evolved from the two frameworks in question. The model belonging to framework A can be historically traced back to Ancient Greek philosophy and is in its modern forms rooted in dual representation models such as Cartesian dualisms, in which oppositional notions (body and mind, matter and idea, substance and phenomena, subject and object, and so on), negate and exclude each other and are thus strictly and radically separated both formally and logically. Although in Hegel's theory the two oppositional concepts still form a correlative unity, they are seen as static momenta within this entirety. In the ultimate instance, this unity is nothing more than the sum of its parts, which contradict and exclude each other. In such models, the two oppositions are often denoted *thesis* and *antithesis*. The tension that results from the mutual negation and contradiction of both poles leads to the synthesis, which can be reached through *Aufhebung* or sublation in Hegel. This third stage is a qualitatively different and "higher" stage of development, in which parts of the previous opposition are preserved and the other eliminated. In essence, the dialectical thought in framework A is conceptual (i.e., containing fixedly defined contents). In framework B it is a process, based on categories (the concrete content of which is exchangeable and replaceable, not only in the semantic but also in the axiological sense). In its earliest form, this latter model goes back to the oldest Chinese proto-philosophical classic, the *Book of Changes* (*Yi jing* 易經), where it appears as a model of "continuous change" or "continuity through change" (*tongbian* 通變, Tian, Chenshan 2002, 126). It functions by applying binary categories and the principle of correlative complementarity. The oppositions it contains are interdependent and do not negate but rather complete each other. They are oppositional dualities, but not dualistic contradictions. Hence, the model of their mutual relationship and interaction cannot be denoted as an abstract form of dualism, but rather as a process of a dynamic duality. Furthermore, each of them represents the very essence of the other and none of the two can exist without the other. In contrast to the synthesis belonging to framework A, the totality or unity of both oppositions in framework B is to be found in the very process of their interaction as such. It does not lead to a qualitatively new and higher stage or form of reality, idea, or even its understanding (which is the tendency of framework A).[9]

Framework A presupposes a metaphysic of transcendence. In framework B, it is not possible to distinguish between noumenon and phenomena. Although both are recognized as specific states of being, the demarcation line between immanence and transcendence is blurred and subjected to a dynamic process of all-embracing change.[10] Instead, there is an omnipresent unity of culture and nature, of human beings and the cosmos, and of transcendence and immanence in the Unification of Heaven and Humans.

In its epistemological aspects, framework A proposes a distinction between knowable and the unknowable reality. While the latter is represented, for instance, by the thing-in-itself, the knowledge of the former can be obtained either through experience or through *a priori* mental forms. In framework B, the realm of the unknowable is also accepted, but it does not represent an object of investigation or any kind of elaboration. However, there is also in framework B—similarly as in framework A—a distinction between innate knowledge (which mostly pertains to axiological contents) and external knowledge, which is mainly empirical. The main distinction between the *a priori* (A) and innate (B) knowledge lies, once again, in the static (A) and dynamic (B) nature of their respective forms. Framework B shows that knowledge about both external and internal reality is obtained through the structural compatibility of human mind and external world. Knowledge within the constructs of framework B can never be separated from practice. Meanwhile in framework A, reason is the main method for gaining knowledge. Framework B allows for it to be additionally obtained through intuition, emotions, and intentions.

Ethics in framework A is closely related to the notions of freedom and moral responsibility. This framework suggests that to act morally is to act from a principle. Freedom, responsibility, and ethics can mainly be maintained through the regularity and rationality of universal rules. Ethics here is a social reality, a spiritual entity, or a fact of reason—it is something external to human inwardness.[11] In framework B, ethical rules are less normative and much more contextual and situational. This framework views the universe as permeated with meaning and therefore also as encompassing ethical implications reflected in the humanness as a central virtue of humaneness. In concrete human life, this humaneness must be properly learned and cultivated through social customs and especially through rituality, which rationalizes the instinctual essence of human natural feelings. However, since humans are seen as being in unity with heaven, nature, or the universe, humaneness is both the basis of ethics and the core of individual morality. Its external cultivation simultaneously means the realization of one's own individual and personal self.

In framework A, contents pertaining to the above-mentioned fields of philosophical investigation are structured and ordered into mutually distinct disciplines (logic, ontology, metaphysics, and epistemology). There are no strictly defined disciplines in framework B, but rather contexts (or discourses) belonging to these fields. In this framework epistemological thought, is intermingled, blended, and mixed with ideas from many other fields of philosophical inquiry, particularly with ontology, ethics, and phenomenology.

Referring to Li's theory as a whole, we can determine that there are great similarities between his own system and that of framework B. One of the main characteristics of Li's anthropo-historical ontology is namely the dynamic nature of all his central paradigms, concepts, and categories. They are highly historicized, contextual, and relational.

Li also opposes dogmatic views on the existence of absolute truth, though warning at the same time against the dangers of a radical postmodern relativization of reality in the form of cultural relativism. The emphasis on radical relativity of reality and its perception pertains more to Daoist than to Confucian referential frameworks. An important part of Confucian referential frameworks is the idea of "proper(ness)," "correct(ness)," or simply of that which is "right" (zheng 正). In a variety of different situations properness or correctness serves as the central, criteria or the main norm of understanding and acting. However, relativeness as something that is in sharp contrast with the idea of absoluteness is certainly also an important part of the Confucian referential framework. This kind of dynamic relativeness cannot be understood as a form of relativity that eliminates the axiological value of objects (or subjects) in question, but rather as a congruence between different views, positions, and understandings. This relativeness manifests itself in the notion of "the state of equilibrium" or the "mean." It is important to see this notion as something in constant movement and not as a fixed norm judging fast-frozen relations between opposite possibilities or objects. Such a highly dynamic vision of a complementary interaction—from the vibrant, interactive, and interchangeable unity of absoluteness and relativeness—can be found in the notion of *proper measure*.

Li also criticizes the Western division of reality into the two strictly separate realms of noumenon and phenomena. He emphasizes the ontological and metaphysical significance of the holistic Chinese view of the unity of Heaven (or Nature) and humans and follows the paradigm of the one-world view in his entire philosophy.

Regarding his epistemological thought, Li proceeded from the originally Marxist notion of human practice, which he did not see merely as the main trigger for human development, but also for human recognition and comprehension. His thoughts remained safely posited in the Confucian referential framework, which emphasizes the unity of knowledge and action, theory, and practice.

Concerning the ethical realm, Li admires Kant's categorical imperative. Li also emphasizes that the belief that human beings are always the goal, and not the means of any understanding, action, or judgment is simultaneously the very kernel of Confucian ethics and the very grounds for the construction of the central Confucian virtue of humaneness. In addition, his theory of the two kinds of morality can be viewed as a modernized development of the traditional Chinese binary category of the inner sage and the external ruler.

It is quite obvious that Li's system cannot be constricted to one or two philosophical disciplines. His theory cannot even completely fit into one entire field of "strict" or "pure" philosophy, since it reaches into and flirts with discourses on literature, art criticism, history, psychology, and anthropology.

Li Zehou's system can be seen as a system rather belonging to the B-type of referential frameworks. However, there are some specific features that do not precisely fit into any of the above described models. In these aspects, Li mainly attempts to construct or "transformatively create" a new theoretical system rooted in, but by no means limited to, Confucian, Marxist, Kantian, and Hegelian discourses. As mentioned, Li's theory cannot solely be seen as a combination of these philosophies. His work surpasses a mere "synthesis of Kant and Marx" through his combination of these two theoreticians with Hegel and, above all, with Confucius (Bruya 2003, 134). Besides, Li's theory contains numerous innovative fundamental elements that cannot be found in the work of any other philosopher.

Most of his attempts to construct a new philosophy based on anthropo-historical ontology are methodologically either directly or indirectly, tightly or loosely, linked to the binary structure of reasoning, which is common to the previously described referential frameworks, although the concrete operational mode of this structure varies depending on the respective frame.

Toward a New Model of Duality

It is interesting and revealing to analyze Li's model of dealing with dual (binary) categories. The structure of opposition—or, in a less determined sense, of relation—between two or more different ideas, beliefs, notions, presumptions, images, or concepts influences the developmental mode of any theory. The mode of development is particularly crucial for his theory His thought is rooted in an explicitly dynamic, resilient, and flexible framework. The concepts and ideas he shapes occur within this framework in a highly contextual and situational manner, continuously fluctuating and modifying the structural pattern of thought into which they are embedded. Such a system allows (and even necessitates) dynamic changes and the continuous evolution of the all-inclusive structure of the theory. Hence, the understanding of his theoretical system is conditioned by the understanding of his dialectical model. An insight into the latter offers a key to the perception of the former.

Dual oppositions are an important foundation of dialectical thought. Because it allows dynamic alternations and offers possibilities of multifaceted insights into the complex nature of reality, dialectics facilitates and advances the development of philosophic reasoning. It is not surprising that, as a method of examining opposing ideas to reach a new level of reasoning, dialectics is present in both traditional Euro-American and in traditional Chinese thought. As discussed, the concrete method of dialectical thought differs in both discourses that have most profoundly influenced Li. In the modern European form, which crystalized with Hegel, the two oppositional notions negate each other. However, they appear in the traditional Chinese model as binary categories, mutually complementary, and correlative. As previously discussed, the conception of this model goes back to the earliest proto-philosophical works of ancient China, as far back as the *Book of Changes*. The Chinese model is first introduced in this ancient classic through the concept *tongbian* (Zhou Yi 2009; Xi Ci I, 229), which in this context can be translated as "continuity through change" (Tian, Chenshan 2002, 126). Explanations of this dynamic philosophical paradigm can also be found in Laozi's *Book of the Way and the Virtue* (*Daode jing* 道德經).[12]

With this in mind, let us examine Li Zehou's theoretical system through the lens of his declaratively materialist orientation.

> I raised the controversial topic of "a return to classical Marxism" and entitled my philosophy jokingly as "a philosophy of eating." "Food before morals" is a plain, homily, but important truth. Some people, especially intellectuals (who have no problem with food) easily forget it. So it seems to me that it is still important to repeat that economic development, especially the development of science and technology (according to classical Marxism this is the determinative element of the productive force), is a presupposition for essential changes of other aspects of civilization. The material life of common people is the foundation of any civilization. It is economy, not culture, which decides the modern appearance of peoples everywhere, and this is the real reason why modernization is so powerful that it destroys almost every kind of obstacle and causes a series of cultural shifts. (Li, Zehou 1999a, 1)

In order to obtain an insight into this materialist level of his theory, and simultaneously into the nature of his theoretical model of complementarity, we will take another look upon Li Zehou's view of the *ti—yong* (substance and function) relation, this time from the perspective of their respective relations to matter and idea.[13] In the contexts of traditional Western theory (or in the context of referential framework A), the duality of matter and idea represents a fundamental distinction in the modes of being. Hence, the specific characteristics of the traditional Chinese (framework B) and Li's model of complementarity might become visible if approached through the lens of this distinction.

If we take into account Li Zehou's demonstratively emphasized materialist worldview, we could typically presuppose that, in his view, the material basis must be primary, and that this primary role would not only be logical, but also ontological. The framework of such logic, substance, would necessarily consist of matter, and function would, as a juxtaposition of substance (i.e., of matter), necessarily represent the elements pertaining to the sphere of ideas, (i.e., to human consciousness and its products), as ideology, theory, culture, art, and so on. Following the Marxist materialist structure, this would naturally imply that substance could be equated with the material base, and function with the ideational superstructure.

Indeed, such logic is typical for framework B. However, we must abandon this framework if we want to obtain a genuine insight into Li Zehou's system. But to prevent too much pain and suffering we shall leave it slowly, step by step.

As we already know, Li often notes that *ti* pertains to "social existence,"[14] which has an ontological position in regard to society, for it is its ultimate substance (*shehui benti* 社會本體) (Li, Zehou 1999c: 1160). According to the strictly materialist view, the "ontology of society" is the same as the "material being of society." Connecting these two presumptions should lead us to the premise that Li's *ti* could well be equated with the Marxist material basis, which is different from and external to its negated apposition—the ideal superstructure. Nevertheless, Li also notes that in his understanding, the substance *ti* includes not only material, but also ideational production (ibid.). As a representation of "social existence" Li's *ti* is something that does "*not chiefly* consist of ideologies," and this certainly means that ideologies must also be a part of it (ibid.).[15] For a Western reader, such a theoretical construction is unusual and can be confusing and difficult to grasp. As an example, let us look at Wang Jing's interpretation (Wang, Jing 1996, 98). Wang argues that although Li subscribes to the vulgar Marxist theory of levels and gives more weight to the infrastructure in his proposition of Western substance and Chinese function, Li cannot resist making sporadic references to Western "superstructure" (identified as "self-consciousness" or "ontological consciousness"). In Wang's view, Li identifies this superstructure as a necessary part of the "Western substance" that must be transplanted to China simultaneously with means of technological and material production. According to Wang, such integration of an "idealist perspective" into an otherwise "materialist framework" reveals apparent imprints of eclecticism: "At times, it is difficult to tell if one doctrine really gains the upper hand over the other in this seemingly harmonious picture of ideological conjugation" (ibid).

Li's application of *ti* and *yong* cannot be identified with the Marxist juxtaposition between matter and idea (or basis and superstructure) in the first place. According to Li, the substance of any society embraces its material practice, labor relations, technology, and its ideational production (*jingshen shengchan* 精神生產)—theories and ideologies. For Li, substance is basis that constitutes all elements of everyday life. While in Marxist thought, the contradiction between matter and idea comprise a central dual opposition within his ontology, in Li's model there is only a duality between the social existence and the mode of its realization, or, in other words, the substance of social life (*ti*) and the method of its fulfillment (*yong*). To Li, material and ideal stuff are intermingled, amalgamated, and correlative. The same is true for the category of function (*yong*), it is the implementation of substance or that, which brings it into a concrete existence. It is only natural that function can also appear as both matter and idea. Just as substance represents the material and ideal basis of (everyday) life, function—which also embraces material and ideal factors—is the concrete way of life, the *modus vivendi*, that is culturally, linguistically, historically, and environmentally conditioned.

It is doubtful whether the material base and ideational superstructure can truly be incorporated into Li's model of substance, as some interpreters consider. Wang, for instance, believes that Li subscribes to the "fundamentally materialist law of cause and effect," a fact that is revealed, for instance, in Li's definition of *xiti* as the sum total of both spiritual (ontological consciousness) and material (science and technology) production (ibid.). According to Wang, the former should be understood as a superstructural system that mirrors and reproduces the latter—the base (ibid.).

Although Li's theory is materialist in terms of cause and effect, he actually never speaks about the ideational elements of his system in terms of superstructure. All he says is that different modes of spiritual substance (*Jingshen benti* 精神本體)[16] and ontological consciousness (*Benti yishi* 本體意識)[17] do not belong to the substance. This is also the main reason for his insisting on the shorter version of the slogan.[18]

> Whether we talk of the Confucian "Chinese learning," or the Marxist "Western learning" . . . neither belongs to the substance, neither is the ultimate reality. They are only the substance of mind or the consciousness of substance. They belong to the forms of mind and to systems of cognition.
>
> 不管是孔夫子的「中學」，還是馬克思的「西學」......都不是體，都不能作為最後的體。他們只是心理本體或本體意識，即一種理論形態和思想體系。 (Li Zehou 1999c, 1161)

No matter how tempting it is for Western-educated researchers to interpret Li's "substance" in terms of the material basis, and his "function" in terms of ideal superstructure, Li has never mentioned such an ontology in his elaborations on *ti* and *yong*. He limits the Marxist materialist ontology to the "social existence," which appears in form of the "social substance" (*shehui benti* 社會本體).

For Li substance (*ti*) refers to his idea of the ontology of human beings and their social practice. As mentioned, Li's "substance comprises material as well as ideational or spiritual productions" (Li Zehou 1999c, 1160). On a larger scale, matter and idea both participate equally in a broader structure of complementary dual collaboration, namely in the correlative process of interaction between substance and function.

> Substance and function cannot be separated. Chinese tradition also emphasizes that *ti* and *yong* are not two things. Substance cannot exist outside of the function for it is a part of it.
>
> 實體與功能，即「用」本不可分，中國傳統也講「體用不二」，沒有離用的「體」，「體」即在用中。 (ibid.)

It is hardly possible to reproach Li with the application of an "orthodox Marxist faith in the one-to-one correspondence between base and superstructure" (Wang, Jing 1996, 98). It is even less so considering that Li, as previously discussed, openly distances himself from economic determinism. He highlights that he does not believe that social existence necessarily defines social ideologies, cultures, values, or politics (Li Zehou 2016c, 387).[19]

Considering the specific characteristic of Li's dialectical model, in which the substance of society implies its material, as well as ideational elements, it is difficult to understand why Li Zehou still regards himself as a materialist philosopher. To answer this requires an approach from two angles. First, from the external viewpoint of the historical and ideational background that has necessarily influenced the shaping of Li's ideas, and, second, from the internal viewpoint of his own system.

In the Chinese tradition (even after the introduction of Marxist thought at the beginning of the twentieth century) dialectics has always been chiefly understood as a model, described previously, as a corelative interaction of complementary oppositions. The modern European model of dialectic thought was slightly, but significantly altered. This holds true for the interpretations of Hegel, as well as works of Marx and Engels. The specific characteristics of the Chinese language led the debate of Marxist dialectics through a new process, into a new context, and onto a new field of focus. Nevertheless, Marxist variations of Western dialectics have had a huge doctrinal effect on *tongbian* discourse, the consequence of which was the application of a completely new terminology to a school of traditional thought. In this way, a new, genuinely Chinese version of Marxist dialectics was born. One that can be seen to have existed as far back as the *Yi jing*. This shows that there are elementary differences between the original European terminology and the Chinese translations. As soon as Chinese scholars began to employ Chinese philosophical expressions in their readings and especially as they became engaged in the campaign to Sinicize Marxism, the Chinese concept of dialectics thus came closer to the concept of *tongbian* (Tian, Chenshan 2002, 126).

It was in such, then prevailing discourses and modes of reasoning, that Li received his education. Within these frameworks, traditional Chinese variations of dialectical thought were, more or less unconsciously, incorporated into the model of Marxist dialectics, replacing in this process some parts that did not "fit well with the model of correlative dialectics" (ibid., 137). Understanding Li requires comprehending that in these patterns of synthesizing Marxism and Chinese thought, the traditional correlative worldview, which was based upon a presumption of an interconnectedness of all things, naturally led to an elimination of the ontological split between the determinative principle and that which is determined by this principle (ibid.). In Chenshan's analysis of the semantic connotations and development of the terminology, with concepts such as "matter" and "materialism" being translated into Chinese (*wuzhi, weiwulun* 物質、唯物論), that the "conceptual significance of 'materialism' and 'matter or substance' is not given any significance in the Chinese translation" (ibid., 134).

A crucial difference between Marx's ontological and Li's empirical materialism manifests itself in Li's specific dialectical relation between matter and idea, in which the social and existential substance (*ti*) is not something that absolutely determines the concrete mode of existence or the function (*yong*) that serves as its antipode.[20] Even worse (or better), in Li's view, the two oppositional notions still seem to be interdependent. In spite of the primary role of the substance (*ti*), Li often highlights the significance of the function (*yong*). Following this, without the method of its implementation, there can be no substance. Function can only be preserved, maintained and developed through interaction with substance. Substance and function are situated in a complementary interrelation that fits into the traditional description of the correlative association between *ti* and *yong* as provided by the pioneer of Modern Confucianism, Xiong Shili.

> While we can say that substance is a substance of function, this does not mean that it is an independent entity, which can go beyond function or exist somewhere outside it. The fact that substance is the very substance of function means it cannot be found outside it.
>
> 所以說他是用的本體, 絕不是超脫於用之外而獨存的東西。因為體就是用的本體, 所以不可離用去覓體。 (Xiong Shili 1992, 362)

This is why Li Zehou's reversed slogan of Western substance and Chinese function differs substantially from the Marxist concept of basis and superstructure. Li sees correlative interplay between the two oppositional notions in a similarly traditional way as Xiong, even though he denotes *ti* as the (material) social existence and *yong* as the function that defines its realization.

What is important here is the fact that the notion *ti*—even when in the position of the primary level of existence—lacks an ontologically determinable dimension. Although mostly translated as "substance," *ti* as a part of the dual opposition (or binary category) in which it appears as the antipode of *yong* (function), has no ontological dimension and cannot be identified with noumenon in the traditional European sense.[21] It is fundamental in the sense of the ultimate reality, which, however, is not something external to human life. This specific feature belongs to the basic differences between the Western "two worlds" and the Chinese "one world" theory.

Li's materialism is not ontological but rather pertains to the empirical realm and is rooted in life itself.[22] In contrast to modern European understandings of materialism, Li sees the primary role of matter (or physicality) in a very direct and elementary way. For example, without food—which is very material and guarantees one's survival—no one can create art, construct science, or investigate philosophical theory. This is also the main reason that Li named his materialist viewpoint the "philosophy of eating." This empirically materialist position is actually based upon the well-known Marxist presumption that Marx wrote of in a letter to Engels in 1868: "it is absolutely impossible to transcend the laws of nature. What can change in historically different circumstances is only the form in which these laws expose themselves" (Marx, cf. Swiderski 1979, 159). It is also grounded in pragmatic Confucian philosophy, which was also focused upon material or better physical life. This was the starting point of Confucian philosophy, which often implied that we should first try to master life before trying to understand death (Lunyu 2009, Xian Jin, 569).

Li's elementary starting point, which he expressed in the axiom that "people are alive" and his situational, emotion-based substance was formed on this very elementary, existential basis. For Li, it is the strictly material practice that gives rise to the life, evolution, and progress of human beings. However, the basic material circumstances that enable human life are only the sufficient but not the necessary conditions for the development of humankind. They do not mechanically determine human life and even less directly define the particular mode of human existence.

In Li's anthropo-historical ontology of human life, the concept of subjectality is the very link that connects the multifarious dualities of human existence, which includes social existence and its *modus vivendi*, the material and the ideal sphere of human life, human reason, and emotion. In Li's system the subject of humanity appears and manifests itself in various activities of human subjectality through the social realization of material reality, which is based on material production. This is the elementary, objective level of subjectality, which manifests itself in the structural link between technology and society and in concrete social existence. At the same time, subjectality also generates the subjective level of social consciousness, which manifests itself in mental structures that differ from period to period, from culture to culture and from one language to another. In this sense, subjectality is precisely the magic link that sophisticatedly, but powerfully, connects not only the material sphere with the ideal one, but also, on a more basic level, connects the complexity of human life with its existential foundations. In Li's framework, the material basis does not determine human life, but provides the essential conditions for its realization. This material basis is an origin of existence and must be maintained and sustained through human practice, but the existential level of the material basis does not imply that it also possesses ontological nature. The categories *ti* and *yong*, or the substance and the function of (contemporary) human societies, refer to the sublime material and ideational implications, to the innumerable exquisite products of human subjectality. This framework places technology and culture in an active mutual correlation equally rooted in the physical world that provides basic necessities for human existence.

It is on this level, where existence itself is already guaranteed, that Li constitutes a complementary relation between matter and idea.

Even though Li's own worldview is materialistic, it is not materialistic ontologically, but rather in pure empirical or causal logical terms. Li's materialism refers to the basic and general material conditions of existence. The substance, which underlies Li Zehou's anthropo-historical ontology, comprises material and spiritual production. It cannot be separated from the given conditions in which human beings live—who represent and incorporate the meaning, the elementary criterion, and the ultimate goal of all existence. This substance incorporates various ontological components in which material and ideal factors are intermingled and difficult to separate. The elementary constituent, which makes human beings human and surpasses the limitations of the empirical realm, is human emotion. In Chinese culture, this emotion assumes the position of the emotion-based (or situation-based) substance.

Humankind prevails on the basis of the material circumstances of existence, which preconditioned its entire empirical reality. These material preconditions of (human) existence represent the foundation of Li's specific materialism. However, humanity could only be realized as essentially human through the agenda of subjectality, the driving force for both the humanization of nature and the naturalization of humans.

Substance and function are a pair of categories representing the level (and the structure) of technological development (including the productive forces and productive relations), and the method of its implementation—the given *modus vivendi*. They appear in Li's philosophical system as a correlative model, typical and necessary for the survival of any human society. In different societies and cultures these models can be structured in different ways. For Li, the decisive factor that enables the best possible interaction between existence and *modus vivendi* is the concept of proper measure. This is the very principle that enables human society to choose the "middle way" according to each given situation and, hence, to achieve the "equilibrium" of all life-influencing aspects. In Li's view, this is how humankind should proceed towards progress, well-being, and harmony. In Li pattern of dialectic development, synthesis is not an automatic product of mechanistic laws of reason, but rather a result of human subjectality and its actively chosen decisions and practices. Ultimately, the development of human societies and cultures is to a large degree defined by such decisions and the actions resulting from them. As we discussed, the best way to choose is always to choose in accordance with the proper measure. Li describes its potential in the following way:

> This is what I often defined as the "Chinese dialectics." It is not P v 'P, but rather P ≠ P±. If you do something exaggeratedly well, it is the same as doing it in a lousy way. This is the State of Equilibrium or the Mean.
>
> 這是我常講的「中國辯證法」。不是 P v 'P 而是 P ≠ P±。認為「過猶不及」，即中庸是也。 (Li Zehou 2015, 38)

This principle arises in the process of the humanization of consciousness (*yishide renhua* 意識的人化), which

> creates the dialectics of the oppositional concepts of yin and yang as well as the idea of the "proper measure" of the Equilibrium or the Mean. The "proper measure" contains the ability or potential of choosing names and organizing explanations. This is a model, a structure, a form of reason, constructed by people.
>
> 產生辯證法――即陰陽兩分的矛盾觀念和中庸的「度」觀念。「度」包含選擇名且織解釋諸功能，它也是一種人所建立的模型、結構、理性形式。 (Li Zehou 2016, 130)

With subjectality, Li aims to emphasize that it is people's decisions and actions that shape the mode of human life and that the multifarious effects of human decisions and actions also influence their environment and the existence of the universe. Subjectality is the very bridge that connects human beings with cosmic existence.

Life is not entirely governed by the mechanic laws of reason or by the will of an external supernatural power. It is us, human beings, who can and should try to find in our lives and in the development of our societies the proper measure that enables us to choose the way of equilibrium. Li maintains that this is the only way that guarantees human progress and well-being.

In Li's dialectical model, there is no negation, no sublation, and no higher stages or phases of development. A synthesis is latently hidden in the very process of correlative interaction between opposing antipodes and must be created, brought out, and realized by subjectality, humankind's conscious activity that is able to choose the main direction of further development by virtue of proper measure. Unlike the Hegelian or Marxist model, Li's Chinese dialectics does not lead to anything qualitatively new. Its procedures, which guide humans to advanced ways of life, are as old as the history of humankind. Precisely because they are old, they are also verified and deep-rooted. Hence, they can lead humankind to always-new forms of well-being and progress.

To a certain degree, Li's theory supplemented Kant by Marx and the importance of empirical, historical. and social materialism. It also supplemented Marx by Kant and his ultimate concern and respect for the autonomous human subject. In the mechanistic scheme of Marxist dialectics, even revolution as such is predetermined. The unequal and unjust conditions in class societies, the mutual negation and contradiction between the owners of the means of production on the one hand, and the productive forces who have "nothing to lose, but their chains" on the other, must necessarily lead to revolution (Marx and Engels 1992, 34). In this model, revolution is the necessary social and economic outcome of class contradictions, which determine all class societies. The final sublation—and the final resolution—of these social contradictions can only be achieved in socialism, which is a preparatory phase for a genuinely communist society. In contrast to such a view, Li emphasizes that people can choose by themselves how they want to resolve existing conflicts in their societies. As discussed, Li recommends reforms instead of revolution, reason instead of violence.

For a Western reader, Li's dialectics seem a bit unusual and extremely complex. In reality, it is simple and clear. It is always human life that preconditions all levels of existence. On this basis of logical and empirical conditionality, which can by no means be confused with ontological determination, there evolve multifarious models of correlative binary complementarities.

Above, we have tried to demonstrate Li's mode of dialectical theory through the lens of his understanding of the traditional binary category of *ti* and *yong*. However, the same dialectical model of mutually independent and congruent relations rooted in basic conditions of human existence and including changing roles of prevalent and secondary elements are equally present in most of his innovative paradigms. In Li's philosophy, this configuration manifests itself in the relations between heaven and human beings, emotion and reason (*qingli* 情理), religious and social morals, individual and society, and so on.

Li started elaborating upon this model already in his first theoretically important essay, "On the Aesthetic Feeling, Beauty, and Art." His critique of idealism, which predominates the first few pages of the essay, is crucial for understanding his dialectical model. He reproaches the idealists with continuous separations of binary oppositional notions through contradictions and with an absolute division of reason from intuition. His view holds that materialists understand the methods as one and the same cognitive potential. In this harmony of oppositions, however, everything that is individual, ideational, or subjective is of secondary nature, and reason always dominates over intuition.

The important thing here is that Li explains why two oppositional notions must not necessarily be in mutual contradiction. At that time other Chinese theoreticians who were working on theoretical models suitable for the Sinification of Marxism were not aware of the importance of this differentiation (as they were similarly unaware of the importance of the determining elements or the question of ontological versus empirical materialism). Although two elements in mutual contradiction can still be seen as a part of a totality, the formula of their mutual negation always suggests a flaw or incompleteness in any initial thesis. Besides, this abstract procedure neither explains why the thesis requires the antithesis. The unity of two correlative binary oppositions is fundamentally different. The two oppositional antipodes are correlative and complementary because they are mutually interdependent and, at the same time, each is also interdependent with the unity that both of them form together. In other words, in this dialectical model the two antipodes are in a dynamic opposition and this opposition as such already forms a totality, which, however, is also dynamic and different in each moment.

In "On the Aesthetic Feeling, Beauty, and Art" Li links the model of dynamic complementarity to his interpretation of the aesthetic feeling (Li Zehou 1956, 45). He explains that there is no need to place the two aspects—the individual and the social—in mutual contradiction. However, they are necessary in mutual opposition, which is correlative and complementary, for without society there can be no individual and vice versa. As soon as the opposition is complementary and interdependent, the concept, which is shaped by the two antipodes, is necessarily and automatically a unity.

In this, as well as all the other complementary structures, there is always a dominant and prevailing element that triggers the complementary interchange in a certain direction and along a certain trend. Some scholars have criticized this predomination, arguing that it actually devaluates or destroys the theoretical complementarity: "Eventually, it is the subjugation of the senses to reason, the natural to the sociocultural, the individual to the community, rather than the harmonious coexistence of the two" (Wang, Jing 1996, 104). Even the predominant position of one of the two elements within the mutually oppositional structure is not absolute and eternal, but changeable and modifiable as all the concepts and categories of framework B. They cannot be judged as isolated moments in a certain frozen and fixed formula, taken out of time and space. This predominant element conditions the genuine development of the model and its dialectical progress.[23] Besides, the predominant element, which is in each particular model of Li's complementary dialectics connected to the permanent variable of human life, is never a necessary, but nonetheless a sufficient condition of its own oppositional antipode. This also means that although this predominant element conditions its oppositional antipode, it does not determine it. This is a small, but significant difference in comparison with Marxist theory, which is grounded not only on empirical and logical, but also on ontological materialism.

It is also important to note that in Li's dialectical models the predominant element is always the one that contributes most—in a given situation and a particular context—to sustainable nature, to the preservation and evolution of human life. In his dialectics of anthropo-historical ontology, the decisive instance, which always operates in accordance with these goals, is human subjectality. The more we are responsive to the effects of proper measure, the easier it is to live our everyday lives. By virtue of our human sensibility and rationality we can solve our dilemmas and make our decisions in accordance with this viable element. Choosing in congruence with the proper measure will allow us to preserve the balance between all aspects embedded into the innumerable structures of the multifarious complementary relations comprising our individual and social lives.

His Own Path

In his short story *Homeland*, Lu Xun (1881–1936), a leading figure of modern Chinese literature, wrote:

> Hope cannot be said to exist, nor can it be said not to exist. It is like a path in the countryside: originally there was no path—yet, as people walk all the time in the same spot, a way appears.
>
> 希望是本無所謂有，無所謂無的。這正如地上的路；其實地上本沒有路，走的人多了，也便成了路。 (Lu Xun 2016, 143)

This famous saying is inspiring and thought-provoking for it opens new questions about the nature of the human mind, about human feelings and aspirations. It makes us wonder about this mysterious riddle called human life. It raises the question of whether hope for a better life is really always linked to the creation of new paths, new ways of thinking, and new methods of inquiry. It leaves us wondering who will be the first person struggling their own way through uncultivated and rough country, hoping to successfully create a new, better way for people who might follow. Deep in their inner heart-mind such people must be somehow different from the majority of those who prefer to walk along and follow others. Some of them are simply driven by a desire for power, longing to become leaders, while such considerations are completely irrelevant for others. We are not dealing here with the first category of overly ambitious people, for both Lu Xun and Li Zehou certainly belong to the second one. When starting to search for a new way on untrodden ground, such people must strongly believe in their hopes and have faith in the importance of their goals, which must be worthy of their strenuous efforts. However, we might still wonder what the fundamental driving force is that makes them leave their safe and comfortable grounds of predictability. Is it just curiosity? Is it stubbornness? Or is it loyalty to oneself?

Lu Xun was never satisfied with walking the old, well-known, beaten paths that can only lead to old and known destinations, without any surprises or challenges. He was against any form of conservativism for he believed that the Chinese ideational and political tradition was based upon "cannibalistic" rituals, which cruelly oppress deprived minorities, relentlessly strangle the free individual spirit, and eliminate every single innovation in order to protect, maintain, and reproduce the interests and the privileges of the ruling elite. Lu Xun was certainly following his own path, constructing a new way for himself and for China. Li does the same, although in a different manner.

As discussed, Li never agreed with the radical presumption that premodern Chinese tradition was absolutely mistaken. He certainly clearly saw its weaknesses and its obsolescence, and rather strove for its reasonable transformation, through which the new Chinese society could find a good way to unify and fruitfully synthesize tradition and modernity. But even in this fragment of his intellectual endeavors, he took his own path that promoted new ideas, which were quite different from almost everything that had been proposed before. It was a way that was oriented against both complete Westernization and a complete revival of Chinese tradition without simultaneous considerations of the material and technological progress, which had to be imported from the Western world. Hence, it is not a coincidence that his work is significant in the constructs of China's post-Mao Enlightenment movement, since it exemplifies the most essential contradictions and dilemmas that sprang from the processes of Chinese economic liberalization and social transition.

Li has thoroughly remained faithful to his own way. He often claimed that he did not take honor or disgrace too seriously, which enabled him to maintain a certain degree of independence even in the harshest times of political repression. From a very young age, Li considered independent thinking the central component of his work. His intellectual interests frequently contained unorthodox perspectives, novel ideas, and new methods. The path he followed was truly unique. We saw that it was a path of numerous innovations. In Li's view, the production of new concepts and novel ideas could open new perspectives that allow us to find new methods of investigating phenomena (Li Zehou 2015, 3). Such investigations seek to react to an era that is determined not only by the efforts to preserve and recover different traditions, but also by determinations to reconcile such cultural heritages with the requirements of the prevailing economic, political, and axiological structures of a globalized world. By recommencing and reconsidering numerous important facets of ancient and traditional Chinese values and knowledge, Li made a significant impact on contemporary theoretical debates in the fields of Chinese and comparative philosophies. His work is a continuous effort to revive and reconstruct the Confucian intellectual tradition, thus not only assisting China on its way to future material and spiritual progresses, but also making an exceptional and valued input to world philosophy.

Li often mentions that he sees philosophy as science imbued with poetry. As science, it offers a systematic way of exploring and comprehending reality. As poetry, it wanders with us through the opaque jungle of our existence—a long and intimate journey that not only offers us beauty and pleasure, but also forces us to confront fear and melancholy. Philosophy is a way of life that is rational and artistic at the same time. It not only urges us to search for answers to eternal questions of being, but also to unceasingly raise new ones. It does not remain limited to discovering the world, but also allows for its ongoing creative change.

In more than sixty years of his active theoretical work, Li's philosophy as a coherent system never substantially altered. Although the range of his accomplishments is enormously extensive, it is important to note that the fundamental conceptual structure, the logical pattern, and above all, the basic theoretical framework employed by him are always consistent. He outlined the main structure of his theoretical system well before the third decade of his life. By that point he had already created the methodological foundations and coined most of the crucial concepts on which his theory was based. In the following decades, he continuously and persistently elaborated upon them, constantly improving and completing his thought without slipping away from the main structural principles of its theoretical scheme.[24] As discussed, this system represents a complex relational arrangement, in which all parts are interconnected, forming a broad framework of specifically "Li Zehouian" thought, the name he gave the practical philosophy of subjectality or anthropo-historical ontology. It included his philosophy of pragmatic reason and the emotion-based substance, his theory of practical aesthetics, his sedimentation based anthropological, psychological, and cultural studies, his ethics of emotio-rational structures, his political philosophy of the two kinds of moralities, the epistemology of sensibility and reason, as well as the psychology of dynamic mental formations. In a certain sense Li's entire system is an anthem of autonomous human subjectality and its ability to continuously shape, evolve, and improve humanity and the world in which we are living. This progress can effectively be achieved through the application of the proper measure, a second central and pivotal concept that took center stage in Li's theory and simultaneously a personal compass, showing him ever new paths through the complex labyrinths of his own life. It never fails to help him find the right direction towards his final destination, the peace of mind, in which he could rest in a unity of reason and feeling through the restless and continuous widening and deepening of his ideational system.

If we now look back on Li Zehou's own long and winding path, we quickly see that creating and following such a way is anything but simple. It not only requires strength and courage, intellect and creativity, but it also calls for subtle but powerful sensitivity, marked by an eternal, never fully realized longing for beauty. What Li's philosophy has shown us, among other things, is that beauty is not only the ultimate realm of our human values, nor is it limited to the ultimate sphere of our humanness—our being human. It also offers us autonomy and liberation from estrangement. Li offers us the assurance that we ourselves possess our freedom, not only regarding free choices, but also in a broader and much more complex sense of our free will, which can only be fully realized through the complete recognition and implementation of our responsibilities.

This freedom, which is actually based on limitations and on enriching commitments, enhances even more the feeling of togetherness in a multitude of differences. Seen from a broader intercultural perspective, Li's way of thinking points to a common human way regardless of the differences in our individual preferences, cultures, languages, and traditions. His philosophical thought, which is thoroughly reflected in his special intellectual path, reminds us of our belonging to humankind. With his sensible explanations and sharp theoretical syntheses, Li makes us appreciate the complex, rich, and diverse intellectual heritage that his old home, the Chinese culture, can offer to our globalized world.

Appendix

General Scheme of Ethics
(Lunlixue zong lanbiao 倫理學總覽表)

Table A.1. General Scheme of Ethics (Lunlixue zong lanbiao 倫理學總覽表)

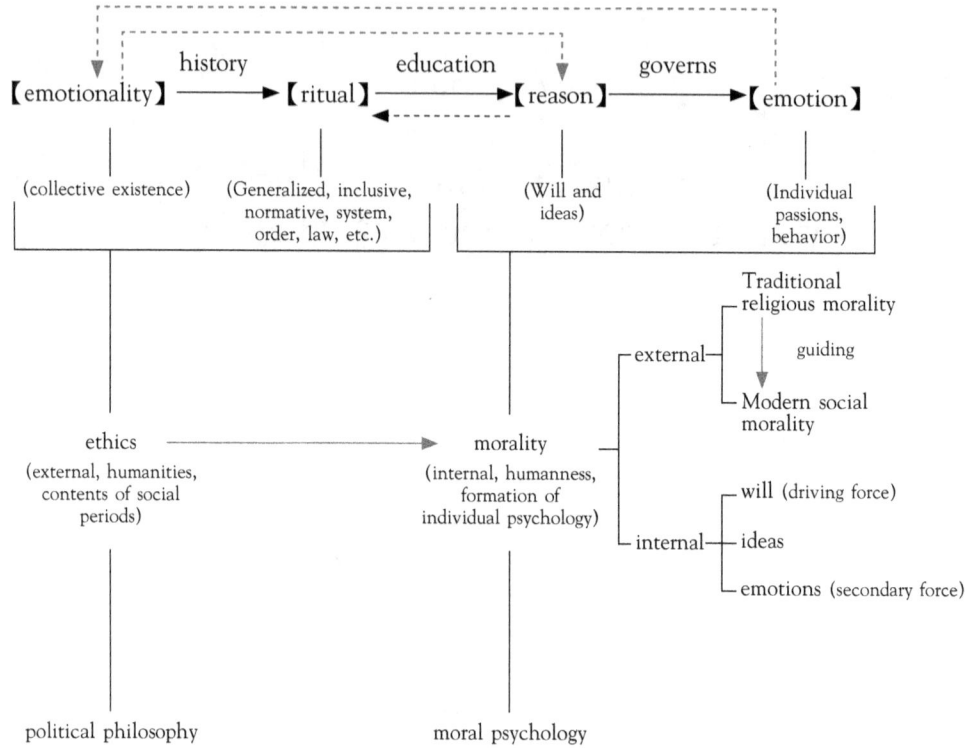

Notes

Introduction

1. Li certainly belonged to the most inspirational and charismatic intellectual figures of this period, which lasted approximately from 1984 until 1989. As we shall see later, he argued that Chinese Enlightenment had already begun in the 1890s but was extinguished at the urging of the so-called national salvation. However, "at this second juncture of Enlightenment with its unusual receptiveness to Western philosophy, especially aesthetics, Li made much of this fortuitous East–West confluence in his oft-quoted *Xiti zhongyong* 西體中用 (Western substance, Chinese application)" (Jensen 2005, 463), which will be explained in detail later in this book. With this idea, he offered an image of "humans as agents of craft to a generation looking beyond the meaningless, overpoliticized bromides of state ideology" (ibid.).

2. In his view, even though both currents were established in opposition to each other, they were still linked as two complementary philosophical streams. The complementary and mutual roles played by Confucianism and Daoism are an important thread that has run through all traditional Chinese aesthetic thinking. Chinese philosophy, including aesthetics, has been guided by the practical rationality of daily life, human relations, and political concepts, rather than by any abstract rationalist theory (Ding 2002, 253).

3. Although Li has acknowledged that modernization cannot be equated with Westernization (Li Zehou 1998: 170) he also opposed radical neo-conservative opinions, which advocated a "purely Chinese" path to modernization, pointing out that all the material conditions for this social transformation came to China from the West (ibid.).

Chapter 1

1. This is a shortened version of the phrase *Zhongxue wei ti, Xixue wei yong* 中學為體, 西學為用, which means "Chinese learning for essence (fundamental

principles) and Western learning for function (practical application)." Zhang pointed out this phrase in his work *Exhortation to Study* (*Quanxue Pian* 勸學篇).

2. These demands did not signify a sexual revolution based upon promiscuity, but only the free choice of marriage partners, as opposed to traditional weddings based upon agreements between families or clans.

3. They were later published in a collection entitled *Talks at the Yan'an Forum on Literature and Art* (*Zai Yan'an wenyi zuotan huishangde jianghua* 在延安文藝座談會上的講話).

4. This was especially true during the so-called Anti-Rightist Movement and the Cultural Revolution.

5. This "first wave," which begun in the late 1950s was not yet called "Aesthetic Fever" but "The Great Debate on Aesthetics (*Meixue da taolun* 美學大討論)." The second wave, i.e., the "real" Aesthetic Fever followed in the 1980s.

6. The translator of this English version is Gong Lizeng. Even before the English translation, this book has also been translated into German by Karl-Heinz Pohl and Gudrun Wacker (see Li, Zehou 1992).

7. Together with Liang Qichao 梁启超 (1873–1929), they were initiators of the *Wuxu reform movement* (戊戌變法), better known in the West as the Hundred Days Reform (百日維新) in 1898. The reforms failed after just 100 days when the Empress repealed them and sentenced their main proposers to death. Kang Youwei and Liang Qichao managed to escape abroad (to Hong Kong, Japan, America, and Mexico), where they would remain until the First Republic was established in 1911. Although Tan Sitong was offered the same protection and the possibility of foreign asylum by various foreign missions, based on his belief that sweeping social change needed martyrs, he allowed himself to be imprisoned and executed.

8. In a revised version that includes some recently written parts, these works were compiled, slightly reworked, and republished in 2016 in a monumental monograph under the new title *Anthropo-Historical Ontology* (*Renleixue lishi bentilun* 人類學歷史本體論). On the cover of the book, the English translation of the title slightly differs from my own and reads *A Theory of Anthropo-Historical Ontology*. (In my opinion, however, the word "theory" in this translation is somehow tautological, since the word *lun* 論, which is commonly translated as "theory," is already implied in the notion of ontology, which means a theory of being or existence).

9. These two books are prohibited still in the People's Republic of China.

10. This work was translated into English by Paul D'Ambrosio and Robert A. Carleo. It was published in 2016 as a part of a special issue of the journal *Philosophy East and West* (see the section "Sources and Literature").

11. He was always very much interested in mathematics, physics, and chemistry, and was extremely successful at these subjects in school. Many of his friends, including several former classmates, still claim that it was a pity he did not further pursue a career in the natural sciences and technology (Li Zehou 2003a, 19).

12. See section "From *Zhongti Xiyong* to *Xiti Zhongyong*."

13. This was the great debate on aesthetics, which took place in China in the late 1950s and in the beginning of the 1960s.

14. For a detailed explanation of the issue, see chapter 5, "Toward a New Model of Duality."

15. A member of the infamous "Gang of Four" and of the Politburo of the Central Committee of the Communist Party of China during the Cultural revolution, mainly in charge for the cultural propaganda.

16. For the ideological background of the campaign, see Yang Guorong 2016.

17. Even the other (or original) name of his "anthropo-historical ontology," namely, the "theory of practical subjectality," reveals the synthesis of Kant and Marx, for the element of practice is a typical Marxist one, while the aspect of subjectality can doubtless be prescribed to Kant's influence.

18. Li has elaborated on the difference between these two categories of knowledge in greater detail. In his view the experts were good in storing, systemizing, and ordering the information, while the thinkers could also process it in the sense of analyzing and, above all, synthesizing the data, therefore transforming quantitative information into qualitative knowledge. In a later essay, which he also wrote to and for young readers, he points out that in the future experts could be replaced by computers and artificial brains, while thinkers would always remain nonpareil (Li Zehou 1996, 85).

19. The so-called Practice School was established in the 1960s in Yugoslavia. It called for radical social change and was a living example of a socialist movement based on such Marxist humanism.

20. When speaking of Li's philosophy, we should differentiate between subjectivity (*zhuguanxing* 主觀性) and subjectality (*zhutixing* 主體性). These differences, however, will be explained in detail in later chapters, especially in the chapter on subjectality.

21. In chapter 1 of the *Capital*, Marx wrote: "Along with the useful qualities of the products themselves, we put out of sight both the useful character of the various kinds of labor embodied in them, and the concrete forms of that labor; there is nothing left but what is common to them all; all are reduced to one and the same sort of labor, human labor in the abstract" (Marx 2015, 28).

22. Kant defines transcendental illusion as an illusion, "which influences principles whose use is not ever meant for experience, since in that case we would at least have a touchstone for their correctness, but which instead, contrary to all the warnings of criticism, carries us away beyond the empirical use of the categories, and holds out to us the semblance of extending the pure understanding" (Kant 1998, 385).

23. Li uses the term *jiegou* 結構 (structure) to mean mental structures. He preferred to translate it into English as "formation" rather than "structure" because in his view, formations belong to dynamic concepts, whereas structures were more fixed and static. However, in Western structuralist, and even more

so in the poststructuralist, theories, the concept of structure can also be seen as a changeable and dynamic one (see Rošker 2012, 3).

24. The Duke of Zhou was an early leader of the Zhou Dynasty. He played a major role in consolidating the kingdom established by his elder brother King Wu (Zhou Wu Wang 周武王). He is famous for acting as a capable and devoted regent for his young nephew and for overturning a series of rebellions, pacifying the nobility of the defeated Shang Dynasty with high titles and positions. He is also well-known for creating the *Rites of Zhou* (*Zhou li* 周禮); as the alleged author or compiler of other Confucian classics that include the *Book of Changes* (*Yi jing* 易經), and the *Book of Poetry* (*Shi jing* 詩經); and as the establisher of the *Elegant music* (*Ya yue* 雅樂), a form of classical Chinese music.

25. For a detailed explanation of these traditions, the differences between them and the ideational consequences of this distinction see the section "The Four Periods of Confucianism and the Culture of Pleasure."

26. In the original version of his "Economic and Philosophical" manuscripts, Marx writes about *Menschlichkeit* (2005, 59), which is translated as "human nature" in the English version (2007, 46), although "human nature" is *menschliche Natur* in German.

27. The concept *ren xing* 人性 refers to inborn human-specific features or inclinations that "makes us distinctively human," and thus separate our species from other living beings (Ames 2017). The term has mostly been translated as "human nature." However, in traditional Western understanding, this term has predominantly static or fixed connotations, while the Chinese *ren xing* is changeable and dynamic. In Christian theology, which belongs to the main ideational pillars of classical Western thought, human nature is viewed as originating in God (or creator). Translating *ren xing* as human nature does not seem to be very appropriate. I propose replacing the phrase "human nature" in the English translation of *ren xing* the term "humanness." In the sense of something that makes us human, or simply in the sense of being human (for a comprehensive explanation and discussion of the *ren xing* problem see Ames 1991, 143–75 and Ames 2017).

28. Li points out: "Sedimentation flows from history into psychology, from rationality into sensuousness, from sociality into individuality" (Li and Cauvel 2006, 167).

29. According to Li's anthropology of human practice, as described in his article "A Supplementary Explanation of Subjectivity (*Guanyu zhutixingde buchong shuoming* 關於主體性的補充說明)," which was first published in 1985, mankind evolved by developing two basic formations, namely the technological-social (or techno-social) formation, which is external, and the cultural psychological formation, which is innate (Li Zehou 2006; 1985, 15). Later on, the former term was changed into *gonju benti* 工具本體 (techno-social substance) and the latter into *qingan benti* 情感本體 or *qing benti* 情本體 (emotion-based substance) (Yu Chuanqin 2016, 3).

30. These two notions were first introduced in his book *Critique of Critical Philosophy: A New Approach to Kant*. Here, Li Zehou is citing Kang Youwei's 康有為 notions of the great (society) (*da wo* 大我) and small (individual) self (*xiao wo* 小我) (Li Zehou 2001, 52). However, at the turn of the twentieth century, both notions were also frequently applied by Liang Qichao 梁啟超 and Sun Yat-sen (Sun Zhongshan 孫中山).

31. As we shall see later, however, the pragmatic nature of this rationality was tightly linked to and intertwined with human emotions.

32. In the chapter on the humanization of nature and naturalization of humans.

33. Here, Liu Kang is probably implying the notion of subjectality.

34. Speaking of psychoanalysis, as Slavoj Žižek's compatriot, I cannot help but quote one of his infamous jokes, as it fits well in this context. The joke is about "a group of historians of language who, in order to support the hypothesis that God created man out of apes by telling them a joke (he told apes who, up to that moment, were merely exchanging animal signs, the first joke that gave birth to spirit), try to reconstruct this joke, the 'mother of all jokes.' Incidentally, for a member of Judeo-Christian tradition, this work is superfluous, since we all know what this joke was: 'Do not eat from the tree of knowledge!'—the first prohibition that clearly is a joke, a perplexing temptation whose point is not clear" (Žižek 2014, viii).

35. *Histomat* is an abbreviation for historical materialism. Actually, *histomat* mainly refers to the Stalinist reinterpretation of Marxist methodology, which is, in comparison with the original, quite limited and reduced. Hence, the term *histomat* seems rather unsuitable for denoting the method of historical materialism that was applied by Li.

36. If a theory is falsified, this falsification can subsequently certainly imply that one or more of the applied methods are inoperable, inapplicable, or ineffective.

37. On the other hand, this problem cannot be solved without investigating the specific essential nature of Li's materialism. In the last chapter of this book, we will problematize Li's materialism through the lens of traditional Chinese holism in order to investigate the modes of their possible interaction.

Chapter 2

1. For instance, see Husserl, Heidegger, Merleau-Ponty. In their famous book, *The Social Construction of Reality: A Treatise on the Sociology of Knowledge*, Peter Bergman and Thomas Luckmann also apply and describe the term sedimentation in a similar way. In the following years, the term sedimentation gradually became a common expression with which various theoreticians from the field of sociology, anthropology and other related fields have described the process

in which information and experiences were encoded and stored in the human mind (see for instance Giddens 1981 and 1984, Butler 1988 etc.).

2. In this first description, Li has not yet used the word sedimentation. He was merely writing about accumulations of a river.

3. Li points out: "Sedimentation flows from history into psychology, from rationality into sensuousness, from sociality into individuality" (Li and Cauvel 2006, 167).

4. The term "external techno-social formation" was changed into *gonju benti* 工具本體 (techno-social substance) and "internal cultural-psychological formation" was changed into *qinggan benti* 情感本體 or shortened into *qing benti* (emotion-based substance) (Yu Chuanqin 2016, 3) and *xinli benti* 心理本體 (psychological substance) (Li Zehou 1999b, 30).

5. These two notions were first introduced in his book, *Pipan zhexuede pipan: Kangde shuping* (*Critique of Critical Philosophy: A New Approach to Kant*). Here, Li Zehou is citing Kang Youwei's 康有為 notions of the great (society) (*da wo* 大我) and small (individual) self (*xiao wo* 小我) (Li Zehou 2001, 52). However, at the turn of the twentieth century, both notions were also frequently employed by Liang Qichao 梁啟超 and Sun Yat-sen (Sun Zhongshan 孫中山).

6. See for instance, Li Zehou 1994, 464. According to Li, Piaget also remained limited to the individual level without trying to explore the role of social subjectality and humanness in the process of learning and developing.

7. This concept will be explained in detail in the next section.

8. In her article, "Li Zehou, Kant and Darwin: The Theory of Sedimentation," Marthe Chandler shows that "the evidence from anthropology, studies of child development, primatology, linguistics and the behavior of our closest living primate relatives is highly suggestive and appears consistent with Li's theory of sedimentation" (Chandler 2016, 141).

9. As Chandler (2016, 134) points out, Marx believes that people became different from animals when we started to produce the things we need in order to live, but he says little more than this about primitive humans. Li's theory of sedimentation fills in this lacuna, describing the "humanization of nature," the process of creating a human nature (humanness) that is different from that of every other animal, which began when our early ancestors started systematically making and using tools.

10. According to Liu Kang (1992, 125) there is, however, a basic difference between Li's "cultural-psychological formation" and the Freudian "unconscious." While in his understanding, Li's psychic formation is a thoroughly rational and cultural product, in Freud and Lacan the "unconscious" signals an irreconcilable hiatus between cultural constraints and natural instincts and drives (see Lacan 2006, 52).

11. However, Li's historical view of sedimentation is compatible with early Marx and is also to a greater extent consistent with Darwin's theory.

12. In this context, Li rejected the orthodox Marxist supposition of class struggle as the crucial and sole driving force of historical development.

13. Gu Xin (1996, 215) asserts that in his *Philosophic and Aesthetic Writings* (*Zhexue meixue wenxuan* 哲學美學文選). Li also emphasizes the dialectical nature of this reciprocal process by pointing out that sedimentation is by no means a linear, one-way process, but rather a process characterized by a dialectical triad of sedimentation, breakthrough, and resedimentation (Li Zehou 1984, 393–402).

14. Li believes that, while in Western cultures people proceeded from shamanistic rituals to science and religion, Chinese culture directly upgraded them by developing their basic Confucian rituality (*li*) and (co)humaneness (*ren*, Li Zehou 2015, 13). To illustrate this supposition, we shall quote a sequence from the Confucian *Analects* that explicitly refer to this process: 顏淵問仁。子曰:「克己復禮為仁。一日克己復禮, 天下歸仁焉。」. Yan Yuan asked about humaneness. The Master said, "Humaneness means to subdue one's self and to restore rituality. If you can subdue yourself and restore rituality for one single day, then all under heaven will return to humaneness."

15. These culturally determined differences are, of course, not limited to mutually distant cultures like China and the United States. Cauvel (1999, 160) explains this phenomenon further, pointing out that "two Chinese scholars reading the same painting will (likewise) apply their own unique interpretations to it because of their separate life experiences, but since they share common cultural and artistic assumptions, they will take certain artistic conventions for granted."

16. These limiting layers of mental sedimentations can be broken or superseded by highly cultivated individuals through the implementation of various practices belonging to the naturalization of humans. Because they are able to direct experience towards the harmonic unity of human beings and nature, the cultural-psychological formations of their mental forms are developed in a way that enables the forming of new sedimentations, new sentiments, and new thought patterns. According to Jane Cauvel (1999, 164), they become "freer beings, less constrained by their history and culture."

17. German *subjektivität* and French *subjectivité* likewise have only one word for both meanings. However, my native tongue, Slovene, like Chinese, differentiates between the epistemological (subjektivno *zhuguanxing* 主觀性) and ontological (subjektno *zhutixing* 主體性) connotations of the term.

18. In his essay "An Outline of Kant's Philosophy and the Construction of Subjectality," Li stresses that for him, the main contribution of Kant's philosophy is precisely in his elaboration of the notion of subject and in his aprioristic system, not in his purely epistemological questions regarding the thing in itself (Li Zehou 1994, 461).

19. Li's critique of Kant's interpretation of knowledge, morality, and aesthetic judgment is centered upon its lack of any social and historical dimension. In Li's view, Kant's philosophy reduces the human subject to the fixed, *a*

priori relationships between transcendental principles, subjective structures, and objective products. "In giving Kant's notion of subjectivity a holistic, historicist turn, Li argues that all subjective structures are the products of historical process. They are not empty, but have their concrete, historical contents. As for the formation of these structures, the material, productive activities of practice are the determining factor" (Gu, Xin 1996, 224).

20. Here, Li was referring to his essay "An Outline of Kant's Philosophy and the Construction of Subjectality *(Kangde zhexue yu jianli zhutixing lungang* 康德哲學與建立主體性論綱)."

21. In this work, Marx frequently uses two similar German terms, *Entäußerung* and *Entfremdung*, to express the notion of alienation or estrangement. In Chinese translations of the *Manuscripts*, the term *Entäußerung* is usually translated with the term *waihua* 外化 and *Entfremdung* with the term *yihua* 異化. Although in his later works, Marx himself used the word "alienation" as the English equivalent of the term *Entäußerung* (ibid., 32). In this book, I am mainly using the term alienation for the former, and estrangement for the latter notion. First, the term *estrangement* is the most comprehensive translation of the German word *Entfremdung*, and second, in modern social studies, the term *alienation* mainly refers to isolation of human beings in societies with a low degree of integration or common values and is hence mainly referring to a state, which is a product or consequence of estranged labor (or estrangement as such). The English translation of *Entäußerung* (or *waihua* 外化) is externalization.

22. According to Marx (2007, 29), the estrangement of the workers from their products means not only that their labor becomes an object, an *external* existence, but that it exists *outside them*, independently, as something alien to them, and that it becomes a power that confronts them on its own. It means that the life they have conferred upon the object confronts them as something hostile and alien. The workers put their lives into the object and, consequently, their life no longer belongs to them but to the object.

23. In developing his theory on estranged labor and alienation, Marx described the phenomenon of the estrangement (*Entfremdung*) of human beings as a species from their human essence or their species-being (*Gattungswesen*). In Marx's view, this phenomenon is a consequence of forced, exploitative labor and of stratified social classes, because being a part of such institutions estranges them from their humanity (Marx 2007, 28–32).

24. In the 1980s, an intense debate arose in China about what constitutes *ren xing* or "humanness," mainly in reaction to the idea prevailing in the Cultural Revolution that it is identical to class (Chong 1999, 122).

25. Li points out that although both expressions have different connotations (the former refers to the narrower, and the latter to the broader meaning of the notion) they have both been translated into Chinese with the word *shijian* 實踐. Hence, this term refers to praxis as the surpassing of human beings' biological constitution on the one hand, and the practices that serve to satisfy their basic,

biologically determined—the instinctual, needs on the other. These narrow and broad meanings are mutually intertwined in real life—this differentiation only serves for the sake of an easier theoretical categorization. Nevertheless, the pure material practice in the narrower, Marxist sense, is more elementary, for people existentially depend on it.

26. Li points out (Li Zehou 1999e, 174) that in the Chinese tradition the separation between subject and object is not very clear, it is not important, and it is sometimes even overlooked, especially in epistemology.

27. In this regard, Li Zehou's philosophy is also congruent with the Chinese holistic tradition, in which ontology is inseparable from epistemology, as in its view of the world every object of cognition is also cognition itself—the manner of its existence is thus linked to our understanding of it. Because this connection goes both ways—their relation is not a relation of single-sided dependency and determination, but an interaction that includes mutual co-dependency—it cannot be seen as a purely solipsistic conceptualization of the world. Likewise, the perception of the existing world also holds true for its perception and interpretation. These also cannot be separated from the wholesome but changeable and much individualized existence of various objects of cognition (Rošker 2016, 51).

28. This close connection between individual and social virtue and between ethics and epistemology, which is included in the notion of self-completion, is clearly visible in numerous traditional texts, for instance, in the Confucian classic *The State of Equilibrium or the Mean*, which describes the concept of *cheng ji* as follows "Sincere people do not only accomplish the self-completion of themselves, but also strive to complete the others.' The completing of one's Self shows that a person possesses humaneness. The completing of others' shows that a person possesses knowledge" (誠者非自成己而已也，所以成物也。成己，仁也；成物，知也) (Zhong Yong 2013, Zhang ju da quan, 180).

29. We should also mention that Li also distinguishes between two types of morality, namely religious and modern (see Li Zehou 2015a, 6; Li Zehou and Liu Yuedi 2014, 207).

30. The concepts of humanized nature (or the humanization of nature) and of naturalized humans (or the naturalization of humans) will be treated in detail in the next chapter.

31. The word *aesthetic* derives from an ancient Greek word-family referring to perception.

32. However, since *meixue* 美學 is the most conventional term, Li has often preserved and applied it in his writings, incorporating into it the ideas of perceiving and recognizing beauty.

33. Even by introducing the concept of sedimentation, Li originally attempted to achieve a dialectical solution to the antinomy of content and form in aesthetics (Gu, Xin 1996, 215).

34. This presumption was first indicated already by Wang Guowei 王國維 (1877–1927) and Liang Qichao 梁啟超 (1873–1929) and was formulated

in more detail by Cai Yuanpei 蔡元培 (1868–1940) (see, for instance, Davies 2010, 209–10).

35. Marx was actually—though not explicitly—applying the aesthetic dimension as the key to imagining what a nonalienated world would look like. "In this ideal world, the economic and aesthetic dimensions of human life really do form a single, seamless entity; here artistic activity can no longer be separated from other forms of human production" (Gu, Xin 1996, 217). According to Gu Xin the most exquisite expressions of this aesthetic utopianism can be found in the works of Adorno and Marcuse (ibid., 218).

36. In fact, Li was the first Chinese Marxist who discovered the aesthetic implication of the *Manuscripts*, although the problem of alienation, which is widely seen as one of the central concepts in the *Manuscripts*, did not attract his attention until the 1980s. Even though the main theme of the book is a development of a revolutionary economic political theory, it is nevertheless grounded in philosophical impulses with distinctly aesthetic features (Gu, Xin 1996, 217). "In Marx's view, human beings are distinguished by their creative powers, and human creativity, in turn, is what lies at the heart of productive practices" (ibid.).

37. Li regards these doctrines as an "unfortunate product of Marx's successors that is incompatible with Marx's own doctrine because it is mechanistic and deterministic, ignoring the role of human agency" (Chong 1999, 127).

38. Li viewed humanism as a significant element of human ethics that has to be preserved and further developed (1985a, 19).

39. While Li employed Marx's early writings to support his technology-oriented view of social development, Wang Ruoshui and others put these self-same writings in the service of "socialist humanism" (Chong 1999, 122).

40. For a detailed description of this ideologically muddled transformation of the Chinese notion of harmony, see Rošker 2012, 3–10 and 2016, 153–64.

41. Unlike Mao's socialist hero, whom Li argues was mainly modeled after traditional Chinese philosophical and literary paradigms, the subject in Li's own philosophy, while active, creative, and concrete, always operates within objective boundaries (Chong 1999, 140). Li was well aware of the fact that in Chinese culture there is a "longstanding belief that the purified human will and consciousness alone are sufficient to overcome the inertia of both untamed nature and deeply ingrained sociocultural habits and dispositions. This is why Maoist ideology held that the key to the ordering of the universe was moral education or the transformation of individual consciousness rather than labor and technology—a tenet which, according to Li, could be traced back directly to Confucianism" (Chong 2005, 246).

42. Brian Bruya (2003, 135) notices that Li Zehou found the crucial correction of such voluntarist trends in Kant's notion of the subject, who is confined by the limits of the *a priori* structures of human understanding, which actively and autonomously constructs experience.

43. On the other hand, Lin Min (1992, 974) argues that Li Zehou has personally told him in a private conversation that he was indeed deeply influenced by Lukács's later work. According to Lin, Lukács's search for a new philosophical ontology in the later years of his life became the theoretical inspiration for and the source of Li's exploration of social ontology on which his theory of human subjectality is based (ibid.).

44. In this context, Marx writes: "Just as only music awakens in man the sense of music, and just as the most beautiful music has *no* sense for the unmusical ear—is [no] object for it, because my object can only be the confirmation of one of my essential powers, therefore it can only exist for me insofar as my essential power exists for itself as a subjective capacity because the meaning of an object for me goes only so far as *my* sense goes (has only a meaning for a sense corresponding to that object)—for this reason the *senses* of the social man *differ* from those of the nonsocial man. Only through the objectively unfolded richness of man's essential being is the richness of subjective *human* sensibility (a musical ear, an eye for beauty of form—in short, *senses* capable of human gratification, senses affirming themselves as essential powers of *man*) either cultivated or brought into being" (Marx 2007, 46).

45. However, the relationship between humanization of nature and the human subject is a complementary and reciprocal one. If we say that the humanization of nature is a condition for the evolution of the subject, we must also be aware that it is at the same time also conditioned by it, for without a developmental progression of the latter the former could not proceed as a continuous and significant historical process.

46. The phrase *tian ren heyi* is, in fact, a rather modern term, for it does not occur in this form in any work of classical Chinese philosophy. It refers to the holistic nature of the classical Chinese worldview, which is inherent in most of the prevailing currents of traditional Chinese ideational history. In this context, the epistemological aspects of bodily recognition (*tiren* 體認) or the unity of body and mind as developed by, for instance, by Xu Fuguan 徐復觀, were also of utmost importance (see Sernelj 2014, 86).

47. In his earliest published theoretical essay "On Aesthetic Feeling, Beauty and Art," Li distanced himself from the notion that at the time he saw as an expression of bourgeois psychologisms. When discussing the social nature of beauty he wrote: "Hence, this transference is much more than a simple outward projection. It is by no means a kind of mystical 'unification of the objects and myself,' nor a 'unification of nature and human beings'" (「所以,『移請作用』不是一種簡單的外射,不是什麼神秘的『我物同一』、『天人合一』」).

48. Later on, Zhuangzi's emphasis on the naturalization of humans was taken up by the proponents of popular or religious Daoism, who used various spiritual training methods to strengthen the body and prolong life.

49. These basic emotions include joy, anger, sorrow, fear, love, hate, and desire.

50. However, we must note that Li Zehou strongly opposes seeing Marxism as absolutely deterministic: "In the past, Marxist theory was often seen as a kind of 'economic determinism.' This determinism, however, can only be understood in the relatively long lasting period of human societies as a whole. It is an expression of an anthropologic-philosophical perspective, and cannot be seen as a static, unchangeable formula or an empirical principle, which could be directly and mechanistically applied to concrete historical circumstances." s(馬克思上述理論曾被人稱之為「經濟決定論」,其實這個「決定」,只能從整個人類社會較長時期來看。它所表述的只是一種人類學的哲學視角,而不是直接套用在具體歷史上的不變公式或實證原理) (Li Zehou 2006, 2).

51. Li points out that Kantian teleology, in which "man is seen as the ultimate purpose of nature, is still, in a sense, an objective teleology, while Kant's subjective purposiveness exists only in the aesthetic realm" (Li Zehou 2010, 189).

52. Liu Kang points out that in this context Li did not only draw on Kant, but also on the cognitive psychology of Piaget and Wittgenstein's theory of language-game as social practice (1992, 124).

53. In this context, Li also lays stress on the philosophical layers of classical Chinese thought, pointing out that the Five Phases Theory (*wu xing shuo* 五行說), the origins of which reach back to the Shang Dynasty (1600–1066 BC), already represented a theoretical scheme containing both rational and irrational elements: "The fact that tastes, sounds and colors are analyzed and divided into categories, and connections are drawn between these and various social contents and social elements, actually constitutes the theoretical establishment of the unity of reason with the perceptions, and of nature with society" (Li Zehou 2010, 9). According to Li, "this is of great philosophical significance" (ibid.).

Chapter 3

1. However, we have to emphasize in this context that "Li Zehou's ideas on the relationship between Confucianism and other schools of thought is meant to show that there are inner connections among all the traditional Chinese schools of thought and it is feasible to creatively integrate the useful sources from the various schools into a reconstructed Confucianism in its broad sense" (Gu Ming Dong 2015, 21).

2. Here, Li has once again shown his predilection for reversed slogans and phrases. By exchanging the position of the two characters that compose the Chinese word for Enlightenment (from *qimeng* to *mengqi* 蒙啟), he tried to show that the Enlightenment movement (literary means "opening up or awakening

from the ignorance and dullness") was replaced by "covering up the enlightened state of mind," which is the meaning of the reversed phrase.

3. As opposed to the "Three periods of Confucianism (*ruxue san qi* 儒學三期)," a classification that was advocated by Tu Wei-ming and his teacher Mou Zongsan.

4. Even though Li admits that he is not interested in establishing a system of Confucianism, "he nevertheless offers his vision, insights, inspirations, theoretical approach, and practical strategies for interested scholars to read, understand, and creatively transform Confucianism, and supplies concrete guidelines for the common people" (Gu 2015, 3).

5. Li Zehou inverted Lin Yusheng's 林毓生 concept of "creative transformation," which was assumed by many Chinese scholars, including Tu Wei-ming, in the reversed phrase "transformative creation." We shall introduce the difference between both concepts in the chapter on Chinese modernization, since originally both phrases were applied in the context of China's modernization.

6. These bamboo slips were excavated in 1993 in the Guodian tombs in the Hunan province and published in a restored form in 1998. The texts include many previously unknown versions of the pre-Qin thought, and thus the unearthing of them has provided new information on the history of thought in ancient China. In the chapter "*Yu cong*," there is a passage stating that "emotions were born from inner nature, and rituals were generated from emotions" (情生於性, 禮生於情), see *Guodian chu mu zhu jian* 1998; Yu cong II, 203.

7. While the nomadic origin of the Zhou continues to be debated in both the Chinese academic world and in Western Sinology, strong support for this thesis can be found in the chapter *Zhou benji* of *Shi Ji* (Historical Notes), see next footnote. In their philosophical and religious approaches, the representatives of the second generation generally subscribed to Xu Fuguan's historical studies, especially those found in the chapter, "The pre-Qin Period (*Xian Qin bian*)," in his study, *The History of Human Nature Theories in China (Zhongguo renxing lun shi)*.

8. Recently this notion has been introduced and described as a paradigmatic foundation of relating individuals and society in traditional Chinese culture by several Western Sinologists (see for instance, Lai 2016, 109).

9. As opposed to both individualism and collectivism.

10. The traditional Chinese character *xin* 心 in a literal sense means heart. But traditionally it mostly refers to the human mind. It was chiefly used in the sense of such an emotio-rational structure in classical works of Chinese literature and philosophy. This is also the reason why this character has mostly been translated as "heart-mind" in modern Western Sinology.

11. However, Li also firmly believes that this inseparability of religion, ethics, and politics, which is still prevalent in modern Chinese society, must be changed to achieve a "Chinese style of separation of religion and state" (Li Zehou 2015: 69).

12. Although the notion *legan wenhua* has mostly been translated into English as "culture of optimism," I prefer to use the term "culture of pleasure," since, as we shall see below, optimism is only one of the crucial characteristics by which it is defined. I also suspect that the first translator (whoever that might be) possibly confused the Chinese terms *leguan* 樂觀 (which means optimism or optimistic) and *legan* 樂感 (feeling of pleasure or joy), since they sound very similar.

13. See Jaspers 2003, 98.

14. Chen Lai (1996, 4), for instance, explains this counter-tendency by the fact that in China the great religious crisis occurred before the emergence of the "axial period" (Chen Lai 1996, 4). Because this morally-defined religion, dating from the early Zhou Dynasty, had gradually lost all its moral luster and because Heaven itself, in the role of the highest God and the ultimate moral instance, had lost all credibility, overcoming citizens' prevailing skepticism and reestablishing some form of theological thought that would permit the development of a monotheistic faith was extremely difficult. This "religious" faith was instead replaced by a faith in the rational structure of the universe, and "Heaven" became "Nature."

15. This supposition is not an entirely new idea in existing scholarship, as Confucianism is often defined as a "secular religion" in Sinology. "What is novel in his work is the accompanying analysis that supports his ideas from a conceptual point of view. Li states that as a semi-religion, it does not lay emphasis on revelation, personal god, miracles, etc., but at the same time, it is endowed with the qualities of a religion, in which people find their spiritual consolation, life's purpose and emotional home" (Gu 2015, 3–4).

16. On the other hand, Confucianism is not just a compendium of common-sense sayings and aphorisms for life. As Ming Dong Gu emphasizes, for Li, it is also endowed with a strong sense of religiosity due to its "ultimate concerns" (Gu, Ming Dong 2015, 4).

17. Therefore, quite astoundingly Chinese culture celebrates neither Christian guilt nor Japanese shame. In their place it enshrines pragmatic reason in a "culture attuned to pleasure," which duly accommodates intense feelings, even as it focuses on harmony, beauty, and proportion.

18. Here, we have to note that the character *le* 樂—the first character in the phrase *legan wenhua*—means joy or pleasure on the one hand, but also music on the other. In the latter case it is pronounced *yue*. Hence, in the spoken language, the character 樂 can be read either as *le* (meaning joy or pleasure), or as *yue* (meaning music). Wang Keping points out that both are commonly understood as parts of humanness (human nature). "Hence such culture helps facilitate the final accomplishment of human nature by virtue of musical appreciation and aesthetic feeling at its best" (Wang Keping 2016, 189).

19. In this context, Li speaks about the so-called peak-experience (Li Zehou 2016, 190).

20. According to the *Historical Notes* (*Shi ji* 史記), there were six main schools of thought in pre-Qin China, namely, Confucianism, Daoism, Moism, Nomenalism (School of names), Legalism, and the Yinyang School (see Taishi gong zixu 1988, 7–8). The *Book of Han* (*Han Shu* 漢書) added four more: the Diplomats, Agriculturalists, Syncretists, and the School of the Minor Talks (Han Shu xinyi 2013, Yiwen zhi, 2162).

21. Li denotes this holistic view as the "one-world view."

22. In this context, Li points to the fact that on numerous occasions Zhuangzi quotes Yan Hui (an important disciple of Confucius) and in the inner chapters he even borrows the role of Confucius himself to expound his own ideas. He also claims that the view of scholars who presuppose that Zhuangzi was a disciple of Yan Hui is not without merit (Li and Cauvel 2006, 86).

23. This line is mainly represented by the interpretations of the Wei Jin scholar Guo Xiang (died AD 312).

24. Li coined the term non-Dionysian tradition to mark a clear distinction between the Chinese "culture of (sensory) pleasure" on the one hand, and the Dionysian licentiousness or saturnalia for, in contrast to the latter, the Chinese aesthetic and intellectual tradition emphasized the moderation of violent sensuality, the rationalization inherent in the perceptual senses, and the inherent social present in the natural (Li and Cauvel 2006, 10). The joy people can feel in the culture of pleasure is hence not an ordinary sensual pleasure. On the other hand, however, it is also not a form of rational happiness, but rather refers to an aesthetic attitude toward life.

25. Li opposes the common (and in some discourses still prevailing) view that Daoism is closer to Buddhism than to Confucianism, and even more the view, which was immensely popular among several Japanese scholars at the threshold of the twenty-first century, which held Zhuangzi to have been an early representative of existentialism.

26. Following the famous Chinese historian Chen Yinke 陳寅恪, Li points out that many famous Chinese scholars and literati (e.g., Tao Qian) were "Confucian on the inside, but Daoist on the outside" (內儒而外道) (Chen Yinke 1977, 1035).

27. This supposition cannot be reduced to the fact that he was the teacher of the two most important legalist thinkers, namely Han Feizi and Li Si, but can also be seen in many of his philosophical ideas. See for instance: "A human being who likes the law and acts in accordance with it, is noble and educated. . . . But people without law are wild savages. And those who know the law but are unwilling to act in proper way are unsteady. We should live in accordance with the law and be well aware of our respective classes: only in this way can we achieve gentleness (Xunzi s.d.; Xiu shen, 9). (好法而行, 士也; . . . . . . 人無法, 則倀倀然; 有法而無志其義, 則渠渠然; 依乎法, 而又深其類, 然後溫溫然). In his main work, *Xunzi*, the character *fa* (law) appears 183

times. Li even points out Chen Yinke's claim that Xunzi has been "assisting in the establishment the system of the Qin Dynasty" (受旬卿之學, 佐成秦制) and that this was a system to which a certain fraction of Confucianism was attached (Chen Yinke 1977, 1032).

28. As noted, Modern Confucians have generally followed a Neo-Confucian philosophy based upon Mencius's, rather than Xunzi's development of the original teachings. Xunzi was thus often viewed as something of a heretic who did not profess or elaborate upon "proper" Confucianism in his own discourses.

29. Although the Han emperors acted as patrons of Confucianism, their policies and their closest advisers were largely Legalist.

30. Even though the first official exams were established as early as in the Han Dynasty, the system only became the major path to office in the period of the Tang Dynasty and remained as such until its closure in 1905. Precisely because the exams were based on knowledge of the Confucian classics and literary style, and not on some technical or professional expertise, successful candidates were mostly members of the higher classes, who shared a common language and culture. This general culture, which was based upon syncretic Confucianism, helped to unify the state and to legitimize imperial rule.

31. Ming Dong Gu pointedly remarks: "In this regard, Li Zehou is truly a pioneer who has not only studied Confucianism in relation to other Chinese schools of thought including Daoism, Legalism, and Buddhism, but also engages in reconstruction of Confucianism by infusing ideas from Western philosophical thinking including Kant, Hegel, Marx, Heidegger and others. His approach should inspire us to re-construct Confucianism in its broadest possible sense" (Ming Dong Gu 2015, 17).

32. We will elaborate on this specifically Chinese nontranscendental form of moral reasoning later in a separate section.

33. Some theoreticians, especially those from Taiwan, sometimes prefer to use the term *cunyoulun* 存有論 as a more proper translation for ontology.

34. Here, Lee Ming-Huei is referring to Modern Confucians.

35. For the full controversy between Lee, Hall, and Ames, see Lee Ming-Huei, 2001a and 2002 (especially chapter 1), as well as Hall and Ames 1987 and 1998 (especially chapter 9).

36. One could certainly presuppose that human heart-mind is not completely restricted by concrete given sensual experiences, even though it is rooted in the actual limitations of the human physical body. Even according to the strictly materialistic worldview, the human brain has limitless potential to construct new, previously inexistent knowledge by shaping new synapses, which arise from innumerable possibilities of new relations between different neurons. Besides, new relational knowledge is also created by every single new idea that is being shaped by the human heart-mind. Since all these relations can occur in countless combinations, it could be claimed that human consciousness—the very foundation of the

Chinese heart-mind, is epistemologically and axiologically infinite. In this sense it is immanent, but in this immanence there is also the possibility of transcendence. Following Levine, Husserl, and Whitehead, some scholars also translate the Chinese term *neizai chaouye* 內在超越 as "transcendence in immanence," instead of "immanent transcendence," which seems to be a more appropriate translation.

37. Although this model is by no means dualistic, it is still binarily structured and dynamic. We could also consider it as a kind of an alterable model in which pairs of entities (whether they belong to objects, qualities, patterns, or realms) can interact according to the correlative principle of complementarity. In such a model, immanence and transcendence are not necessarily in a mutual contradiction—although they are, of course, in mutual opposition. Here, immanence (similar to Confucianism) is demarcated by a forceful ability of assimilation, which enables it to integrate within itself its dual opposition (whereby this opposition cannot be equated with negation), and therefore to unite within itself their mutual differences. In this continuously changing, dynamic, and correlative holistic model, immanence is still dominant (similar to Confucianism in relation to Daoism). However, in Chinese philosophy, both realms can still be seen as mutually interdependent and complementary. Here, we could also consider some of Li's own statements, in which, by describing Confucianism, he writes that in these discourses, the Way of Heaven and the Way of Humans are "two in one and one in two" (「天道與人道是一而二、二而一的東西」, see Li Zehou 2008, 247).

38. There is some evidence for the proposition that Li did not distinguish between the English terms "transcendent" (in Chinese *chaoyue* 超越) and "transcendental" (in Chinese *chaoyan* 超驗), because the two adjectives are written and pronounced in the same way in the noun form (see for instance, Yang Guorong 2009, 323–24).

39. Because the character *qing* 情 also contains situational connotations, it is also possible to denote this elementary substance as "situation-based substance."

40. Although material practice is the very origin of any cognition and rationality, human reasoning is developing further and does not remain in this origin. Hence "laws, standards, values come from the historic building up of pragmatic reason, and they do so in the interaction of humans with the world; they do not depart from it" (Lynch 2016, 719).

41. However, in a footnote, he has already pointed to the fact that Kant's notion of practical reason is different from his own (Li Zehou 1980a: 89, footnote 3). Prior to that, he simply applied a more general term "Chinese rationalism" (*Zhongguo lixingzhuyi* 中國理性主義) to highlight the specific nature of this kind of reason (Li Zehou and Liu Yuedi 2014a, 4).

42. In his book *Outline of Philosophy* (*Zhexue gangyao* 哲學綱要) Li also emphasizes that his philosophy cannot be regarded as pragmatism, but rather as an anthropological ontology (Li Zehou 2011, 159).

43. The chapter, "On Music (*Yue ji* 樂記)" of the Confucian *Book of Rituals* (*Li ji* 禮記) contains the following passage: "This is why the ancient kings instituted their ceremonies and music and regulated them by the consideration of human needs" (「是故先王之制禮樂, 人為之節」, Li ji 2016, Yue ji. 476).

44. Li always emphasizes that original, instinctive human feelings have been made to be the norm (or, in a Confucian terminology, cultivated) by sensitive, rational regulations. He never explicitly defines the criteria of such reasonableness. In other words, he fails to demonstrate the actual standards of deciding what is actually "crazy," "evil," "ugly," or "deconstructive," and hence must be eliminated by the activation of pragmatic reason. Although, he highlights the importance of the dynamic nature of pragmatic reason, its utilitarian tendency, and especially its openness toward innovations and alternations, it still remains difficult to understand what underlies this kind of regulations, which in fact mostly manifest themselves in restrictions (this is also the primary criticism directed against Confucianism by most representatives of classical Daoism). Although Li mentions that (similar to Dewey's pragmatism), the truth is determined by what is positive and useful for a society, and although the concrete content of this usefulness is subject to continuous alternations, the question about what (or who) has the actual power of determining this usefulness (or this truth) remains open. In other words, Li seems—at least in this context—to disregard the function of power structures and relations in the development of human cultures and societies.

45. This tendency is especially visible in the famous Neo-Confucian phrase that advocates "the preservation of the (moral and rational) cosmic structure and the elimination of human desires" (*cun tianli mie renyu* 存天理滅人欲).

46. "The failure of the Song and Ming Neo-Confucian quest for transcendentalism" (*Song Ming lixue zhuiqiu chaoyande shibai* 宋明理學追求超驗的失敗).

47. Jia Jinhua points out that the *Shuowen jiezi* 說文解字 explanation of the etymological meaning of the character *ren* 仁 (human being and the number two) has led several scholars "to assume that the meaning implied in *ren* in the *Analects* is not based on a psychological notion, and the psychological, subjective use of *ren* in Chinese is a later development" (Jia Jinhua 2016, 761). She offers a lengthy, in-depth, and very detailed analysis of the etymological development of this concept to prove the opposite. However, I think that the psychological (or emotional) dimension is perfectly clear even if we consider Xu Shen's original explanation, for it suggests that human beings can only exist in communities with other people (here, the radical element signifying "two" can be understood as a plural form or simply as an expression of other people, for humans can only be humans when there are at least two of them). The original meaning implies that nobody is an island, that we all depend on each other, and that we therefore simply cannot afford not to love, cherish, and help each other. What the original meaning expresses, is—in my own view—simply a deep feeling of mutual inter-human empathy.

48. In this context, emotion-based substance refers mainly to positive feelings and resulting social attitudes. As Jia Jinhua noted, however, this was not the case in the Western tradition, in which "the study of moral psychology had traditionally focused on moral reasoning. Since the 1980s there has been a 'moral-emotional correction,' and emotion has gradually become a central subject in moral psychology research. However, researchers have placed more weight on 'negative' moral emotions such as contempt, anger, shame, and guilt than on 'positive' moral emotions, and it is still under debate as to whether some major emotional experiences such as love can be seen as moral emotion. Li Zehou's study of the Confucian ethics of emotion with the general love of *ren* as its core provides a rich source for filling this gap" (Jia Jinhua 2016, 780).

49. Actually this structure is rooted in emotions and ultimately returns into it. In short, Li Zehou schematized it as follows: emotion → ritual → reason → emotion (*qing* 情 → *li* 禮 → *li* 理 → *qing* 情).

50. See for instance, Li 2016b, 151.

51. We can speak of joy, anger, sadness, concern, love, hate, and desires. These are all the seven emotions. 曰喜怒，曰哀懼。愛惡欲，七情具。(San zi jing ju jie 2015, 50).

52. The transcendent (morally cultivated) subject and the empirical (social and political) self.

53. However, this would require a timely "transformative creation" of contemporary Chinese culture, a topic that will be elaborated in detail in the following chapters.

54. See, for example, the final chapter entitled "We Want Reforms, Not Revolutions (要改良，不要革命)" in his *Farewell to Revolution* (Li Zehou and Liu Zaifu 1999, 371–92).

55. See, for instance, the recent ideological manipulation of the Confucian concept of harmony (Rošker 2013, 3–20).

56. Here, we are not referring to traditional modernity (for example, the Western "New era"), but to modernity understood as a process of general social transformation or social revival, linked to certain specific conditions that dictate modernization (e.g., the Enlightenment, the dominant role of reason in philosophy, industrialization, and so on). This process has followed diverse trajectories depending on the specific cultural environment or tradition and has always involved the transformation of the specific conditions of transitional societies.

57. As we will see later, the slogan was not actually created by Zhang Zhidong, but became famous in the context of his essay "Exhortation to Study (*Quanxue pian* 勸學篇)."

58. I will introduce this inversion and its implications in detail later in this chapter.

59. Although some scholars, including Liang Shuming in his *Dongxi wenhua jiqi zhexue* 《東西文化及其哲學》 (1921), claimed exactly the opposite.

60. In his books and essays on modern Chinese philosophy, especially in those dealing with the problem of Xiti Zhongyong (see the next section), Li mainly distinguishes between two oppositional currents—the stream of complete Westernization (*quan pan xihua*) and the stream that advocated Chinese essence and Western function. He sees the latter as a neo-conservative one and views his own proposal as a reasonable middle way between the two radical oppositions. In his view, a similar "middle way" was already advocated by Kang Youwei 康有為 in his *Book of Great Unity* (*Datong shu* 大同書) (see Li Zehou 2016b, 374).

61. The reform, which led to the gradual introduction of the market-capitalist economy, began in 1978 under the leadership of Deng Xiaoping. Like the first two social modernization programs, Deng's reforms also began in technology and economics, and avoided cultural reforms as such. However, Hua Shiping has shown how the increasingly successful reforms were often reflected in cultural terms, as confirmed by phenomena such as the "Cultural Fever" (*wenhua re* 文化熱) and the "Great Debate on Culture" (*wenhua da taolun* 文化大討論) (Hua Shiping 2001, 4). Of course, following Tiananmen, these theoretical reflections on modernization processes were violently suppressed.

62. According to Wang Hui, the epistemological sources that formed the basis for New Enlightenment theory mostly derived from (predominantly liberal) Euro-American economic, political, and legal theories. In the historic perspective, it becomes evident that these thought processes served as the basic ideology for economic reforms (Wang Hui 2000, 16).

63. Possibly because of his huge influence on students and his indirect, but important function in the theoretical origins of the 1989 student movements, some scholars count Li Zehou among the representatives of the New Enlightenment movement, but such a view is by far too superficial. Precisely due to his thoroughly critical attitude towards instrumental reason (see previous sections), Li can hardly be understood as an advocate of this intellectual stream.

64. Obviously, the representatives of the movement had a merely superficial understanding of the tradition, which was evidently insufficient to actually supersede or transform it. This superficial view was inherently connected to an idealized image of science, which was seen as the incorporation and a vehicle of an omnipotent reason. Science was thus understood as a kind of surrogate that could resolve the "transcendental homelessness" and loss of cultural identity that inevitably followed upon the total negation of Chinese traditional culture.

65. In his article "A Short Explanation of the Motto 'Western Essence, Chinese Functions' (《「西體中用」簡釋》)," Li states that Li Shu 黎澍 was the first to "invert" this slogan (Li Zehou 2002, 154). Both were widely criticized for proposing this "inversion" (Li Zehou 2002, 154).

66. Because of this reversal, Li was criticized for advocating wholesale Westernization. He was labeled a traditionalist, for he was one of the first Chinese intellectuals who emphasized, as early as the beginning of the 1980s, the impor-

tance of not only the Confucian revival, but also the revival of all traditional philosophical discourses. By the end of the 1980s he was again condemned as being conservative, for he insisted on the theoretical value of early Marxism.

67. *Zai shuo Xiti Zhongyong* 再說西體中用 (*Western Substance and Chinese Function Revisited*), in Li Zehou 1998: 168–201. See also "Manshuo Xiti Zhongyong 漫說西體中用 (*A Simple Lecture on Western Substance and Chinese Function*)" in Li Zehou 1987, 311–41 or Li Zehou 2016c, 334–66. In this book, I used an earlier version of the latter essay, published in the journal *Kongzi Yanjiu* in 1987; see Li Zehou 1987a. In the most recent reprint of his book *On Contemporary Chinese Intellectual History* (of which this essay is also a part) Li has added an appendix, in which he explains the issue in an even greater detail (ibid., 369–94).

68. Zhang elaborated upon this phrase in a very traditionalist manner in his famous essay, "Exhortation to Study (*Quanxue pian* 勸學篇)," which advocated a conservative reform.

69. Here, we could add, in terms that are more concrete, that it is certainly by no means irrelevant what kind of food we find in our refrigerators or what kind of programs can be watched on our televisions.

70. Here, Li is influenced by Immanuel Kant: "While Marx focused on the crucial aspect of the capacity of the collective human subject to engage in economic production by the use of 'tools,' Kant provided Li with the philosophical framework to reflect on the mental and ideal aspects of human nature—the faculties of knowledge, ethics, and aesthetics" (Chong 1999, 121).

71. In his *Theses on Feuerbach* (1845) Marx criticized the Young Hegelians for misunderstanding "the essence of human beings" as abstract, isolated entities. Marx argued that human nature could only be understood in the context of the economic and social relations in which people actually lived. He also argued that it was the underlying social and economic conditions that gave rise to religious beliefs and other ideational superstructures.

72. See, for example, Li and Liu Zaifu 1999, 65, 69, 75, 331; Li Zehou 2002c: 3, 7; Li Zehou 1985, 154, 298, etc.

73. None of the most influential Neo-Marxist theorists ever questioned the intrinsic nature of the Marxist dialectical model in such a radical (even if unconscious) way. Although Li was often described as a "Neo-Marxist," by other intellectuals, he preferred to define himself as a proponent of the early Marx (Li Zehou 1998, 175).

74. The original passage in German reads "Es ist nicht das Bewusstsein der Menschen, das ihr Sein, sondern umgekehrt ihr gesellschaftliches Sein, das ihr Bewusstsein bestimmt" (Marx 1971, 9. English translation assumed from Marx 2009).

75. He wrote: "In order to prevent a conceptual confusion I had coined a new formulation of the notion "*ti*." However, this does not mean that I was generally advocating the view, according to which "learning" represents the "basis" (Li Zehou 2016, 110).

Chapter 4

1. In this context, Li often recalls that Kant also emphasized the importance of the line as the most elementary and simultaneously the most superior aesthetic visual element (Kant 1998, 161).

2. Gao's theory clearly rejected the objective existence of beauty, which was "obviously in opposition to the official view of Marxist dialectical materialism" (Man 2001, 51). Hence, it was not surprising that Gao was labeled a political Rightist. Many years later Gao expressed his gratefulness to Li, who never criticized him for holding a different opinion and who never claimed that subjectivity was automatically equal to idealism. In Gao's view, and especially considering the iron times of the period, this was an incredibly tolerant and respectful attitude (Gao Ertai 2014, 1).

3. Zhu Guangqian's earlier theory proceeded from paradigms belonging to subjective idealism, for which he was harshly criticized. Although he tried to place it on a materialist foundation, he was unable to fully agree with Cai Yi's pure and absolute objectivism. He later tried to elaborate on a dialectical paradigm in which both aspects were in mutual interaction.

4. The essay "On the Aesthetic Feeling, Beauty and Art" was first published in the fifth issue of the 1956 volume of the famous journal *Philosophy Research* (*Zhexue yanjiu* 哲學研究). It was originally subtitled "Also on Zhu Gauangqian's Idealistic Aesthetic Thought" (*Jian lun Zhu Guangqiande weixinzhuyi meixue sixiang* 兼論朱光潛的唯心主義美學思想). Although the essay included many serious criticisms on his aesthetic thought, Zhu (in a letter written to He Lin later acknowledged that "among numerous critiques that were directed against him during that time Li Zehou's was the most substantial and well-grounded" (Yang Bin 2015, 19).

5. Almost four decades after the publication of this essay, in 1990 Cai Yi proclaimed critically that Li's most severe problem began in 1956 when he started proposing the "duality of aesthetic feeling" (Yang Bin 2015, 19).

6. If we hadn't known that Li belonged to the founders of *Zhexue yanjiu*, it would be almost unbelievable that this best, most important, and most authoritative theoretical journal from the field of philosophy would publish an essay written by such a young scholar, especially considering the fact that it contains several grammatical and stylistic errors. However, due to the relative complexity of the language, it seems that the linguistic copyeditors and technical editors might have easily overlooked them. At the end of the essay Li even apologized for them, blaming the rush and hurry under which the essay had to be written. At the same time, he apologized because he had no time to improve and supplement the essay because "he was now too busy doing other things" (Li Zehou 1956, 73). (As a twenty-first century European researcher, one might wonder what "other things" might be more important than a publication in the nation's

best academic journal of one's own research field). It is obvious that the editors were eager to publish the essay in spite of its formal shortcomings and notwithstanding the young age and unimportant position of the author. This eagerness might be the result either of short-term political decrees, for instance, because of a need for a clear—including theoretical—distance from the Soviet Union, with which the People's Republic of China had some milder conflicts at the time. These were mostly due to the fact that Soviet Premier Nikita Khrushchev officially denounced the legacy of Stalin. Li's essay provided a Marxist theory of aesthetics, which differed from the official Soviet interpretation (Yang Bin 2015, 19). But on the other hand the reason might have been the simple fact that the essay was theoretically brilliant and that official Chinese ideology was in bitter need of establishing a Sinicized, but theoretically solid, "scientific" link, between Kantian, Hegelian, and Marxist theories of perception.

7. Like most of his contemporaries, Marx was—in a conscious or unconscious way—definitely a successor of Kant's intellectual heritage, although in his *Manuscripts* he never even mentions this "idealist philosopher," in the above-cited statement he was referring to Feuerbach and not directly to Kant.

8. In the German Ideology, for instance, Marx and Engels write: "Kant was satisfied with 'good will' alone, even if it remained entirely without result, and he transferred the *realization* of this good will, the harmony between it and the needs and impulses of individuals, to *the world beyond*. Kant's good will fully corresponds to the impotence, depression, and wretchedness of the German burghers, whose petty interests were never capable of developing into the common, national interests of a class and who were, therefore, constantly exploited by the bourgeois of all other nations" (Marx and Engels s.d., III/5).

9. Although many scholars believe that Marxism as a communist theory is "fundamentally aesthetic in character," the parts regarding aesthetics are only fragmentary and nearly epigrammatically scattered among Marxist texts, never amounting to a systematic disquisition in any sense (Swiderski 1979, 48). On this scattered basis Georgi Valentinovich Plekhanov managed to construct a comprehensive theoretical system and is thus considered to have been the founder of Marxist aesthetic theory (ibid., 60).

10. In this earliest aesthetic work, Li was still stuck within the formal limitations of the orthodox Soviet aesthetic theory and its concepts such as "typicality" or "*tipichnost*" (*dianxing* 典型).

11. This information provided by Yang Bin is not completely accurate, as the concept sedimentation as such never occurs in the text (Yang Bin 2015, 18). However, Li mentions several times in the essay words like "to accumulate" (*jilei* 積累, Li Zehou 1956, 48) or "compact accumulation" (*jijin* 積緊 ibid., 71).

12. The article is "The Objective and the Social Nature of Beauty (*Meide keguanxing he shehuixing* 美的客觀性和社會性)." Altogether Li published ten essays on aesthetics in the years between 1955 and 1959.

13. Here, it must be clarified that in the Marxist (and more general, in the modern or post-Enlightenment German) tradition, humanities continue to be seen as a kind of science, although not belonging to the "natural" sciences (*Naturwissenschaften*), but rather to "intellectual or spiritual sciences" (*Geistewissenschaften*). While the former investigates the empirical world by applying quantitative methodologies, the latter were supposed to work with qualitative methodologies and to explore human action and the human mind in their multifarious relations to cultures and arts in past and present societies. As long as Marxism was dominant in Chinese academia as the only theoretical model in the absolute forefront of any serious research, the academic authorities (via the Soviet Union) adopted this German methodological categorization. Any research in the humanities accordingly had to follow a certain "materialistic scientific methodology" to be treated as a serious theoretical discourse. Philosophy was only credible when it was written in a scientific way, either as analytic or pragmatic philosophy, as long as it dealt with provable elements of the phenomenal world. All metaphysical speculations were excluded from the realm of "real" philosophy. Now Chinese academia no longer follows this model, although such categorical framework to a certain degree and with certain adaptations has been applied in continental Europe.

14. However, this tight connection did not mean that aesthetics could be equated to epistemology. In all his years of academic and theoretical activity Li has always and constantly emphasized that aesthetics cannot be reduced to epistemology and that it represents another independent discipline.

15. It is of course clear that these diametrically opposed methodologies and referential frameworks are a natural consequence of different valuations of reality—of profoundly different worldviews and beliefs. This paradigmatic ontological difference, however, does not influence the very concept by which philosophies (irrespectively of their materialistic or idealistic nature) work.

16. According to Li, a similar problem occurs with idealistic misuses of Kant's concept of intuition. While the German philosopher first described it as a form of direct perception, a momentous pure experience that is not processed by human reason or logical cognition, the idealistic philosophers have assumed this notion and misinterpreted, manipulated, and misused it by defining it as something absolute and mysterious (Li Zehou 1956, 45). In their eyes it "transcends all utilitarianism," for it is "without any purpose" (ibid.). Although, Marxism is seen by Li as strongly opposing such misapplication of aesthetic feeling, as this is based upon a misinterpretation of intuition, it does not reject the existence of this primary phenomenon per se. By the same token, Li points out that materialist psychology also does not deny the existence of mental perceptional processes. Materialism never rejects facts. Further, such a pure intuition, a pure appearance of a certain form beyond any utilitarian, moral or any other purposes definitely exists. This idealist misinterpretation of intuition also has, of course, further

epistemological consequences, for it leads advocates of the idealistic paradigm to a complete and absolute separation of reason and intuition. Knowledge in their understanding is either a product of intuition (imagination, appearances), or a product of purely rational cognitive understanding. Li has shown that in the materialist framework reason and intuition both exist, but not in absolute separation from each other. They merely represent two different methods of how human beings perceive the world (ibid., 46).

17. The Chinese title reads *Xiao luoji* 小邏輯; see Hegel 1981.

18. Here, Li is probably referring to the following sequence: "Everything that exists stands in correlation, and this correlation is the veritable nature of every existence. The existent thing in this way has no being of its own, but only in something else: in this other however it is self-relation; and correlation is the unity of the self-relation and relation-to-others" (Hegel 1981 § 135a, 224), although He Lin's Chinese translation, which he quotes, is somehow ambiguous (存在之反映他物與存在之反映自身不可分 . . . . . . 存在 . . . . . . 包含有與別的存在之多方面的關係於其自身, 而它自身卻反映出來作為根據, 這樣性質的存在便叫作「物」或「東西」).

19. Many scholars have misunderstood this crucial point in Li's theory—mostly because it is (much too) common to automatically link objectivism with internal qualities of objects. Woei Lien Chong, for instance, writes: "The young Li held that beauty is not a construct of the perceiving subject, but a property of concrete things" (Chong 1999a, 72). This is her interpretation of an article in which Li clearly says that "nature as such is not beautiful. The beauty of nature is a result of the socialization of nature" (自然本身並不是美, 美的自然是社會化的結果, Li Zehou 1956, 57). It is of utmost importance to see that even though the young Li stood firmly on an objectivist starting point, his view of objectivity was a social one and external to the object regarded to be beautiful: the criteria for judgments were a common and universally human issue and were evolving in accordance with the development of society. In this sense, Li's objectivity was in absolute opposition to subjectivity only because subjectivity is necessarily linked to individual judgments.

20. Here, Li mentions Cai Yi as belonging to such objective idealists.

21. Or concrete "image-nature."

22. The official aesthetic theory that was predominant in China from the late 1940s on leaned heavily on Lukács and the Soviet theories of "typicality," which emphasized the developmental laws of history, whereas the cognitive functions of art were mostly described as "image-thinking" (see Zhou, Xiaoyi 2005, 107). Although these art theories did not completely deny any kind of emotions or feelings, and even though they advocated the viewpoint that every "type" has to be "aesthetic" and distinctive—that it has to possess specific, unique characteristics, in essence they have mostly still demanded a "transcending of individuality and feelings."

23. See especially chapter 3, "Pragmatic Reason and Emotion-Based Substance."

24. Li seized upon this opportunity immediately. In January 1978, i.e., a few days after this speech, he published the essay "Continuing the Debate on Image-Thinking (*xingxiang siwei xutan* 形象思維續談)" in the prestigious academic journal *Xueshu yanjiu*.

25. According to Li (2016, 73–74), there were four kinds of "fever" that erupted in China in the final decades of the twentieth century. Apart from the "aesthetic" and the "cultural" fevers in the eighties, there were also the "national studies" (*guoxue re* 國學熱) and the "Western studies" (*xixue re* 西學熱) fevers in the nineties.

26. In a 2011 interview, Li explained that the cultural fever of the eighties was an attempt to cover up political questions through cultural issues. Everyone was passionately debating cultural problems, but, in fact, they were interested in issues regarding the reforms and openness policies (see Xu Youyu in Zhao Shilin 2012: 207).

27. This slogan was by no means invented by Deng Xiaoping. He merely popularized it anew to promote an empirical basis for his economic and political reforms. The slogan was quoted by Mao Zedong back in 1938 but it is in fact a proverb that was first mentioned in the history of the Han Dynasty *Han shu* (Han shu 2013; Jing shisan wang chuan, 02–678).

28. In the *Afterword* to the second edition of his Critique on Kant's transcendental philosophy, Li wrote that he was himself positively surprised when this campaign broke out only one year after his book was published (Li Zehou 1984a, 116–17). Although he was very skeptical at the academic level of the debate, he was nevertheless glad because it was a sign that his book had a certain influence and a certain educational impact.

29. We cannot forget, however, that in these two decades (especially after 1966) it was practically impossible in the People's Republic of China to publish serious or solid academic work. This does not mean, however, that Li stopped reasoning and working on his theories. On the contrary, precisely during this period, in which he could not freely read, let alone publish anything critical, innovative, or controversial, he must have secretly conducted a huge amount of intellectual work, because if we compare his writings from the mid-1950s with those from the end of the 1970s, it becomes very clear that such a theoretical maturation cannot be achieved overnight.

30. Li wrote his first study of this concept even earlier in 1963, when it was published in the journal *Academic research*. In this early work he connected art with emotions (see Li Zehou 1980b, 29).

31. "Continuing the Debate on Image-Thinking" (*Xingxiang siwei xutan*).

32. "A New Continuation of the Debate on Image-Thinking" (*Xingxiang siwei zai xutan* 形象思维再续谈).

33. Although his primary interest in aesthetics later shifted to other subjects, Li never completely distanced himself from the notion of image-thinking. Occasionally he dedicated some pages to the explanation of this concept as late as in the first decade of the twenty-first century, for instance, in his short article "On Image Thinking (*Guanyu xingxiang siwei* 關於形象思維)" from 2008.

34. "Under these economic conditions" (Marx 2007, 29).

35. Here we must point out that even when writing about alienation in his later periods, Li mostly referred to the sociological (and not to economic-political) connotations of the term. When mentioning alienation he mostly understands it as a state of inter-human isolation in modern societies with a low degree of integration or common values. This is of course also a partial consequence of the estranged system of labor in Marxist sense; however, Li almost never described the concept of alienation in a strictly Marxist terminology.

36. Li mentioned Plekhanov in this paper only passingly, in a quotation of Lu Xun (Li Zehou 1956, 51).

37. See for instance, Li Zehou 2016a, 16 and 21.

38. Despite the same name, this Chinese notion is not to be confused with Kierkegaard's concept of aesthetic realm.

39. Besides being the first scholar to introduce to China the works of Nietzsche, Schopenhauer, and Kant, Wang Guowei initiated the comparative study of Western and Chinese aesthetics. Similar to Li Zehou's thoughts, the idea of human life was the basic foundation of all aesthetic studies also for Wang Guowei. On this basis, he created an aesthetics of life in the sense of modern humanitarianism and purposelessness by elaborating Zhuangzi's category of "the use through the useless" (*wu yong zhi yong* 無用之用) in aesthetic activities. (Zhuang Zhou 2014; Nei pian. Renjian shi, 81).

40. Here, we can see an important difference between the majority of the Modern New Confucian philosophers and Li Zehou. Whereas the Modern Confucians mostly follow the Kantian equation according to which beauty is a symbol of morality and thus emphasize the union of goodness and beauty, the fusion of aesthetics and morality, Li believes that because of its all-embracing nature, the aesthetic realm is higher than the domain of morality.

41. In *The Path of Beauty*, Li Zehou describes this ontological dimension of emotion in the chapter on the aesthetics of the Wei Jin period (220–589): "Since emotion is already linked with the noumenal inquiry and experience of the human personality, its aesthetic significance has already surpassed that of social ethics" (Li, Zehou 2010, 137).

42. In his aesthetic theory, Li Zehou's shows, inter alia, how the Chinese tradition develops a sense of dynamic, moral and sophisticated beauty, which functions similarly to the concept of sublime in the Western tradition. This kind of beauty is embodied in the inherent moral strength of the sage, and it manifests itself in the unity of heaven (nature) and humans. In this unity, "the

intercommunication and resonance between heaven and humans, or the correspondence between heaven and humans, is a very widespread and long-lasting notion in Chinese aesthetics and artistic creation. From today's perspective, however, this principle can be seen as simply a roughhewn and roundabout expression of the idea of the 'humanization of nature' in Chinese philosophy and aesthetics" (Li, Zehou 2010, 72).

43. Here we are mainly referring to the notion of dynamically (rather than to the mathematically) sublime (see Pluhar 1987, ixix–ixx).

44. In *Critique of Judgement*, Kant describes the difference between the notions beautiful and sublime in the following way: "The beautiful in nature concerns the form of the object, which consists in (the object's) being bounded. But the sublime can also be found in a formless object, insofar as we present *unboundedness*, either (as) in the object or because the object prompts us to present it, while yet we add to this unboundedness the thought of its totality. So it seems that we regard the beautiful as the exhibition of an indeterminate concept of the understanding, and the sublime as the exhibition of an indeterminate concept of reason" (Kant 1987, 98).

45. Li mentions this comparison several times and in different contexts. This ideational contrast was actually pointed out by the founder of modern Chinese aesthetics, Kang Youwei (1858–1927) and later many times by the first president of the Peking University Cai Yuanpei (1868–1940): "He regarded Westerners to be largely shaped by religion, whereas for China, he held aesthetics (a combination of ritual, art and ethics) to be the functional 'spiritual' equivalent to religion in the West. For this reason the demanded for modern China 'aesthetic education in place of religion' (Pohl 2009, 93). See also Cai's article "Replacing Religion with Aesthetic Education (*Yi meiyu dai zongjiao* 以美育代宗教)" in Cai Yuanpei 1984, 30–35.

46. Li explains that the phrase is a popularized description of the historical materialist worldview (see Li Zehou 1999b, 20).

47. There are three books that bear the name of this paradigm—one with the shorter title (*Historical Ontology*) and two with the longer title (*Anthropo-Historical Ontology*). Most of the content of the latter is a reworked, expanded, and completed versions of the material collected in his book *An Outline of my Philosophy*.

48. Confucius said that "We cannot (even) know life, so how could we know (anything about) the death" (未知生, 焉知死?) (Lunyu 2009; Xian jin, 569).

49. In this context, Li Zehou points out that similar ideals can also be found in the works of Modern Confucians (e.g., Liang Shuming, Feng Youlan and Qian Mu) and in the ideals of Dewey, who claimed that art is experience (Li Zehou 2016b, 401).

50. He claims that the central epistemological question of Kant's first *Critique*, namely the question of how synthetic *a priori* judgments are possible, implies, in fact, the question of how the universal necessity of scientific truth

is possible. For Li, the core aim of Kant's critical philosophy was to invalidate all dogmas and skepticisms, to posit the investigation of the human forms of knowledge in the center of philosophical inquiry and to highlight the problem of their limited scope to establish a clear distinction between science and religion (Li Zehou 1996b, 13).

51. Of the ten chapters included in the book, chapters 2–7 deal with epistemology; chapters 8 and 9 critically introduce Kant's ethics (his second *Critique*), and chapter 10 discusses his aesthetic thought (his third *Critique*).

52. According to Lionel Jensen (2005: 463), this "return to Kant" was a 1980s phenomenon and extended, as well, to Japan where Kojin Karatani's *Transcritique* read Kant's first *Critique* to disclose the ethical foundations of socialism (Jensen 2005, 463).

53. Li describes this feature with the term "humanization of nature."

54. However, proper measure was not only a basic epistemological paradigm but also a primary and fundamental concept of Li Zehou's anthropo-historical ontology. As we see in the chapter on Li Zehou's theoretical system, his thought was—although modern and quite up-to-date—firmly rooted in the dynamic framework of specifically Chinese thought, in which the demarcation lines between ontology and epistemology (as well as ethics) were changeable and hence blurred.

55. He claims that he raised this question because it highlights the central onto-epistemological problem. In this context, Li could neither agree with *a priorism*, were God created humans, nor with social biologism, were humans evolved from apes. Although numerous scholars believe Li based his studies upon Darwin's theory of evolution, he emphasized several times that he was never dealing with questions connected to the human body, but with questions regarding the establishment of external civilizations and the shaping of humanness, including epistemology. For Li, these phenomena were not merely results of biological evolution (Li Zehou 2012b, 1).

56. In addition, this elementary idea was further completed by integrating into it an "anthropological version of Piaget's child developmental theory" (Li Zehou 2008e, 318).

57. Li went as far as establishing a hypothesis stating that the basic laws of formal logic, namely the law of identity and the law of contradiction, are the results of first ethical orders. In such a framework ethics exists prior to epistemology.

58. During the first four decades of the twentieth century this issue became one of the most important subjects in the controversies that arose regarding the Marxist historical materialism. Chinese scholars seemed to reflect upon it much more deeply than was the case in the rest of the world. One of the main critiques directed against Marxist theory was its problematic projection from a theoretical logical model of formal development to the historical evolvement of concrete societies, see for instance, Zhang Dongsun 1931 and 1933.

59. This work has been translated by Paul D'Ambrosio and published in *Philosophy East and West* in 2016. D'Ambrosio is currently working on a translation of Li Zehou's *An Outline of Philosophy*.

60. To only name a few: *Lunli wenti ji qita* 倫理問題及其它 (About Ethics and Other Issues, 2014); *'Qing benti' de wai tui yu neitui* 「情本體」的外推與內退 (The Extension and Intention of the Emotion-based Substance, 2012); *Guanyu 'Youguan lunlixuede dawen' de buchong shuoming* 關於「有關倫理學的補充說明」 (2008) (Additional Explanation to "Some Questions and Answers regarding Ethics" 2008, 2009); With Liu Yuedi: *Cong 'Qing benti' fansi zhengzhi zhexue* 從「情本體」反思政治哲學 (Reflecting on Political Philosophy from the Perspective of Emotion-based Substance, 2014); *Cong 'Liangde lun' tan pushi jiazhi yu Zhongguo moshi* 從「兩德論」談普世價值與中國模式 (On Universal values and the Chinese Model from the Perspective of the "Theory of two Moralities," 2011); *Goujian zhengyi jichushangde hexie—cong Sangdeerde 'Gongzheng' shuoqi* 構建正義基礎上的和諧——從桑德爾的「公正」說起 (Constructing Righteousness on the Basis of Harmony—On Sandel's Concept of Justice, 2013), etc.

61. Li emphasizes that Kant is the first and foremost representative of deontological ethics, and that any discussion of ethics must address him (Li Zehou 2016, 71).

62. For a more detailed explanation of these categories, see chapter 4, "Two Kinds of Morality and Proper Measure."

63. See Li Zehou 2016, 1079. A more detailed schematic overview on Li's ethical thought can be found in the appendix.

64. Li excluded Carol Gilligan from these anti-rationalist stream because he believed she was not rejecting the importance of reason.

65. The concept of the so-called Confucian role-ethics was constituted and developed by David Hall and Roger Ames (see Hall and Ames 1987 and especially Ames 2011). However, because in the Western world the term "role" is mostly understood as "playing a part or a character that is different from one's true self," which can lead to a misunderstanding of the essence of Confucian ethics, I prefer to denote it with the (although a bit vague) phrase "Confucian relational ethics" or simply with "Confucian ethics of relations."

66. Partly this is also due to the recent ideological misuses of the concept. However, in original Confucian teachings and in other dominant traditional discourses, the concept has nothing to do with conflict avoidance or "social peace, discipline and order," nor with unification. On the contrary, the Confucian notion of harmony is based upon diversity (see Rošker 2013; Li, Chenyang 2014).

67. In contrast to Paul D'Ambrosio, the translator of Li's *Reply to Sanders* (which I am quoting here), I translate this term (*guanxizhuyi* 關係主義) as "relationalism."

68. This diversion does not only pertain to the concept of class struggle—after 1964 he even completely stopped operating with even most basic categories of such discourses, as for instance, with the category of social classes.

69. Besides the issue of these different dialectical models, Li has repeatedly emphasized that he also highly valued the materialist basis of Marxist thought. He claimed that the materialistic disposition of Marxist thought is reflected in his own "philosophy of eating," which represents an attempt to bring materialism closer to ordinary and uneducated people and is furthermore allegedly rooted in Confucian philosophy. In this framework, he especially valued early Marxist ideas about alienation and has thoroughly highlighted the "constructive" elements of Marxism. However, the question of whether Confucianism can be regarded as a materialist philosophy will also remain open for now.

70. Note that the work was published one year before the massacre at Tiananmen Square. In this book I use a reprinted version published in Taiwan two years later.

Chapter 5

1. These "static forms" that needed to be "creatively transformed" include even such patterns of thought that come closest to a kind of (at least cognitive) dynamics, namely the pattern of dialectics, based upon the thesis-antithesis-synthesis model. This is because these models are still based upon dualisms with static demarcation lines clearly separating body and mind, idea and matter, subject and object, nature and culture, and so on.

2. This does not mean that Li does not highly respect the precious contribution of Western liberal discourses to the progress of human societies and social systems, and to the development of humanism in general. He writes: "But on the other hand, these theories, programs and slogans decidedly oppose pre-modern despotic rules as well as post-modernism, which wants to protect the absolute power under the banner of nations, states, peoples and democracies. This is very valuable and significant" (ibid.). (但這些理論、綱領和口號在堅決反對前現代的專制統治和後現代以民族、國家、人民民主等作招牌維護絕對權力的鬥爭中, 具有極大的價值和意義。).

3. Here, I am specifically referring to frameworks of reference that define theories and other forms of abstractly ordered cognitive constructions within sciences and humanities. A referential framework in this sense can be defined as a relational structure of concepts, categories, terms, and ideas, as well as values, which are applied in perceiving, comprehending, and interpreting reality, but also the paradigms and perspectives that influence and define the comprehension and evaluation of semantic elements within the structure, as well as the structure as a whole. This defining role of a referential framework does not only pertain to the meaning of notions, but also to their mutual relations. Hence, it is a comprehensive tool used to filter perceptions and to create meaning. In this intercultural philosophic debate, it is important to consider that different referential frames can lead to different descriptions and interpretations of the same objective reality.

4. The following description or contrastive analysis of these two referential frameworks is of course based upon rather bold generalizations and, as such, is rather essentialist. Neither of the philosophical systems belonging to any of the two frameworks fulfils all the requirements for a "pure" A or B framework or possess all the attributes described in them. The present schematic differentiation and none of the two frameworks should or can be viewed as a precise and accurate summary of the central characteristics of Confucian or modern European thought. They are not based on definite factual parameters, but rather imply theoretic tendencies and chief guidelines of thought that are not necessary parts of all theoretical systems in the respective discourse. Thus, this schematic overview will serve us only as an additional tool for a better understanding of the complex intercultural syntheses and multifaceted fusions of tradition and modernity contained in Li Zehou's thought.

5. These two frameworks are based upon differences in the "causal" and "correlative" cosmology as elaborated by David Hall and Roger Ames (1995). In this context, they were building on A. C. Graham's (1989) idea of different "contested spaces." Similar ideas were discussed by earlier pioneers of Sinology such as Marcel Granet (1934) and Joseph Needham (1974). Although they are an important part of the standard literature in Sinology and Chinese philosophy, I think the contrastive and comprehensive illustration or summary of these dissimilarities can be quite helpful in understanding Li's philosophical system, in which certain aspects of both frameworks are sometimes combined or synthesized. The information included in these frameworks is a necessary base for the understanding of the following section.

6. For a more detailed elaboration of this method see Rošker 2013.

7. This is probably because binary contrasts and patterns are an elementary condition and characteristic of human cognition and that a dialogue or confrontation between two different ideas is a precondition for the evolution of any thought or understanding.

8. Binary categories belong to the basic features of traditional Chinese philosophy. Such categories can be seen as dualities that seek to attain a state of actuality through relativity, which is expressed through the relation between two oppositional notions. The mutual interactions between the two poles that form such a category are governed by the principle of correlative complementarity, which belongs to the fundamental paradigms of Chinese reasoning and which led to the formation of patterns of specific Chinese analogous reasoning. Some of the generally best known Chinese binary categories are: *yinyang* 陰陽 (sunny and shady), *tiyong* 體用 (essence and function), *mingshi* 名實 (names and actualities), *liqi* 理氣 (structure and vitality), *benmo* 本末 (roots and crown), and so on.

9. In the process of the intensive Sinification of Marxism, this feature of the dialectical model, belonging to framework B (which was typical for traditional China), was highly problematized by Maoist theoreticians. Hence,

they used to call this form of dialectics "simple" (see Lü Xiaolong 1993, 58) or "primitive" (see Pan Tianhua 1995, 14) dialectics (*pusu bianzheng fa* 樸素辯證法, *yuanshi bianzheng fa* 原始辯證法) and criticized it for its conservative nature—for its lacking of the component of progress.

10. Many modern Chinese philosophers have focused upon this difference, aiming to solve the alleged contradiction of simultaneous immanence and transcendence in Chinese philosophy. Here, we could mention the controversial Modern Confucian paradigm of "immanent transcendence," which is also linked to Mou Zongsan's concept of "double ontology," or the "one-world" view proposed by Li Zehou.

11. In several philosophical systems belonging to framework A—for instance, in Kant's philosophy—it could be claimed that ethics is an important part of the human self. But even in such contexts, it is only a part of the noumenal nature of the Self, whereas in framework B it is part and parcel of the self that pertains to a concrete human being in any situation of a given human life.

12. Particularly in chapters 2, 40, and 42. Li Zehou often points out that the system of yin-yang and the five phases (*Yinyang wuxing* 陰陽五行) is also a form of specific Chinese dialectics.

13. As previously mentioned, *ti* and *yong* were applied as a binary category in the Chinese tradition. In this tradition, categories (*fanchou* 範疇)—in contrast to concepts (*gainian* 概念)—do not possess fixed content, but usually serve as empty molds for different, interchangeable content within theories (see Zhang Dainian 2003, 118). It seems that Li did not see this specific feature, which determines the difference between concepts and categories. In one of his argumentations, he noted that "the contents of *ti* and *yong* are unclear and blurred" (*hanyi mohu* 含義模糊; Li Zehou 2016c, 370). In fact, these contents cannot be blurred, since as categories, *ti* and *yong* have no fixed contents at all. But in other sources he mostly denotes *ti* and *yong* as categories (see for instance, Li Zehou 1999c, 1160). In spite of this minor methodological deviation, his theory regarding *ti* and *yong* is very significant and instructive for the clarification of problems, linked to the actualization of traditional Chinese dialectics, as well as to many hitherto unsolved questions in the discourse of Sinicizing Marxism.

14. Here we are already confronted with the first of many linguistic difficulties that occur in the processes of discursive translations—the transmitting of concepts and categories from one referential framework (or one socio-cultural context) to another. In the German original of his *Preface to a Contribution to the Critique of Political Economy* (1859) Marx writes about "*gesellschaftliches Sein*" (Marx 1971, 9), which is translated as "social being" (Marx 1977, n.p.) or as "social existence" (Marx 2009, 2.). Since Marx does not speak about "*gesellschaftliche Existenz*," it is clear that the first translation is correct and the second is not, for in the Euro-American philosophic tradition the notions of "being" and "existence" are not always the same. However, in Chinese, there is

still no consensus regarding the question of how to translate the two terms, since in the relational-holistic worldview the distinction between the two concepts is rather difficult to establish (see Rošker 1995). For example, the words "being" and "existence" are commonly both translated with the term "*cunzai* 存在." Li Zehou seems to express the notions of substance with the term "*benti* 本體," which refers to the ultimate existence. The ultimate existence in the Chinese one-world view is, however, always the existence of something and does not dwell in the sphere of pure concepts or ideas. But "*benti*," on the other hand, is also not purely material, for it embraces and pertains to material and ideal entities.

15. Emphasis by the author.

16. Besides "spiritual substance" the term is sometimes also translated as the "substance of mind."

17. The term could also be translated as "consciousness of the substance" or "substantial consciousness."

18. The shorter version only speaks about Western substance and Chinese function, while the longer would (analogous to Zhang Zhidong's original version) refer to the Western and Chinese teachings.

19. As already mentioned, he does not believe, for example, that the establishment of a market economy automatically leads to the establishment of a democratic system. However, he still believes that the opposite is true, namely that a market economy is a necessary precondition for the establishment of a democratic system.

20. We must bear in mind that speaking of Marx's "ontology" and in this context about his "ontological materialism" is controversial, because in a certain sense Marx also understood ontology in a "historical" way—as an anthropological or empirical discourse (which is linked to human material practice). We must be careful when applying later interpretations, which attempted to draw various "ontologies" directly from Marx's theories. The shallowest (and unfortunately, also the most widely known) version of these attempts is the Stalinist *diamat*. For a more detailed explanation of these problems, see Karl Korsch's book, *Marxism and Philosophy*. According to Korsch, the crucial notion of Marx's theory was the so-called principle of historical specification, meaning that we should understand all things as being social in terms of a concrete historical period (see Korsch 2008). In this context, Korsch also stresses that Marx treats all categories of his socio-historical and economic theories in that specific form and in that specific context in which they occur in modern bourgeois society. He never deals with them as with formal, eternal, and universal categories. However, in spite of these issues (which ultimately lead to problems of terminology, or, better, of philology), Li's materialism differed substantial from Marx—not only regarding the above-mentioned dialectical relations, but also regarding Li's highlighting the role and function of human subjectality and incorporating it into his dialectical system.

21. Li translates the term *ti* in the sense of substance with the word *shiti* 實體 (Li Zehou 1999c: 1161). The term *benti*, a notion, which also commonly serves as a translation of the Western term substance, was commonly applied in Li's philosophy to substantial consciousness, emotion-based substance, the psychological substance, and so on. *Shiti* refers to the actual, and *benti* to the original substance. In this context, it is clear that both kinds of substances belong to the one-world scheme (or immanent metaphysics), which means that none of them is static or isolated and they are all rooted in empirical life, they are profoundly different from one another. The former (which is also the *ti* in the correlative relation with *yong*) is namely a category whose content is modifiable, whereas the compounds composed by the term *benti* are categories.

22. One of Li's main critiques of the Marxist model is also its direct connection between ontology and empirical life, for Marx (like Hegel) projected his theoretical models upon history and society, which was, in Li's view, a very problematic flaw (Li Zehou 2016a, 13).

23. The original form of the complementary dialectical model (as described in the Yi Jing or Laozi), is limited to dynamic interchanges of both antipodes. The emergence of the primary or decisive element can be traced back to the Song Dynasty Neo-Confucianism, or, more precisely, to Zhu Xi's interpretation of the relation between the structural (*Li* 理) and the creative (*Qi* 氣) potential.

24. Li Zehou himself has divided his philosophical development into three phases (see Li Zehou and Liu Xuyuan 2011b, 75–76):

1. 1950–1962, the period in which he learned to carry our research work independently;

2. 1962–1990, the phase of transformative creations;

3. From 1990, the mature period.

Bibliography

Li Zehou's Works in Chinese

Li Zehou 李澤厚. 1956. "Lun meigan, mei he yishu (Yanjiu tigang)—Jianlun Zhu Guangqiande weixinzhuyi meixue sixiang 論美感、美和藝術 (研究提綱)——兼論朱光潛的唯心主義美學思想 (On the Aesthetic Feeling, Beauty, and Art (A Research Proposal)—Also on Zhu Guangqian's Idealist Aesthetic Thought)." *Zhexue yanjiu* 5: 43–73.

———. 1957. "Meide keguanxing he shehuixing 美的客觀性和社會性 (The Objectivity and the Social Nature of Beauty)." *Renmin ribao* January 9.

———. 1957a. "Guanyu dangqian meixue wentide zhenglun 關於當前美學問題的爭論 (About the Current Controversies on Aesthetics)." *Xueshu yuekan* (10): 25–42.

———. 1958. *Kang Youwei Tan Sitong sixiang yanjiu* 康有为谭嗣同思想研究 (Studies on the Thoughts of Kang Youwei and Tan Sitong). Shanghai: Shanghai renmin chuban she.

———. 1959. "Shilun xingxiang siwei 試論形象思維 (On Image-Thinking)." *Wenxue pinglun* (2): 101–17.

———. 1978. "Xingxiang siwei xutan 形象思維續談 (Continuing the Debate on Image-Thinking)." *Xueshu yanjiu* (1): 94–102.

———. 1978a. "Guanyu Kangdede 'wu ziti' xueshuo 關於康德的「物自體」學說 (On Kant's Theory of the 'Thing in Itself')." *Zhexue yanjiu* (6): 43–52.

———. 1980. *Meixue lunji* 美學論集 (A Collection of Essays on Aesthetics). Shanghai: Shanghai wenyi chuban she.

———. 1980a. "Kongzi zai pingjia 孔子再評價 (A Re-evaluation of Confucius)." *Zhongguo shehui kexue* 2: 77–96.

———. 1980b. "Xingxiang siwei zai xutan 形象思維再續談 (A New Continuation of the Debate on Image-Thinking)." *Wenxue pinglun* (3): 29–40.

———. 1984. *Zhexue meixue wenxuan* 哲學美學文選 (Philosophic and Aesthetic Writings). Changsha: Hunan renmin chuban she.

———. 1984a. "Pipan zhexuede pipan (Kangde shuping): Xiuding zaiban houji 批判哲學的批判 (康德述評): 修訂再版後記 (Critique of the Critical Philosophy [A New Key to Approach to Kant]: Afterword to the Second, Revised Edition)." *Du shu* 1984 (4): 114–18.

———. 1985. *Zhongguo gudai sixiang shilun* 中國古代思想史論 (On Traditional Chinese Intellectual History). Beijing: Renmin chuban she.

———. 1985a. "Guanyu zhutixingde buchong shuoming 關於主體性的補充說明 (A Supplementary Explanation of Subjectality)." *Zhongguo shehui kexue yuan yuanjiushengyuan xuebao* 1: 14–21.

———. 1985b. "Zhongguo sixiang shi zatan 中國思想史雜談 (Various Conversations on the History of Chinese Thought)." *Fudan xuebao (Shehui kexue ben)* 5: 31–39.

———. 1985c. "Xin chun hua zhishi—zhi qingnian pengyoumen 新春話知識——致青年朋友們 (Knowledge in the New Spring: For My Young Friends)." *Wenshi zhishi* (1): 3–7.

———. 1985d. *Shilun renlei qiyuan* 試論人類起源/提綱/ (On the Origin of Mankind [An Outline]). Changsha: Hunan renmin chuban she.

———. 1987. *Zhongguo xiandai sixiang shilun* 中國現代思想史論 (On Contemporary Chinese Intellectual History). Beijing: Dongfang chuban she.

———. 1987a. "Manshuo Xiti Zhongyong 漫说西體中用 (A Simple Lecture on Western Substance and Chinese Function)." *Kongzi Yanjiu* 4: 15–28.

———. 1987b. "Guanyu zhutixingde di san tigang 关于主体性的第三个提纲 (The Third Outline on Subjectivity)." *Zouxiang weilai* 1987 (3): 10–21.

———. 1989. *Dangdai sichao yu Zhongguo zhihui* 當代思潮與中國智慧 (Contemporary Currents of Thought and Chinese Wisdom). Taibei: Fengyun shidai chuban she.

———. 1990. *Meixue he weilai meixue* 美學和未來美學 (Aesthetics and Future Aesthetics). Beijing: Zhongguo shehui kexue chuban she.

———. 1990a. *Pipan zhexuede pipan (Kangde shuping)* 批判哲學的批判 (康德述評) (Critique of the Critical Philosophy [A New Approach to Kant]). Taibei: Fengyun sichao.

———. 1994. "Kangde zhexue yu jianli zhutixing lungang 康德哲学与建立主体性论纲 (An Outline of Kant's Philosophy and the Construction of Subjectality)." In *Li Zehou shi nian ji*, vol. 2, 459–75. Hefei: Anhui wenyi chuban she.

———. 1994a. "Di si tigang 第四提綱 (The Fourth Outline)." *Xueshu yuekan* (10): 18–40.

———. 1996. *Zou wo zijide lu* 走我自己的路 (Following My Own Way). Taibei: Sanmin shudiuan.

———. 1996a. *Wode zhexue tigang* 我的哲學提綱 (The Outline of My Philosophy). Taibei: Sanmin shuju.

———. 1996b. *Pipan zhexuede pipan (Kangde shuping)* 批判哲學的批判 (康德述評) (Critique of the Critical Philosophy [A New Approach to Kant]). Taibei: San min.

———. 1998. *Shiji xin meng* 世紀新夢 (The New Dream of the Century). Hefei: Anhui wenyi chuban she.

———. 1998a. *Li Zehou xueshu wenhua suibi* 李澤厚學術文化隨筆 (Essays on Li Zehou's Academic Culture). Beijing: Zhongguo qingnian chuban she.

———. 1999. *Zhongguo sixiang shilun* 中國思想史論 (On Chinese Intellectual History). Hefei: Anhui wenyi chuban she.

———. 1999a. *Li Zehou zhexue wencun* 李澤厚哲學文存 (A Deposit of Li Zehou's Philosophy). Hefei: Anhui wenyi chuban she.

———. 1999b. *Jimao wushuo* 己卯五說 (Five Essays from 1999). Beijing: Zhongguo dianying chuban she.

———. 1999c. "Man shuo 'Xiti Zhongyong' 漫說「西體中用」(A Simple Lecture on 'Western Substance and Chinese Function')." In *Zhongguo sixiang shilun*, part 3, 1139–69. Hefei: Anhui wenyi chuban she.

———. 2000. *Tanxun yusui* 探尋語碎 (Exploring Fragments). Shanghai: Shanghai wenyi chuban she.

———. 2001 (1988). *Meixue si jiang* 美學四講 (Four Essays on Aesthetics). Nanning: Guangxi shifan daxue chuban she.

———. 2001a. *Huaxia meixue* 華夏美學 (The Chinese Aesthetic Tradition). Nanning: Guangxi shifan daxue chuban she.

———. 2002. *Meixue san shu* 美學三書 (Three Books on Aesthetics). Hefei: Anhui wenyi chuban she.

———. 2002a. *Meixue jiu zuo ji* 美學舊作集 (Earlier Writings on Aesthetics). Tianjin: Tinajin shehui kexue yuan chuban she.

———. 2002b. *Zou wo zijide lu* 走我自己的路 (Going My Own Way). Beijing: Shenghuo dushu xinzhi Sanlian shudian.

———. 2002c. *Lishi benti lun* 歷史本體論 (Historical Ontology). Beijing: Sanlian shudian.

———. 2003. *Mei de licheng* 美的歷程 (The Path of Beauty). In *Meixue sanshu* 美學三書 (Three Books on Aesthetics), edited by Yi Jing, 3–193. Tianjin: Tianjin shehui kexue yuan chuban she.

———. 2003a. "Wo zoude lu 我走的路 (My Own Way)." *Yuwen shijie* (Z1): 19–20.

———. 2006. "2004 Chuantong wenhua fuxing sichao 2004 传统文化复兴思潮 (The Revival of Traditional Culture in 2004)." *Asixiang*. Accessed December 11, 2006. http://www.aisixiang.com/data/12137.html.

———. 2006a. *Makesizhuyi zai Zhongguo* 馬克思主義在中國 (Marxism in China). Hong Kong: Minbao chuban she.

———. 2007. *Pipan zhexue de pipan: Kangde shuping* 批判哲學的批判: 康德述評 (Critique of Critical Philosophy: A New Approach to Kant). Beijing: Shenghuo dushu xinzhi Sanlian shudian.

———. 2008. *Shiyong lixing yu legan wenhua* 實用理性與樂感文化 (Pragmatic Reason and the Culture of Pleasure). Beijing: Shenghuo dushu xinzhi Sanlian shudian.

———. 2008a. *Lishi bentilun: Jimao wu shuo* 歷史本體論: 己卯五說 (Historical Ontology: Five Essays from 1999). Beijing: Shenghuo dushu xinzhi Sanlian shudian.

———. 2008b. *Lunyu jindu* 論語今讀 (Reading the Analects Today). Beijing: Shenghuo dushu xinzhi Sanlian shudian.

———. 2008c. *Za zhu ji* 雜著集 (A Collection of Various Essays). Beijing: Shenghuo dushu xinzhi Sanlian shudian.

———. 2008d. "Wo he bashi niandai 'meixue re' 我和八十年代「美學熱」 (The 'Aesthetic Fever' from the 1980s and Me)." *Jingji guancha wang*, August 6. Accessed May 25, 2016. http://www.eeo.com.cn/2008/0609/102665.shtml.

———. 2008e. *Renleixue lishi bentilun* 人類學歷史本體論 (Anthropological Historical Ontology). Tianjin: Tianjin shehui kexue yuan chuban she.

———. 2008f. *Li Zehou ji* 李澤厚集 (A Collection of Li Zehou's Works), 10 vols. Beijing: Sanlian shuduan.

———. 2008g. "*Guanyu xingxiang siwei* 關於形象思維 (On Image-Thinking)." *Zhonghua huoye webxuan* (9): 23–25.

———. 2009. *Zhongguo gudai sixiang shilun—Zhongguo jindai sixiang shilun—Zhongguo xiandai sixiang shilun (quan san ce)* 中國古代思想史論·中國近代思想史論·中國現代思想史論(全三冊 (On Ancient Chinese Intellectual History, On pre-Modern Chinese Intellectual History, On Modern Chinese Intellectual History: 3 vols.). Beijing: Sanlian shudian.

———. 2009a (1981). *Mei de lichen* 美的歷程 (The Path of Beauty). Beijing: Shenghuo dushu xinzhi Sanlian shudian.

———. 2009b. *Li Zehou meixue gailun* 李澤厚美學概論 (An Introduction to Li Zehou's Aesthetics). Beijing: Sanlian shudian.

———. 2009c. "Guanyu 'Youguan lunlixuede dawen' de buchong shuoming 關於「有關倫理學的答問」的補充說明 (2008) (Additional Explanation to 'Some Questions and Answers Regarding Ethics' [2008])." *Zhexue dongtai* (11): 26–33.

———. 2010. *Lunlixue gangyao* 倫理學綱要 (An Outline of Ethics). Beijing: Renmin ribao chuban she.

———. 2010a (1997). "Zhong Ri wenhua xinli bijiao shi shuo lüe gao 中日文化心理比較試說略稿 (A Small Experimental Draft on the Comparison of Chinese and Japanese Cultural Psychology)." *Huawen wenxue* 100(5): 15–36.

———. 2011. *Zhexue gangyao* 哲學綱要 (An Outline of Philosophy). Beijing: Beijing daxue chuban she.

———. 2012. *Shuo wenhua xinli* 說文化心理 (On Cultural Psychology). Shanghai: Shanghai wenyi chuban she.

———. 2012a. *Shuo Xiti Zhongyong* 說西體中用 (On Western Substance and Chinese Application). Shanghai: Shanghai wenyi chuban she.

———. 2012b. "Renshilun dawen 認識論答問 (Q&A about Epistemology)." *Zhongguo wenhua* (1): 1–11.

———. 2012c. "'Qing benti' de wai tui yu neitui 「情本體」的外推與內退 (The Extension and Intention of 'Emotion-Based Substance')." *Xueshu yuekan* 44(1): 14–21.

———. 2013. "Goujian zhengyi jichushangde hexie—cong Sangde'erde 'Gongzheng' shuoqi 構建正義基礎上的和諧——從桑德爾的「公正」說起 (Constructing Righteousness on the Basis of Harmony—On Sandel's Concept of Justice)." *Shanghai Shehui kexue bao*, December 31. Accessed August 7, 2016. http://blog.sina.com.cn/s/blog_63959b6d0101d444.html.

———. 2014. "Zai tan shiyong lixing 再談實用理性 (Another Talk about Practical Rationality)." *Wucu qinghuade boke*, April 25. Accessed May 22, 2016. http://blog.sina.com.cn/s/blog_a404f6dd0101ra3j.html.

———. 2014a. "Xingshi ceng yu yuanshi jidian 形式層與原始積澱 (Formal Layers and Elementary Sedimentation)." *Meixue* 1: 5–8.

———. 2014b. *Li Zehou duihua ji–bashi niandai* 李澤厚對話集·八十年代 (A Collection of Dialogues with Li Zehou from the 1980s). Beijing: Zhonghua shuju.

———. 2014c. *Li Zehou duihua ji—jiushi niandai* 李澤厚對話集·九十年代 (A Collection of Dialogues with Li Zehou from the 1990s). Beijing: Zhonghua shuju.

———. 2014d. *Li Zehou duihua ji—Ershi yi shiji (yi)* 李澤厚對話集·廿一世紀(一) (A Collection of Dialogues with Li Zehou: The Twenty-first Century—Part 1). Beijing: Zhonghua shuju.

———. 2014e. *Li Zehou duihua ji—Ershi yi shiji (er)* 李澤厚對話集·廿一世紀(二) (A Collection of Dialogues with Li Zehou: Twenty-first Century—Part 2). Beijing: Zhonghua shuju.

———. 2014f. *Li Zehou duihua ji—yu Liu Zaifu duitan* 李澤厚對話集·與劉再復對談 (A Collection of Dialogues with Li Zehou: Conversations with Liu Zaifu). Beijing: Zhonghua shuju.

———. 2014g. *Li Zehou duihua ji—Fushenglun xue* 李澤厚對話集·浮生論學 (A Collection of Dialogues with Li Zehou: On the Science of the Floating Life). Beijing: Zhonghua shuju.

———. 2014h. *Li Zehou duihua ji—Zhongguo zhexue dengchang* 李澤厚對話集·中國哲學登場 (A Collection of Dialogues with Li Zehou: Chinese Philosophy Is Appearing on the Stage). Beijing: Zhonghua shuju.

———. 2014i. *Huiying Sangde'er ji qita* 回應桑德爾及其他 (A Response to Sandel and Other Writings). Beijing: Sanlian shudian.

———. 2014j. *Li Zehou huayu* 李澤厚話語 (Li Zehou's Discourse). Shanghai: Huadong shifan daxue chuban she.

———. 2014k. "Gao Ertaide zhiyi 高爾泰的質疑 (Gao Ertai's Question)." *Xinlan boke*. Accessed August 29, 2016. http://blog.sina.com.cn/s/blog_676299b-b0102wubg.html.

———. 2015. *You wu dao li, shi li gui ren* 由巫到禮、釋禮歸仁 (From Shamanism to Rituality, Explaining Rituality as a Return to the Humanness). Beijing: Sanlian shudian.

———. 2015a. "Da 'Gauguin san wen' 答「高更 (Paul Gauguin) 三問」(The Answer to 'Three Questions Posed by Paul Gauguin')." *Zhonghua dushu bao*, April 11.

———. 2015b. *Shenme shi daode* 什麼是道德 (What is Morality). Shanghai: Huadong Shifan daxue chuban she.

———. 2016. "Li Zehou duitan lu 李澤厚對談錄 (Recordings of Li Zehou's Conversations)." *Dai yue ting yu zhu jilu*. http://www.doc88.com/p-7030124841.html.

———. 2016a. "Guanyu Makeside lunli ji qita (xia) 關於馬克思的倫理及其他 (下) (On Marxist Ethics and Other Issues, Part 2)." *Tongsu wenda—zai tan makesizhuyu zai Zhongguo*, May 2. Accessed May 22, 2016. http://blog.sina.com.cn/s/blog_63959b6d010182uw.html.

———. 2016b. *Renleixue lishi bentilun* 人類學歷史本體論 (Anthropo-historical Ontology). Qingdao: Qingdao chuban she.

———. 2016c. *Zhongguo xiandai sixiang shilun* 中國現代思想史論 (On Contemporary Chinese Intellectual History). Beijing: Sanlien shudian.

Li Zehou's Coauthored Works in Chinese

Li Zehou 李澤厚, and Liu Gangji 劉鋼紀. 1999. *Zhongguo meixue shi* 中國美學史 (A History of Chinese Aesthetics). Hefei: Anhui wenyi chuban she.

———, and Liu Zaifu 劉再復. 1999. *Gaobie geming—Ershi shiji Zhongguo duitan lu* 告別革命——二十世紀中國對談錄 (Farewell to Revolution: A Critical Dialogue on Twentieth Century China). Taibei: Maitan chuban.

———, and Chen Ming 陳明. 2002. *Fusheng lun xue* 浮生論學 (On the Science of Floating Life). Beijing: Huaxia chuben she.

———, et al. 2004. *Ziran shuo hua* 自然說話 (*Nature Speaking*). Changsha: Hunan meishu chuban she.

———, and Liu Xuyuan 劉緒源. 2011. *Gai Zhongguo zhexue dengchang le?* 該中國哲學登場了? (Should Chinese Philosophy Appear on the Stage?). Shanghai: Shanghai yiwen chuban she.

———. 2011a. "'Qing benti' shi yizhong shijiexing shijiao「情本體」是一種世界性視角 ('Emotion-based Substance' Is a Global Perspective)." *Juece yu xinxi* 3: 9–13.

———. 2011b. "Li Zehou tan xueshu sixiang san jieduan 李澤厚談學术思想三階段 (Li Zehou Discusses the Three Phases of His Academic Thought)." *Shanghai wenxue* (1): 72–77.

———. 2012. *Zhongguo zhexue ruhe dengchang?* 中國哲學如何登場? (How can Chinese Philosophy Appear on the Stage?). Shanghai: Shanghai yiwen chuban she.

———, and Liu Yuedi 劉悅笛. 2014. "Cong 'qing benti' fansi zhengzhi zhexue 從「情本體」反思政治哲學 (Reflecting on Political Philosophy from 'Emotion as Substance')." *Kaifang shidai* 4: 194–215.

———. 2014a. "'Qing benti' shi shijiede「情本體」是世界的 ('Emotion as Substance' Belongs to the World)." *Tansuo yu zhengming* (4): 4–9.

———, and Yang Guorong 楊國榮. 2014. "Lunli wenti ji qita 倫理問題及其他 (About Ethics and Other Issues)." *Shehui kexue* (9): 117–28.

Li Zehou's Works in English and German

Li, Zehou. 1986. "The Philosophy of Kant and a Theory of Subjectivity." *The Phenomenology of Man and of the Human Condition, II: The Meeting Point between Occidental and Oriental Philosophies*, edited by Anna-Teresa Tymieniecka, 135–49. Dordrecht, Boston, Lancaster, Tokyo: D. Reidel Publishing Company.

———. 1992. *Der Weg des Schönen: Wesen und Geschichte der chinesischen Kultur und Aesthetik*. Translated by Karl-Heinz Pohl and Gudrun Wacker. Freiburg: Herder.

———. 1994. *The Path of Beauty: A Study of Chinese Aesthetics*. Translated by Gong Lizeng. Hong Kong: Oxford University Press.

———. 1999 (1987). "The Western Is the Substance and the Chinese Is for Application: (Excerpts)." *Contemporary Chinese Thought* 31(2): 32–39. doi: 10.2753/CSP1097-1467310232.

———. 1999a. "Modernization and the Confucian World." Address given at the Colorado College's 125th Anniversary Symposium, "Cultures in the Twenty-First Century: Conflicts and Convergences," in a discussion forum entitled "The Confucian World," Colorado Springs, February 5. Accessed January 20, 2004. http://www.topicdiscussion.org/article/9753920641/.

———. 1999b (1985). "A Few Questions Concerning the History of Chinese Aesthetics (Excerpts)." Translated by Peter Wong Yih Jiun. *Contemporary Chinese Thought* 31(2): 66–78. doi: 10.2753/CSP1097-1467310266.

———. 1999c (1987). "A Supplementary Explanation of Subjectivity." Translated by Peter Wong Yih Jiun. *Contemporary Chinese Thought* 31(2): 26–31. doi: 10.2753/CSP1097-1467310226.

———. 1999d (1985). "An Outline of the Origin of Humankind." Translated by Peter Wong Yih Jiun. *Contemporary Chinese Thought* 31(2): 20–26. doi: 10.2753/CSP1097-1467310220.

———. 1999e. "Subjectivity and 'Subjectality': A Response." *Philosophy East and West* 49(2): 174–83. doi:10.2307/1400201.

———. 1999f. "Human Nature and Human Future: A Combination of Marx and Confucius." In *Chinese Thought in a Global Context: A Dialogue Between Chinese and Western Philosophical Approaches*, edited by Karl-Heinz Pohl, 129–44. Leiden: Brill.
———. 2010. *The Chinese Aesthetic Tradition*. Translated by Maija Bell Samei. Honolulu: University of Hawai'i Press.
———. 2016. "A Response to Michael Sandel and Other Matters." Translated by Paul D'Ambrosio and Robert A. Carleo. *Philosophy East and West* 66(4): 1068–1147.
———, and Jane Cauvel. 2006. *Four Essays on Aesthetics: Toward a Global View*. Lanham: Lexington Books.

Secondary Materials

1988. "Taishi gong zixu 太史公自序注譯 (Preface to Historical Notes)." In *Shiji*. Xining: Qinghai renmin chuban she.
2009. *Lunyu* 论语 (*The Confucian Analects*). In *Si shu da quan jiaozhu /shang/* (An Annotated and Complete Collection of the Four Books: Part One), 322–756. Wuhan: Wuhan daxue chuban she.
2013. *Shi ji* 史記 (Historical Notes). Beijing: Zhonghua shuju.
2016. *Li ji* 禮記 (The Book of Rituals). Beijing: Zhonghua shuju.
Ames, Roger T. 1991. "The Mencian Conception of *Ren xing* 人性: Does it Mean 'Human Nature'?" In *Chinese Texts and Philosophical Contexts: Essays Dedicated to Angus C. Graham*, edited by Henry Rosemont, Jr., 143–75. La Salle, IL: Open Court.
———. 2011. *Confucian Role Ethics: A Vocabulary*. Honolulu: University of Hawaii Press.
———. Forthcoming 2017. "Reconstructing A.C. Graham's Reading of *Mencius* on *xing* 性: A Coda to 'The Background of the Mencian Theory of Human Nature' (1967)." In *Having a Word with Angus Graham: At 25 Years into His Immortality*, edited by Roger T. Ames and Carine Defoort. New York: State University of New York Press.
Arendt, Hannah. 1998 (1958). *The Human Condition*. Chicago and London: University of Chicago Press.
Balter, Michael. 2015. "Human Language May Have Evolved to Help our Ancestors Make Tools." *Science, AAAS*, January 13. doi: 10.1126/science.aaa6332.
Berger, Peter. 1988. "An East Asian Developmental Model?" In *In Search of an East Asian Developmental Model*, edited by Peter Berger and Hsin-huang Michael Hsiao, 3–11. New Brunswick, NJ: Transaction Books.
Berger, Peter L. and Luckmann, Thomas. 1991 (1966). *The Social Construction of Reality. A Treatise in the Sociology of Knowledge*. London: Penguin

Blencowe, Anthony. 1993. "Li Zehou, Confucius and Continuity with the Past in Contemporary China." Thesis (B.A. [Hon.]), University of Adelaide.

Bourdieu, Pierre. 1989. "Social Space and Symbolic Power." *Sociological Theory* 7(1): 14–25.

Bruya, Brian. 2003. "Li Zehou's Aesthetic as a Marxist Philosophy of Freedom." *Dialogue and Universalism* 13(11/12): 133–40.

Bunnin, Nicholas. 2002. "Introduction." In *Contemporary Chinese Philosophy*, edited by Chung-ying Cheng and Nicholas Bunnin, 1–15. Oxford: Blackwell.

Burnham, Douglas. 2016. "Immanuel Kant: Aesthetics." In *The Internet Encyclopedia of Philosophy*. http://www.iep.utm.edu/kantaest/.

Butler, Judith. 1988. "Performative Acts and Gender Constitution: An Essay in Phenomenology and Feminist Theory." *Theatre Journal*, 40(4):519-531.

Cai, Zhen. 2011. Review of *Lunlixue gangyao* 倫理學綱要 (Ethics), by Zehou Li 李澤厚. *Dao* 10(2): 255–57. doi: 10.1007/s11712-011-9209-2.

Cai Yuanpei 蔡元培. 1984. "Yi meiyu dai zongjiao 以美育代宗教 (Replacing Religion with Aesthetic Education)." In *Cai Yuanpei quanji* (The Complete Collection of Cai Yuanpei), vol. 3 (1917–1920), edited by Gao Pingshu, 30–35. Beijing: Zhonghua shuju.

Carleo, Robert A., and Paul D'Ambrosio. 2015. "Confucianism in Contemporary Contexts: Li Zehou and Twenty-First Century Philosophy." Paper presented at the conference "Li Zehou and Confucian Philosophy," The East-West Center, University of Hawai'i at Manoa, Honolulu, October 8–11.

Cauvel, Jane. 1999. "The Transformative Power of Art: Li Zehou's Aesthetic Theory." *Philosophy East and West* 49(2): 150–73.

Chan, Sylvia. 2003. "Li Zehou and New Confucianism." In *New Confucianism: A Critical Examination*, edited by John Makeham, 105–28. New York: Palgrave Macmillan.

Chandler, Marthe. 2016. "Li Zehou, Kant in Darwin: teorija sedimentacije (Li Zehou, Kant, and Darwin: The Theory of Sedimentation)." In *Li Zehou in sodobna kitajska filozofija—zgodovinska ontologija, estetika in nadgradnje marksizma*, edited by Jana S. Rošker and Katja Kolšek, 131–76. Ljubljana: Znanstvena založba FF.

Cheek, Timothy. 1999. "Introduction: A Cross-Cultural Conversation on Li Zehou's Ideas on Subjectivity and Aesthetics in Modern Chinese Thought." *Philosophy East and West* 49(2): 113–19.

———, ed. 1999a. "'Subjectality': Li Zehou and his Critical Analysis of Chinese Thought." *Philosophy East and West* 49(2), April: 113–84.

Chen Lai 陳來. 1996. *Gudai zongjiao yu lunli—ru jia sixiangde genyuan* 古代宗教與倫理——儒家思想的根源 (*Ancient Religions and Ethics: The Foundation of Confucian Thought*). Beijing: Sanlian shudian.

———. 2014. *Renxue bentilun* 仁學本體論 (*The Ontology of Humaneness*). Beijing: SDX Joint Publishing.

Chen Yinke 陳寅恪. 1977. *Chen Yinke xiansheng quanji* 陳寅恪先生全集 (*The Complete Collection of the Works of Sir Chen Yinke*). Taibei: Jiusi chuban she.

Cheng, Chung-ying. 2002. "Recent Trends in Chinese Philosophy in China and the West." In *Contemporary Chinese Philosophy*, edited by Chung-ying Cheng and Nicholas Bunnin, 349–404. Oxford: Blackwell.

Cheng Hao 程顥, and Cheng Yi 程頤. 1981. *Er Cheng ji* 二程集 (Collected Works of the Cheng Brothers), vol. 4. Beijing: Zhonghua shuju.

Chong, Woei Lien. 1999. "Combining Marx with Kant: The Philosophical Anthropology of Li Zehou." *Philosophy East and West* 49(2), April: 120–49. doi: 10.2307/1400199.

———. 1999a. "Kant and Marx in Post-Mao China: The Intellectual Path of Li Zehou." (PhD diss., Leiden University).

———. 2002. "Philosophy in an Age of Crisis: Three Thinkers in Post-Cultural Revolution China: Li Zehou, Liu Xiaobo, and Liu Xiaofeng." In *China's Great Proletarian Cultural Revolution: Master Narratives and Post-Mao Counternarratives*, edited by Woei Lien Chong, 215–54. Boulder/New York/Oxford: Rowman and Littlefield.

———. 2005. "Hubris in Chinese Thought: A Theme in Post-Mao Cultural Criticism." In *The Magnitude of Ming: Command, Allotment, and Fate in Chinese Culture*, edited by Christopher Lupke, 245–71. Honolulu: University of Hawai'i Press.

D'Ambrosio, Paul. 2016. "Approaches to Global Ethics: Michael Sandel's Justice and Li Zehou's Harmony." *Philosophy East and West* 66(3): 720–38.

———, Robert Carleo, and Andrew Lambert. 2016. "On Li Zehou's Philosophy: An Introduction by Three Translators." *Philosophy East and West* 66(4): 1057–67.

Davies, Gloria. 2012. "Discontent in Digital China." In *Red Rising, Red Eclipse*, edited by Geremie R. Barme, Jeremy Goldkorn, and Carolyn Cartier, 119–23. Canberra: The Australian National University, Australian Center on China in the World.

Davis, Walter B. 2014. "Art, Aesthetic and Religion in Modern China." In *Modern Chinese Religion II: 1850–2015*, edited by Jan Kiley and Vincent Goossaert, 197–260. Leiden: Brill NV.

Ding Yun 丁耘. 2008. "Qimeng zhutixing yu sanshi nian sixiang shi—yi Li Zehou wei zhongxin 啟蒙主體性與三十年思想史——以李澤厚為中心 (*The Enlightened Subjectality and Thirty Years of Ideational History: Focused upon Li Zehou*)." *Fudan daxue.* http://jpkc.fudan.edu.cn/s/221/t/426/20/04/info8196.htm.

Ding, Zijiang John. 2002. "Li Zehou: Chinese Aesthetics from a Post-Marxist and Confucian Perspective." In *Contemporary Chinese Philosophy*, edited by Chung-ying Cheng and Nicholas Bunnin, 246–57. Oxford: Blackwell.

Eliade, Mircea. 1991. *Images and Symbols: Studies in Religious Symbolism*. Princeton, NJ: Princeton University Press.

———. 2004. *Shamanism*. Princeton, NJ: Princeton University Press.

Elstein, David. 2015. "Contemporary Confucianism." In *The Routledge Companion to Virtue Ethics*, edited by Lorraine Besser-Jones and Michael Slote, 237–51. New York: Routledge.

Falkenstein, Lorne. 1995. *Kant's Intuitionism: A Commentary on the Transcendental Aesthetic*. Toronto: University of Toronto Press.

Feng Qi, ed. 1985. *Zhexue da cidian: Zhongguo zhexueshi juan* 哲學大辭典: 中國哲學史卷 (The Great Encyclopedia of Philosophy: The History of Chinese Philosophy Volume). Shanghai: Shanghai cishu chuban she.

———, ed. 2001–2002. *Zhexue da cidian (shang xia) (Xiuding ben)* 哲學大辭典 (上下) (修訂本) (The Great Encyclopedia of Philosophy, An Actualized and Expanded Edition in Two Volumes). Shanghai: Shanghai cishu chubanshe.

Flynn, Bernard. 2011. "Maurice Merleau-Ponty." In *The Stanford Encyclopedia of Philosophy*, fall edition, edited by Edward N. Zalta. https://plato.stanford.edu/archives/fall2011/entries/merleau-ponty/.

Gao Ertai 高爾泰. 2014. "Shui ling qi ma ke jing hua? 誰令騎馬客京華? (Why Did I Have to Ride to the Capital Just to Spend Here Such Lonely Days?)." *Aisixiang*. Accessed August 30, 2016. http://www.aisixiang.com/data/78787.html.

Gao, Jianping. 2006. "Sto let kitajske estetike (Hundred Years of Chinese Aesthetics)." *Filozofski vestnik* 27(6): 103–12.

Gao Jianping 高建平. 2014. "Meixue zai dangdaide fuxing 美學在當代的復興 (The Contemporary Aesthetic Renaissance)." *Wenshi zhishi* (11): 15–20.

Geist, Beate. 1996. *Die Modernisierung der Chinesischen Kultur: Kulturdebatte und kultureller Wandel im China der 80er Jahre* (The Modernization of Chinese Culture: Cultural Debate and Cultural Change in China in the 1980s). Hamburg: Institut für Asienkunde.

Giddens, Anthony. 1981. *A Contemporary Critique of Historical Materialism: Vol 1: Power, Property, and the State*. London: Macmillan.

———. 1984. *The Constitution of Society: Outline of the Theory of Structuration*. Cambridge: Polity Press.

Gilligan, Carol. 1982. *In a Different Voice: Psychological Theory and Women's Development*. Cambridge MA: Harvard University Press.

Graham, Angus Charles. 1989. *Disputers of the Dao: Philosophical Argument in Ancient China*. Peru, IL: Open Court Press.

Granet, Marcel. 1934. *La pensée chinoise* (Chinese Thought). Paris: La Renaissance du livre.

Gu, Ban, ed. 2010. *Han Shu* 漢書 (The Book of Han). 2010. In *Bei Song jing you kan ben*, vol. 2. Taibei: Shangwuyinshu guan.

Gu, Ming Dong. 2015. "Modernizing Confucianism: Li Zehou's Vision and Inspiration for an Unfinished Project." Paper presented at the Conference "Li Zehou and Confucian Philosophy," The East-West Center, University of Hawai'i at Manoa, Honolulu, October 8–11.

Gu, Xin. 1996. "Subjectivity, Modernity, and Chinese Hegelian Marxism: A Study of Li Zehou's Philosophical Ideas from a Comparative Perspective." *Philosophy East and West* 46(2), April: 205–45.

Guang, Hu, ed. (Ming Dynasty). 2013. *Zhong yong zhang ju da quan* 中庸章句大全 (The Whole Chapter of The Book of Equilibrium). Xinbei: Guangwen shuju.

Guodian chu mu zhu jian 郭店楚墓竹簡 (Guodian Chu Bamboo Slips). 1998. Jingmen: Wenwu chuban she.

Habermas, Jürgen. 1998. *Die postnationale Konstellation—Politische Essays* (The Postcolonial Constellation: Political Essays). Frankfurt/Main: Suhrkamp.

Hall, David L., and Roger T. Ames. 1987. *Thinking through Confucius*. Albany: State University of New York Press.

———. 1995. *Anticipating China: Thinking through the Narratives of Chinese and Western Culture*. Albany: State University of New York Press.

———. 1998. *Thinking from the Han: Self, Truth, and Transcendence in Chinese and Western Culture*. Albany: State University of New York Press.

———. 2001. "Chinese Philosophy." In *Routledge Encyclopedia of Philosophy*, edited by Edward Craig. London: Routledge. doi: 10.4324/9780415249126-G001-1.

Hegel, Georg Wilhelm Friedrich. 1975. *Hegel's Aesthetics: Lectures on Fine Arts*. Translated by T. M. Knox. Oxford: Oxford University Press.

———. 1981. *Xiao luoji* 小邏輯 (The Shorter Logic). Hsinchu: Yinzhe chuban she.

———. s.d. *Hegels Encyclopaedia of the Philosophical Sciences, Part One: The Shorter Logic*. Available at Marxist Internet Archive Library. Accessed August 31, 2016. https://www.marxists.org/archive/marx/works/1845/theses/index.htm.

Heidegger, Martin. 1967. *Sein und Zeit* (Being and Time). Tübingen: Max Niemeyer Verlag.

Held, Virginia. 1993. *Feminist Morality: Transforming Culture, Society, and Politics*. Chicago: The University of Chicago Press.

———. 2006. *The Ethics of Care: Personal, Political, and Global*. Oxford: Oxford University Press.

Hobsbawm, Eric, and Terence Ranger, eds. 1995 (1983). *The Invention of Tradition*. Cambridge: Cambridge University Press.

Hove, Thomas. 2009. "Communicative Implications of Kant's Aesthetic Theory." *Philosophy and Rhetoric* 42(2): 103–14.

Hu Shi 胡適. 1990. *Hu Shi wencun* 胡適文存 (Hu Shi's Essays), vol. 2. Taibei: Yuandong chuban she.

Hu Weixi 胡偉希. 2002. *Guanniande xuanze: 20 shiji Zhongguo zhexue yu sixiang touxi* 觀念的選擇: 20世紀中國哲學與思想透析 (A Selection of Ideas: A Critical Analysis of Chinese Philosophical Thought in the Twentieth Century). Kunming Shi: Yunnan renmin chuban she.

Hua, Shiping. 2001. "Introduction: Some Paradigmatic Issues in the Study of Chinese Political Culture." In *Chinese Political Culture 1989–2000*, edited by Hua Shiping, 3–17. London: M. E. Sharp, East Gate Books.

Huang, Chenxi. 2017. "Li Zehou's Life and Works." In *Li Zehou and Confucian Philosophy*, edited by Roger T. Ames and Jinhua Jia, 618–24. Honolulu: Hawai'i University Press.

Jaspers, Karl. 2003. *The Way to Wisdom: An Introduction to Philosophy*. New Haven, CT: Yale University Press.

Jensen, Lionel. 2005. "Li Zehou." In *Encyclopedia of Contemporary Chinese Culture*, edited by Edvard L. Davis, 461–65. London: Routledge.

Jia, Jinhua. 2016. "Li Zehou's Reconception of the Confucian Ethics of Emotion." *Philosophy East and West* 66(3): 757–87.

Jie, Wang, et al., eds. 2002. *Xunzi* 荀子 (Master Xun). With commentary by Wang Jie and Tang Jing. Beijing: Huaxia Chuban she.

Jung, Byung-seok. 2017. "Li Zehou's Theory of Emotion as Substance and Confucianism." *Journal of Confucian Philosophy and Culture* (27): 87–109.

Jung, Carl Gustav. 1990. *The Archetypes and the Collective Unconscious*. London: Routledge.

Kant, Immanuel. 1987. *Critique of Judgement*. Translated by Werner S. Pluhar. Indianapolis: Hackett.

———. 1998. *Critique of Pure Reason*. Translated by Paul Guyer and Allen W. Wood. Cambridge: Cambridge University Press.

———. 2000. *Critique of the Power of the Judgement*. Edited by Paul Guyer, translated by Paul Guyer and Eric Mathews. Cambridge: Cambridge University Press.

———. 2006 (2001). *Kritik der Urteilskraft* (Critique of the Power of Judgement). Hamburg: Meiner.

Korsch, Karl. 2008. *Marxism and Philosophy*. Translated by Fred Halliday. New York: Monthly Review Press.

Lacan, Jaques. 2006. *Écrits: The First Complete Edition in English*. Translated by Bruce Fink. New York: W. W. Norton & Company.

Lai, Karin. 2016. "Close Personal Relationships and the Situated Self: The Confucian Analects and Feminist Philosophy." In *The Bloomsbury Research Handbook of Chinese Philosophy and Gender*, edited by Ann A. Pang-White, 111–26. London: Bloomsbury Academic.

Laozi 老子. s.d. *Daode jingxi shuo* 道德经 (The Book of the Way and the Virtue). Edited and commentary by Cao Feng. Kaifen: Henan daxue chuban she.

Lee Ming-Huei 李明輝. 2001. *Dangdai ruxuede ziwo zhuanhua* 當代儒學的自我轉化 (The Self-Transformation of Contemporary Confucianism). Beijing: Zhongguo shehui kexue chuban she.

———. 2002. "Zai lun Rujia sixiang zhongde 'neizai chaoyuexing' wenti 再論儒家思想中的「內在超越性」問題 (A Revisited View of the Problem of 'Immanent Transcedence' in Confucian Thought)." In *Zhongguo sichao yu wailai wenhua* (Chinese Thought Currents and Foreign Cultures), edited by Liu Shu-hsien, 223–40. Taibei: Zhongyang yanjiu yuan, Zhongguo wenzhe yanjiusuo.

———. 2016. *Kangde zhexue zai Dongya* 康德哲學在東亞 (Kantian Philosophy in East Asia). Taibei: Guoli Taiwan Daxue chuban zhongxin.

Legge, James, ed. and trans. 2011. *Shang shu* 尚書 (Book of Documents). In *The Shoo King*, vol. 1 of *The Chinese Classics*. Shanghai: Huadong shifan daxue chuban she.

Lenk, Hans. 1993. "Introduction." In *Epistemological Issues in Classical Chinese Philosophy*, edited by Hans Lenk and Gregor Paul, 1–10. New York: State University of New York Press.

Li, Chenyang. 2014. *The Confucian Philosophy of Harmony*. New York: Routledge.

Li, You-Zheng. 1997. *Epistemological Problems of the Comparative Humanities: A Semiotic/Chinese Perspective*. Frankfurt/Main: Peter Lang, Europäischer Verlag für Wissenschaften.

Lin Daoqun 林道群, and Li Zhihua 李志華. 1991. "Fangwen Li Zehou xiansheng 訪問李澤厚先生 (Visiting Sir Li Zehou)." In *Wu si duoyuande fansi* (Pluralistic Reflections on the May 4th Movement), edited by Wang Yuanhua. Taibei: Fengyun shidai chuban she. Lin, Min. 1992. "The Search for Modernity: Chinese Intellectual Discourse and Society, 1978–88: The Case of Li Zehou." *China Quarterly* 132: 969–98.

———, and Maria Galikowski. 1999. *The Search for Modernity: Chinese Intellectuals and Cultural Discourse in the Post-Mao Era*. London: MacMillan Press.

Lin, Tongqi, Henry Rosemont, and Roger T. Ames. 1995. "Chinese Philosophy: A Philsophical Essay on the 'State-of-the-Art'." *The Journal of Asian Studies* 54(3): 727–58.

Liu, Huiru. 1993. "Die 4. Mai Bewegung aus heutiger Sicht (The May 4th Movement from the Present Point of View)." In *Chinesische Intellektuelle im 20. Jahrhundert: Zwischen Tradition und Moderne* (Chinese Intellectuals in the Twentieth Century: Between Tradition and Modernity), edited by Karl-Heinz Pohl, Gudrun Wacker, and Liu Huiru, 37–55. Hamburg: Institut für Asienkunde.

Liu, Kang. 1992. "Subjectivity, Marxism, and Culture Theory in China." *Social Text* 31/32: 114–40. doi: 10.2307/466221.

———. 2000. *Aesthetics and Marxism: Chinese Aesthetic Marxists and their Western Contemporaries*. Durham: Duke University.

Liu, Shu-hsien. 1972. "The Confucian Approach to the Problem of Transcendence and Immanence." *Philosophy East and West* 22(1): 45–52.

Liu Zaifu 劉再復. 2016. "Tuijian Yang Binde Li zehou xueshu nianpu 推薦楊斌的「李澤厚學術年譜」 (Recommending 'A Chronicle of Li Zehou's Academic Work' by Yang Bin)." *Xinlang boke*. Accessed November 1, 2016. http://blog.sina.com.cn/s/blog_4cd081e90102wohz.html.

Luo Rongqu 羅榮渠, ed. 2008. *Cong "Xihua" dao xiandaihua* 從「西化」到現代化 (From Westernization to Modernization). Hefei: Huangshan shu she.

Lü Xiaolong 呂孝龍. 1993. "Yinyang bian yi shengsheng bu xi—lun 'Yi jing' zhong pusu bianzhengfa sixiangde meixue jiazhi 陰陽變易生生不息——論「易經」中樸素辯證法思想 的美學價值 (The Change of Yinyang and the Continuity of Life: On the Aesthetic Value of the Simple Dialectical Thought in the *Book of Changes*)." *Yunnan shifan daxue xuebao Zhexue shehui kexue ban* (3): 58–65.

Lu Xun 魯迅. 2016. "Gu xiang 故鄉 (Homeland)." In *A Q zheng zhuan* 阿Q正傳 (The True Story of Ah-Q), 143–61. Taibei: Zhexue tang wenhua.

Lynch, Catherine. 2016. "Li Zehou and Pragmatism." *Philosophy East and West* 66(3): 704–19.

Man Kit Wah, Eva. 2001. "A Critical Reflection on a Suggested Return to Aesthetic Experience in Socialist China." *The Journal of Aesthetic Education* 35(4): 47–55.

Mao, Zedong. 1942 (1967). "Zai Yan'an wenyi zuotanhui shang di jianghua (Talks at the Yan'an Forum on Literature and Art)." In *Selected Works of Mao Tse-tung*. Peking: Foreign Languages Press.

Marx, Karl. 1859. *Zur Kritik der Politischen Ökonomie, Erstes Heft* (A Contribution to the Critique of Political Economy), vol. 1. Berlin: Franz Dunder.

———. 1971. *Zur Kritik der Politischen Ökonomie* (A Contribution to the Critique of Political Economy). In Marx, Karl and Friedrich Engels, *Werke*, vol. 13. Berlin: Karl Dietz Verlag.

———. 1977. "Preface to A Contribution to the Critique of Political Economy." Translated by R. Rojas. Moscow: Progress Publishers. http://www.marxists.org/archive/marx/works/1859/critique-pol-economy/preface.htm.

———. 2005. *Ökonomisch philosophische Manuskripte (1844)* (Economic and Philosophic Manuscripts of 1844). Köln: Verlag Internationale Sozialisten.

———. 2007. *Economic and Philosophic Manuscripts of 1844*. Translated and edited by Martin Milligan. Mineola, New York: Dover.

———. 2009. "Preface to A Contribution to the Critique of Political Economy." Proofed and corrected by Matthew Carmody. Moscow: Progress Publishers. https://www.marxists.org/archive/marx/works/1859/critique-pol-economy/preface.htm.

———. 2015. *Capital: A Critique of Political Economy, Vol. I, Book One: The Process of Production of Capital*. Translated by Samuel Moore and Edward Aveling, edited by Frederick Engels. Moscow: Progress Publishers.

Marx, Karl, and Friedrich Engels. (1845). *The German Ideology*. Available at Marxist Internet Archive Library. Accessed August 29, 2016. https://www.marxists.org/archive/marx/works/1845/german-ideology/.

———. 1992. *The Communist Manifesto*. Translated by Samuel Moore. Oxford: Oxford University Press.

McGrew, William. 1993. "The Intelligent Use of Tools: Twenty Propositions." In *Tools, Language, and Cognition in Human Evolution*, edited by Kathleen R. Gibson and Tim Ingold, 151–70. Cambridge: Cambridge University Press.

Meissner, Werner. 1990. *Philosophy and Politics in China: The Controversy over Dialectical Materialism in the 1930s*. Translated by Richard Mann. London: C. Hurst.

Merleau-Ponty, Maurice. 1962. *The Phenomenology of Perception*. Translated by Colin Smith. New York: Humanities Press.

Misra, Kalpana. 1998. "Deng's China: From Post-Maoism to Post-Marxism." *Economic and Political Weekly* 33(42/43): 2740–48. http://www.jstor.org/stable/4407298.

Mithen, Steven. 2006. *The Singing Neanderthals: The Origins of Music, Language, Mind and Body*. Cambridge, MA: Harvard University Press.

Moody, Peter R., Jr. 1974. "The New Anti-Confucian Campaign in China: The First Round." *Asian Survey* 14(4): 307–24.

Moritz, Ralf. 1993. "Denkstrukturen, Sachzwänge, Handlungsspielräume—Die Chinesische Intelligenz im Konflikt der Ordnungsmuster (Structures of Thought, Constraints, Maneuvers: Chinese Intellectuals in the Conflict of the Patterns of Order)." In *Chinesische Intellektuelle im 20. Jahrhundert: Zwischen Tradition und Moderne* (Chinese Intellectuals in the Twentieth Century: Between Tradition and Modernity), edited by Karl-Heinz Pohl, Gudrun Wacker, and Liu Huiru, 59–108. Hamburg: Institut für Asienkunde.

Mou Zongsan 牟宗三. 1990. *Zhongguo zhexuede tezhi* 中國哲學的特質 (Specific Features of Chinese Philosophy). Taibei: Taiwan xuesheng shuju.

Navarro, Zander. 2006. "In Search of a Cultural Interpretation of Power: The Contribution of Pierre Bourdieu." *IDS Bulletin* 37(6): 11–22.

Needham, Joseph. 1974. *Science and Civilization in China*. Cambridge: Cambridge University Press.

Nylan, Michael. 2016. "Li Zehou's Lunyu Jindu (Reading the Analects Today)." *Philosophy East and West* 66(3): 739–58.

Pan Tianhua 潘天華. 1995. "'Sunzi binfa' biyuju tese 「孫子兵法」比喻句特色 (The Characteristics of the Metaphor Sentences in *The Art of War*)." *Xiuci xuexi* (1): 14–15.

Penglin, Yu, Zhang Liangyi, and Liao Jianhua, eds. 2003. *Zhexue xiao cidian* 哲學小辞典 (A Small Philosophical Dictionary). Shanghai: Shanghai cishu chubanshe.

Pluhar, Werner S. 1987. Translator's Introduction to *Critique of Judgement*, by Immanuel Kant, xxiii–cix. Indianapolis: Hackett.

Pohl, Karl-Heinz. 2001. "An Intercultural Perspective on Chinese Aesthetics." In *Frontiers of Transculturality in Contemporary Aesthetics: Proceedings Volume of the Intercontinental Conference, University of Bologna, Italy, October 2000*, edited by Grazia Marchianò and Raffaele Milani, 135–48. Turin: Trauben.

———. 2009. "Identity and Hybridity: Chinese Culture and Aesthetics in the Age of Globalization." In *Intercultural Aesthetics: A Worldview Perspective*, edited by Antoon Van den Braembussche, Heinz Kimmerle and Nicole Note, 87–103. Brussels: Springer.
Ramachandran, Vilayanur. 2009. "Self-Awareness: The Last Frontier." *Edge*. Accessed May 23, 2016. https://www.edge.org/conversation/self-awareness-the-last-frontier.
Rongzeng, Wu, and Liu Huazhu, eds. 2013. *Han Shu xinyi* 漢書新譯 (Book of Han with New Annotations), vol. 4, Zhi 2. Taibei: Sanmin shuju.
Rosemont, Henry, Jr., and Roger T. Ames, trans., eds. 2009. *The Chinese Classic of Family Reverence: A Philosophical Translation of the Xiaojing*. Honolulu: University of Hawaii Press.
Rosenthal, Sandra B., and Patrick L. Bourgeois. 1991. *Mead and Merleau-Ponty: Toward a Common Vision*. Albany: State University of New York Press.
Rošker, Jana S. 1995. "Laozi yu Haidegede duihua: shitan yixie youguan Zhong Xi chuantong cunyoulun bijiaode wenti 老子與海德格的對話: 試探一些有關中西傳統存有論比較的問題 (A Dialogue between Laozi and Heidegger: Some Problems Regarding a Comparison between the Notions of Ontology in Chinese and Western Traditions)." *Hanxue Yanjiu* 1995 (2): 189–213.
———. 2008. *Searching for the Way: Theory of Knowledge in Pre-Modern and Modern China*. Hong Kong: Chinese University Press.
———. 2012. *Traditional Chinese Philosophy and the Paradigm of Structure (Li* 理*)*. Newcastle upon Tyne: Cambridge Scholars Publishing.
———. 2013. "The Concept of Harmony in Contemporary P.R. China and in Taiwanese Modern Confucianism." *Asian Studies* 1(2): 3–20.
———. 2013a. "Specific features of Chinese Logics: Analogies and the Problem of Structural Relations in Confucian and Moist Discourses." *Synthesis Philosophica* 57(1): 23–40.
———. 2016. *The Rebirth of the Moral Self: The Second Generation of Modern Confucians and their Modernization Discourses*. Honolulu: University of Hawai'i Press.
———. 2016a. "Modern Confucianism and the Concept of Asian Values." *Asian Studies* 4(1): 153–64.
———. 2016b. "Li Zehou and the Contemporary New Confucianism: A Philosophy for New Global Cultures." Paper presented at the Conference "Li Zehou and Confucian Philosophy," The East-West Center, University of Hawai'i at Manoa, Honolulu, October 8–11.
———. 2018. "Li Zehou's Notion of Subjectality as a New Conception of the Human Self." *Philosophy compass* 13(5): 1–10. doi: 10.1111/phc3.12484.
Ruddick, Sara. 1989. *Maternal Thinking: Toward a Politics of Peace*. New York: Beacon.
Samei, Maija Bell. 2010. Translator's Introduction to *The Chinese Aesthetic Tradition*, by Li Zehou, ix–xix. Honolulu: University of Hawai'i Press.

Sernelj, Tea. 2010. "Estetizacija ideologije: rekonstrukcija sodobne kitajske umetnosti in kulture (The Aesthetization of Ideology: Reconstructing Contemporary Chinese Art and Culture)." *Azijske in afriške študije* 14(2): 91–109. doi: 10.4312/as.2010.-14.2.91-110.

———. 2014. "The Unity of Body and Mind in Xu Fuguan's Theory." *Asian Studies* 2(1): 83–95.

———. 2016. "Medkulturni pristop k Li Zehoujevi teoriji sedimentacije (Intercultural Approach to Sedimantation)." In *Li Zehou in sodobna kitajska filozofija—zgodovinska ontologija, estetika in nadgradnje marksizma*, edited by Jana S. Rošker and Katja Kolšek, 75–100. Ljubljana: Znanstvena založba FF.

Shan Si 杉思. 1961. "Jinian lai guanyu meixue wentide taolun 幾年來關於美學問題的討論 (The Debates on Aesthetics during Recent Years)." *Zhexue yanjiu* (5): 73–85.

Shuangdi, Zhang, et al. 2011. *Lü shi Chunqiu yi zhu* 呂氏春秋. (Master Lü's Spring and Autumn Annals). 2011. Commentary by Zhang Shuangdi, Zhang Wanli, Yan Guoguang, and Chen Tao. Beijing: Beijing daxue chuban she.

Swiderski, Edward M. 1979. *The Philosophical Foundations of Soviet Aesthetics: Theories and Controversies in the Post-War Years*. Dordrecht: D. Reidel.

Tian, Chenshan. 2002. "Tongbian in the Chinese Reading of Dialectical Materialism." *Philosophy East and West* 52(1): 126–44.

Tomasello, Michael. 1999. *The Cultural Origins of Human cognition*. Cambridge, MA: Harvard University Press.

Wang, Ban. 1997. *The Sublime Figure of History: Aesthetics and Politics in Twentieth-Century China*. Stanford: Stanford University Press.

Wang Guowei 王國維. 2013. *Renjian cihua* 人間詞話 (Poetic Remarks in the Human World). Beijing: Fenghuang chuban she.

Wang Hui 汪暉. 2000. "Dangdai Zhongguode sixiang zhuangkuang yu xiandaixing wenti 當代中國的思想狀況與現代性問題 (Contemporary Chinese Thought and the Question of Modernity)." *Taiwan shehui yanjiu* 37(1): 1–43.

Wang, Jing. 1996. "Li Zehou and the Marxist Reconstruction of Confucianism." In *High Culture Fever: Politics, Aesthetics, and Ideology in Deng's China*, 93–117. Berkeley: University of California Press.

Wang, Keping. 2006. "Interactions between Western and Chinese Aesthetics." In *The Pursuit of Comparative Aesthetics*, edited by Mazhar Hussain and Robert Wilkinson, 113–26. Hants: Ashgate Publishing.

———. 2007. "A Rediscovery of Heaven and Human Oneness." *American Journal of Economics and Sociology* 66 (1): 237–60. http://www.jstor.org/stable/27739629.

———. 2016. "Li Zehoujev pogled na pragmatični razum (Li Zehou's View of Pragmatic Reason Revisited)." In *Li Zehou in sodobna kitajska filozofija—*

zgodovinska ontologija, estetika in nadgradnje marksizma, edited by Jana S. Rošker and Katja Kolšek, 117–206. Ljubljana: Znanstvena založba FF.

Wang Ruoshui 王若水. 1986. *Wei rendaozhuyi bianhu* 為人道主義辯護 (In Defence of Humanism). Beijing: Sanlian shudian.

Wang, Yunping. 2008. "Confucian Ethics and Emotions." *Frontiers of Philosophy in China* 3(3): 352–65.

Whitehead, Alfred North. 1978. *Process and Reality*. New York: The Free Press.

Winkelman, Michael. 2011. "Shamanism and the Evolutionary Origins of Spirituality and Healing." *NeuroQuantology* 9(1): 54–71.

Wittgenstein, Ludwig. 1975. *On Certainty*. Oxford: Basil Blackwell.

Wu Ji 吳忌. 2016. "Li Zehou meixue pipan 李澤厚美學批判 (A Critique of Li Zehou's Aesthetics)." In *Li Zehou duitan lu* 李澤厚對談錄 (Recordings of Li Zehou's Conversations), 276–289. http://www.doc88.com/p-7030124841.html.

Xi, Zhu, ed. 2009. *Zhou yi benyi* 周易本意 (The Original Meaning of the *Book of Changes*). Commentary by Zhu Xi. Beijing: Zhonghua shuju. Xiong Shili 熊十力. 1992. *Xiong Shili lunzhu zhiyi: Xin weishi lun* 熊十力論著集之一：新唯識論 (Collected Works of Xiong Shili, Part 1: The New Theory of Pure Consciousness). Beijing: Zhonghua shuju.

Xiurui, Hong, ed. 2015. *San zi jing ju jie* 三字經句解 (Three Character Classic with Explanations). Xinbei: Duo shijie tushu wenhua.

Xu Fuguan 徐復觀. 1987. "Zhongguo renxing lun shi—Xian Qin pian 中國人性論史――先秦篇 (The Theory of Human Nature: The Pre-Qin Chapter)." In *Xiandai xin rujia xue'an* 現代新儒家學案 (A Study of Modern Confucianism), vol. 3, edited by Fang Keli 方克立 and Li Jinquan 李錦全, 647–62. Beijing: Zhongguo shehui kexue chuban she.

Yang Bin 楊斌. 2015. *Li Zehou xueshu nianpu* 李澤厚學术年譜 (A Chronicle of Li Zehou's Academic Work). Shanghai: Fudan daxue chuban she.

Yang Guorong. 2008. "Being and Value: From the Perspective of Chinese-Western Comparative Philosophy." *Philosophy East and West* 58(2): 267–82.

Yang Guorong 楊國榮. 2009. *Renshi yu jiazhi* 認識與價值 (Recognition and Value). Shanghai: Huadong shifan daxue chuban she.

———. 2016. "Liang Han shidai weiwu lun fandui weixin lun xianyan lunde douzheng 兩漢時代唯物論反對唯心先驗論的鬥爭 (The Materialist Struggle Against Idealism and Apriorism during the Period of the Two Han Dynasties)." *Wenge ziliao*. Accessed October 5, 2016. http://blog.sina.com.cn/s/blog_73767cad0100y4b9.html.

Yang Zebo 楊澤波. 2007. "Mou Zongsan chaoyue cunyou lun boyi—cong xian Qin tianlunde fazhan guiji kan Mou Zongsan chaoyue cunyou lunde quexian 牟宗三超越存有論駁議――從先秦天論的發展軌跡看牟宗三超越存有論的缺陷 (A Critique of Mou Zongsan's Transcendental Ontology: A

View on the Flaws of Mou Zongsan's Transcendental Ontology through the Lens of the Development of the Discourse on Heaven in the Pre-Qin Period)." *Zhongguo lunwen xiazai zhongxin*. Accessed July 15, 2012. http://www.studa.net/guoxue/060407/11563323.html.

Yu Chuanqin 於傳勤. 2016. "Li Zehou xueshu sixiang gai shuo 李澤厚學术思想概說 (A Summary of Li Zehou's Academic Thought)." In *Li Zehou duitan lu* 李澤厚對談錄 (Recordings of Li Zehou's Conversations), 248–60. http://www.doc88.com/p-7030124841.htm.

Zhang Dainian 張岱年. 2003. *Zhongguo zhexue shi fangfalun fafan* 中國哲學史方法論發凡 (Introduction to the Methodology of the History of Chinese Philosophy). Beijing: Zhonghua shuju.

Zhang Dongsun 張東蓀. 1931. "Wo yi tantan bianzhengde weiwu lun 我亦談談辯證的唯物論 (I Would Also Like to Speak About Dialectical Materialism)." *Da gong bao* 大公報 (*Xiandai sichao* 現代思潮), September 18. Hong Kong: Zhonggong Gang Ao gongwei 中共港澳工委.

———. 1933. "Dongde luoji shi kenengde ma? 動的邏輯是可能的嗎? (Is a Moving Logic Possible?)." *Xin Zhonghua* 新中華 1(18): 1–11.

Zhao Shilin 趙士林, ed. 2012. *Li Zehou sixiang pingxi* 李澤厚思想評析 (An Analytical Evaluation of Li Zehou's Thought). Shanghai: Shanghai yiwen chuban she.

Zhao Wenhe 趙文河. 2016. "Zhongguo chuantong shenmei guannian yu xifang zhelimeixuede qubie yu lianxi 中國傳統審美觀念與西方哲理美學的區別與聯繫 (Differences and Connections between Traditional Chinese Aesthetic Ideas and Western Philosophical Aesthetics)." *Jinri toutiao*, May 28. http://toutiao.com/i6289683794219762178/.

Zhengying, Xu, and Chang Peiyu, eds. 2014. *Zhou li* 周禮 (The Rites of Zhou). 2014. Commentary by Xu Zhengying and Chang Peiyu. Beijing: Zhonghua shuju.

Zhou, Xiaoyi. 2005. "The Ideological Function of Western Aesthetics in 1980s China." In *Cultural Studies in China*, edited by Tao Dongfang and Jin Yuanpu, 98–115. Singapore: Marshall Cavendish Academic.

Zhuang Zhou 莊周. 2014. *Zhuangzi* (Master Zhuang). Beijing: Zhongguo Huaqiao chuban she.

Zongxiang, Zhang, and Zheng Zhaochang, eds. 2010. *Lun heng jiao zhu* 論衡校注. (The Book *"On Balance"* with Comments and Annotations). Shanghai: Shanghai guji chuban she.

Žižek, Slavoj. 2014. *Žižek's Jokes: (Did You Hear the One About Hegel and Negation?)*. Cambridge, MA: MIT Press.

Glossary of Specific Terms, Phrases, and Titles (Chinese-English)

Bai hua 白話	Colloquial language
Bai hua qi fang, bai jia zhengming 百花齊放, 百家爭鳴	Hundred Flowers Movement
Bai hua yundong 白話運動	Colloquial Movement
Beijing daxue 北京大學	Peking University
Ben 本	Root, origin
Bengen 本根	Root, basis, origin
Benmo 本末	Roots and crown
Benti 本體	Root, origin, substance, noumenon
Benti yishi 本體意識	Ontological consciousness
Bentilun 本體論	Ontology (in Chinese philosophy)
Bian zhe 辯者	Dialecticians
Changsha 長沙	Changsha (city)
Cheng ji 成己	Completing oneself
Chi fan zhexue 吃飯哲學	Philosophy of food (or eating)
Chigan wenhua 恥感文化	Culture of shame
Chuangzaoxing 創造性	Creativity
Chuangzaoxingde zhuanhua 創造性的轉化	Creative transformation
Chuantong wuyishi 傳統無意識	Traditional unconscious

Chun guan zongbo 春官宗伯	*The Overseer of Ritual Affairs in the Spring Offices*
Cun tianli mie renyu 存天理滅人欲	The preservation of the (moral and rational) cosmic structure and the elimination of human desires
Cunyoulun 存有論	Ontology
Da wo 大我	The great self (community)
Da yuejin 大躍進	Great Leap Forward
Dangdai sichao yu Zhongguo zhihui 當代思潮與中國智慧	*Contemporary Currents of Thought and Chinese Wisdom*
Dao 道	The Way
Dao jia 道家	Daoists, Daoist philosophers
Daode jing 道德經	*The Book of the Way and the Virtue*
Datong shu 大同書	*Book of Great Unity*
Di si tigang 第四提綱	*The Fourth Outline*
Dianxing 典型	Type, typical example, typicality
Dianxinghua 典型化	Typification or exemplification
Du 度	Dynamic proper measure
Duili fanchou 對立範疇	Binary categories
Duixianghua 對象化	Objectification
Fa 法	Law
Fa jia 法家	Legalism
Fan you yundong 反右運動	Anti-Rightist Movement
Fan youpai yundong 反右派運動	Anti-Rightist Movement
Fanchou 範疇	Category
Fandao he shidang goujian 範導和適當構建	Guide by example and appropriately construct
Fugu pai 復古派	The conservative intellectual current
Fuguzhuyi 復古主義	The renewal and rebirth of the (classical Chinese) tradition
Fuhaoxue meixue 符號學美學	Aesthetics of semiotics
Gainian 概念	Concept
Gan 感	Emotional responsiveness

Glossary of Specific Terms, Phrases, and Titles

Ganxing 感性	Sensibility
Gaobie geming 告別革命	Farewell to revolution
Genben 根本	Root, basis, foundation
Geti jidian 個體積澱	Individual sedimentation
Getixing 個體性	Individuality
Gongchan dang 共產黨	Communist Party
Gongju 工具	Tools
Gongju benti 工具本體	Techno-social substance, instrumental substance
Gongyi—shehui jiegou 工藝——社會結構	Techno-social formation (technological-social formation)
Guanxi 關係	Relationships, relations
Guanxizhuyi 關係主義	Relationalism
Guanyu zhutixingde buchong shuoming 關於主體性的補充說明	*A Supplementary Explanation of Subjectivity*
Guodian Chu mu zhu jian 郭店楚墓竹簡	*Guodian Chu Bamboo Slips*
Guomin dang 國民黨	Nationalist Party
Guoxue re 國學熱	National studies
Han Shu 漢書	*Book of Han*
Hankou 漢口	Hankou (city)
Hanyi mohu 含義模糊	Blurred content
He 和	Harmony
Hei shou 黑手	Black hands
Hexie gaoyu Zhengyi 和諧高于正義	Harmony is higher than justice
Hong qi 紅旗	*Red Flag*
Hou Ji 後稷	The mythological founding ancestor of the Zhou Dynasty
Hou zhexue 後哲學	Post-philosophy, post-philosophical
Huaxia meixue 華夏美學	*The Chinese Aesthetic Tradition*

Huiying Sangde'er ji qita 回應桑德爾及其他	*Response to Michael Sandel and Other Matters*
Hunan 湖南	Hunan province
Jidian 積澱	Sedimentation
Jidian shuo 積澱說	Theory of sedimentation
Jiefang sixiang 解放思想	Liberation of thought
Jiegou 結構	Structure
Jimao wu shuo 己卯五說	*Five Essays from 1999*
Jingjie 境界	Aesthetic realm
Jingshen benti 精神本體	Spiritual substance
Jiti shehui yishi 集體社會意識	Collective social consciousness
Jiuwang 救亡	Saving (the country from foreign aggression)
Jutide xingxiangxing 具體的形象性	Concrete figurativeness, the nature of concrete images
Kang ri zhanzheng 抗日戰爭	Anti-Japanese war
Keguan jiegou 客觀結構	Objective structure
Keguande shehuixing 客觀的社會性	Objective sociality
Kong Meng zhi dao 孔孟之道	School of Confucius and Mencius
Kongzi zai pingjia 孔子再評價	*A Re-evaluation of Confucius*
Legan 樂感	Pleasure
Legan wenhua 樂感文化	Culture of pleasure (culture of optimism, culture of happiness)
Li 理	Structure, structural pattern
Li 禮	Ritual, (Confucian) rituality
Li fa jiaorong 禮法交融	Blending of ritual and law
Li ji 禮記	*The Book of Rituals*
Li sheng yu qing 禮生於情	Rituals were generated from emotionality
Liang de lun 兩德論	Theory of the two kinds of morality
Liangge shijie guan 兩個世界觀	Two-worlds view
Liangzhi 良知	Inborn knowledge
Liangzhong daode 兩種道德	Two kinds of morality

Liqi 理氣	Structure and vitality
Lishi bentilun 歷史本體論	Historical ontology
Lixing ningju 理性凝聚	Condensation of reason
Lixing ronghua 理性融化	Melting of reason
Lixue 理學	School of the structural principle
Lü shi Chunqiu 呂氏春秋	*Master Lü's Spring and Autumn Annals*
Lun meigan, mei he yishu 論美感、美和藝術	*On the Aesthetic Feeling, Beauty, and Art*
Lunli daode erfen 倫理道德二分	Differentiation between ethics and morals
Lunli xue gangyao 倫理學綱要	*An Outline of Ethics*
Lunyu 論語	*The (Confucian) Analects*
Lunyu jindu 論語今讀	*Reading the Analects Today*
Manshuo Xiti Zhongyong 漫說西體中用	*A Simple Lecture on Western substance and Chinese Function*
Mao Zedong sixiang 毛澤東思想	Maoism
Meide keguanxing he shehuixing 美的客觀性和社會性	The objective and the social nature of beauty
Meide licheng 美的歷程	*The Path of Beauty*
Meigan liangchongxing 美感兩重性	Duality of aesthetic feeling
Meigan 美感	Aesthetic feeling, sense of beauty
Meigan zhijue 美感直覺	Aesthetic intuition
Meixue 美學	Aesthetics as the (originally Western) academic discipline
Meixue da taolun 美學大討論	The great debate on aesthetics
Meixue re 美學熱	Aesthetic Fever
Meixue sanshu 美學三書	*Three Books on Aesthetics*
Meixue sijiang 美學四講	*Four Essays on Aesthetics*
Meixuede duixiang yu fanwei 美學的對象與範圍	*The Subject and the Scope of Aesthetics*
Mingshi 名實	Names or concepts and actualities

Neihua 内化	Internalization
Neisheng 内聖	The inner sage
Neisheng waiwang 内聖外王	The inner sage and the external ruler
Neizai chaoyuexing 内在超越性	Internal (or immanent) transcendence, transcendence in immanence
Pi Lin pi Kong 批林批孔	Criticize Lin Biao, criticize Confucius
Pipan xianyanlun 批判先驗論	Criticize apriorism
Pipan zhexuede pipan: Kangde shuping 批判哲學的批判:康德述評	*Critique of Critical Philosophy: A New Approach to Kant*
Pusu bianzheng fa 樸素辯證法	Simple dialectics
Qi 氣	Creative potential
Qi qing 七情	Seven feelings or emotions
Qi qing zheng 七情正	Rectification of seven human emotions
Qimeng 啟蒙	Enlightenment
Qing 情	Emotion, situation
Qing benti 情本體	Emotion-based substance, emotion based substance
Qing bentide neitui 情本體的内推	Intention of emotion-based substance
Qing bentide waitui 情本體的外推	Extension of the emotion-based substance
Qinggan 情感	Emotion, feeling
Qinggan benti 情感本體	Emotion-based substance
Qingjing 情境	Situation or context
Qingjing jiaorong 情景交融	Fusion of emotion and scene or situation
Qingli 情理	Emotion and reason
Qingli jiegou 情理結構	Emotio-rational structure
Quan pan xihua 全盤西化	A complete Westernization (of culture and thought)
Quan xue pian 勸學篇	*Exhortation to Study*
Ren 仁	(Co)humaneness, Chinese humanism

Ren dao 人道	Way of Humans
Ren huode zenmeyang 人活得怎麼樣?	How do humans live?
Ren huozhe 人活著	The human being is alive
Ren jiegou 仁結構	The structure of humaneness
Ren qing 人情	Human feelings
Ren ruhe huo 人如何活?	How is it that humans are alive?
Ren wei shenme huo 人為什麼活?	Why do humans live?
Ren xing 人性	Humanness, human nature, human inborn qualities, inborn humanness
Rende ziranhua 人的自然化	Naturalization of humans
Renlei qunti 人類群體	Human community
Renlei zhutide bentilun 人類主體的本體論	Ontology of human subjectality
Renleixue bentilun 人類學本體論	Anthropological ontology
Renleixue lishi bentilun 人類學歷史本體論	Anthropological historical ontology, anthropo-historical ontology
Renmin ribao 人民日報	*People's Daily*
Renyi 仁義	Humaneness and justice (a general denotation of Confucian morality)
Rudao hubu 儒道互補	Complementary relation between Confucianism and Daoism
Rufa huyong 儒法互用	Reciprocal utilization of Confucianism and Legalism
Ruxue san qi 儒學三期	Three periods of Confucianism
Ruxue si qi 儒學四期	Four periods of Confucianism
San min zhuyi 三民主義	Three National Principles
Sange daibiao 三個代表	Three Representations
Shang shu 尚書	*Book of Documents*
Shehui benti 社會本體	Social substance
Shehui chonggao 社會崇高	Social sublime

Shehui cunzai 社會存在	Social existence
Shehuixing daode 社會性道德	Social morality
Shehuixing gongde 社會性公德	Social public virtues
Shenghuo jidian 生活積澱	Vital sedimentation
Shenmei 審美	Aesthetics (referring to concepts, ideas and values that tend to be linked to the specific features of the Chinese ideational tradition)
Shenmei yishi 審美意識	Aesthetic awareness
Shenmeixue 審美學	Aesthetics (as the study of the process of recognizing and perceiving beauty, derived from the Chinese tradition)
Shi Ji 史記	*Historical Notes*
Shi jing 詩經	*Book of Poetry*
Shijian 實踐	Practice, praxis
Shijian lixing 實踐理性	Practical reason
Shijian meixue 實踐美學	Aesthetics of practice, practical aesthetics
Shijian shi jianyan zhenlide weiyi biaozhun 實踐是檢驗真理的唯一標準	Practice as the only criterion for finding truth
Shijianlunde renleixue 實踐論的人類學	Anthropology of human practice
Shilun xingxiang siwei 試論形象思維	*On Image-Thinking*
Shishi qiushi 實事求是	Seeking the truth in the facts
Shiyong lixing 實用理性	Pragmatic reason, pragmatic rationality
Shiyong lixing yu legan wenhua 實用理性與樂感文化	Pragmatic Reason and a Culture of Pleasure
Shu jing 書經	Book of Documents
Shuowen jiezi 說文解字	*Interpreting Texts and Explaining Characters* (The oldest Chinese etymological dictionary from the Han dynasty)

Glossary of Specific Terms, Phrases, and Titles

Si pai 四派	Four currents
Si ren bang 四人幫	Gang of Four
Taiwan 台灣	Taiwan, Formosa
Ti 體	Stem, root, body, ultimate reality
Tian 天	Heaven, nature
Tian'anmen guangchang 天安門廣場	Square of heavenly peace
Tian ming 天命	Decree of heaven
Tiandao 天道	Way of heaven
Tian ren heyi 天人合一	Unity (or unification, reconciliation) of heaven (or nature) and humans
Tiren 體認	Bodily recognition
Tiyong 體用	Substance (essence) and function
Tiyong bu er 體用不二	Substance and function cannot be separated
Tongbian 通變	Continuous change or continuity through change
Waihua 外化	Alienation, externalization ("Entäußerung")
Waiwang 外王	The external ruler
Waizai chaoyuexing 外在超越性	External transcendence
Wen yan 文言	Ancient or classical Chinese
Wenhua—xinli jiegou 文化——心理結構	Cultural-psychological formation
Wenhua da taolun 文化大討論	Great debate on culture
Wenhua geming 文化革命	Cultural revolution
Wenhua jidian 文化積澱	Cultural sedimentation
Wenhua re 文化熱	Cultural fever
Wode zhexue tigang 我的哲學提綱	*An Outline of My Philosophy*
Wu 巫	Shamanism, magicians
Wu 無	Absence

Wu qing bianzheng fa 無情辯證法	Emotionless dialectics, Impassive rational laws of dialectical development
Wu xing shuo 五行說	Five phases theory
Wu yong zhi yong 無用之用	The use through the useless
Wu zi ti 物自體	Thing-in-itself
Wuchan jieji wenhua da geming 無產階級文化大革命	Great proletarian cultural revolution
Wujun heyi 巫君合一	Unity of shaman and (Confucian) gentleman
Wushi chuantong 巫史傳統	Shamanistic historical tradition
Wusi yundong 五四運動	May 4th Movement
Wuxu bianfa 戊戌變法	Hundred days reform
Wuzhong jidian 物種積澱	Sedimentation of species
Xiandai shehuixing daode 現代社會性道德	Modern social morality
Xiao 孝	Filial respect and love
Xiao wo 小我	The small self (individual)
Xin Guoxue 新國學	New National Studies
Xin qingnian 新青年	*New Youth*
Xin ruxue 新儒學	Modern Confucianism (New Confucianism)
Xin wenhua yundong 新文化運動	New Culture Movement
Xing 性	Nature, inborn qualities
Xingshi 形式	Form
Xingxiang siwei 形象思維	Figurative thinking, image thinking
Xingxiang siwei tezheng 形象思維特徵	Specific features of the figurative thought (or image-thinking)
Xingxiang siwei xutan 形象思維續談	*Continuing the Debate on Image-Thinking*
Xingxiang siwei zai xutan 形象思維再續談	*A New Continuation of the Debate on Image-Thinking*

Xinhai geming 辛亥革命	Xinhai revolution
Xinli benti 心理本體	Psychological substance
Xinxing 心性	Heart-mind and inner nature
Xiti Zhongyong 西體中用	Western substance, Chinese application (or function)
Xixue re 西學熱	Western studies
Xue 學	Learning
Ya yue 雅樂	Elegant music (a form of classical Chinese music)
Yangqi 揚棄	Sublation or "Aufhebung" (Hegel)
Yangwu yundong 洋務運動	Westernization movement
Yijing 易經	*Book of Changes*
Yi mei chu shan 以美儲善	Preserving the good through beauty
Yi mei qi zhen 以美啟真	Illumination of truth through beauty
Yi meiyu dai zongjiao 以美育代宗教	*Replacing Religion with Aesthetic Education*
Yige shijie guan 一個世界觀	One-world view
Yihua 異化	Estrangement ("Entfremdung"), commonly (wrongly) translated as "alienation"
Yijing 意境	Artistic conception
Yinyang 陰陽	Yin and yang, "sunny and shady"
Yinyang wuxing 陰陽五行	Yin and yang and the Five Phases (or Five Agents)
Yishide renhua 意識的人化	Humanization of consciousness
Yishu jidian 藝術積澱	Artistic sedimentation
Yong 用	Function
You 有	Presence
You qing yuzhou guan 有情宇宙觀	Emotional view of the universe, emotional cosmology
You wu dao li, shi li gui ren 由巫到禮, 釋禮歸仁	*From Shamanism to Rituality, Explaining Rituality as a Return to the Humanness*

Yu 欲	Desire, wish
Yuanshi bianzheng fa 原始辯證法	Primitive dialectics
Yuanshi jidian 原始積澱	Elementary (original, primitive) sedimentation
Yue ji 樂記	On music
Yue or le 樂	Music or joy
Yue yu zheng tong 樂與政通	Music is integrated into the governance
Za zhu ji 杂著集	A Collection of Various Essays
Zai Yan'an wenyi zuotan huishangde jianghua 在延安文藝座談會上的講話	Talks at the Yan'an Forum on Literature and Art
Zheng 正	Proper(ness), correct(ness)
Zhenli biaozhun da taolun 真理標準大討論	Discussion of the Criteria of Truth
Zhexue gangyao 哲學綱要	An Outline of Philosophy
Zhexue meixue wenxuan 哲學美學文選	Philosophic and Aesthetic Writings
Zhexue yanjiu 哲學研究	Philosophy Research
Zhide zhijue 智的直覺	Intellectual intuition
Zhixing heyi 知行合一	The unity of knowledge and action
Zhong 中	The middle, the mean, equilibrium
Zhong yong 中庸	The state of equilibrium or the mean
Zhongguo benwei wenhua 中國本位文化	Chinese (tradition) as a new, leading culture
Zhongguo gudai sixiang shilun 中國古代思想史論	On Classical Chinese Intellectual History
Zhongguo jindai sixiang shilun 中國近代思想史論	On Pre-modern Chinese Intellectual History
Zhongguo meixue shi 中國美學史	A History of Chinese Aesthetics

Zhongguo shehui kexue yuan zhexue yanjiu suo 中國社會科學院哲學研究所	Research Institute of Philosophy at the Chinese Academy of Social Sciences (CASS)
Zhongguo sixiang shilun 中國思想史論	*On Chinese Intellectual History*
Zhongguo xiandai sixiang shilun 中國現代思想史論	*On Modern Chinese Intellectual History*
Zhongguo zibenzhuyi mengya 中國資本主義萌芽	Germs of capitalism in China
Zhongti Xiyong 中體西用	(Preserving) Chinese essence and (applying) Western functions
Zhongxue wei ti, Xixue wei yong 中學為體, 西學為用	Chinese learning for substance (fundamental principles) and Western learning for function (practical application)
Zhou gong 周公	Duke of Zhou
Zhou Kong zhi dao 周孔之道	School of Duke of Zhou and Confucius
Zhou li 周禮	*Rites of Zhou*
Zhuanhuaxingde chuangzao 轉化性的創造	Transformative creation
Zhuanhuaxinde chuangzaozhe 轉化性的創造者	Transformative creator
Zhuguan cengmian 主觀層面	Subjective level
Zhuguan lun 主觀論	Theory of subjectivity
Zhuguanxing 主觀性	Subjectivity
Zhuti 主體	Subject
Zhutide nengdongxing 主體的能動性	Human agency
Zhutixing 主體性	Subjectality
Zhutixing shijian zhexue 主體性實踐哲學	Pragmatic (or practical) philosophy of subjectality
Ziqiang yundong 自強運動	Westernization movement
Zirande renhua 自然的人化	Humanization of nature

Ziwo xuanze 自我選擇	Individual choice
Ziwo yishi 自我意識	Self-consciousness
Ziyou yizhi 自由意志	Free will
Zongjiaoxing daode 宗教性道德	Religious morality
Zongjiaoxing side 宗教性私德	Religious private virtues
Zou wo zijide lu 走我自己的路	*Following My Own Way*
Zui hou shizai 最後實在	Ultimate reality
Zuigan wenhua 罪感文化	Culture of sin

Index

Absence: as *wu* (無), 123; in relation to presence (*you* 有), 123
Aesthetic awareness: as *shenmei yishi*, 37; as ultimate meaning of life, 222
Aesthetic craze, 200. *See also* Aesthetic feeling
Aesthetic feeling, 16, 37, 63, 79, 95, 97, 120, 185, 187, 196, 206–7, 211, 271; as *meigan*, 36; origin and genesis of, 188, 210. *See also* Duality of aesthetic feeling; Sense of beauty
Aesthetic Fever (movement), 19, 186, 197–202, 204, 208–9, 280n5; as *meixue re*, 8, 9. *See also* Aesthetic craze
Aesthetic intuition, 192
Aesthetic realm, 78, 80, 87, 95, 97, 100, 188, 102, 214, 218, 224, 226, 290n51; as *jingjie*, 213–14; Wang Guowei's, 213–14
Aesthetics, as the (originally Western) academic discipline, 8, 203, 213, 229; as *meixue*, 77–78
Aesthetics of practice (practical aesthetics), 189, 275; as *shijian meixue*, 50, 79

Alienation, 20, 70–71, 79, 82, 84, 86, 95, 97, 120, 167, 172, 185, 194, 199–200, 210–11, 231, 286n23, 288n36, 305n35, 309n69; as externalization (*Entäußerung*, *waihua*), 286n21. *See also* Estrangement
Analects, The (Confucian), 103, 105, 112, 118, 142, 285n14, 296n47
Ancient or classical Chinese (language), 3
Anthropo-historical ontology, 19–20, 25, 216, 222–24, 228–29, 239–40, 251, 258, 260, 267–68, 272, 275, 281n17, 307n54. *See also* Anthropological ontology
Anthropo-historical ontology (Li Zehou), 12, 237, 280n8, 306n47
Anthropological historical ontology, 123. *See also* Anthropological ontology
Anthropological ontology, 50, 56, 83, 86, 168, 185, 215, 295n42; as *renleixue benti lun*, 32. *See also* Historical ontology; Ontology
Anthropology of human practice, 282n29; as *shijianlunde renleixue*, 71
Anti-Japanese War, 3

Anti-Rightist Movement, 4, 85, 280n4
Arendt, Hannah, 86
Artistic conception, 214; as *yijing*, 212
Artistic sedimentation, 49; as *yishu jidian*, 48. See also Sedimentation

Bai hua yundong (Colloquial Movement), 3. See also Hundred Flowers Movement
Benmo (root and branch, roots and crown), 124, 310n8
Binary categories, 163, 173, 182, 256, 259, 260, 266, 270, 310n8; as *duili fanchou*, 124
Black hands (*hei shou*), 22
Blending of ritual and law (*li fa jiaorong*), 245
Bodily recognition, 120; as *tiren*, 289n46
Book of Changes (*Yi jing*), 93, 256, 260, 265, 282n24, 313n23
Book of Documents (*Shu jing* or *Shang shu*), 114
Book of Great Unity (*Datong shu*, Kang Youwei), 298n60
Book of Han (*Han shu*, Ban Gu), 293n20, 304n27
Book of Poetry (*Shi jing*), 282n24
Book of Rituals, The, 139, 145, 296n43
Book of the Way and the Virtue, The (Laozi), 261
Buzhu, 108

Cai Yi, 16, 185, 193, 197, 201, 208, 300n3, 300n5, 303n20
Cai Yuanpei, 288n34, 306n45
Cauvel, Jane, 33, 48–49, 57, 62–64, 78, 89, 92, 96–97, 109, 111, 114–15, 125–27, 131, 199, 201–2, 282n28, 284n3, 285n16, 293n22, 293n24
Chandler, Marthe, 48–49, 58–60, 66, 70, 109–10, 284n8, 284n9
Changsha (city), 8
Chen Duxiu, 2, 172
Chen Yinke, 293n26, 294n27
Cheng Hao, 144
Cheng ji (Completing oneself), 76
Chinese aesthetic tradition, 100, 183, 213, 215, 218
Chinese Aesthetic Tradition, The (Li Zehou), 10, 211
Chinese essence (substance) and Western function (application), 170, 174, 178; as *zhongti xiyong*, xiv, 1, 39, 172–73; Chinese learning for substance (fundamental principles) and Western learning for function (practical application) (*zhongxue wei ti, xixue wei yong*), 163, 178; reversal of, xiv, 298n60. See also Western essence, Chinese function
Chinese tradition, 2, 5, 7, 24, 31, 37, 79, 104, 111, 120–21, 129–30, 138, 146, 158, 161, 163, 169–70, 173, 181, 216–18, 237, 251, 264, 274, 287n26, 305n42, 311n13; as a new leading culture, 2
Chongbai Moluo, 140
(Co)humaneness, 120; as *ren*, 60
Collective social consciousness, 59, 252; as *jiti shehui yishi*, 110
Colloquial language (*bai hua*), 2
Colloquial Movement (*Bai hua yundong*), 3. See also Hundred Flowers Movement
Communist Party, 3, 200, 281n15; and New China, 17; renewed the system of high education, 4
Complementary relation between Confucianism and Daoism, 38, 92,

106, 123–24, 126, 279n2; as *rudao hubu*, 125
Completing oneself (*cheng ji*), 76
Concrete figurativeness (*jutide xingxiangxing*), 195
Condensation of reason, 97; as *lixing ningju*, 238; grounded in sedimentation, 64
Contemporary Currents of Thought and Chinese Wisdom (Li Zehou), 11
Continuous change (continuity through change), 52; as *tongbian*, 256, 261. See also *Tongbian*
Creative transformation, 171; as *chuangzaoxingde zhuanhua*, xiv. See also Transformative creation
Criticize Apriorism (campaign), 18
Criticize Lin Biao, Criticize Confucius (campaign), 18
Critique of Critical Philosophy: A New Approach to Kant (Li Zehou), xiv, 11, 17, 21, 44, 66, 86, 198, 205, 229, 231, 235–36, 237, 239, 283n30, 284n5, 304n28
Cultural Fever, 167, 199, 304n26; as *wenhua re*, 298n61
Cultural Revolution (Great Proletarian Cultural Revolution), xiv, 4, 10–11, 17, 19, 21, 41, 82, 85, 197, 199, 203, 208–9, 280n4, 281n15, 286n24
Cultural-psychological formation, 28, 48–50, 51–53, 56, 58, 65, 98, 121, 143, 147–49, 151, 168, 174, 188, 201, 218–19, 242, 252, 285n16; as *wenhua—xinli jiegou*, 29, 33, 35; as transcendental forms, 28. See also Techno-social formation
Culture of pleasure (optimism, happiness, joy), 106, 119–23, 124, 131, 137, 146, 159, 221, 253, 293n24; as *legan wenhua*, 29, 35. See also Legan wenhua
Culture of shame (*chigan wenhua*), 119
Culture of sin (*zuigan wenhua*), 119

Da wo (the great self, community), 33, 48, 59, 78, 112, 283n30, 284n5. See also Great self
Dao (the Way), 126, 243. See also Way; Way of Heaven; Way of Humans
Daoism, 37, 93–94, 106, 116–17, 124–29, 289n48, 293n20, 293n25, 294n31, 295n37, 296n44. See also Complementary relation between Confucianism and Daoism
Daoists (Daoist philosophers), 38, 92, 124–25, 293n26
Datong shu (Book of Great Unity, Kang Youwei), 298n60
Decree of Heaven, 142; as *tian ming*, 135. See also Way of Heaven
Deng Xiaoping, 4, 46, 166, 201, 298n61
Dewey, John, 142, 296n44, 306n49
Dialectics, 6, 179, 189, 225, 235, 249, 260, 265, 270, 272, 309n1; Chinese (*tongbian*), 260–61, 264–65, 269–70, 311n13; Marxist, 98, 177–78, 182, 265, 270; simple (primitive), 311n9. See also Continuous change; *Tongbian*
Discussion of the Criteria of Truth (*Zhenli biaozhun da taolun*), 200
Dong Zhongshu, 117–18, 127–28, 136, 245
Du (Proper measure), 36, 101, 159. See also Proper measure
Duality of aesthetic feeling, 191–93, 195, 210, 212, 300n5; as *meigan liangchongxing*, 189

Duke of Zhou, 29, 106, 108–9, 116. See also Zhou Gong

Eliade, Mircea, 109
Emotion (feeling), 156; as *qinggan*, 146
Emotion (situation), 156; as *qing*, 146; as *qingjing*, 146
Emotional cosmology (emotional view of the universe), 24, 226, 248; as *you qing yuzhou guan*, 107
Emotional responsiveness (*gan*), 107
Emotion-based substance, 35, 106, 120, 127, 131, 140–41, 146, 148–49, 154, 157–58, 196, 205, 210, 226, 242, 246, 252, 267, 275, 297n48, 313n21; as *qing benti*, 19, 29, 119, 243, 282n29, 284n4
Emotio-rational structure, 74, 111–12, 131, 140, 148, 150, 151, 154–57, 215, 226, 228, 238, 242–43, 252, 275; as *qingli jiegou*, 29, 35
Engels, Friedrich, 71, 161, 177, 265, 267, 270, 301n8
Enlightenment, 2, 20–21, 23, 30, 59, 82, 87–88, 104, 150, 153–54, 164, 166–68, 169–70, 201, 238, 243, 274, 297n56, 298n62; as *qimeng*, xiii, 290n2
Equilibrium, 101, 127, 268, 270; or the mean, 101, 159, 258, 269; the state of, 159, 258, 269
Estrangement (*Entfremdung*), 24, 65, 71, 79, 86, 187, 199, 210–11, 276, 286n22; as *yihua*, 286n21. See also Alienation
"Exhortation to Study" (Zhang Zhidong), 280n1, 297n57, 299n68
External ruler, 158; as *waiwang*, 129. See also Inner sage
External transcendence (*waizai chaoyuexing*), 133

Farewell to Revolution (Li Zehou and Liu Zaifu), 12, 249, 297n54
Feng Qi, 34, 37
Feng Youlan, 15–16, 306n49
Filial respect and love (*xiao*), 220
Five Essays from 1999 (Li Zehou), 11
Five Phases Theory (*wu xing shuo*), 290n53. See also Yin-yang and the Five Phases
Following My Own Way (Li Zehou), 12
Form: as *xingshi*, 57; of art (artistic), 52, 63; dynamic, 25, 35–36, 51, 53, 66, 141, 194, 231, 233, 257, 275, 282n23; mental forms (formations), 25, 29, 33, 47–48, 50, 54, 56–57, 62, 64, 68, 72, 75, 257, 275, 285n16; of subjectality, 68
Four Essays on Aesthetics (Li Zehou), xv, 10
Four periods of Confucianism, 106; as *Ruxue si qi*, 105, 116–17; as historical development, 105, 116, 119
From Shamanism to Rituality, Explaining Rituality as a Return to the Humanness (Li Zehou), 11, 107
Function, 268; as *yong*, 39–40, 173, 175, 177, 261–67, 271, 310n8; as application, 39, 173
Fusion of emotion and scene or situation (*qingjing jiaorong*), 214

Gang of Four, 18, 167, 200, 281n15
Gao Ertai, 185, 193, 201
Gao Jianping, 197, 201, 203, 208–9
Germs of capitalism in China, theory of the (*Zhongguo zibenzhuyi mengya*), 161
Gongyi-shehui jiegou (techno-social or technological-social formation),

33, 35, 48. *See also* Techno-social formation
Great Debate on Aesthetics, the, 184, 209, 281n13; as *Meixue da taolun*, 7, 185, 280n5; and Marxist aesthetics, 15
Great Debate on Culture (*wenhua da taolun*), 298n61. *See also* Cultural Fever
Great Leap Forward (campaign), 4, 85
Great Proletarian Cultural Revolution. *See* Cultural Revolution
Great self, the (community), 215, 226; as *da wo*, 33, 48, 59, 78, 112, 283n30, 284n5
Guanxizhuyi (relationalism), 110, 308n67. *See also* Relationalism
Guide by example and appropriately construct, 246; as *fandao he shidang goujian*, 243. *See also* Religious morality; Social morality
Guo Xiang, 293n23
Guodian Chu Bamboo Slips, 107, 118, 243

Habermas, Jürgen, xiv, 162
Han Feizi, 293n27
Han Shu (Book of Han, Ban Gu), 293n20, 304n27
Hankou (city), 8
Harmony, 93, 107, 114, 120, 126, 154–55, 183, 215–16, 244, 249, 269, 271, 288n40, 292n17, 297n55, 301n8; as *he*, 159; is higher than justice, 243, 248
He Lin, 300n4, 303n18
Heart-mind, 137–39, 227, 238, 273, 294n36; as *xin*, 291n10
Heart-mind and inner nature, 118, 136; moral metaphysics of, 119

Hegel, Georg Wilhelm Friedrich, xiv, 18, 24, 30, 45, 73, 79, 103, 162, 177, 187–88, 191, 195, 230, 234–36, 249, 254, 256, 259, 260, 265, 294n31, 313n22
Hei shou (black hands), 22
Heidegger, Martin, xiv, 43, 222, 224, 283n1, 294n31
Historical Notes (*Shi ji*), 108, 291n7, 293n20
Historical ontology, 10, 103, 131, 147, 159, 223, 228, 229. *See also* Anthropological ontology; Ontology
Historical Ontology (Li Zehou), 12, 120, 222, 306n47
Hou Ji, 108
Human agency, xiv, 31, 53, 57, 66, 102, 288n37; as *zhutide nengdongxing*, 86
Humaneness, 29, 45, 60, 81–82, 112, 116, 127, 133, 137, 141, 143, 148–49, 167, 200, 220, 242, 258–59, 285n14, 287n28; and justice (or righteousness, *renyi*, a general denotation of Confucian morality), 126, 176. *See also* (Co)humaneness
Humanization of consciousness (*yishide renhua*), 269
Humanization of nature, 16, 34, 36, 38, 48, 50, 56, 63–65, 68, 77, 88–95, 97, 98, 101, 193, 219, 268, 284n9, 289n45, 306n42, 307n53; as *zirande renhua*, xiv, 32. *See also* Naturalization of humans
Humanness, 44, 66, 75, 78, 82, 107, 139, 226, 228, 239, 243, 258, 276, 284n6; as *ren xing*, 28, 32, 36, 42, 48, 71, 220, 282n27; as human inborn qualities, 42, 133, 282n27; as human nature, 70–71, 75,

Humanness (*continued*)
    82, 136, 200, 228, 242, 282n27,
    284n9, 292n18
Hunan province, 8, 291n6
Hundred Flowers Movement, 4. See
    also Colloquial Movement
Hundred-Days Reform, 280n7; as
    Wuxu bianfa, 168

Illumination of truth through beauty
    (*yi mei qi zhen*), 97, 216
Image-thinking, 17, 189, 197, 206–
    10, 212, 213, 303n22; as *xingxiang
    siwei*, 16, 196, 205. See *also*
    Specific features of image-thinking
Impassive rational laws of dialectical
    development (*wu qing bianzheng
    fa*), 226
Inborn knowledge (*liangzhi*), 137
Inner sage, 95, 158–59, 225, 259;
    as *neisheng*, 129. See *also* External
    ruler
Inner sage and external ruler (king),
    159, 225, 259; as *neisheng waiwang*,
    158
Intellectual intuition (*zhide zhijue*),
    140
Internal (immanent) transcendence,
    134–38, 140, 217, 311n10; as *neizai
    chaoyuexing*, 133; as transcendence
    in immanence, 295n36
Internalization, 30, 42, 50, 54, 58,
    64, 90, 97, 144, 148, 205, 227,
    232, 234; as *neihua*, 49
*Interpreting Texts and Explaining
    Characters* (the oldest Chinese
    etymological dictionary), 296n47

Jiang Qing, 104
Jidian (sedimentation), 16, 32, 37.
    See *also* Sedimentation

Jingjie (aesthetic realm), 213–14. See
    also Aesthetic realm
Jung, Carl Gustav, 51–53

Kang Youwei, 10, 15, 283n30,
    284n5, 298n60, 306n45
Kant, Immanuel, xiv–xv, 11, 14,
    17–20, 24–25, 27–28, 30, 31, 35,
    41–42, 45, 49, 53, 56–58, 67,
    70–73, 77–81, 85, 88, 98–102,
    119, 130, 132, 140–41, 153,
    156–57, 187–90, 199, 205, 213,
    215–17, 219, 223–26, 228–40, 246,
    249, 251, 254, 259, 270, 281n22,
    290n51, 294n31, 299n70, 300n1,
    301n7, 302n16, 304n28, 305n39,
    306n44, 306n50, 307n51, 311n11
King Wu of the Zhou Dynasty (*Zhou
    Wu Wang*), 282n24

Lacan, Jacques, xiv, 284n10
Learning, 30, 72, 133, 178–79, 181,
    263, 284n6; as *xue*, 180
Legalism, 106, 117, 124, 128–29,
    293n20, 294n31; as *fa jia*, 245
Legalists, 18, 124, 127, 293n27,
    294n29
Legan wenhua (culture of pleasure,
    optimism, happiness, joy), 29, 35,
    292n12, 292n18. See *also* Culture
    of pleasure
Li Si, 293n27
Liang Qichao, 280n7, 283n30,
    284n5, 287n34
Liang Shuming, 172, 297n59, 306n49
Liberation of thought, 4
Lin Yusheng, xiv, 171, 291n5
Liu Gangji, 201–2, 297n54
Liu Huiru, 170
Liu Yuedi, 252, 287n29, 295n41,
    308n60

Liu Zaifu, 12, 141, 249, 299n72
Lixing ningju (Condensation of reason), 238. *See also* Condensation of reason
Lu Xun, 216, 273–74, 305n36
Lukács, György, xiv, 86–87, 162, 289n43, 303n22

Mao Zedong, 3–4, 85, 101, 166–67, 195, 197, 200, 208, 288n41, 304n27
Marx, Karl, xiv, 14, 18–19, 24–27, 30, 32, 35, 41, 45, 50, 57, 67, 68, 71, 79–81, 84, 87–91, 98, 100–2, 103, 154, 161–62, 174, 177, 179, 185, 187–89, 193, 199–200, 210–11, 213, 228–32, 234, 236, 249, 251, 254, 259, 265, 267, 270, 282n26, 284n9, 284n11, 286n22, 286n23, 288n35, 288n36, 288n37, 288n39, 289n44, 294n31, 299n70, 299n73, 311n14, 312n20, 313n22
May 4th Movement (May 4th Cultural Revolution), 3, 88, 104, 146, 167, 168–70, 172; as *Wusi yundong*, 2. *See also* New Culture Movement
Meixue da taolun (the Great Debate on Aesthetics), 7, 15, 185, 280n5. *See also* Great Debate on Aesthetics
Melting of reason, 227–28; as *lixing ronghua*, 238
Mengzi (Mencius), 109, 116–18, 133, 294n28
Min Ze, 201–2
Modern Confucianism, 137; as *xin ruxue*, 117; as New Confucianism, 166
Modern social morality, 19, 157; as *xiandai shehuixing daode*, 153, 248.
See also Religious morality; Social morality
Moism, 117, 293n20
Moists, 124
Mou Zongsan (Mou Tsung-san), 117, 119, 133–37, 158, 291n3, 311n10
Music or joy (*yue* or *le*), 183

Names or concepts and actualities (*mingshi*), 124, 310n8
Nationalist Party, 3
Naturalization of humans, 38, 48, 92, 94–97, 98, 101, 126, 268, 285n16; as *rende ziranhua*, xiv, 32. *See also* Humanization of nature
Neisheng (Inner sage), 129. *See also* Inner sage
Neisheng waiwang (Inner sage and external ruler or king), 158. *See also* Inner sage and external ruler
New Culture Movement, 3, 168; as *Xin wenhua yundong*, 169. *See also* May 4th Movement
New National Studies (*Xin Guoxue*), 166
New Youth (journal), 2
Noumenon, 35, 130, 133, 136, 146, 214, 217–18, 235, 257, 259, 266; as *benti*, 131

Objectification, 36, 70, 102, 159, 210–11, 214
"Objective and the Social Nature of Beauty, The" (Li Zehou), 301n12
Objective sociality, 16, 215, 231, 239; as *keguande shehuixing*, 194
Objective structure (*keguan jiegou*), 72
On Chinese Intellectual History (Li Zehou), xi
On Classical Chinese Intellectual History (Li Zehou), 144

On Image-Thinking (Li Zehou), 206, 208–9
On Modern Chinese Intellectual History (Li Zehou), 10
"On Music" (chapter in the Book of Rituals), 145, 296n43
On Pre-Modern Chinese Intellectual History (Li Zehou), 10
"On the Aesthetic Feeling, Beauty and Art" (Li Zehou), 10, 16, 187, 205–6, 271, 289n47, 300n4
One-world view, 78, 119, 129–33, 137, 139, 217, 225–26, 259, 266, 293n21, 311n10, 312n14; as *yige shijie guan*, 29, 91
Ontology, xv, 35, 86, 131, 140, 149, 215, 217–18, 223, 232, 243, 258, 262–64, 289n43, 311n10, 312n20, 313n22; as *cunyoulun*, 294n33; in Chinese philosophy (*bentilun*), 131, 133, 287n27, 307n54; of human subjectality (*renlei zhutide bentilun*), 71. See also Anthropological ontology; Historical ontology
"Overseer of Ritual Affairs in the Spring Offices, The" (chapter in the Rites of Zhou), 113

Path of Beauty, The (Li Zehou), xv, 10, 37, 125, 198, 305n41
Peking University, 8, 10, 14, 16, 306n45
People's Daily (newspaper), 189, 197, 208
Philosophic and Aesthetic Writings (Li Zehou), 285n13
Philosophy of food (eating), 176, 221, 228, 261, 266, 309n69
Philosophy Research (journal), 9, 47, 187, 300n4, 300n6
Piaget, Jean, xiv, 49–50, 290n52, 307n56

Pleasure, 49, 62–63, 78, 80, 95, 98–100, 121–22, 131, 145, 194, 211, 214, 219, 275, 293n24; as *legan*, 120, 292n12. See also Culture of pleasure
Plekhanov, Georgi Valentinovich, 188, 212
Practical reason, 122, 142, 147, 226, 238, 240, 295n41; as *shijian lixing*, 141
Practice, xv, 16, 26, 30, 33, 35, 42–43, 45, 49, 50, 52, 54–56, 58, 62–63, 65, 66–67, 69–71, 72–75, 79–81, 85, 88, 91, 96–97, 98, 100, 102, 104, 107–9, 111, 114, 142–43, 186, 200–1, 205, 212, 213, 215, 222, 223, 225, 228, 229, 231, 233–36, 257, 259, 262, 264, 267, 269, 281n17, 285n16, 286n19, 288n36, 290n52, 295n40, 312n20; as *shijian*, 68, 286n25; as praxis (*shijian*), 71, 228, 286n25
Pragmatic (practical) philosophy of subjectality, 19, 69, 83, 86, 222, 275; as *zhutixing shijian zhexue*, 67
Pragmatic reason, xv, 75, 106, 122, 140, 142–48, 150, 158, 226, 232, 238, 252, 275, 292n17, 295n40, 296n44; as *shiyong lixing*, 29, 35, 141; as pragmatic rationality, 42, 116, 119, 132, 142, 144
Pragmatic Reason and a Culture of Optimism (Li Zehou), 11, 146
Presence: as *you* (有), 123; in relation to absence (*wu* 無), 123
Preservation of the (moral and rational) cosmic structure and the elimination of human desires, the (*cun tianli mie renyu*), 296n45
Preserving the good through beauty (*yi mei chu shan*), 97, 216

Proper measure, 15, 87, 154–55, 157, 168, 201, 216, 226, 232–34, 249, 252, 259, 268–70, 272, 275, 307n54; as *du*, 36, 101, 159

Psychological substance, 36, 227, 313n21; as *xinli benti*, 34–35, 66–67, 68, 284n4. See also Substance

Public social virtues, 158; as *shehuixing gongde*, 151

Qian Mu, 306n49

Qin Shi Huangdi, 116

Qing benti (emotion-based substance), 19, 29, 119, 243, 282n29, 284n4. See also Emotion-based substance

Qingli jiegou (Emotio-rational structure), 29, 35. See also Emotio-rational structure

Rawls, John Bordley, 246

Reading the Analects Today (Li Zehou), 11, 119, 242

Reciprocal utilization of Confucianism and Legalism, 106, 245; as *rufa huyong*, 128

Reconciliation of seven human emotions, 64; as *qi qing zheng*, 97

Red Flag (journal), 197, 208

Relationalism, 154–55, 157–58, 246–47, 251; as *guanxizhuyi*, 110, 308n67

Religious morality, 19–20, 128, 152, 154, 156–58, 243; as *zongjiaoxing daode*, 151; as private religious morality, 245–46. See also Modern social morality; Social morality

Ren dao (Way of Humans), 130. See also Way of Humans

Ren xing (humanness), 28, 32, 36, 42, 48, 71, 220, 286n24. See also Humanness

Rende ziranhua (naturalization of humans), xiv, 32. See also Naturalization of humans

"Replacing Religion with Aesthetic Education" (Cai Yuanpei), 306n45

"Response to Michael Sandel and Other Matters" (Li Zehou), 12, 130, 150, 237

Rites of Zhou (book), 113–14, 282n24

Ritual, 52, 111, 125, 144–45, 239, 273, 291n6, 306n45; as *li*, 29, 297n49; as (Confucian) rituality (*li*), 106–8, 111–12, 115, 116, 126, 141, 148, 176, 220, 245, 285n14; as shamanistic ceremonies, 29, 59, 106–14, 152, 253, 285n14

Root and branch (*benmo*), 124; as roots and crown, 310n8

School of the structural principle, 144, 152; as *lixue*, 138, 296n46

Sedimentation, xv, 28, 33, 42, 47–53, 54–58, 61–64, 66, 75, 77, 79, 98, 143, 158, 189, 201, 204–5, 218–20, 226, 228, 232, 252, 275, 284n11, 285n13, 285n16, 287n33; as *jidian*, 16, 32, 37; artistic (*yishu jidian*), 48–49; cultural (*wenhua jidian*), xv, 29, 33, 48, 51, 55, 64–65; elementary (original, primitive, *yuanshi jidian*), 48–49, 60, 61–62, 96, 112; individual (*geti jidian*), 33, 48, 55–56; of species (*wuzhong jidian*), 33, 48, 55, 64; theory of (*jidian shuo*), 42, 49, 52, 56, 60, 61, 284n8, 284n9; vital (*shenghuo jidian*), 48–49

Seeking the truth in the facts (*shishi qiu shi*), 201

Self-consciousness, 114, 262

Sense of beauty, 37, 49, 62, 90; as *meigan*, 36

Seven feelings (or emotions, *qi qing*), 156
Shaman, 109, 112, 114–15; shamanism (*wu*), 29, 31, 106–9, 113–14, 129, 171, 253; shamanistic historical tradition (*wushi chuantong*), 106–7, 110, 247. *See also* Ritual; Unity of shaman and (Confucian) gentleman
Shang shu (Book of Documents), 114. *See also* Book of Documents
Shi ji (Historical Notes), 108, 291n7, 293n20
Shi jing (Book of Poetry), 282n24
Shiyong lixing (Pragmatic reason), 29, 35, 141. *See also* Pragmatic reason
Shu jing (Book of Documents), 114. *See also* Book of Documents
Small self, the (individual), 34, 139, 226; as *xiao wo*, 33, 48, 59, 67, 78
Social existence, 34, 39, 68, 75, 168, 174, 179–80, 194, 253, 262–64, 266–67
Social morality, 20, 111, 152, 154, 157–58, 226, 243, 245–46; as *shehuixing daode*, 151. *See also* Modern social morality; Religious morality
Specific features of image-thinking (*xingxiang siwei tezheng*), 189
Square of Heavenly Peace (Tiananmen Square), 2, 4, 9, 15, 22–23, 66, 167, 298n61, 309n70
Stem, body (*ti*), 131
Structure (*jiegou*), 57, 281n23. *See also* Emotio-rational structure; Objective structure
Structure and phenomena (*liqi*), 310n8
Structure, structural pattern, 260; as *li*, 144, 297n49, 313n23
Subject, xiv–xv, 21, 25, 30–31, 34, 36, 42, 51, 55–56, 60, 62, 66–67, 71, 72–74, 78–79, 81, 85, 87, 91, 94–95, 97, 98–102, 133, 180, 193, 214, 230–31, 235, 237, 256, 258, 267, 270, 285n19, 287n26, 288n41, 288n42, 297n52, 299n70, 303n19, 309n1; as *zhuti*, 68
Subjectality, xv, 19, 30, 33, 35–36, 48, 50, 65, 67, 68–71, 73–83, 85–88, 91, 98–99, 101, 159, 217, 222–24, 230–31, 267–70, 272, 275, 281n17, 283n33, 284n6, 312n20; as *zhutixing*, xiv, 11, 20–21, 31–32, 34, 66, 72, 281n20, 285n17
Subjectivity, 11, 16, 25, 30, 36, 42, 67, 70–71, 76, 78–80, 82, 91, 98, 185–86, 189, 193, 286n19, 289n43, 303n19; as *zhuguanxing*, 31, 66, 281n20, 285n17
Sublation (Hegel's *Aufhebung*), 177, 230, 249, 256, 270; as *yangqi*, 235
Substance, 48, 69, 76, 79, 120–21, 123, 131, 136, 144, 147, 149, 164, 168, 195, 232, 235–36, 256, 262–64, 295n39, 312n16; as essence, 39, 131, 137, 173–74, 179–80, 195, 262–63, 313n21; origin, 35, 131; psychological (*xinli benti*), 34–36, 66–67, 68, 227, 284n4, 313n21; root, 35, 131, 146, 231; techno-social (instrumental, *gongju benti*), 34–35, 66, 68, 225, 252, 282n29, 284n4
Substance and function cannot be separated, 181, 264; as *tiyong bu er*, 137
Substance (essence) and function, 39, 172, 175, 177, 261–62, 264, 266–68, 271; as *tiyong*, 124, 310n8, 311n13
Sun Zhongshan (Sun Yat-Sen), 283n30, 284n5

Taiwan (Formosa), 3, 166, 294n33

Talks at the Yan'an Forum on Literature and Art (Mao Zedong), 4, 280n3
Tao Qian, 293n26
Techno-social (instrumental) substance, 34, 225, 252, 282n29, 284n4; as *gongju benti*, 35, 66, 68. See also Substance
Techno-social (technological-social) formation, 29, 66, 252, 282n29, 284n4; as *gongyi—shehui jiegou*, 33, 35, 48. See also Cultural-psychological formation
Thing-in-itself, 236, 257; as *wu zi ti*, 235
Three Books on Aesthetics (Li Zehou), 10
Three periods of Confucianism, 118, 136; as *ruxue san qi*, 291n3; in contrast to four periods of Confucianism, 117
Tian ming (Decree of Heaven), 135. See also Decree of Heaven
Tian ren heyi (Unity of heaven/nature and human beings), xv, 38, 45, 78, 91, 97, 102. See also Unity of heaven and humans
Tiandao (Way of Heaven), 130. See also Way of Heaven
Tiren (bodily recognition), 289n46. See also Bodily recognition
Tongbian (Continuous change, continuity through change), 256, 261, 265. See also Continuous change
Tools, xv, 28, 43, 49, 57, 68, 233, 299n70; as *gongju*, 49; making and using, 26–28, 30, 33, 35, 42–43, 49, 56, 57–58, 63, 68, 70, 72, 75, 80, 141, 219, 225, 228, 231, 234, 284n9; as technology, 71, 91
Traditional unconscious (*chuantong wuyishi*), 110, 247

Transformative creation, 171, 204, 245, 252, 291n5, 297n53, 313n24; as *zhuanhuaxingde chuangzao*, xiv, 29, 31. See also Creative transformation
Tu Wei-ming, 117, 204, 291n3, 291n5
Two kinds of morality, 128, 151–52, 157–58, 243, 245, 252, 259, 275
Two-worlds view, 136; as *liangge shijie guan*, 91; as opposed to the one-world view, 91, 119, 130, 138, 266
Typicality, 196, 303n22; as *dianxing*, 301n10
Typification (exemplification), 206; as *dianxinghua*, 196

Unity of knowledge and action, 259; as *zhixing heyi*, 73
Unity of shaman and (Confucian) gentleman (*wujun heyi*), 24
Unity (unification, reconciliation) of heaven (nature) and humans, 60, 62, 118–19, 130, 136–37, 145, 184, 257, 259, 285n16, 305n42; as *tian ren heyi*, xv, 45, 78, 97, 102; in Chinese aesthetics, 38, 90–93, 289n47
Use through the useless, the (*wu yong zhi yong*), 305n39

Waiwang (External ruler), 129. See also External ruler
Wang Guowei, 108, 213–14, 287n34
Wang Keping, 58, 64, 97, 102, 120, 202, 211, 292n18
Wang Ruoshui, 200, 288n39
Way, the, 134; as *dao*, 126, 243
Way of Heaven, 134, 137, 139, 142, 295n37; as *tiandao*, 130
Way of Humans, 295n37; as *ren dao*, 130

Wenhua da taolun (Great Debate on Culture), 298n61
Wenhua—xinli jiegou (Cultural-psychological formation), 29, 33, 35. See also Cultural-psychological formation
Western essence (substance), Chinese function (application), 15, 170, 266, 312n18; as *Xiti Zhongyong*, xiv, 39, 172–73, 279n1, 298n60. See also Chinese essence and Western function
Westernization movement (*Yangwu yundong, Ziqiang yundong*), 168
Wittgenstein, Ludwig, 43, 229, 290n52
Wu. See Absence
Wu Ji, 185
Wuxu bianfa (Hundred Days Reform), 168, 280n7

Xiao wo (the small self, individual), 33, 48, 59, 67, 78. See also Small self
Xin Guoxue (New National Studies), 166
Xingxiang siwei (image-thinking), 16, 196, 205. See also Image-thinking
Xinhai revolution, 168
Xinli benti (Psychological substance), 34–35, 67, 68, 284n4. See also Psychological substance
Xiong Shili, 119, 266
Xu Fuguan, 108, 116, 289n46, 291n7
Xu Shen, 296n47
Xunzi, 116–18, 127–28, 225

Yang Guorong, 132, 281n16, 295n38
Yangwu yundong (Westernization movement), 168
Ye Lang, 201–2
Yi jing (Book of Changes), 256, 265, 282n24, 313n23. See also Book of changes

Yijing (artistic conception), 212. See also Artistic conception
Yin and yang ("sunny and shady"), 105, 117, 124, 269, 293n20, 310n8
Yin-yang and the Five Phases, 127–28; as *yinyang wuxing*, 117, 311n12. See also Five Phases Theory
Yinyang wuxing (Yin-yang and the Five Phases), 117, 311n12. See also Yin-yang and the Five Phases
You. See Presence
You Xilin, 210

Zhang Dainian, 311n13
Zhang Zhidong, 1, 15, 163, 173, 297n57, 312n18
Zheng Jiadong, 137
Zheng Jiqiao, 209
Zhenli biaozhun da taolun (Discussion of the Criteria of Truth), 200
Zhixing heyi (Unity of Heaven/Nature and human beings), 73. See also Unity of heaven (nature) and humans
Zhou Gong, 29, 31. See also Duke of Zhou
Zhou Wu Wang, 282n24
Zhu Guangqian, 16, 185–86, 190, 197, 201, 208, 300n4
Zhu Xi, 117, 144, 313n23
Zhuanghuaxingde chuangzao (Transformative creation), xiv, 29, 31. See also Transformative creation
Zhuangzi, 38, 92–95, 125–27, 289n48, 293n25, 305n39
Zhutide nengdongxing (Human agency), 86. See also Human agency
Ziqiang yundong (Westernization movement), 168
Zirande renhua (Humanization of nature), xiv, 32. See also Humanization of nature
Zong Baihua, 201

www.ingramcontent.com/pod-product-compliance
Lightning Source LLC
Chambersburg PA
CBHW071826230426
43672CB00013B/2769